MW00965713

LESSONS FROM IMPLEMENTATION OF EDUCATIONAL REFORMS IN PAKISTAN

Implications for Policy and Practice

LESSONS FROM IMPLEMENTATION OF EDUCATIONAL REFORMS IN PAKISTAN

Implications for Policy and Practice

Edited By

Takbir Ali and Sarfaroz Niyozov

OXFORD
UNIVERSITY PRESS

Oxford University Press is a department of the University of Oxford.
It furthers the University's objective of excellence in research, scholarship, and education by publishing worldwide. Oxford is a registered trade mark of Oxford University Press in the UK and in certain other countries

Published in Pakistan by
Oxford University Press
No.38, Sector 15, Korangi Industrial Area,
PO Box 8214, Karachi-74900, Pakistan

First Edition published in 2017

ISBN 978-0-19-940608-1

Second Impression 2018

Typeset in Adobe Garamond Pro
Printed on 80gsm Local Offset Paper

Printed by Mas Printers, Karachi

Dedication

Dedicated to the 25th anniversary of the Aga Khan University-Institute for Educational Development, Pakistan, in recognition of the difference it has made to the lives of educators and children through improved quality of education. The Institute has come a long way, from enrolling just 21 students in its flagship programme in 1993 to educating more than 35,000 teachers, teacher educators, and school leaders; producing knowledge to inform educational policies and practices and improving educational opportunities for thousands of children in under-served areas.

Contents

Acknowledgements

The publication of this volume is inspired by the experiences gained through the implementation of the STEP project. The STEP project was implemented with generous financial support from the Global Affairs Canada and the Aga Khan Foundation, Canada. We are grateful to these organizations for their generous support, which enabled AKU-IED to ignite hope and determination in a wide range of public sector educational stakeholders, including students, teachers, head teachers, managers, parents, community members, and women in disadvantaged rural communities of Sindh, Balochistan, and Gilgit-Baltistan to change themselves and the world around them.

The volume arises out of research studies undertaken by AKU-IED's faculty and project team to document experiences and lessons learnt about the impact of various interventions and innovations undertaken by the STEP project. We are thankful to all those people (government officials, district coordinators, investigators, data enumerators and research officers, and project's support staff) who contributed to these studies in various ways. We are grateful to the authors of chapters for extracting insightful lessons from their research reports and reflecting deeply on the implications of these lessons for policy and practice.

We would like to extend our gratitude to the people who assisted in copyediting of the manuscript, including Nida Dossa, Rozina Gulzar, Dr Alnaaz Kassam, and Sumera Veljee. We would also like to express special gratitude to our mentors, mentee, head teachers, and lead-teachers whose persistent efforts and unrelenting commitment made a positive change in schools and classrooms possible.

The list of the people, whose contributions made the publication of this volume possible, is too long to mention individually by name; they will know their contributions and deserve our special thanks.

Finally, for financial assistance for the production and printing of this book, we are grateful to the Global Affairs Canada and the Aga Khan Foundation (Canada and Pakistan).

Takbir Ali and Sarfaroz Niyozov
Karachi
August 2017

Acronyms

ADELM	Advanced Diploma in Educational Leadership and Management
ADI	Assistant District Inspector
ADOE	Assistant District Officer, Education
AKDN	Aga Khan Development Network
AKES	Aga Khan Education Service
AKF, C	Aga Khan Foundation, Canada
AKF, P	Aga Khan Foundation, Pakistan
AKPBS	Aga Khan Planning and Building Services
AKRSP	Aga Khan Rural Support Programme
AKU-HDP	Aga Khan University-Human Development Programme
AKU-IED	Aga Khan University-Institute for Educational Development
ASER	Annual Status Education Report
BBCM	Broad Based Community Mobilisation
BoC	Bureau of Curriculum
CBMP	Cluster-Based Mentoring Programme
CBOs	Community-Based Organizations
CPD	Continuing Professional Development
CSRC	Civil Society Resource Center
CT	Certificate in Teaching
CTLA	Curriculum Teaching Learning and Assessment
DDEO	Deputy District Education Officer

DDO	Draw Disbursement Officer
DEO	District Education Officer
DFATD	Department of Foreign Affairs, Trade and Development
DoE-GB	Deportment of Education-Gilgit-Baltistan
EC	European Commission
ECED	Early Child Education and Development
EDOE	Executive District Officer of Education
ELM	Education Leadership and Management
ESR	Education Sector Reform
ESP	Education Sector Plans
FBTDP	Field-Based Teacher Development Programme
FEOs	Field Education Officers
GAC	Global Affairs Canada
GB	Gilgit-Baltistan
GBES	Gilgit-Baltistan Education Strategy
GBLA	Gilgit-Baltistan Legislative Assembly
GCE	Government College of Education
GECE	Government Elementary College of Education
HEC	Higher Education Commission
INGOs	International Non-Governmental Organizations
ISP	Institutional Strengthening Programme
KKH	Karakorum Highway
KPK	Khyber-Pakhtunkhwa
LLIs	Local level Institutions
LRC	Learning Resource Centre
LRS	Learning Resource School
MEd	Master of Education
MSG	Mother Support Group
MPA	Member of Provincial Assembly
NDIE	Notre Dame Institute of Education
NEP	Northern Education Project

NOWPDP	Network of Organizations Working with People with Disabilities, Pakistan
PDCN	Professional Development Centre North
PDT	Professional Development Teacher
PEAC	Provincial Examination and Assessment Cell
PITE	Provincial Institute for Teacher Education
PNTD	Professional Network of Teacher Development
PPIU	Policy Planning and Implementation Unit
PTC	Primary Teacher Certificate
PTSMC	Parent Teacher School Management Committee
RSU	Reform Support Unit
SLOs	Students Learning Outcomes
SMC	School Management Committee
STEP	Strengthening Teacher Education in Pakistan
TA	Teaching Associate
TEO	Taluka Education Officer
TTIs	Teacher Training Institutions
UC-TRC	Union Council-Teachers' Resource Centre
UN	United Nations
UNDP	United Nations Development Programme
UNICEF	United Nations International Children Emergency Fund
USAID	United States Agency for International Development
WSIP	Whole School Improvement Programme

Editors and Contributors

Takbir Ali, Editor of this volume, is presently working as an Assistant Professor and Head, Outreach at the Aga Khan University-Institute for Educational Development (AKU-IED), Karachi, Pakistan. He obtained his PhD and MEd degrees from the University of Toronto, Ontario Institute for Studies in Education and the Aga Khan University-Institute for Educational Development, respectively. He started his career with the Aga Khan Education Service, Pakistan, as a school teacher and moved to higher education after earning his master's degree in education. He worked with the Professional Development Centre North (PDCN) as a Professional Development Teacher and later as a Core Faculty. Moreover, Dr Ali has extensive work experience in designing and executing developmental projects in the education sector. He coordinated the Strengthening Teacher Education in Pakistan (STEP) project (2008–2016) of AKU-IED. His research interests are in teachers' change experiences, teacher development, curriculum implementation, school improvement, and teaching and learning science in schools. He has published his research in a research monograph, several journal articles, and book chapters. Email: takbir.ali@aku.edu

Sarfaroz Niyozov, Co-Editor of this volume, is the Director of the Institute for Educational Development of the Aga Khan University, Karachi (AKU-IED). Born and raised in Tajikistan, Dr Niyozov worked and studied in countries of the Middle East and South

Asia. He has a BA in Arabic from Tajik State University, MEd from the Aga Khan University and PhD from the University of Toronto. From 2001 to 2005 Dr Niyozov worked at the Institute of Ismaili Studies where he founded its Central Asian Unit. In 2005, he joined the University of Toronto and is an Associate Professor at the University. He assumed the roles of the Co-Director of the Center for Comparative, International and Development Education and editor of the *Journal of Curriculum Inquiry* at University of Toronto. Dr Niyozov has been an active member of professional associations such as Central Eurasian Studies and Comparative International Education Societies. Since August 2015 he assumed the role of the Director of the Institute for Educational Development of the Aga Khan University in Karachi for a period of three years. His research and teaching experiences include comparative international education, Islamic and cultural studies education and teacher development. He has authored several articles, two books, and numerous reports in these areas of research.
Email: sarfaroz.niyozov@aku.edu

Sadrudin Pardhan is currently working as a Special Advisor to the Provost of the Aga Khan University. He obtained his doctoral and teacher education studies from Uppsala University, Sweden and completed his MBA from the University of Alberta, Canada. Starting his career as a Chemistry lecturer at Kenyan Science Teachers College, Nairobi, Kenya, he moved on to assume various leadership roles as a professional in various institutions particularly in the education sector in East Africa, Canada, and Pakistan. Of prominence are his services to the Aga Khan Education Service, Pakistan (AKES, P) as the CEO, and his contribution towards the establishment of AKU-IED in Karachi and its Professional Development Centres in Gilgit-Baltistan, Chitral, and East Africa. In recognition of his outstanding services to the education sector and particularly to the university, AKU presented him the prestigious *Professor Emeritus* award in November 2012. Email: sadrudin.pardhan@aku.edu

Mola Dad Shafa is an Associate Professor at AKU-IED and is working as the Head of AKU-IED's Professional Development Centre, North (PDCN) in Gilgit. He earned his PhD in Teacher Education from the University of Toronto, Ontario Institute for Studies in Education. He obtained his MEd (Teacher Education) from AKU-IED, Karachi, Pakistan. As the Head of PDCN, he has earned a great reputation by introducing numerous innovative teacher/head teacher professional development programmes and by reaching out to some of the hard-to-reach and resistant-to-change communities in Gilgit-Baltistan to improve their access to education.
Email: moladad.shafa@aku.edu

Sharifullah Baig is a Senior Instructor at AKU-IED's Professional Development Centre North (PDCN), Gilgit-Baltistan. He earned a master's degree in Public Administration from Gomal University in Khyber-Pakhtunkhwa and obtained his MEd degree from AKU-IED. He has played a leading role in the implementation of school improvement projects and programmes, including the recent landmark Education Development and Improvement Programme (EDIP) implemented in Gilgit-Baltistan. He is a global scholar with the 2013 International Editorial Advisory Board of the National Council of Educational Administration (NCPEA) in educational leadership and administration, Greensboro, NC 27402.
Email: sharifullah.baig@aku.edu

Zeenat Shah is presently working as a Senior Instructor with AKU-IED's Professional Development Centre North (PDCN). He did his MEd from AKU-IED, Karachi, Pakistan. He has over 25 years working experience in education, including 15 years as a school

teacher and 10 years as a teacher educator. Recently, he completed his tenure working as a Senior Coordinator in the EDIP project.
Email: zeenat.shah@aku.edu

Sadia Muzaffar Bhutta is an Assistant Professor and Head of the Research and Policy Studies at AKU-IED, Pakistan. She holds a Doctor in Education (DPhil) degree and a master's degree in Research from Oxford University, UK. She completed her MEd degree (Teacher Education) from AKU-IED. She started her career as a secondary school Science teacher. She teaches courses about Research Methods and Science Education at graduate level. In recent years she has focused on the development and validation of assessment tools as well as conducted large-scale studies in the field of education—a journey that started during her studies at the University of Oxford.
Email: sadia.bhutta@aku.edu

Nahid Parween Anwar earned her MSc and MEd degrees from Karachi University and the Aga Khan University-Institute for Educational Development respectively. She worked with AKU-IED as faculty and later as Teaching Associate with the STEP project of AKU-IED. She has diversified experiences of teaching at school, college, and university levels. Her main areas of interest are science education, teacher education, and school improvement.
Email: nahidkoko@yahoo.com

Ayesha Bashiruddin worked as an Associate Professor and Head, Research and Policy Studies at AKU-IED. She has a master's degree in English from the University of Peshawar and a master's degree in Applied Linguistics from the University of Durham, UK. She obtained her PhD from Ontario Institute for Studies in Education, University of Toronto (OISE/UT). Her research interests are in English Language Education, teacher learning, qualitative research

methods including autobiographical research (self-study research, narrative inquiry, and arts-based research).
Email: aaaabbbb57@gmail.com

Mir Afzal Tajik is an Associate Professor at the Nazarbayev University Graduate School of Education (NUGSE). He obtained his PhD from the Ontario Institute for Studies in Education, University of Toronto, Canada and Master of Education from the Aga Khan University Institute for Education development (AKU-IED), Pakistan. Before joining NUGSE in September 2016, Dr Tajik worked as an Association Professor and held leadership positions including Interim Director, Associate Director, Head of Graduate Programmes, and Head of Outreach Programme at AKU-IED. He has also led AKU-IED's capacity building programmes in Afghanistan and Tajikistan. Dr Tajik brings over 25 years of experience in teacher education, educational leadership and management, school improvement and community-based education. He is the recipient of AKU's Award for Sustained Excellence in Scholarship of Application, 2009.
Email: afzal.mir@nu.edu.kz

Naureen Madhani is currently an Adjunct Lecturer at New York University and coordinates Learning Communities at the City University of New York, Kingsborough Community College. She holds a Master's of Education in Higher Education from the University of British Columbia, Canada and an MBA in Educational Management from the University of Leicester, UK. She is pursuing a PhD in Higher and Postsecondary Education at the New York University, USA. Her doctoral research focuses on international academic partnerships from the perspective of South African faculty. She has extensive experience in academic administration of higher education in Pakistan, East Africa, and North America.
Email: nmadhani@gmail.com

Dilshad Ashraf is an Associate Professor at the AKU-IED. She has done her PhD in Education from the Ontario Institute for Studies in Education, University of Toronto, Canada and her MEd from AKU-IED. She has extensive experience of managing research and scholarship endeavours of AKU-IED. Her work over a decade includes leading numerous research and educational development projects. More recently, she led 'knowledge generation for social cohesion and resilience' project, gender equality strategy of Strengthening Teacher Education Project, and the education component of AKDN's Multi-input Earthquake Reconstruction Programme in Khyber Pakhtunkhwa and Azad Kashmir. Her research and teaching focuses on curriculum, teaching and learning, teacher development, educational governance, social cohesion and equity (gender) issues in education.
Email: dilshad.ashraf@aku.edu

Nusrat Fatima Rizvi is an Assistant Professor at AKU-IED. She holds a DPhil (Doctor of Philosophy) in Mathematics Education from the University of Oxford, UK; Master of Education and Master of Art (by research) from Flinders University of South Australia. She teaches Mathematics Education at the graduate level. Her research interests include exploring effective models of teaching and learning, curriculum development, Mathematics teachers' subject matter, pedagogical content knowledge and their influence on students' learning, different orientations of Mathematics curricula and their influence on students' reasoning. She is one of the founding members of the Mathematics Association of Pakistan.
Email: nusrat.fatimarizvi@aku.edu

Zubeda Bana (late) worked as an Assistant Professor and Head, Outreach at AKU-IED. She had earned a master's degree in education from the University of London. She had extensive work experience in the public sector in Pakistan. She had rich experience of designing and teaching teacher education and educational leadership and management programmes in a variety of settings within and outside Pakistan. Her research interests were in improving schools in disadvantaged rural areas. She passed away in July 2017.

Kulsoom Jaffer is an Assistant Professor at AKU-IED. She holds a Doctor in Education (EdD) degree and a Master's in Arts, Educational Management and Administration from University College London, Institute of Education. She teaches Educational Leadership and Management courses at the graduate level, and also offers continuing professional education courses. Her research interests include monitoring and review of school performance, institutional leadership and management, teacher professional development and performance appraisal.
Email: kulsoom.jaffer@aku.edu

Khushal Khan is currently associated with the CARE Foundation Pakistan and working as a Campus Incharge in Karachi at DHA Campus. He has earned his MEd degree from the Notre Dame Institute of Education, Karachi, Pakistan. He worked with the STEP project of AKU-IED as a Teaching Associate. Currently he is studying towards his MPhil degree at AKU-IED. In this role, he designed and conducted continued professional development courses for teachers and educational managers and supported school improvement initiatives in projects schools.
Email: khushalyasin@gmail.com

Foreword

This remarkable book offers an optimistic but realistic and challenging research-grounded account of the implementation of a wide array of initiatives supported and undertaken under the auspices of two major multi-year international donor funded education improvement projects in Pakistan—the Strengthening Teacher Education in Pakistan (STEP) and the Educational Development and Improvement Programme (EDIP). The Aga Khan University-Institute for Educational Development (AKU-IED) was the key in-country organization responsible for planning, mobilising, organizing, and delivering programmatic interventions associated with the two projects in the provinces of Sindh, Balochistan, and Gilgit-Baltistan. The editors and authors of the book are teaching and research faculty of AKU-IED and were directly associated with the design and implementation, research and evaluation, and supervision of many of the education improvement initiatives that provide the topical focus of different chapters. The projects overall were designed as multi-level and multi-constituency capacity building initiatives largely directed towards the public school sector and targeting various groups of education stakeholders including teacher educators, teachers, head teachers, district education authorities, parents, and education system policy makers. The uniqueness of these efforts stems in part from the fact that they built upon and extended to a wider scale AKU-IED and the Aga Khan Development Network's efforts to positively influence education access, quality, and equity over the previous two decades, which are comprehensively described in Chapters 3 and 4 of this book. I was personally involved as a partner in the first decade of AKU-IED's development between 1994 and 2006, and have been an interested observer of ongoing developments since then.

The book presents findings from a selection of distinct research studies carried out by AKU-IED faculty on different focuses of STEP and EDIP project supported intervention, as well as some chapters that provide more comprehensive overviews of the projects with summaries of implementation and outcome findings and recommendations from the project monitoring and evaluation reports and the authors' personal experience with the projects. The chapters address a variety of education improvement focused interventions which are internationally touted as innovative and effective ways of improving education quality, including: developing teacher leaders to model and lead change in professional practice in cooperating schools, leadership development for head teachers and other education managers, organizing school clusters to promote collaborative professional development and improvement activities, establishing field-based learning resource centres, and implementing Whole School Improvement processes (e.g. teacher development, leadership, curriculum, teaching and learning materials, physical facilities, community involvement). The chapters also describe, investigate, and reflect upon the implementation of professional development strategies such as teacher mentoring, action research, and professional networks of teachers and school administrators within the local organizational, cultural, and political contexts.

At a macro-level, several of the authors provide evidence of promising positive results of the overall projects in terms of educators benefitting from professional development programmes delivered at AKU-IED, its outreach centres, and in the field; of the numbers of schools and teachers affected; and even of important indicators of student impact such as access, attendance, and results on local assessment measures in comparison to similar schools in Pakistan not involved in project interventions. At a micro-level, several of the authors provide closer to the ground accounts of the daunting challenges of integrating innovative ideas, practices, and attitudes cultivated in their professional development experiences into practice in teacher education institutions, schools and classrooms, communities, and levels of school system administration and support beyond the school. Some of these challenges arise from the gaps between local cultural beliefs and traditions, especially concerning gender relations and education, and traditional school culture norms (e.g. hierarchical authority, seniority, teacher isolation, no tradition or enabling conditions for reflective practice and professional inquiry). These accounts speak strongly about the need to be sensitive, persistent, respectful, and patient while addressing such challenges. Other challenges relate more to organizational issues, in particular, the generalised absence of effective governance and leadership and the influence of local politics that constrain or derail efforts to introduce more effective and sustainable ways of working in schools. To their credit, the book contributors do not shy away from the very real political and resource issues of sustainability and continuous improvement and of local adaptation of innovations in school management, professional development, community involvement, curriculum, and methods of teaching and learning. At the same time, the authors demonstrate continued commitment and optimism about the potential for improvement in access, quality, and equity in Pakistani public and community schools, drawing lessons from these projects and from empirical research that has characterised the work of AKU-IED since its inception in 1993. This book and the lessons it highlights are a must read, not only for stakeholders in the future of education in Pakistan, but also for education reformers in other developing countries.

Stephen Anderson, PhD
Director, Comparative, International and Development Education Centre
Department of Leadership, Policy and Adult Education
Ontario Institute for Studies in Education University of Toronto
Toronto, Canada

PART I:
INTRODUCTION AND AKU-IED'S ROLE IN EDUCATIONAL REFORM

1

Imperatives of Educational Reform in Pakistan: Towards an Analytical Framework

Takbir Ali

Introduction

Pakistan is the sixth most populous country in the world, inhabited by over two hundred million people.[1] Corresponding to its demographic realities, the country operates a large system of education, which unfortunately is in shambles. The multifarious socio-economic challenges and the fast changing demographics seem to have made it difficult for the government and the international community to achieve noteworthy successes in reforming the public education system in the country. Despite efforts by the federal and provincial governments, consistent donor support over decades, education indicators related to both access and quality have not improved, but rather deteriorated further, as the evidence suggests.[2] For example, the recurring patterns of low enrolment (more worrisome for girls and rural communities), increasing dropout rates at primary level, decreasing retention rates at middle and secondary levels, and deplorable poor student achievements at all levels are some of the critical indicators accounted for the ostensible failure of reform in the public sector education in the country (Aziz et al., 2014; RSU, 2015).

Experience and evidence from the Pakistani context, which broadly resonate with experiences from other developing countries, suggest that educationally effective reform initiatives in the public sector are often obstructed by a wide variety of obstacles. Some of these obstacles are necessarily rooted in the 'absence' of reform support policy framework at national as well as at province levels.

In this introductory chapter, while providing a conceptual base for reflections, experiences, and research-based evidences, discussed in the volume's subsequent chapters, I give a brief overview of donor supported reforms. I also discuss some of the experiential evidences and lessons so as to paint a broader picture of the past, present, and future of educational reforms in Pakistan.

The chapter consists of three sections. The first section takes a bird's eye view of the socio-economic context, including the demographic conditions and social realities and their interface with educational reform. Next, a brief overview of the reforms undertaken by the government with support from international donors/aid agencies is provided. I highlight a number of notable successes achieved at macro level and critically reflect on the perils and pitfalls of the donor supported educational reforms. The second section, building on an analysis of the local experience and the existing scholarship on educational reform, examines the imperatives of educational reform and proposes an analytical reform policy framework for guiding the reader through the rest of the volume. It also draws the contours and directions of the systemic and effective educational reform in Pakistan. The last section concludes with book and chapters overview.

Pakistan: A Country of Socio-Cultural Diversities and Paradoxes

Before presenting my analytical stance on the political dynamics of educational reform, I provide a brief overview of the context, its demographic and social realities and their interface with the efforts to create a milieu for comprehensive and lasting educational reforms in the country.

As mentioned above, Pakistan is one of the most densely populated countries in the world. The population is growing at the rate of two per cent a year, which is one of the highest in the world. Looking at the size and the growth speed of the population, it is not difficult to imagine the magnitude and the complexity of the challenges the country is facing in its efforts to fulfil educational and other basic needs of the people. The socio-economic problems have further been exacerbated by the long-standing internal conflicts, civil-military tensions, and religious/tribal warfare, resulting in an invariably deteriorating law and order situation. Numerous flaws inherent in the governance and policy structures (e.g. pervasive culture of nepotism, lack of accountability, and misuse or abuse of power at all levels of governance) and imprudent or inefficient use of resource, etc., are a few but serious issues facing the country throughout the seventy years of its existence as an independent state.

From a more critical perspective, lack of good/effective governance and a functional accountability system, coupled with deeply rooted and wide-spread social inequities have resulted in proliferation of corruption and corrupt practices, lack of social cohesion, and ideological polarization, thereby causing disruptions and ruptures in the social order of the country (International Crisis Group, 2014). On top of all these challenges, reforming the overall education system or developing schools for improved student learning outcomes have not been the 'number-one-priority' of the successive governments in Islamabad and in the provinces. Barber (2010) has attributed this to the lack of political 'will' to transform the education system.

Pakistan is a culturally rich country in terms of geography, ethnicity, language, and religious diversity. It has promising economic potential, mainly hidden in its agricultural resources and burgeoning youth population. Unfortunately, however, diversity and resources, instead of being taken as strengths of the country, have been used by politicians, religious leaders and other power groups as tools to exploit national resources and perpetuate hegemonic interests of the elites (for more details, see chapter 9). As a result, Pakistan has become a country of paradoxes. On one hand, Pakistan claims to be an atomic power, while on the other hand, it sits at the bottom on the global index of social indicators, such as education, health, and gender parity. While there are many people who go abroad and spend extravagantly on regular routine health screening, there are millions of poor people who do not have access to basic health care services. They consequently suffer from curable and preventable diseases. Similarly, there are schools for elites which have every imaginable facility, including luxurious swimming pools for students. These posh schools co-exist with hundreds of thousands of impoverished public schools, which do not have basic facilities. For these schools safe drinking water is a luxury. In sum, these and many other paradoxes explain the depth and breadth of social inequities and the widening gap between haves and have-nots, thus generating complex insurmountable challenges for both educational and social reforms. Ironically, they also explain the vitality of equitable and quality education systems in the country. In such environments, reforming the education system in a comprehensive and systematic manner is undertaking.

A Bird's Eye View on the History of Educational Reforms in Pakistan

A look at the history of educational reforms in the country suggests that in the past various governments have formulated and launched national education polices[3], five year plans, and special reform projects/programmes[4] aimed at bringing about positive change in the public education system. These policies and plans look good on the paper. They appear to be as comprehensive enough in analysing problems and envisaging solutions with wide subsector (e.g. teacher education, curriculum, management, community, etc.) coverage. In reality, however, these policies and plans have yielded very little or no significant positive results. Numerous issues emanating from this policy 'implementation' are held responsible for rendering these policies and plans irrelevant and ineffective.

Since the devolution of the mandate of education to provinces in 2010, Pakistan's provinces have begun taking greater responsibility for the delivery and improvement of their educational services. Starting from 2013, the provinces have designed their comprehensive Education Sector Plans (ESP)[5], which envisage radical reforms in some areas or subsectors of the education system. Given that the implementation of the education sector plans is still in progress, it is too early to judge the impact of these reforms on the education system's quantitative and qualitative indicators. Nevertheless, a critical look at the ways these plans have been conceptualised and the manner in which they are being executed so far, raise serious conceptual and implementation concerns. These, in my view, include: (i) short duration of interventions; (ii) low quality of inputs; (iii) illogical sequencing of activities; (iv) lack of follow-up; (v) dependency on extrinsic motivation; (vi) undue leverage of government bureaucracy and external consultants; and (vii) no genuine grass-roots level participation in decision-making. These are important symptoms that predict success or failure of donor supported large-scale reforms.

Research-based scholarship on educational reform and change has grown into almost a mature science. Applying its evidence and experiential insights, one can easily predict the fate of reforms. For example, in an approach to reform, where the power of decision-making and other aspects of reform management are concentrated in the nexus of government bureaucracy and international or national consultants (who every so often consider themselves as redeemers of the ailing education systems in the developing countries), may not produce the intended outcomes in the long run. There is a serious shortage of participation by the grass-root level beneficiaries such as children, parents, communities, teachers, and disadvantaged ethnic and social groups in decision-making at school and district levels (for more details, see chapter 9). What change do people want? What do they think about a particular change? How it can be brought about and sustained within the local conditions? How can they be a part of and benefit from the reform? These are the questions which, according to the 'science' of reform/change, are important considerations for making reform successful in the long run.

Contribution and Impact of Donor supported Reform

A closer look at the history of the donor supported projects/ programmes implemented in Pakistan reveals the extent to which the governments at both federal and provincial levels have relied on foreign aid in developing and improving the country's education system. Over the past many decades, the international donor community and aid agencies have provided substantial financial and technical support to Pakistan in order to improve school infrastructure, access, quality of teaching, teacher competencies, and curricular materials.

Moreover, the donor community's interventions have germinated a fresh thinking in Pakistan and other developing countries where age-old local practices and 'hit and run' strategies adopted by donor-aided project have been challenged often. There is an increasing realisation among the education fraternity in the country about the need for seeking innovative, contextually appropriate and grounded solutions to educational problems. The other notable contribution of the donor supported reform programmes has been the introduction of innovative practices and models of teacher education and professional development, capacity building of school leaders, school improvement, and cluster-based mentoring. Some of these models or 'global best practices' (e.g. decentralisation of teacher training, integration of teacher in-service training with school improvement) and theories of change (e.g. capacity building at all levels, community involvement, and whole school approach to change), have been tested and modified to make them more relevant to local needs (for more details, see chapter 2). In this way, reforms initiated or supported by international donors and aid agencies in collaboration with the private sector and government institutions offer an opportunity for cross fertilization of ideas and integrate indigenous and external theories and practices to make them relevant to the local context. Admittedly, this is not an easy task as the field of policy borrowing and contextualization of global practices is a highly contested one (for a critical discussion, see chapter 13).

Last but not the least, the education sector has been a priority recipient of donor funding. The funds received through donor aids, have contributed significantly to employment generation and mobilisation of economic activities in the resource starved countries such as Pakistan, which had significant tangible impact on the country's educational and social developments.

Perils and Pitfalls of the Donor supported Educational Reform

There prevails a strong perception that despite consistent engagement of the donor community and funding agencies in the educational reform, the accessibility and quality indicators in public education sector have not improved significantly (Burki, 2005; Mitchell, Humayun & Muzaffar, 2005). Contrary to this, the evidence on the quality of education shows a decline and deterioration in both students' learning achievement and enrolment/retention. The public system's primary and elementary schools, despite being the foundation of the education system, are poorly managed and are imparting an education of deplorably low quality to millions of boys and girls.

Hence, a closer look at the current state of affairs in Pakistan's public education system and the long history of the donor community's engagement does not present an optimistic picture. The picture reinforces the comparative international development's disbelief about the long-term impact of donor supported interventions on schools and students' learning outcomes. These interventions are ill-conceived, short-term, and poorly implemented due to political pressures and expediencies. That is why some critics, including myself, who have closely witnessed the work done through projects or have had first-hand experience of working in these projects, tend to contest the sustainable impact of donor supported projects, and would go to the extent of describing Pakistan's education sector as 'the graveyard' of poorly implemented developmental projects. Arguing about people's resistance to change, Andy Hargreaves (2002), an esteemed scholar of educational change, puts it as follows: '...history continually repeats itself. This repeated failure becomes more than a set of disconnected episodes. In the minds and the memories of teachers, the failure of change becomes a cumulative phenomenon' (p.190).

Reforms, initiated in various areas of the public education system through donor supported projects, usually have a short life (on average 1–3 years). The trend is that, as soon as the project completes its life and the flow of funds stops, the attrition of changes begins and old practices start reasserting themselves. This all makes change a 'zero-sum' game. Ideally, to sustain change, the government needs to step in to replenish resources and use 'support' and 'pressure' combination (Fullan, 2000) to sustain the momentum of the change. The real fate of reforms, however, is contingent upon the commitment, motivation, and capacity of teachers and head teachers who are the real custodians of school and classroom-based changes.

More often than not, short-term donor supported projects rely heavily on monetary incentives to involve teachers and head teachers in the school/classroom-based changes and to get the buy-in of the district officials into these changes. Donor supported projects tend to consider this an easy way or a short cut to garner support for change. This has made public system teachers and education officials the habit of seeking personal benefits (money, foreign tours or so-called study tours/exposure visit, gifts, and employments for their family members, relatives and friends) in exchange for their active participation in and support to the project. I call this as an induced 'ventilator effect'; using money to gain support of teachers/head teachers or education officials is akin to putting a terminally sick person on a ventilator knowing that the person will die if the ventilator (temporary support) is removed. This, as I have seen in many cases, happens to the changes which are not internally induced because change agents' intrinsic motivations are not engaged. Rather, changes are made to happen and sustained through the use of conditional incentives—the 'killer' of change, I would say. This is usually done in donor supported reform projects to achieve short-term objectives rather than paying attention to the complex process of educational change, which is rife with ambiguities, anxieties, and uncertainties.

Reform projects are considered to be 'knowledge mobilisers' (Levin, 2012). Donor supported reform projects are best placed to put theories of reform and development to the test of practice. Most of the short-lived (usually 1–3 years) projects and programmes, developed and implemented in a haphazard fashion, tend to make inadequate to generate grounded knowledge and use it to influence government policy with regards to institutionalisation of models and practices. According to Healey and DesStefano (1997):

> ...most school reform initiatives are, in one sense or another, "demonstration" projects that are designed to generate concrete information about good educational and pedagogical practice. And in fact, these pilot projects often do provide models of what schools and school districts need to do (p.3).

Yet, they can not only be conduits of knowledge transfer and tests but also play a major role in generating useful knowledge that is grounded in practice and local culture. To do this, these projects need to engage the various stakeholders such as the policy community to produce new knowledge and enable them to deliberate about the structural and political conditions for sustaining and replicating educational reforms. It is through this process that, contextually grounded knowledge can be generated and brought to bear upon policy discourses and decisions.

Reform Policy Framework

The biggest challenge to educational reform in Pakistan is that there is no coherent policy framework at national or provincial level to guide and regulate small or large reforms that are undertaken through donor support. This absence of a strong and coherent reform policy framework leads to lack of consensus and cohesion among the different donors, governments, and clientele groups on the broader principles and imperatives that derive comprehensive educational reform. In the environment where there is a lack of coordination and synergy among stakeholders and programmes which normally results in duplication of programmes. There is hardly any sharing of experience and no learning from each other's good practices, negative competition among donors and local partners (private sectors players and NGOs) and 'repetition' of mistakes (use of strategies and solutions that have not worked). This all underscores the need for having a coherent policy framework (at national or provincial level) in place, which serves as a road map to provide direction for systematic, progressive, real, lasting, and multi-faceted improvements in the education system in Pakistan.

Imperatives of Educational Reform: Towards an Analytical Policy Framework

A policy framework is needed to steer educational reform at the national or provincial level. It should be used by the government and the donor community as a road map to envision the impact of reform and strategies, and adopt choices and approaches to achieve the envisaged impact through government's initiatives and donor supported reforms. The policy framework should lay out broad parameters for gauging the outcomes and determining the ultimate impact of reform. Taking into account the current scenario of education in the country and the lessons learnt from reform implementation, the reform policy framework should also spell out the prioritisation of needs at national, province, district, school, and classroom levels.

There are no agreed upon principles to judge the quality indicators of a successful reform. However, there are recurring patterns of empirical evidence, emanating from case studies of successful or failed reforms in Pakistan and other developing countries, that helps identify some success indicators for donor supported large-scale reforms. Drawing upon the existing knowledge base, research evidence, and my personal experiences, I can attest to at least the following four success indicators that may be used as loosely defined benchmarks for judging the success or effectiveness of a large-scale educational reform. These are: (i) 'greater impact' (on receiving-end users such as students and schools); (ii) 'long-term sustainability' (long-lasting use and continuity of reform practices, examples, legacies, and gains); (iii) 'widespread usage' (expansion and proliferation of reform results, and of the ideas, values, and strategies that underpin it); and (iv) 'sustained commitment' of the frontline change agents (teachers, head teachers, and educators) to reform. These benchmark indicators in fact have been discussed so widely and consistently in the literature that they have almost appeared to be 'gold standards' for determining effectiveness of donor supported educational (large-scale) reforms (e.g. Fullan, 2000; Levin, 2012; Stoll, 1999).

Once we have a settled opinion about the benchmarks (outcome/impact indicators), we will need to know what, at the input level, helps to achieve these successes. My own experience and a scrutiny of the worldwide research about successful educational reform suggest the following four key factors to be present essentially at input level for such reforms to succeed in terms of yielding the above four success indicators. First, there needs to be 'government or local/beneficiary ownership' of the reform. Second, the reform needs to be 'demand-driven' and not 'supply driven' (needs to come from the target beneficiary, while solutions are negotiated, not imposed by the supplier). Third, a 'broad representation of the grass-roots level educational stakeholders' (involvement in choosing, planning, and executing reform) from its early stages is critical. Lastly, there has to be 'capacity building at the local level' (which includes involving people as local change agents, champions, and actors).

There is a wide agreement on these factors (input variables), which collectively help create the necessary conditions for substantive educational reform (e.g. Hargreaves, 2002; Sherry, 2003). As shown in Figure 1, they are intricately interlinked and have a direct effect on the above four outcomes or 'markers' (benchmarks) of successful and effective educational reform. The complex interface of the four input variables (preconditions) and the four key markers (output quality indicators) of effective educational reform, as explained in Figure 1, provide an analytical framework for understanding the interactive dynamics and the imperatives of donor supported educational reform in Pakistan and elsewhere in low income developing countries. The four input variables (preconditions), considered to be important determinants of substantive and impactful educational reform, are briefly discussed to see how they are mutually dependent and bear direct or indirect influence on the outcomes of reform.

Government/Local Ownership of Reform

The large-scale project-based reforms that do not enjoy institutional patronage or ownership of the government, after project life, prove less effective in terms of achieving long-term results such as breaking the inertia inside schools and classrooms and challenging the status quo in the public sector education system (Fullan, 2000). On the other hand, the educational reforms that can enjoy the system's or the government's ownership have a greater chance of sustainability and expansion after the project's life (Fullan, 1993). Therefore, it is imperative to take all the necessary measures and adopt well-thought-out strategies to ensure the government's ownership of the reform and its gains at all levels of governance.

As discussed above, various reform projects do make efforts to ensure the government's buy-in and ownership in their own ways, and according to their own understanding. However, the experiences

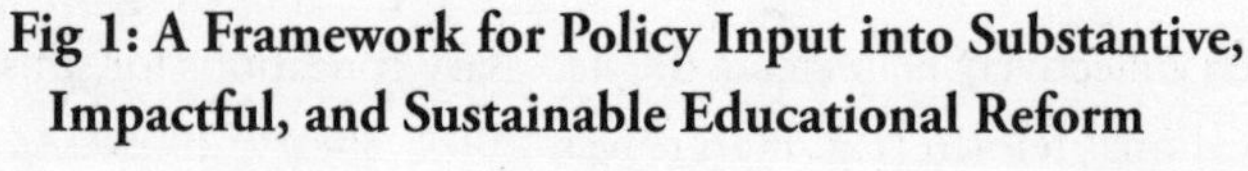
Fig 1: A Framework for Policy Input into Substantive, Impactful, and Sustainable Educational Reform

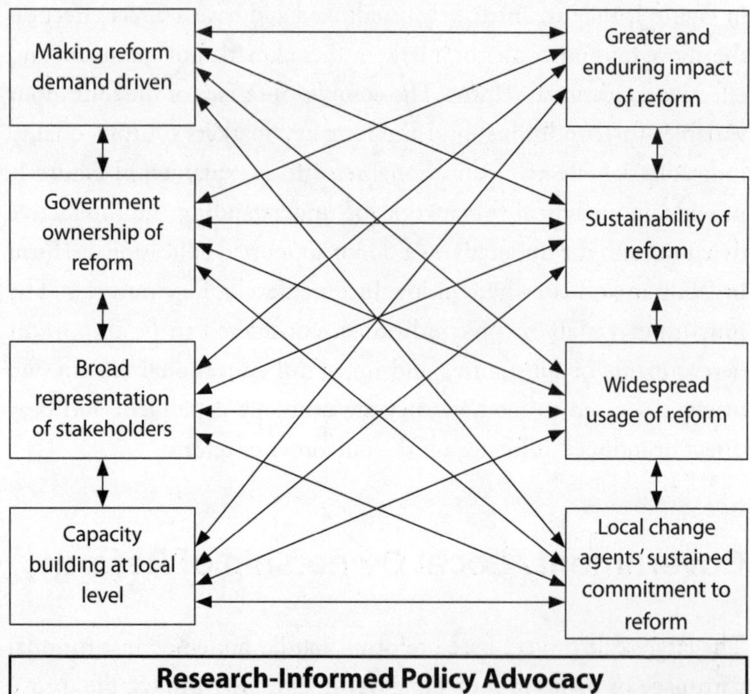

suggest that these efforts yield little or no long-term results. Enhancing the government's ownership of the reform needs more soul searching and more focused and intelligent efforts on the part of all parties involved in the reform including, donors, implementing agencies, and government institutions, and local community.

An example from recent experience would suffice to explain the difficulties involved in ensuring government's ownership of educational reform. Backed by one of the leading international development/donor agencies, a couple of years ago, the government introduced an Associate Degree in Education (ADE), as a substitute to the existing pre-service teacher training programmes in Pakistan e.g. Primary Teacher Certificate (PTC) and Certificate in Teaching (CT). Despite the apparent successful implementation of the initial two cycles, the programme is now in a limbo, and the symptoms of the predictable failure of the innovation have begun to appear. Staring from its inception, the decreasing patterns of enrolment in the programme and increasing dropouts in each successive year, and some provincial governments' search for alternate models for teacher education and professional development under donor-supported reforms, suggest that the programme has already started losing its credibility. Due to poor implementation, it may soon become an 'old wine in a new bottle' (for more details, see chapter 12). From the academic and scholarship point of views (e.g. long duration, richness of curriculum, and emphasis on practicum), the programme has well-thought-out ideas, which have the potentials to produce good results, if implemented according to programme's true spirit and rigor. But the issue lies with the 'government or local ownerships' because the government (governments in all four provinces and federally administered regions) have failed to fulfil their promises to sustain their commitment of providing financial support (stipends) and employment guarantees to the prospective teachers (Muhammad, 2017). If this is the fate of a well-planned reform, initiated with policy support and patronised by an influential and powerful international development/donor agency, one can imagine how the future of other less fortunate reforms in this country might look like.

Making Reforms Demand-Driven

The lessons derived from the experiences of working through reforms and the scholarly perspectives on their effectiveness underscore the need for making reform 'demand-driven'. When a donor-funded project is conceived and implemented by private sector organisations

(NGOs/INGOs) and government institutions without input from the widespread grass-roots level beneficiaries they become 'supply-driven'. Thus, the projects having no genuine representation of end-users and have little chance to survive and thrive after the project's life. The demand-driven approach emphasises that solutions to educational problems in a given context should be found locally. '...the specific answers that constitute reform should be home-grown. *Local answers* not only address specific educational needs and aspirations, but also engender a sense of *ownership* that enhances the overall viability of implementation of reform' (Healey & DesStefano, 1997, p. 10).

Broad Representation of Grass-Roots Level Stakeholders

The role of the government system and institutions in the post-project scenario is to provide an environment conducive to the meaningful and active involvement of the broader, grass-root level stakeholders at the district and local levels (Tehsil, Union Council, Taloqa in case of Pakistan). In educational reform, these stakeholders include teachers, school leaders, educators, students, managers, parents, community members, women, marginalised/disadvantaged groups (ethnic, religious, and rural communities).

Without engaging the local dynamics i.e. involving grass-roots level beneficiaries and mobilising local influences in identifying problems and their solutions in accordance with the principles of democracy (participation, equality and equaity, liberalism, diversity, and pluralism), the government, change agents, and different interest groups in Pakistan and elsewhere will have a hard time in ensuring long-lasting and impactful reforms.

In conformity with these principles of inclusion, and in collaboration with the donors, the government education systems in Pakistan (federal, provincial) and elsewhere in developing countries also need to develop the capacities of the above mentioned primary stakeholders. This will ensure wider representation of legitimate partners and beneficiaries in policy negotiations, policy-making, and policy implementation processes in the public sector education system.

Capacity Building at the Local Level

It is essential to win the hearts and minds of the people who lead reform as active and frontline change agents. It is important for these people to acquire a certain level of 'professional competence', which combines knowledge, skills, and dispositions. It is indispensable for change agents, change workers, change champions, change sympathisers, and change advocates at the grass-roots level to be knowledgeable about reform and its underlying purpose and demands. Training, professional development programmes, critical reflection on actions, action research, analytical problem solving, and other activities during the reform projects are intended to build the capacity of key players such as teachers, head teachers, administrators, managers, and community members. However, as suggested by experience, capacity building at the local level alone must not be used as a panacea for the problems associated with sustainability; rather it should be used as one among many other favourable conditions for reform sustainability. There are numerous other factors involved in how change agents, or more precisely, the 'custodians' of change, endeavour to hone and translate their capacities into actual outcomes.

Sustained Commitment of the Change Agents towards Reform

It is imperative to develop a critical mass of key actors and champions at the institutional (school) level so as to sustain their commitment to reform. The experience suggests that an adequate number of motivated teachers, head teacher, parents, and district officials in a school context can constitute the required critical mass to support and sustain reform initiatives at the school level. In Pakistan and other developing countries, it has been observed that financial incentives (e.g. additional allowances for participation in training or other incentives such as compensation for any additional undertaking) during project life help generate a great deal of interest, enthusiasm, and motivation in teachers and other stakeholders towards change. However, as already discussed, the motivation for becoming change agents and change custodians dwindles when financial incentives, rewards, and compensations are reduced or withdrawn towards the project's conclusion.

As discussed earlier, sustaining the key actors' motivation and commitment towards change without additional financial incentives after project life has been the *single most important dilemma* of both external and local reforms in the context of Pakistan. Unfortunately, some of the externally funded projects throughout Pakistan have extravagantly invested in getting 'mock' support from local stakeholders and government bureaucracy for short-term gains. The trends and traditions set by these projects by paying extravagant allowances (travel allowances and per diems) and sponsoring lavish foreign tours for bureaucrats have proven counterproductive in the long run. We are reminded by Hargreaves (2002) that:

> ...sustainable improvement contributes to the 'growth and the good of everyone, instead of fostering the fortunes of the few at the expense

> of the rest. It does not channel water to prosperous villages while their poorer neighbours die of thirst (p.191).

The undue dependency on financial and other incentives, which are often related to short-term change, do not only create hurdles for long-term sustainability of reform but also contribute to the proliferation of malpractices, often leading to moral degradation within the system and the society at large. The donor community and implementing partners from the public and private sector unfortunately have been oblivious to this bitter reality.

In the chapters that follow, the authors will demonstrate that the four primary determinants, namely government/local ownership, demand driven reform, grass-roots level representation of local stakeholders, and capacity building at the local level are vital to the success of large-scale educational reforms in developing countries. Together with the four outcomes (e.g. greater impact, long-term sustainability, widespread usage, sustained commitment of change agent towards change), they provide a conceptual grounding for the analysis and discussions presented throughout the volume's distinct chapters.

Envisioning a New Direction for Educational Reform

The perspectives and reflections on experience and research evidence, as discussed above, underscore the need for envisioning a new direction for impactful, lasting, and comprehensive educational reform in Pakistan. This requires assessing deeper the complexity of reform in order to reinvent policy narratives and raise critical questions about the role of donor supported reform projects/programmes. It also requies understanding globally-construed best practices and their compatibility with the idiosyncrasies of the local context. The focus should be on implementations of innovative, contextually grounded, and culturally engaging approaches and strategies towards increasing enrolment, decreasing gender inequalities, alleviating, socio-economic disparities and improving and sustaining the overall quality of basic primary school education. Working out the new reform policy direction among many other measures would require the comprehensive review of educational reform policy options, assumptions, strategies, and models. It would also require needs re-assessments, and re-definition of priorities for educational reform to strategically align national, regional and global agendas based on the comprehensive reforms and sustainable social development.

Knowledge Base to Inform Reform Policy Framework

A coherent reform policy framework cannot be developed in a vacuum. Research-informed, contextually-grounded knowledge should provide conceptual basis for the development of the reform policy framework. There exists enough expertise, human and institutional capacities and necessary research-informed knowledge in the country to help develop a contextually relevant reform policy framework. There are institutions and organisations in the public and private sector which have a long history of working closely on large-scale educational reforms in collaboration with the donor agencies. The Aga Khan University-Institute for Educational Development (AKU-IED) is one such organisation, which, since its inception in 1993, has been closely engaged in designing, implementing, and researching large-scale education reforms, especially in the public education realm. Chapter two of this volume illuminates the depth and breadth of the experiences that AKU-IED has gained while implementing donor-supported large-scale reforms in most parts of Pakistan, and researching the impact of reform projects with the support from the international donors, government institutions, local partners, and the Aga Khan Development Network. This gives the institution an effective voice to legitimately represent key stakeholders' interests in an effort to create and promote powerful policy narratives. In addition, it leverages policy-makers to be accountable for better policy choices and to influence donors and the development community in terms of adopting effective approaches to educational reform in Pakistan and other developing countries.

Book and Chapter Overviews

This volume has been compiled keeping in mind the interest of a wide range of audience residing both inside and outside Pakistan, these include researchers, educators, and students of educational and developmental studies, donors, development community, policy-makers, teachers, and managers. Inspiring stories about successes achieved through all-encompassing, long-term donor-supported reform projects[6], and critical reflections on the factors that either facilitate or inhibit change in the local context make this volume worth reading. One of the unique features of this volume is its critical stance and sharp focus on issues surrounding the understanding of theory-practice relationship in the context of large-scale education reform. The analysis undertaken and perspectives shared in different chapters are all results of rigorous and informed analysis of issues emerging from empirical evidence. They are presented with the purpose of demonstrating what works and why, as well as what does not work and why not, in the context of multi-dimensional large-scale reform projects.

This unique volume is organised in five parts, comprising

13 chapters. The parts and chapters are thematically or conceptually sequenced. Part One (chapters 1 & 2) includes a sharp situation analysis of the donor supported educational reforms in Pakistan and chronicles AKU-IED's evolving role in the country's educational reforms. Part Two (chapters 3–8) deals with the theme of capacity building for schools, teachers, managers and communities. Part Three (chapter 9) is solely devoted to issues of educational governance; taking school as a focal point of decision-making. It examines, from a deeper level, how, to what extent, and in what ways issues associated with educational governance impinge on educational outcomes. Part Four (chapters 10–12) delves deeper into the opportunities and issues associated with the strengthening of teacher education institutions. Finally, Part Five (chapter 13) synthesises the key deliberations and lessons learnt, presents conclusions, positions them in the international comparative scholarship on 'global best practices', and 'policy borrowing and lending.' The chapter revisits the study's arguments and propositions highlighted in this introductory chapter. It ends with policy implications for locally grounded educational reform.

Chapters Overview

In the **first Chapter**, I have provided a situation analysis of the donor supported large-scale educational reforms and their contribution to the educational improvement in Pakistan. It is argued that educational reforms in school education in the public sector in Pakistan have been heavily dependent on donor-funded initiatives. These initiatives, technically or financially supported by donors and international funding institutions (IFIs), have played a significant role in improving educational access, developing infrastructure, strengthening teacher training and building institutional capacity throughout the country. Notwithstanding, the remarkable contribution made by externally funded reform projects and programmes to educational reform and development in Pakistan, the effectiveness of these programmes and projects are questioned from sustainability and scalability perspectives.

Based on the international literature on educational reform and change, an analytical reform policy framework is presented and discussed. The framework includes four input level imperatives and four output level success markers. It explains the complex and interactive dynamics of these imperatives and the success markers. I then present background in order to set the scene for deliberations and reflections on lessons learnt from various reform initiatives undertaken by the STEP and EDIP projects. In doing so, I examine the policy context in the nexus of donor-funded large-scale educational reform and the forces that either enable or inhibit efforts intended at achieving effective educational reform. This is followed by deliberations for envisioning a future direction for education in the country.

In **Chapter 2**, Sadrudin Pardhan discusses the developmental work undertaken by AKU-IED in the form of reform projects and places it in a historical context. He details the circumstances in which AKU-IED worked with international donors, local partners, and AKDN institutions in its efforts to improve the quality of education in Pakistan. He explains how AKU-IED transited through its three critical phases of development. Pardhan describes AKU-IED's journey towards earning, owning, implementing, and disseminating STEP and EDIP—two large-scale reform projects, as the main focus of this particular volume.

The story about AKU-IED's journey narrated by Pardhan elucidates the growth and maturity of AKU-IED, and its recognition both locally and internationally as a contextually relevant institution of prime quality. It also talks about the institution's deep and enduring commitment, and its reliable partnership with public, private, and civil society institutions, as well as with international donors. An important development in AKU-IED's journey has been engaging public and private education policies which has become more evident and efficient with the passage of time. The STEP and EDIP projects are illustrations of the extension of AKU-IED's efficient and grounded model into other areas of Pakistan. While AKU-IED has been going national and global for a while, STEP, with its remarkable scale and catchment has firmly put the institution on the national map. While addressing the question of sustainability, Pardhan argues that sustainability of gains could be increased by professional development which leads to capacity development and includes opportunities for participants to reflect on theories. It also links them to practices in the field, and provides follow-up support to them in their own environments.

In **Chapter 3**, I highlight some facts about the STEP project, including its sources of funding, areas of intervention, key components, geographical coverage, and beneficiaries. I elaborate on the change model adopted by the STEP project, followed by a description of and reflection on the models of professional development and capacity building espoused by the project. Models of teacher professional development and school improvement, including the Cluster-Based Mentoring Programme (CBMP), Whole School Improvement Programme (WSIP), and Professional Network for Teacher Development (PNTD) are discussed, with reflections on key outcomes.

The STEP project, as portrayed above, has been an all-encompassing large-scale initiative, which concurrently focused on multiple areas of interventions. In **Chapter 4**, I provide details about STEP's interventions in areas of management capacity building and policy advocacy and examine the ways in which STEP's initiatives aimed at human and institutional capacity building influenced practices at individual and institutional levels. The chapter demonstrates the importance of understanding educational issues around opportunities for and challenges to STEP. This process is generated through various activities, including research, policy discussion, and collection of lessons learnt in the project.

Chapter 5 by Mola Dad Shafa, Sharifullah Baig, and Zeenat Shah provides a short break from STEP, the key focus and narrative of this volume. The authors describe another large-scale reform project, also implemented by the AKU-IED (from 2010 to 2015), namely the Education Development and Improvement Project (EDIP). Unlike STEP, which was funded by Canada's Global Affairs and Aga Khan Foundation, this project was funded by the Department of Foreign Affairs and Trade (DFATD) of the Australian government. The project endeavoured to bring about systemic change in public and private (not-for-profit) sector education systems in Gilgit-Baltistan—a geographically and economically challenged region of Pakistan. Presenting details about the demographic conditions in and socio-cultural realities of the context, the chapter presents a comprehensive overview of the project, its areas of interventions, models of professional development and school improvement, achievements and lessons learnt. In this chapter, the authors report on a fascinating story about working with highly disadvantaged, conservative, and traditionalist communities in the Diamer District of Gilgit-Baltistan. Diamer District, inhabited by conservative religious communities, presents the most unique and challenging context for educational intervention in Pakistan, where education literacy is overwhelmingly low, particularly for women and where modern education has been considered a 'forbidden' area for girls.

Returning to STEP, **Chapter 6** describes how the project implemented a wide variety of programmes and innovations under the umbrella of its three key components. Under its second component, *teaching, learning, and educational management*, the project implemented a major field-based large-scale intervention that is the Cluster-Based Mentoring Programme (CBMP), in seven districts of Sindh and one district of Balochistan, focusing on teachers' professional development. Over 1,600 schools and 3,500 teachers benefited from the programme. To determine the effectiveness of the programme, Sadia Muzaffar Bhutta, Nahid Parween, and I conducted a study employing experimental quantitative design. The study collected data from STEP trained and non-STEP teachers' classrooms and compared two sets of data regarding teachers' performance against given sets of indicators. The data and findings presented and discussed in this chapter, reflect a notable, in some instances (indicators), significant positive causal relationship between training through CBMP and teachers' (mentees) in improved classroom practices. The STEP trained teachers overall outperformed their counterparts who did not receive STEP training.

As far as sustainable educational change is concerned, there is no alternate to engaging quality human resource in the process. There is no short-cut to developing quality human resource for institutions, it needs time, resources and, above all, a vision. Ayesha Bashiruddin and Mir Afzal Tajik in **Chapter** 7 suggest that AKU-IED's experience has been transformational for its graduates in multiple ways which include: professional and personal; pedagogical and managerial; technical and intellectual; and cultural and political. The STEP project invested considerable resources in developing quality human resource for schools in general and teacher education institutions in particular through the two-year MEd programme at AKU-IED. A total of 43 teachers and teacher educators completed their MEd studies through STEP-sponsorship and returned to serve their institutions. Using the phenomenological approach within qualitative research paradigm, Ayesha Bashiruddin and Mir Afzal Tajik investigated how and in what ways the MEd graduates have been able to use their newly acquired knowledge and skills to leverage influence on practices in their workplace and in the wider social context. Importantly, however these transformations have been fraught with challenges at personal, familial, school, system, community, and cultural levels. The study provides strong lessons for how a programme, like AKU-IED's MEd, can be further improved in terms of taking reform to schools and classrooms.

Often higher education, particularly in-service professional education, is considered to be a means of improving services and outcomes at the institutional level. However, we often ignore other benefits attached with higher education (professional qualification) while judging or evaluating the impact of advanced level professional education. Higher education (advanced professional qualification) gives private and social returns to graduates and society at large. Using in-depth qualitative case studies and performing meta-analysis on these cases, Naureen Madhani in **Chapter 8** explores the private and social returns to sampled MEd graduates of AKU-IED sponsored by the STEP project. The returns are positive and significant and the implications of these findings are important. Quality advanced professional education, like MEd at AKU-IED not only helps individuals to bring about change in their institutions, but also makes a difference in their personal lives and in their families and communities, implying that social change can be attributed to educational change in the community.

Good governance and effective management are considered to be the backbones of an education system that delivers. In **Chapter 9**, Dilshad Ashraf and I argue that in Pakistan and other developing countries, the deteriorating governance system and failing management structures are perceived to be the main causes behind the education system that is in a parlous state and has failed to deliver. Issues of educational governance are immensely complex, intricately interlinked and deeply rooted in the socio-cultural context and political milieu of the society. In order to understand, some of the key issues involved in the governance conundrum from an ethnographic perspective, under STEP project funding, Dilshad Ashraf and I conducted a research study using a quasi-ethnographic approach, and applied critical discourse analysis, with particular emphasis on decision-making processes, practices, and structures in educational governance. The study yielded interesting findings, having far-reaching implications and recommendations for reforming educational governance. **Chapter 9** presents and examines the findings of the research study and formulates a set of recommendations with regards to improvement of educational governance.

Chapter 10 by Kulsoom Jaffer, Zubeda Bana (late), and Khushal Khan looks at the influence of the capacity building programme conducted through the STEP project for the administrators (principals and vice principals) of teacher education institutions on the participants' leadership and management practices. While applying Thomas Guskey's model of evaluating programmes, they found that although overall, the participants enjoyed the course and learnt a great deal about what an educational leader signifies, they all had a hard time implementing the learning from the course in their workplaces. The influence of training on participants' practices and on their institutions' culture is not as visible or as encouraging as one would expect. According to the authors, one possible explanation of the situation is that there are loopholes in the process of recruitment and nomination of candidates for the professional development course. They suggest that a course cannot be effective if the whole process is not taken seriously.

Nusrat Fatima Rizvi in **Chapter 11** reports on a meta-analysis of the Action Research (AR) projects carried out by the participants of a twelve-day course organised by the STEP project. The chapter discusses how a global best practice on teacher professional development that is Action Research, promoted by the STEP's multi-programmatic interventions, was taught, received, and applied. AR has been promoted as a tool where research becomes professional development. AR has democratised research and makes teachers feel empowered as it allows their voices to be heard and makes them in charge of their practice. The chapter, however, reveals that even such a seemingly easy approach to knowledge generation and practice improvement such as AR can produce multiple challenges to the course instructors and participants. The case shows both the potential and problems of teaching and internalising action research.

Teacher education institutions in the public sector in Pakistan critically lack the capacity to provide quality pre-service and in-service education to prospective and practicing teachers. The lack of this capacity, among other aspects, essentially involves the faculty being deficient both in content and pedagogy. The new Associate Degree in Education in replacing the traditional pre-service courses (e.g. Certificate in Teaching and Primary Teaching Certificate) places high demand on the knowledge, skills, and disposition of the educators who teach the ADE courses in Government Elementary Colleges of Education (GECEs). In this context, the STEP project undertook an Institutional Strengthening Programme (ISP) for selected GECEs in Sindh, Balochistan, and Gilgit-Baltistan. The programme involved focused, deliberate, and systematic efforts (capacity gap analysis, planning, and implementation) to strengthen the professional capacity of the management and the faculty members of the target institutions. In **Chapter 12**, drawing on case studies conducted into the implementation of ISP, Sadia Muzaffar Bhutta, Zubeda Bana, and Kulsoom Jaffer present interesting stories about the successes and challenges of capacity building at selected Government Elementary Colleges of Education (GECE) in Quetta (Balochistan), Skardu (Gilgit-Baltistan), and Hyderabad (Sindh). The authors demonstrate how at each GECE, three different conceptual frameworks were successfully used to achieve the programme's objectives. The stories depict the joyful and transformative learning the teachers received at the colleges.

In the **last concluding Chapter**, Sarfaroz Niyozov pulls together important experiences, key deliberations, and critical reflections from each chapter, derives meanings from them and consolidates them into important learning outcomes implementation of large-scale educational reforms in Pakistan. He synthesises the implications of these lessons for policy and practice which lead to the formulation of comprehensive yet realistic recommendations. Such recommendations help create a powerful narrative for effective policy-making for sustainable educational reform in Pakistan and other developing countries. Niyozov looks through the tensions that inevitably arise from 'lending and borrowing' of ideas, theories, and practices in educational reforms. He contests the neoliberal approaches to reforming education in developing countries, which strikingly differ from developed countries in their socio-cultural realities.

To summarise, the various chapters in the book present rich information about contexts, programmes, interventions, and views from the beneficiaries about impact, challenges, and lessons learnt. The authors discuss successes, reflect through possibilities and challenges and also raise questions about practices, approaches, and strategies involved in the implementation of reform initiatives.

References

Aziz, M., Bloom, D.E., Humair, S., Jimenez, E., Rosenberg, L., and Sathar, Z., 'Education System Reform in Pakistan: Why, When, and How?' (*The IZA Policy Paper Series no. 76*, 2014).

Barber, S.M., 'Education reform in Pakistan: This time it's going to be different', *Policy Paper, Government of Pakistan, Ministry of Education*, Islamabad, 2010.

Burki, S.J. 'Educating the Pakistani Masses', in R.M. Hathaway, ed. *Education Reform in Pakistan: Building for the Future* (Woodrow Wilson International Center for Scholars, Washington, DC, 2005), 16–32.

Fullan, M., 'The return of large-scale reform', *Journal of Educational Change,* 1/1, (2000), 5–28.

Fullan, M., *Change Forces: Probing the Depths of Educational Reform* (London: Falmer Press, 1993).

Hargreaves, A., 'Sustainability of educational change: The role of social geographies', *Journal of Educational Change,* 3/3, (2002), 189–214.

Healey, F.H., and DeStefano, J., *Education reform support. A framework for scaling up school reform* (Academy for Educational Development, 1997).

International Crisis Group, '*Education Reform in Pakistan*', (ICG, Brussels, 2014), <http://www.crisisigroup.org/en/regions/asi>accessed 13 November 2014.

Levin, B. '*System-wide improvement in education*' (International Institute for Educational Planning & United Nations Educational, Scientific and Cultural Organization/ International Academy of Education, 2012).

Mitchell, J., Humayun, S., and Muzaffar, I. 'Education Sector Reforms in Pakistan: Demand Generation as an Alternative Recipe' in R.M. Hathaway, ed. *Education Reform in Pakistan: Building for the Future* (Woodrow Wilson International Center for Scholars, Washington, DC, 2005), 107–122.

Muhammad, Z., 'An in-depth qualitative inquiry into the key stakeholders' experiences about the implementation of the Associate Degree in Education Programme at a Government Elementary College of Education in Karachi, Pakistan' (Unpublished MPhil thesis, Aga Khan University-Institute for Educational Development, 2017).

Reform Support Unit, '*Standards Achievement Test-Class V & VIII: Sindh Government Schools' Students' Achievement-Class V-VIII*' (Education and Literacy Department, Government of Sindh, 2014–2015).

Sherry, L., 'Sustainability of innovations', *Journal of Interactive Learning Research,* 13/3, (2002), 211–238.

Stoll, L., 'Realizing our potential: Understanding and developing capacity for lasting Improvement', *School Effectiveness and School Improvement,* 10/4, (1999), 503– 532.

Notes

1. The most recent national census conducted during the final stage of writing this book will help determine the actual size of the country's population.
2. ASER, Pakistan, 'Annual Status of Education 2010–2015' (Idara-e-Taleem-o-Aaggahi, Lahore, Pakistan. 2016), <www.aserpakistan.org>accessed 10 May 2016 (ASER—The Annual Status of Education Report is the largest citizen-led household based initiative that aims to provide reliable estimates on the schooling status of children aged 3–16 years residing in all rural and few urban districts of Pakistan). Alif Ailaan, 'Pakistan district education ranking 2016'. (Alif Ailaan is a Pakistan-based NGO working for Education; every year it collects data from selected districts from all over Pakistan and does a

comparative analysis of student achievement across sampled districts), <www.alifailaan.pk> accessed 10 May 2016. 'Education for All 2015 National Review Report: Pakistan' (Trainings and Standards in Higher Education Academy of Educational Planning and Management Islamabad, Pakistan, 2014). The Aga Khan University-Institute for Educational Development (2010). STEP Project baseline report.

3. Since its independence in 1947, Pakistan has launched 16 national education policies.
4. E.g. USAID-funded Education Sector Reform Assistance (ESRA) project implemented from 2001–2006.
5. Sindh Education Sector Plan-SESP (2014–2018); Balochistan Education Sector Plan–BESP (2013–2018); Khyber-Pakhtunkhwa Education Sector Plan-KESP (2015–2020) and Punjab Education Sector Reform Plan-PESRP (2012–2017); Gilgit-Baltistan Education Strategy (2016). These reform plans are being implemented with financial and technical support from major donor agencies.
6. The Strengthening Teacher Education in Pakistan (STEP) and the Education Development and Improvement Programme (EDIP). These two projects, with funding from the Department of Foreign Affairs, Trade and Development (DFATD) of the government of Canada (STEP) and DFATD of the Australian government (EDIP) were respectively implemented in Sindh, Balochistan (small component in KPK and Gilgit-Baltistan). The STEP project was designed solely for the public sector, while EDIP for a large part catered to the public system with a proportion of its funds used to support reform initiatives of a private education system.

2

In Pursuit of Educational Reform and Institutional Growth: AKU-IED's Experience

Sadrudin Pardhan

Introduction

The Strengthening Teacher Education in Pakistan (STEP) was a multi-pronged innovative initiative of the Aga Khan University-Institute for Educational Development (AKU-IED) to improve teacher education in the provinces of Sindh, Balochistan, and Gilgit-Baltistan. The project lasted from 2008 to 2016 and was generously funded by the Global Affairs Canada (GAC)[1]. AKU-IED was the lead agency and worked very closely with the Provincial Departments of Education to implement the project. Their support was outstanding. Support from GAC and the Aga Khan Foundation (both in Canada and Pakistan) was also outstanding to achieve the targets of the project.

Prior to the implementation of STEP, AKU-IED had accumulated a wealth of experience of working with the three beneficiary provinces by developing and implementing innovative, contextually relevant teacher education programmes to develop local capacity. Below is an account of the evolution of the various models developed by AKU-IED before embarking on developing the STEP project which benefited much from the experience gained by AKU-IED.

Towards the end of this chapter is given the process used to develop the STEP proposal and what its expected outcomes were. The remaining chapters of this volume give details about the main programmatic interventions and its actual outcomes.

The Context

The Aga Khan University-Institute for Educational Development (AKU-IED) was established in Karachi, Pakistan, in July 1993 under the charter of the Aga Khan University (AKU)[2]. AKU is a part of the Aga Khan Development Network (AKDN). During its twenty-three years of existence, AKU-IED has emerged as a leading teacher education institution in Pakistan and has taken a lead role in testing innovations in teacher education, educational leadership, influencing policy, conducting research, and promoting scholarship in Pakistan[3]. It is considered as a 'national resource'. A key aspect of AKU-IED's work has been the capacity building of the public sector particularly in Pakistan to implement educational reforms effectively. AKU-IED has also contributed to Public Sector development in other countries like Kenya, Uganda, Tanzania, Afghanistan, Tajikistan, and Kyrgyzstan[4].

Over the past couple of decades, AKU-IED has achieved a great deal of success in Pakistan in terms of developing individual and institutional capacity in initiating and sustaining change. The Institute has developed a series of educational initiatives, which have been nationally and internationally recognised as credible and significant. These form the basis for a coherent programmatic approach to educational improvements and broader social development.

AKU-IED is a relatively small institution confronting major challenges. Its natural constituencies include some of the most impoverished nations of the world. These include regions where access to basic education remains low and where gender disparities in educational access and achievement are large. In such a situation, AKU-IED tries to find ways of 'working smarter' rather than 'working harder' by developing mechanisms for impact multiplication or impact amplification[5]. In such a condition, as the Chancellor's Commission put it nearly 20 years ago, '...the Aga Khan University will not be needed as a sheer quantitative contribution to a generally overcrowded scene in higher education...It must justify its worth through distinctiveness and quality'(1994, p. 27)[6]. Some of AKU-IED's mechanisms for impact multiplication and amplification include: role modelling; viewing programme and course graduates as not only direct beneficiaries but also as active change and impact agents for others; facilitating the participation of faculty and graduates in external and outreach activities such as consultancy, textbook writing, and curriculum development; and emphasising research dissemination; supporting the development of professional teachers associations as major impact multiplication activities.

AKU-IED was established at a time when key education indicators in most countries and in particular, the developing countries, reflected the poor quality of education; low and inequitable enrolment and retention rates; irrelevant curricula compounded by ineffective assessment which in turn fosters rote learning and passive student roles; and poorly resourced schools staffed by inadequately trained and supported teachers[7]. Thus, the institute was established with the aim to show models that would look into increasing the efficiency and effectiveness of schools and other educational institutions in the country through innovation, policy development, practice, training and research.

A considerable amount of time was spent on conceptualising the Institute, as Aga Khan Development Network (AKDN) did not want to establish yet another teacher education institution. It had to be unique and creative. During the 1980s and the early part of the 1990s, AKDN had tested a number of school improvement models in different parts of the world including East Africa, India, and Pakistan (Northern Pakistan and Sindh[8]). Many lessons had been learnt. It had been clearly established that if appropriate field-based support is given to the teachers, their classroom performance improves substantially. It had also been established that in schools, where the leadership was strong, the performance was also good. Field-based practice including teacher education in real classrooms succeeded much better than other forms of teacher education. These kinds of programmes, while very successful, led AKDN to believe that a permanent base was necessary for innovation in educational approaches that could improve schools. Such an institution would be able to credibly certify teachers who put in a lot of hard work to attend courses during the school improvement implementation. After much deliberation around these points, the idea of AKU-IED was conceived. The total time from initial discussion to conceptualisation, stakeholder inputs, getting various approvals from the government, the Aga Khan University and the agencies including the Aga Khan Education Services, the Aga Khan Foundation, the Ministry of Education, Partner Universities of Oxford and Toronto, mobilising start-up funding and actual start-up took about four and a half years.

Phase I: Setting up AKU-IED

AKU-IED's first phase lasted from July 1993 up to June 2001[9]. For this initial phase, AKU-IED received grant funding from the European Commission (EC), the Canadian International Development Agency (CIDA[10]), United Nations Development Programme (UNDP), and the Aga Khan Foundation (AKF). The AKF also provided land on which the institution was built.

A medium-term collaboration was established between the Faculty of Education, the University of Toronto, Canada, and the Oxford

University, Department of Educational Studies (OUDES), UK. Through this collaboration, AKU-IED developed and delivered high quality education programmes, collaborative relevant research in the local context and faculty development. Other than credibility-related support, these institutions were also involved in field-based teacher education in their respective countries. It was an attractive consideration for AKU-IED to forge a partnership with them.

The first programme developed by AKU-IED was its innovative Master of Education (MEd) programme. The emphasis of this programme was on teacher education but it was expected that the graduates of this programme would be exemplary reflective teachers and action researchers. The programme was intensive and spread over two years. The focus of the courses was to create a strong commitment to educational change, developing critical thinking skills, commitment to reflective practice, lifelong learning, and school improvement[11].

During the first phase, the main focus of AKU-IED was on Institutional Development and to test some innovative teacher education models. As the institution's reputation increased, many new opportunities came up. Many of these were unique and AKU-IED ensured that it did not adopt the 'one size fits all' model. AKU-IED worked with stakeholders and developed and tested innovative models of teacher education and school improvement, focusing on the context, reflective practice embedded in critical pedagogy and active learning for the improvement of schools and other educational institutions.

Realizing the increased needs of continuing professional education of teachers and others, AKU-IED adopted an in-service professional education route to collaborate with public, private (not-for-profit), and AKDN schools as well as other educational institutions through school-university partnerships in South Asia (Pakistan and Bangladesh), Eastern Africa (Kenya, Uganda, and Tanzania), and Central Asia (Tajikistan and Kyrgyzstan). Through this model, teachers, who attended various professional development programmes, worked together as teams in their respective schools according to well-developed school plans, which had a shared understanding of the stakeholders. AKU-IED worked closely with schools and the results were very encouraging[12].

This was the first innovation targeting schools. Variations of this model are currently practiced in a number of AKU-IED's collaborating schools in Karachi, Pakistan. A number of case studies were documented of such schools[13].

Professional Development Centre in Northern Pakistan

During the first phase, AKU-IED developed a Professional Development Centre in Northern Pakistan (PDCN), which is a teacher development institution established specifically to serve the remote areas of Gilgit-Baltistan and Chitral[14]. The focus of PDCN is to support teacher education in the rural setting using innovative field-based practices. It is run by MEd graduates of AKU-IED under the leadership of a Head (initially from overseas but replaced by a well-qualified local person with doctoral degree qualification).

This model of PDC was also an innovation which could easily be replicated and was indeed done by a number of partner schools and other organisations. The PDCN tested an innovative model called the Whole School Improvement Programme (WSIP) in Gilgit-Baltistan. For participating schools, the WSI model lasted for three years. Schools were selected so that there were a number of them in a cluster which could be supported easily and which also gave teachers at the schools an opportunity to network. The first year had a school-based focus, followed by less intensive support in the second year as follow-up. Through this model, a pair of PDCN faculty (MEd graduates of AKU-IED) also called Professional

Development Teachers (PDTs) worked in each of the clusters (in the field) for four days a week alongside teachers, head teachers, students, and parents within their contexts, to find appropriate strategies for improvement. Keeping in mind the realities of classrooms and the knowledge base and beliefs of teachers, the PDTs were expected to help teachers maximise the available human and material resources to improve the quality of teaching and learning. They attempted to develop good practice through collaborative work, team teaching, and activity-oriented learning. Additionally, a workshop was held for all cluster-based teachers every week to enhance the teachers' professional knowledge. The schedule of workshop topics included principles of children's learning, methodology and organisation, behaviour and discipline, curriculum development and some content knowledge, and examinations and assessment practices. Through these workshops, it was intended to establish a culture of regular staff meetings the purpose of which was to institutionalise regular professional/academic dialogue about teachers' work. This often was the most difficult challenge in terms of changing the deeply embedded egg box culture of schools, where teachers teach within their own boundaries (Hargreaves & Fullan, 1992).

The focus was also on analysing schools as organisations and questioning age-old practices, which often create barriers to teachers' work. On Fridays, the PDTs came back from the field to attend the 'Friday sessions' at PDCN in order to share their field experiences. The Friday feedback sessions enabled the PDTs to learn from each other, develop strategies for further innovation, and seek support from colleagues[15].

The programme was not only designed as a vehicle for implementing effective practices but also as a research tool for examining the project schools' own effectiveness as an organisation, and the success of the support structures and procedures of the educational systems which manage these schools. For example, what educational resources are given to schools? Are they adequate? Are they effectively used? What is their impact on teaching and learning? What is the impact of the monitoring and support visits by local supervisors such as Field Education Officers (FEOs) and Assistant District Inspectors (ADIs)? Are the human resources in terms of teachers-students ratios adequate?

Both the implementation focus and the research focus in terms of case studies and action research make this a powerful strategy for school improvement. Since, PDCN's emphasis was on whole school improvement and on developing collegiality and cooperation amongst members of the staff and also parents, the concentration was on a small group of schools in a particular area. But because the schools worked in clusters of three or four, the multiplier effect in the long-term in a given area could be significant, especially if the WSI schools were enabled to create partnerships with other uninitiated schools around the original clusters, thereby creating ever increasing circles. Such a model, however, required a strong commitment from the educational systems in terms of following up the project schools and maintaining support and pressure on these institutions.

The key lessons learnt from the WSI model were that field-based work enhanced the quality of teacher education in schools, the teachers worked collegially, the mentors (PDTs) got an opportunity to teach in real classroom situations, the school heads got an opportunity to develop their knowledge and skills as leaders through the programme and the programme also created possibilities of networking through a cluster-based workshop model. An interesting outcome of this model was the enthusiasm with which the parents (particularly mothers) accepted this approach and the appreciation from them of how much the school cared for them. The programme lasted for many years and from the lessons learnt new models evolved, two such models have been discussed in Chapter 3.

Other Models Developed by AKU-IED during Phase 1

There were other significant models developed by AKU-IED that came towards the end of its phase 1.

The education scenario in Balochistan province of Pakistan had been dismal. Efforts were being made by the government with funding from international donors to support in-service teachers. In June 1996, the Primary Education Department (PED) of the Government of Balochistan approached AKU-IED for its support in developing a programme that could develop teachers efficiently and effectively. It was recognised that any programme that was developed had to have long-term sustainability (Memon, Lalwani & Meher, 2006). It was also agreed that there was a need to involve not only teachers and teacher educators but also educational leaders at both the District and the Provincial levels so that they also had 'ownership' in developing these teachers.

So, in collaboration with the Primary Education Department (PED), a strategy was developed by AKU-IED. According to this, AKU-IED agreed to develop teacher educators through its two year innovative MEd teacher education programme. However, the key driving force of field-based development would be primary level teachers who would become mentors after undergoing a tailor-made training. While capacity was being developed through the MEd programme at AKU-IED, the institute developed a curriculum for the primary school teachers who would be the participants of this training and also for Education Managers and Leaders who were expected to support the teachers in the field. In this development activity, AKU-IED faculty (who were themselves IED graduates) participated together with the instructional team from PED. As the trained teachers were going to become mentors at the field level, AKU-IED's Visiting Teacher (VT) programme was designed accordingly with emphasis on mentoring. Whenever it was possible, the course participants of the MEd programme from Balochistan also participated in the curriculum development activities.

At the cluster level, the needs of primary teachers and of potential mentors were identified. These included learning strategies for effective delivery of primary school curriculum in the context of multi-grade teaching, developing low-cost material, enhancing pedagogical content knowledge, and understanding the dual role as classroom practitioners and mentors. Also, materials had to be developed in Urdu as the English language skills of the proposed participants from primary schools in Balochistan were not up to the mark.

To save time, the initial certificate courses, based on AKU-IED's own Visiting Teacher programme, were conducted at AKU-IED in Karachi. Ten teachers were developed from each district of Balochistan (there were 23 districts in Balochistan at that time). In each group there were a minimum of three female teachers. Because of cultural reasons and because of the paucity of female teachers, the numbers for female teachers participating in training were low. Efforts were made to engage the MEd course participants from Balochistan while the VT training was going on so that they could gain experience from the real training situation. Simultaneously, small groups of education supervisors and officers were also brought to AKU-IED to engage in leadership development programmes and to engage in dialogue with teachers from their own districts. This was something that many of them had not done at the field level because of lack of time and long distances to the schools.

By the time the first batch of MEd graduates from Balochistan was ready (in June 1998), four courses had been completed at AKU-IED. The MEd graduates (PDTs) from Balochistan were now almost ready to take more responsibilities to conduct the courses. The next set of courses was held in Quetta, the provincial headquarter. In the Quetta-based programmes, the MEd graduates (PDTs) worked closely with

AKU-IED faculty to gain confidence. By the time the sixth cohort of the VT programme was conducted, the PDTs took full charge of their work with minor support from AKU-IED faculty. Subsequently, the PDTs conducted a couple of other certificate programmes.

The participating teachers after their graduation went back to their schools and in collaboration with education officers and the PDTs, developed cluster-based professional development programmes for their colleague teachers, and they in turn worked with about 30 teachers in the clusters. The group met for two days each month and the programme continued for two years. Substantial capacity was developed at the field level through this process. Teachers got an opportunity to network with other teachers in the system. In all, nearly 6,000 teachers from 20 districts in Balochistan benefited from this programme (Memon, Lalwani & Meher, 2006). More importantly, capacity had been created at the provincial level to support the work of teachers and an opportunity was also created for teachers to network. Most of the PDTs from Balochistan were then posted at the Provincial Institute of Teacher Education (PITE).

While the Balochistan programme was going on, the Aga Khan Foundation, Pakistan (AKF, P) launched a project titled 'Pakistan Non-Government Initiatives' (PNI) with an aim to enhance the capacity of NGOs/CBOs for promoting the quality of pre and primary education, in general, and girls' education, in particular, in rural and semi-urban areas. The programme was funded by United States Agency for International Development (USAID). AKU-IED was involved in: (i) strengthening non-governmental organisations (NGOs)/community-based organisations (CBOs); and (ii) documenting the best practices and lessons learnt in the areas of community management, financing of education, and policy advocacy. In this chapter only the capacity development aspect is discussed.

The project objectives were to develop the capacity of educational management both at the school and the community level, teaching and learning at the classroom level and to develop means for follow-up support to teachers.

AKU-IED worked with fourteen NGOs selected after a comprehensive needs assessment exercise. The focus of capacity building was placed on creating internal conditions for developing 'collaboration', 'empowerment', 'ownership', 'networking', and a sense of 'strategic leadership' among the relevant stakeholders to achieve the overall purpose of the project.

Based on the 'needs assessment' of the fourteen collaborating NGOs, AKU-IED developed and launched a series of innovative contextual professional development programmes ranging from Certificate to Advanced Diploma levels in the areas of teacher education, educational leadership and management, and monitoring, evaluation and documentation for building capacity. A total of five members from the NGO community were also developed through IED's MEd programme to provide long-term teacher education support. Project achievements indicated significant impact of professional development on students' learning that led to improved overall annual examination results of schools. Substantial changes in teachers' attitude and behaviour and their relationship with students and parents were also found. Many female NGO staff received accelerated promotion to senior management positions. They became quite successful in managing and leading their schools effectively. Another achievement of the project was increased enrolment of girls in schools and dramatic reduction in girl students' dropout rate.

An important innovation in the PNI II project was the development of Learning Resource Centres (LRC) for the NGOs. The LRC concept of this project was developed on indigenous models of professional development of teachers. The purpose was to use these as platforms to support teachers' work in the field[16].

While many lessons were learnt from this model, the key was systematic follow-up after each training programme, field-based approach of programme delivery, collaborative vision development between AKU-IED and the communities and thus the 'ownership' by the leadership of NGOs and CBOs, and finally the creation of a PDC like resource centre for each NGO/CBO.

One of the immediate outcomes of this initiative was to establish Learning Resource Centres (LRCs) to provide access to teachers and others for their continuing professional development on the job. Literature on professional development suggests that teachers and others learn more effectively on the job than off their workplaces (Clandinin & Connelly, 1995). Another strength of this professional development model was that teachers and others were able to relate their new learning to their own context and apply it and reflect on the implications. This allowed AKU-IED to develop an 'indigenous' model of professional development of teacher education and educational leadership which can be replicated in other areas of Pakistan. All NGOs/CBOs had strongly recommended that AKU-IED should continue such partnership with them until their LRCs become fully functional and sustainable.

Another model that AKU-IED developed towards the end of phase 1 was the establishment of subject related teacher associations by interested teacher educators and teachers. In Pakistan, there are few opportunities for teachers to come together to network and learn from each other.

In 1995, AKU appointed a Task Force (called Task Force 2) to look at the future direction of AKU-IED, once Phase 1 concluded. One suggestion made by this think-tank was that AKU-IED should inspire its own graduates to form professional associations that were subject related. There was a possibility that these could try and reach out to teachers who did not belong to AKU-IED's collaborating schools and so would get opportunities to access high quality professional development. AKU-IED faculty was looking for an opportunity to encourage the graduates to do this[17]. The first opportunity came up in

July 1997 when a mathematics summer school was organised at AKU-IED to which 35 teachers from AKU-IED's collaborating schools and graduates of AKU-IED were invited. At the end of this course, these mathematics teachers, encouraged by the AKU-IED's leadership, met and developed a proposal to form an association called Mathematics Association of Pakistan (MAP).

They approached AKU-IED to find out how the Institute could support them. After much discussion, it was agreed that AKU-IED would provide space for the activities of MAP. It would provide operational costs in case MAP wanted to develop a newsletter. And it was agreed to provide snacks whenever workshops were organised. MAP felt really encouraged and worked on a strategy of developing workshops once a month on the first Saturday. It was also agreed that people who conducted the workshops would not charge any fees, in other words they were all volunteers. MAP decided to form an executive committee to do the day to day follow-up. The Executive Committee also worked on a constitution and bylaws. The first workshop turned out to be a major success. Soon after that, and as word of mouth spread, a lot of inquiries started coming from teachers who were interested in joining MAP. More importantly, during the second workshop a month later where MAP invited 30 people to participate, nearly 75 turned up! So obviously there was a big demand. None of those 75 was turned away because the whole purpose was for teachers to network and to participate to continue professional education. So, this way MAP got a firm footing and it became very popular.

Similar to what happened with MAP was repeated a year later with science teachers who were attending a summer school at AKU-IED. They formed the Science Association of Pakistan (SAP) with support from AKU-IED[18]. And like MAP, they were also very successful. They decided to meet every second Saturday of the month so that it would not interfere with MAP. Coincidently, between 1997 and

1998, AKU-IED conducted an Advanced Diploma in Education and Leadership Management called ADISM (Advanced Diploma in School Management). At the end of the programme, the head teachers decided to form their own association so they could network. This gave birth to SHADE (School Heads Association for Development of Education).

So within two years, AKU-IED was associated with three very popular associations. They were given space and partial administrative support through a programme officer at AKU-IED. Also, these associations decided that they would ask their member teachers to contribute a small membership fee of PKR 100 ($1) a year. This was to give them ownership of the association and to prepare them for the future when support from AKU-IED may not be forthcoming. The teachers were more than willing to contribute. Considering that the teachers were expected to find their own way to come to AKU-IED, it was remarkable; and this led us to believe that the teachers really valued the work of the associations and networking was important to them. Soon after, schools requested institutional membership to enable more of their teachers to participate.

By 2003, seven associations had been formed. These included Association for Social Studies Educators and Teachers (ASSET), Association for Primary Teachers (APT), Pakistan Association for Inclusive Education (PAIE) and Health Education Association for Learners Teacher Educators and Health Workers (HEALTH) and the three described earlier. These seven associations were formed by 2003. AKU-IED applied for a grant to bring these seven associations under one umbrella called Professional Teachers Associations Network (PTAN) which was subsequently renamed Professional Network for Teacher Development (PNTD). Aga Khan Foundation offices in Pakistan and Canada were very gracious in providing a small grant spread over a period of three years so that these associations could be stabilised.

AKU-IED continued supporting the formation of associations. Two new associations, one for early years called Early Years Learning Association (EYLA) and finally Association for Promotion of Ethics in Education (APEE) were formed. In total, there are now nine associations that are coordinated by PNTD. The associations have become quite vibrant and engage in diverse activities such as regular workshops, Olympiads for children, symposia for teachers, summer sessions, newsletters, consultancies and outreach for both public and private sector teachers. Every weekend, subject teachers come to IED to attend the workshops and to network with colleague teachers. Approximately 2,500 teachers benefit from these associations per year. This model was commended by external evaluators of a funded project as being one of the most efficient teacher education models that also gave opportunities to teachers to network. The model also found place in a Request for Application (RFA) floated by USAID called Linking Education (or EDLINKS) programme.

The contribution of PNTD has been appreciated by teachers, since it has provided a professional platform for sharing experiences and learning from each other. This initiative has created much interest amongst teachers and others to continue finding solutions to their problems and improving teaching learning processes. Inspired by PNTD, university faculty across Pakistan including AKU-IED faculty launched the Pakistan Association of Research in Education (PARE) which contributes towards developing professional networking amongst researchers, academics and others.

At the end of phase 1, AKU-IED was evaluated by a number of agencies who had funded the activities of the Institute. Following are a few excerpts from the evaluators.

The final EC Evaluation report states[19]:

> IED has been successful in building substantial human resources within IED as well as within the co-operating schools… On the qualitative

side, it was observed during site visits as well as from documents and, impact research provided, that considerable changes had taken place at classroom level after teachers and school management participated in IED programmes...(p. 37).

The team of External Evaluators of Phase 1 led by Wilhelm Weidmann (1999) on behalf of the European Commission (EC) noted:

> Since its formation, AKU-IED successfully established a set of educational initiatives within a relatively short time frame, which are nationally and internationally recognised as being credible and significant, and which form the basis for a coherent, programmatic approach to educational improvement and broader social development (p. 27).

The holistic and empirical strategy chosen by AKU-IED to impact the quality of education is unique for Pakistan, effective and efficient and has visible impact at school and student levels. The evaluation report underlined:

> Teachers became 'facilitators' practicing student centred learning styles; students became responsive and demonstrated a confidence in expressing themselves, social behaviour in class was improved by co-operative learning methods and group work, school management and teachers responded more resourcefully in lesson planning and teaching aid preparation and use; school climate improved considerably and collegial spirit among teachers supported their professional work as they practiced peer coaching (p. 37).

Therefore, it is strongly recommended that IED should continue implementing its concept, approach, and strategy of improving the quality of education through school improvement and the professional development of teachers.

On gender equity, the evaluation report stated: 'By empowering teachers through the development of their professional competence, IED also contributes towards the enhancement of teachers' status in Pakistan, particularly of female teachers who represent a large majority of teaching force' (p. 34).

The other agency that evaluated AKU-IED on behalf of UNDP was UNESCO. A Programme Specialist from the UNESCO Regional Office noted that 'the IED at the Aga Khan University is firmly established. It is on its way to become a Centre of Excellence in Teacher Education'[20].

In the final evaluation of Phase 1 conducted by Professor Terrance Boak on behalf of the Canadian International Development Agency and Aga Khan Foundation-Social Institutions Development Programme (AKF-SIDP), he states that 'IED has easily surpassed its expected outcomes (targets) established in 1993 and is an institution in which to be extremely proud'[21] (p. 52).

Phase 2: Developing Models of Teacher Education and Impacting Policy

AKU-IED commenced its second phase from June 2001, which was funded by grants from the European Commission (EC), the United States Agency for International Development (USAID), the Canadian International Development Agency (CIDA), the Aga Khan Foundation (AKF), the Aga Khan University (AKU), small grants, and user fees.

The focus of the second phase was on the following outcomes:

i) To continue developing models of effective teaching and

learning, teacher development, and school management that are relevant to different types of schools in developing countries;

ii) Testing these models under classroom conditions to assess their feasibility and their effectiveness in bringing about improvement at whole school level;

iii) Disseminating outcomes and results of this work through courses, workshops, conferences, papers, and publications; and

iv) Informing and influencing educational policy, through the knowledge and experience gained from the above strategies.

During this phase, AKU-IED continued building institutional capacity of the public sector schools and teacher education institutions, such as Provincial Institutes of Teacher Education (PITE) and Government Elementary Colleges of Education (GECE). AKU-IED also actively participated in Public Sector Education related committees. Just as phase I was coming to an end, Pakistan launched the Education Sector Reforms (ESR) in 2001 aimed at both qualitative and quantitative improvements in the education sector. The plan was very ambitious. The ESRs included programmes to:

- Increase literacy and achieve universal primary education;
- Introduce technical education;
- Improve higher education focusing on science and technology;
- Enable public-private partnerships; and
- Improve the quality of teacher education and training.

It was expected that a National Institute of Teacher Education would be strengthened along with the four Provincial Institutes for Teacher Education. To improve the qualifications of elementary teachers, bridging courses were to be provided for 110,000 teachers. The government also announced a number of other initiatives including improvement in good governance through decentralisation, and substantial devolution of service delivery at district level.

However, there was much anxiety over Pakistan's ability to deliver on such ambitious plans because of a dire lack of implementation capacity on the ground at all levels.

In 2003, USAID in collaboration with the government launched its Education Reform Assistance Programme (ESRA)[22].

USAID advertised a Request for Application (RFA) in 2003 to support ESR through the ESRA programmes.

AKU-IED felt confident that the experiences it had gained in developing innovative models in teacher education for different contexts and its work with the Public Sector particularly in the provinces of Balochistan, Sindh, and NWFP (now Khyber-Pakhtunkhwa) qualified it to participate in the ESRA project. A technical proposal with the following goals was shared with ESRA.

- Deliver effective and relevant teacher education and development programmes;
- Develop capacity at district level to sustain in-service teacher education; and
- Conduct research on the factors which affect the professional development of primary level teachers in selected districts of Sindh and Balochistan.

Based on its proposal, AKU-IED got selected to be a part of the ESRA consortium starting in 2004. AKU-IED worked in nine selected districts (which were further divided into a total of 12 districts over the duration of the project) in Sindh and Balochistan. It was a multi-pronged approach for interventions in these districts to develop skills of education officers, teacher educators, and teachers through a variety of contextualised programmes.

Some of these teacher education and development programmes were customised specifically for the ESRA project, while some were existing programmes offered by AKU-IED. However, innovation was kept in the forefront.

The main focus was on field-based work which was primarily centred on the Cluster-Based Mentoring Programme (CBMP). AKU-IED decided to undertake the Cluster-Based Mentoring (CBMP) approach because of its previous successes in the Balochistan Mentoring Programme and a similar programme conducted for the NGO sector in Sindh. The CBMP through the ESRA project was AKU-IED's first field-based managed programme in rural Sindh and Balochistan. While AKU-IED had tested other cluster-based models, the field work was supported by other partner organisations such as the government and the NGOs. The ESRA Cluster-Based Mentoring Programme and the follow-up fieldwork enabled AKU-IED to shift its focus from academic-based work to developmental work.

As part of the partnership with the government, AKU-IED got the services of PDTs from the government, developed through AKU-IED's MEd programme. They participated in developing the programmes and also worked as District Coordinators in the selected districts of the project. This was mutually beneficial to the government and AKU-IED because AKU-IED's entry into the field was eased since individuals from AKU-IED were not considered to be outsiders in the public sector and resistance to AKU-IED's initiatives by public officials and public school teachers was limited.

Although sustainability of change is a difficult task to accomplish in the short run, through ESRA, AKU-IED attempted to train government officials, particularly the District Officers Education (DOEs), to conduct follow-up monitoring of teachers and to ensure that the change efforts did not come to an end after funding ceased.

In addition to formal training of government officials, communication ties were considerably enhanced at various levels of the public education sector. These private-public partnerships were so effective that many of the government officials themselves stated that they were transformed. By training public school teachers to take a leading role as mentors, the status of primary school teachers was significantly raised in the selected districts of Sindh and Balochistan.

Following a special request from ESRA, AKU-IED began working in the field that not only included establishing AKU-IED district offices, but also institutional development in the form of establishing Learning Resource Centres (LRCs) and Tehsil Resource Centres (TRCs). To this end, AKU-IED provided technical assistance in establishing nine TRCs and 288 LRCs. The LRCs in particular, with the help of AKU-IED, were established by the mentors who had completed their Certificate in Education: Primary Education (Mentoring Focus) to conduct workshops for the mentees in their respective clusters. The TRCs were led by some of the Advanced Diploma graduates so that mentors in turn could seek advice from the diploma graduates of AKU-IED and other colleagues. Moreover, the TRCs provided a forum in which AKU-IED facilitators and diploma graduates could conduct specialised workshops. These included developing low-cost/no-cost materials, creating wall charts, initiating group activities and role play, while moving away from traditional methods of rote memorisation.

School improvement strategies focused on whole school improvement, including teacher training, and head teacher training rather than simply trying to improve classroom learning in isolation without improving the surrounding structures and spaces. The programmes offered through ESRA motivated teachers to actually come to school and teach rather than just record their attendance and leave, as was the existing common practice. Furthermore, teachers were motivated to continue in-service professional development because the ESRA courses whetted their appetite to learn more for their personal and professional growth.

Follow-up and support of teacher education initiatives is one of the key ways in which sustainability was built into the project. Teachers needed a forum to share their experiences and to learn from the experiences of other teachers. They also needed a forum to discuss their successes and challenges with principals and Executive District Officers (EDOs). Seminars and workshops were organised by the graduates of AKU-IED's programmes trained under this project, to enable sharing of experiences, highlighting strengths and weaknesses of various teacher education activities undertaken by the graduates. The PDTs from AKU-IED's programme, with the assistance of AKU-IED faculty helped to organise at least one seminar per year of the project.

There were many successes in the project. A couple of comments from the beneficiaries shed light on these successes.[23] An EDOE from Sukkur, for example, said, 'The AKU-IED's capacity-building programmes have brought significant changes to teachers' attitude, which has resulted in improved classroom practices at the school level. I have witnessed this change while visiting schools in various tehsils of District Sukkur'.

The training conducted by AKU-IED facilitators and the follow-up in the field by the District Coordinators (DCs) was also extremely instrumental in transforming instruction and leadership at the grass-roots level.

The institutional development of LRCs and TRCs proved to be very beneficial to both students and teachers, providing them with considerable resources that were previously unavailable and inaccessible to them. One mentor described the importance of an LRC in the following words:

> The LRC is a place where teachers get the opportunity to work in groups to enhance their content and pedagogical knowledge. Their

joint efforts and creativity result in marvelously creative achievement. My mentees have started bringing raw materials with them, and I am pleasantly surprised by their creativity.

The ESRA project at AKU-IED also helped strengthen AKU-IED itself. As AKU-IED is an English medium institution, virtually all course materials are in English, thereby excluding a significant portion of the population from availing the full potential that these materials have to offer. Urdu materials were developed for the purpose of the CBMP and were very helpful not only to the teachers involved in the ESRA project, but also to AKU-IED itself due to an enhanced library of resources that is more easily understood by the majority of the population. In time to come, this capacity was instrumental in reaching out to teachers.

As can be expected, major interventions also have many challenges. This project had a number of partners and as can be expected it was not always possible to agree on specific approaches. Each organisation had its own priorities. Because we worked with different perspectives, the efficiency of the project was not as robust as we expected. Some of the gaps in and difficulties encountered during the programme may be summarised as follows:

- Because of the ESRA project design the faculty of Government Colleges of Education (GCEs) were not involved so there was a huge lost opportunity;
- The availability of accurate data was an issue but it also gave an opportunity to AKU-IED to develop its own database and share it with the project and the Government;
- Too many partners in the programme created communication gaps, resulting in planning issues; and
- There was also not enough time to take the programme to completion to the satisfaction of AKU-IED. We would have

> needed more time to really institutionalise the innovations. For example, we wanted to enhance the use of Resource Centres. We would have also liked to develop further capacity of the mentors in various clusters. This was not possible as different clusters were supported by different partners, each having a different perspective to teacher development.

The most successful objective of the project was related to strengthening of teachers and administrators of education. However, the policy part of public-private partnership did not work well. The partners looked at the models differently. There was not enough time to engage in policy dialogues and really work out what works and why, and what does not work and why not?

During this hectic period of working with numerous partners, AKU-IED went through a Mid-Term Evaluation. The Mid-Term Evaluation (2004) was carried out by the EC Mission. It noted that Visiting Teacher Programme (a certificate course) contributed to an increased level of confidence, self-assertiveness, and more reflective stance among teachers. The Certificate in Educational Leadership and Management (ELM) has contributed to the changed practices of educational leadership and management. These included moving from an individualistic approach to team building exercises, playing a more active role in curriculum setting and improving monitoring and evaluation and documentation practices[24]. The EC Monitoring Mission (2005) recognised that AKU-IED addressed several issues, which included:

i) The core problem of poor teacher training and weak education system through a set of initiatives supported by the present project as a continuation of Phase I;
ii) Exceptionally sound design of the intervention and a well thought-out change process; and

iii) The attention given to the link between education theory and development practice for ensuring effective change.

The intervention strategies comprised human resource development, construction of models, testing of models, dissemination of its results, and influencing educational policy[25]. The report further highlighted that the graduates were supported to implement change in their own educational context and support was further provided through professional associations[26]. It was also stated that AKU-IED pursued a policy of improving the quality of education in schools, particularly in Pakistan. The initial strategy had been to target professional development of practicing teachers to become change agents; realisation of a better social return from education by achieving better than average quality in the large and sluggishly responsive publicly supported school system; and finding ways whereby high quality private education may radiate effects beyond a few privileged schools. This was further corroborated by the World Bank Representative (2003) who said, 'What AKU-IED has achieved is astonishing. In ten years, it has established a reputation for quality, credibility and independence second to none'[27].

Phase 3: Becoming Partners of Choice and More Large-Scale Intervention Models

In 2003, the Board of Trustees of AKU appointed a new Task Force (III) to start the planning for the future direction of AKU-IED. The TF engaged in discussion with various stakeholders and met a number of times and made recommendations to the Board which accepted them. Based on the TF report, IED developed a proposal for its third phase scheduled to begin in 2007. The proposal stated:

> The broader intention of AKU-IED will be to continue as a *'national resource'*, and would continue taking a lead role in developing credible innovative teacher education and school improvement models, influencing education policy and practice, conducting research and promoting scholarship. It would maintain its international standards in education, research and service and contribute to body of research knowledge and educational reforms in and outside Pakistan for creating an impact on educational development in the respective countries[28] (p. 33).

While the proposal was very detailed, priority was to be given to institutional capacity building of the education sector in Pakistan and other developing countries. It was envisaged that the Institute's new activities and collaboration with public and private organisations would empower individuals and institutions to bring about sustainable reforms in educational systems of Pakistan, as well as in other developing countries. The programmes would be innovative and contextualised.

This proposal was shared with a number of agencies including the Aga Khan Foundation (AKF). The Aga Khan Foundation Canada (AKF, C) informed AKU-IED in June 2006 that the Canadian government had identified Pakistan as a priority country for assistance in the field of education with special focus on teacher education. Canada had just agreed to convert Pakistan's debt to investment in the Education Sector in Pakistan. AKF, C also informed AKU-IED that there had been a discussion between the government of Pakistan and CIDA about how Pakistan and particularly the provincial governments had planned to invest the debt swap money. CIDA's priority area was teacher education and in particular capacity building of Teachers' Colleges. This would enhance the government's capacity to utilise the swap funds. It was suggested by AKF, C as part of phase 3, that AKU-IED could engage public sector institutions like PITE, BoC, and Government Colleges to implement programmes. The Provincial Governments had already commenced the process of preparing their PC-1[29] for that conversion.

The experience of ESRA project was highlighted during discussions with AKF, C. Keeping in mind a number of issues related to ESRA implementation, AKU-IED felt that if a similar innovative project is implemented with AKU-IED as the main implementing partner, the success would be even greater. AKF, C liked the ideas included in the ESRA project and AKU-IED's earlier innovative teacher education programmes. They requested a concept note from AKU-IED[30] which was developed and shared. The goals of the proposed project were highlighted in the concept note which stated:

> The Strengthening Teacher Education in Pakistan (STEP) seeks to improve the quality of basic education in Pakistan by strengthening training and professional development for school teachers and education managers at all three levels-national, provincial/district, and school. At the same time, this project will complement the larger efforts of the Government of Pakistan, particularly the teacher education programme supported by the Government of Canada's Debt for Education Conversion, as well as the process of devolution in the education sector. By drawing on the expertise of Aga Khan University-Institute of Educational Development (AKU-IED) in an innovative public-private partnership, as well as by leveraging Canadian technical resources, STEP will build the capacity of educator training and support programmes (preferably in Sindh and the Northern Areas) by implementing four interdependent and complementary components[31].

The following were four key components envisaged in the above concept note:

1. **Teacher Development** to include cluster-based mentoring, whole school improvement, and Professional Teachers Associations Network
2. **Teacher Support and Supervision** to include educational leadership and management training, follow-up of cluster-based mentoring, and strengthening professional teacher education training
3. **Research and Policy** to influence teacher education related policies
4. **Canadian Component** to seek technical assistance from Canadian institutions

A strong statement was made in the concept note regarding contribution to address gender disparities and to promote increased opportunities for the development of female education managers, trainers, and teachers.

AKF, C in its discussions with CIDA shared the salient features of AKU-IED's initial thoughts. CIDA suggested that the proposed intervention should be in Sindh and Balochistan and, considering AKU-IED's capacity availability in Gilgit-Baltistan, they agreed that some capacity could be developed for teacher education institutions in GB. AKF, C/CIDA commented on the concept note shared with them:

> Overall, we find that this proposed project complements our current education programming in Pakistan very well by focusing on teacher education in the public sector. This project has good potential to complement CIDA's Debt for Education conversion with the Government of Pakistan, which seeks to improve the quality of teacher education and the capacity of teacher education institutions.

Based on the feedback received, the concept note was developed further. The modified concept was discussed with CIDA in November 2006.

There was general agreement that it was difficult to explain some of the ideas within the limited space allotted in a concept note, and that many of CIDA's concerns and comments would be more fully addressed in a full proposal. They were pleased that gender related matters would play a very important role in the project.

It was agreed that CIDA would go ahead with the process to get preliminary approval of the concept note in the new year (2007) while AKU-IED elaborated on some of the more pressing concerns for CIDA's feedback.

By June 2007, a first draft of the proposal was developed by AKU-IED in collaboration with AKF, C, taking into account the comments and suggestions made by CIDA and AKF, C. This was shared with CIDA who sought further clarification on a number of proposed activities and the education scenario at both national and the provincial levels.

There were a number of issues that CIDA raised. Firstly, CIDA was not in a position to fund secondary level teachers. Secondly, it felt that it could not support the implementation of any programme related to English language development at school level as it did not believe that there was enough capacity available in Pakistan to initiate such a programme. The other question raised by CIDA was related to the supervisory staff whose capacity had already been developed. They were also keen to see some work on School Management Committees. On PTAN, CIDA felt that while the model was very good, more participation of public sector teachers was essential. They recognised the problems related to teacher unions but felt that PTAN had proved that its only objective was teacher professional development. They also suggested that the PTAN activities could be developed in other parts of Pakistan.

There was an emphasis that any research conducted should be related to the models developed by AKU-IED, and not on general education. It was also felt that the dissemination of lessons learned from the project in Pakistan, and maybe with other developing countries and other donors, could be interesting, and a small component of the project was devoted to research and knowledge generation, and dissemination.

It was important to have a strong monitoring, evaluation, and research (MER) component under the project. However, it was understood that AKU-IED could clearly align the MER component with the project needs with emphasis on improvement of project interventions and results.

While many of the comments from CIDA were related to clarification on the process and procedure, a couple of interesting comments came up:

Regarding the length of the project, CIDA suggested that the project should be extended to 6.5 years instead of the earlier proposed 5 years. Secondly, CIDA felt that the District Coordinators should be based in the district headquarters and not at AKU-IED to give better support even if it meant an increase in the budget. They also stressed that the WSIP should be based entirely in the rural setting.

Based on these comments, a final proposal was developed in September 2007 and used as the final document[32]. Chapter 3 and 4 in this volume provide further details on the project including, purpose, outcomes, output, and main components.

Educational Development and Improvement Programme (EDIP)

In September 2008, an unexpected opportunity came to AKU-IED just as the faculty was gearing up for the STEP project described above. AKU-IED was invited to a meeting with the Aga Khan Foundation, Pakistan and the representatives of AusAID, (now known as the Department of Foreign Affairs, Trade and Development). In the meeting, the team from AusAID shared that they were looking for partners to develop an innovative programme to improve the quality and efficiency of education in Pakistan. Balochistan was their main priority but they were willing to consider funding education programmes in Sindh and Gilgit-Baltistan (GB). The condition was that the partner would be willing to work with the government. The AusAID team mentioned that Balochistan needed assistance in developing an education strategy.

The AKDN team mentioned that in 2007–2008 the government in GB had developed an education strategy with some assistance from AKDN. However, this had not yet been implemented. The AusAID team felt that this could be considered as part of the overall project that could support further work on the strategy to make it implementable.

It was also shared with AusAID that AKDN institutions, in particular AKU-IED and AKES,P had tested many innovative models and programmes in GB and other parts of Pakistan and could develop a programme for quality improvement and improvement in efficiency of the Education System/Schools.

It was agreed that in the case of Balochistan, AKU-IED could develop quality education programmes after some needs assessments. AKDN was asked by the AusAID team to develop concept papers around these three priorities.

A preliminary concept was developed by AKU-IED and AKF, P and shared with AusAID for intervention in GB. The overall aim of the project was to complement the efforts of the government in Gilgit-Baltistan to build individual and institutional capacity to improve the quality of teaching and learning in schools. It was envisaged that the project would have many partners and bring their specific expertise to bear upon the programme.

After considerable discussion it was decided by AKU-IED that for its part of the intervention, the Institute would use a cluster-based approach to implement its ideas, considering that AKU-IED had successfully implemented a Cluster-Based Mentoring model in Sindh and Balochistan in which more than 7,000 public sector primary school teachers had been developed. Also, AKU-IED had just developed the STEP project in which the cluster-based approach was a central strategy. The model proposed for GB was slightly different. Instead of the Learning Resource Centre model it was decided to use a Learning Resource School (LRS) model in which the school was involved both in its development and in supporting other cluster schools. This was deemed to be of particular importance because of the geographical nature of the region. It would also create a resource that could be used in the long run.

The use of this approach in EDIP was expected to enable support in difficult and remote environments where difficult logistics limit the possibility of wider networking and professional collaboration. It was meant to develop schools as learning organisations that would provide support, academic direction, and mentoring from the centre.

This cluster-based approach would allow for sharing of mutual experiences, best practices, resources, materials and it would maximise the involvement of the community and the government staff at local levels.

It was also proposed that high quality accredited professional development programmes would be developed for teachers, teacher educators, head teachers, education managers, and others in order to build leadership and strengthen their ability to become change-agents within their institutions; introduce viable models of continuous professional development at the grass-roots level; ensure accessibility particularly for females and support teachers within their own contexts for developing learning environments; assist education managers to re-think their roles and responsibilities as 'pedagogical leaders' and to support them in the field as they put these into practice; and to engage the community at large in taking an active role and ownership in promoting quality education in the region.

It was expected that the project would consolidate and build upon earlier progress made in GB and work particularly with children and communities, especially females in seven districts including new and old areas and underserved remote villages.

It was proposed that under the project, in each of the seven districts of Gilgit-Baltistan, namely Gilgit, Ghizar, Hunza-Nagar, Diamer, Astore, Ghanche, and Skardu, two large secondary schools, located at centralised places, would be identified to become LRS. Using Whole School Improvement (WSI) approach, these schools would be transformed as 'hubs of professional development' and would work with around two to three neighbouring primary/elementary schools to develop their capacity. It was expected that this intervention would result in the capacity building of schools for inspiring student learning outcomes, and would also assist in developing sustainable networking between secondary and primary/elementary schools which would be a very important step as the latter works as a feeder for the former.

It was expected that the head teacher of the cluster would be a well-qualified educator preferably a graduate of the AKU-IED MEd or comparable programme. Additionally, it was expected that at each cluster there would be a teacher educator also a graduate of AKU-IED or a comparable institute[33] to support the whole school development of the LRS and the cluster schools. In total, 56 schools were expected to participate in the project.

AKU-IED's Professional Development Centre, North (PDCN) in Gilgit was identified to provide educational services to the teachers and management staff within the region. The centre was to work closely with the government to target communities while building the capacity of the public sector.

The overall expected outcomes of the project[34] were as follows:

- To enhance access and equity for education in target districts of GB
- To improve quality and relevance of education and gender equity for children in selected clusters of schools
- To strengthen governance and management of relevant Government Education Departments

AusAID suggested that the proposal should include a few more elements. These were: (i) the project should address the issue of gender equality (this was in-built in the proposal); (ii) the project should address the issue of inclusion; and (iii) awareness sessions should be organised for communities to better understand the importance of providing opportunities to children with disabilities to access education.

It was decided that other than the government and AKU-IED, AKES, P would also be a key implementation partner. They had also developed a cluster-based model similar to what AKU-IED had done. Support would also be sought from Aga Khan Planning and Building Services (AKPBS) for any construction or retrofitting related aspects. It was also decided that the project would ensure that construction was done only in areas that were considered safe and for this FOCUS Humanitarian Assistance Pakistan (an agency of AKDN) which has expertise in disaster management was also included in the project. Other AKDN institutions included were AKU's Human Development Programme for research, Civil Society Resource Centre (a project of AKF, P) for social mobilisation and Network of Organisations Working with People with Disabilities, Pakistan (NOWPDP) who have expertise in inclusive education.

The overall project also included activities to support the Education Department of GB in its effort to revise the Gilgit-Baltistan Education

Strategy (GBES), thereby reflecting the changing context of the region to provide quality education. Chapter 5 provides further details on the project including purpose, outcomes, output and main components and its impacts.

Summary

STEP and EDIP were, at heart, capacity-building initiatives. As such, both projects had a number of in-built strategies to improve the sustainability of interventions. Firstly, there was an inherent multiplier effect built into several of the components, including the CBM and WSI programmes and the teacher educator training, which ensured that the benefits of project activities extended beyond the individual being directly reached to those that they, in turn, trained and mentored.

Secondly, by involving cadres from different levels of the education system, particularly those who supported teachers at the local level, including head teachers, district education officers, senior government cadres, and teacher educators, there was an increased chance that the 'enabling environment' for sustained change in schools and classrooms would be created.

Thirdly, sustainability of gains could be increased by professional development that extended over a period of time, that included opportunities for participants to reflect on theories and link them to practice in the field, and that provided follow-up support in their own environments.

Fourthly, opportunities to progress up a 'ladder' of professional development through certified training provided many participants with motivation to succeed and think about future learning and improvement, as has been the case with the teacher mentors already trained by AKU-IED.

Lastly, 'networking' opportunities created under the CBM, WSIP, and PTAN (in case of STEP) models are likely to support professional development of teachers beyond the life of STEP and EDIP.

In addition, the active participation and involvement of district government counterparts in managing and coordinating the project built the government's capacity to support those who benefited from the project in appropriate ways and to make better human resource management decisions.

In summary, AKU-IED, with its emphasis on quality, its proven track record, and its longstanding relationship with provincial and national Education Departments, is an indigenous Pakistani institution that deserved to lead both STEP and EDIP and that made both projects into impactful interventions. The real impact will be unfolding in years to come.

References

Clandinin, D.J., and Connelly, F.M. *'Teachers' professional knowledge Landscape'* (New York, Teachers College Press, 1995).

Fullan, M. and Hargreaves A., *Teacher Development and Educational Change* (London, Falmer Press, 1992).

Memon, M., Lalwani, F., and Meher, R., 'Mentoring as an alternative approach to in-service teacher education in Balochistan: some successes and challenges' in I. Farah & B. Jaworski, eds. *Partnerships in educational development* (Karachi: Oxford Symposium Books, 2006), 103–117.

Notes

1. The Aga Khan University-Institute for Educational Development, Karachi, Pakistan. Programme Proposal: Strengthening Teacher Education in Pakistan (2007).

2. The Aga Khan University, Karachi, Pakistan. A proposal to the Board of Trustees (1991).
3. The Aga Khan University-Institute for Educational Development, 'Phase III proposal' (July 2007–December 2013).
4. Ibid.
5. The Aga Khan University-Institute for Educational Development, Karachi, Pakistan, 'Phase II proposal' (2000–2006).
6. The Aga Khan University-Institute for Educational Development, Karachi, Pakistan (1994), 'Report of the Chancellor's Commission: The future of the Aga Khan University: Evolution of a vision.
7. The Aga Khan University, Karachi, Pakistan (1991). A proposal to the Board of Trustees (1991).
8. Ibid.
9. The Aga Khan University-Institute for Educational Development, Karachi, Pakistan (2001): 'EC Project completion report' (1993-2001).
10. Now renamed as Global Affairs Canada.
11. The Aga Khan University, Karachi, Pakistan (1991). 'A proposal to the Board of Trustees'.
12. The Aga Khan University-Institute for Educational Development, Karachi, Pakistan, 'Phase II proposal' (2000–2006).
13. The Aga Khan University-Institute for Educational Development, unpublished case studies of school improvement in Pakistan (Anjum Halai and Stephen Anderson, 2003–2005) and in East Africa (Anjum Halai, Ruth Otieno, Naomi Swai, Zeenat Shariff, 2004–2006).
14. Originally PDCN was supposed to serve both Gilgit-Baltistan and Chitral. Subsequently, it was decided to build a separate PDC in Chitral called Professional Development Centre in Chitral (PDCC).
15. Professional Development Centre North (2003), an unpublished case study of The Whole School Improvement Programme.
16. Ibid.
17. Professional Teacher Association Network—Brochure 2005.
18. The Aga Khan University-Institute for Educational Development, (2005), 'Science Association of Pakistan Brochure'.
19. The Aga Khan University-Institute for Educational Development (1999), 'Final Evaluation of Phase I of AKU-IED.
20. The Aga Khan University-Institute for Educational Development, (1996), 'Proposed Programme for the IED: 1997–2006: Final Report of the Second Task Force'.

21. The Aga Khan University-Institute for Educational Development (1999), 'Final Evaluation of Phase 1—Final report'.
22. Government of Pakistan (2003), 'Education Sector Reform Assistance (ESRA)—Grant Application Guide'.
23. The Aga Khan University-Institute for Educational Development (2007), 'Final Report of ESRA 2004–2007'.
24. The Aga Khan University-Institute for Educational Development (2004), 'Mid-Term EC Evaluation Report'.
25. The Aga Khan University-Institute for Educational Development (2005), 'EC Monitoring Mission Report of AKU-IED'.
26. Ibid.
27. Comments offered by a World Bank's representative during AKU-IED's Task Force III deliberations, 2004.
28. The Aga Khan University-Institute for Educational Development (2006): 'Phase III proposal'.
29. The term PC-1 is used in public sector in Pakistan for a project proposal.
30. The Aga Khan University-Institute for Educational Development (2006/7), 'Internal document on STEP Concept'.
31. Ibid.
32. The Aga Khan University-Institute for Educational Development (2007), 'Programme Proposal: Strengthening Teacher Education in Pakistan'.
33. Graduates of the Notre Dame Institute of Education were also considered at par with AKU-IED graduates.
34. The Aga Khan University-Institute for Educational Development (2010), 'Programme Proposal: Education Development and Improvement Programme (EDIP)'.

PART II:

SCHOOL CAPACITY BUILDING THROUGH STEP AND EDIP PROJECTS

3

An All-encompassing Approach to Educational Reform: A Case of the STEP Project

Takbir Ali

Introduction

Educational change is generally considered to be an immensely complex phenomenon, replete with riddles, dilemmas, and uncertainties. Improving educational processes, practices, and structures, and translating these improvements into improved student learning outcomes, is what matters the most in educational reform and change. Educational reforms vary in their scale and complexity. Large-scale educational reforms require the adoption of a comprehensive approach that brings about change and improvement in policy, processes, practices, and structures intended at institutional capacity building with the ultimate purpose of improved student learning outcomes.

There is a voluminous body of research-informed knowledge about educational reform, and a notable contribution to the existing body of knowledge on educational reform comes from developing countries. Research on educational reform and school change helps us understand the factors primarily needed for authentic, impactful, and sustained reform and development in education.

One of the important lessons learnt worldwide about change suggests that large-scale education reform needs a holistic approach that combines inputs at multiple levels or contexts, focusing on multi-layered interventions and involving a wide range of players and stakeholders. The STEP project is a typical example of a large-scale, multi-dimensional reform initiative of this kind implemented in Pakistan with the purpose of strengthening institutions and improving the systems of primary and elementary education in the public sector.

Focusing on STEP project, this chapter presents a model of large-scale educational reform influenced and informed by local experiences, indigenous knowledge and internationally acclaimed research-informed theories of change and development. The chapter chronicles changes with multilevel inputs through STEP project. The chapter is organised in the following main sections.

The first section describes the project, its geographic, and operational context and also explains the framework of change and the models of teacher development and school improvement adopted in the project.

The second section presents the various multilevel programmatic interventions carried out under the three key components of the project. It further explains the interactive dynamics of these interventions and the resulting changes and improvements at school and classroom levels.

The third section delves into the key lessons derived from the implementation of programmatic interventions and resulting outcomes. Lastly, it presents some recommendations with regards to conceptualisation and implementation of large-scale educational reform in the context of Pakistan and elsewhere in developing countries.

Setting the Context: The Scenario of Education in Sindh, Balochistan, and Gilgit-Baltistan

Sindh, Balochistan, and Gilgit-Baltistan maintain large systems of school education, corresponding to their geographic conditions and demographic realities. In all three provinces, the public sector is the largest provider of education. The public education systems run large networks of primary (Grade 1–5), elementary/middle (Grade 6–8), secondary (Grade 9–10), and higher secondary (Grade 11–12) schools. The majority of primary and most of the middle, secondary, and higher secondary schools are divided by gender. However, primary schools, mainly in rural areas, enrol both girls and boys.

The governments in these provinces with the influence and financial backing of international aid and donor agencies are engaged in efforts towards adding another layer to primary education i.e. Early Childhood Education (ECE). However, no substantial progress has been made thus far in this regard by these governments. The efforts made so far seem to have been limited to developing policy frameworks, with some piloting of ECE classes in selected government schools. The government and the national or international agencies supporting the government systems in provinces in the area of ECD seem to be confused about their strategy because, without improving the quality of primary education system, focus on ECD is likely to remain a false promise. A simple question to be posed is: Where will these children go after completion of their ECD years? Unfortunately, primary education in all three provinces remains the most neglected area in the education system.

In the above backdrop, the STEP project attempted to demonstrate a model of improving the system of primary and elementary education in Sindh and Balochistan, both of which lag behind national quantitative and qualitative educational indicators.

According to the Annual Status of Education Report[1] (2016), in Sindh, Balochistan, and Gilgit-Baltistan, the percentage of children out of school is 29 per cent, 34 per cent and 39 per cent, respectively. In actual fact, the true picture of the enrolment and dropout is far poorer than depicted in these figures. The data used from government sources are doubtful because the processes involved in the collection of these statistics are corrupted by vested interests.

The STEP project's experience of working closely with tens of hundreds of government schools in Sindh and Balochistan over a period of seven and a half years has resulted in a completely different understanding of the 'politics' and practices of collecting statistical information i.e. facts and figures related to student enrolment, gender disaggregated data, retention, dropouts, attendance, and absenteeism (more details in chapter 9).

As far as the quality aspect of school education is concerned, recent national level surveys conducted by the Government (e.g. Reform Support Unit, 2015) and other independent agencies have consistently reported a deplorably lower level of students' achievement against the required basic literacy and numeracy standards in primary curriculum. Low enrolment and high dropouts is caused by the appallingly poor quality of education that hundreds of thousands of children attending government schools experience. To illustrate, approximately 50 per cent of students at the 5th grade level across the nation cannot read a single sentence in English, Urdu, nor the provincial languages (e.g. Sindhi and Pashto[2]).

The comprehensive baseline data on students' achievement collected by the STEP project[3] through a credible and rigorous research process substantiates the claims made by various survey reports about the status of student learning outcomes in primary schools of Sindh and Balochistan. STEP survey findings depict a more deplorable picture of student learning outcomes as these relate to conceptual learning. Students' performance is shockingly low in responding to items in the questionnaire which required them to apply their knowledge or engage their intuitive and independent thinking. Out of seven thousand students tested in the survey, four thousand students scored 'zero' marks in their response to 'Extended Response Questions' (ERQs). This explains the dismal state of primary and elementary education in public sector in the country. This is a quite revealing finding, the federal and provincial governments should pay attention to it, if they are really serious about their responsibility to provide basic quality education to millions of children obligated by the Constitution.

Apparently several factors are responsible for the gloomy picture of delivery of primary and elementary education depicted above. One of the variables that, by any analysis, is central to the invariable deterioration in the quality of education in public sector is 'teacher' factor. There is no substitute to teacher in education delivery whose efforts, underpinned by his or her abilities and values, in the classroom matter the most in student learning. A substantial majority of teachers, who draw salaries from the government treasury, are not in schools. The 'ghost' teacher or 'visa' teacher[4] phenomenon is common in every district, taloqua (village), and school. Also, a good number of teachers, though present in schools, are not actively engaged in the teaching process (more details in chapter 9).

The systematic baseline survey conducted by the STEP project in 2010 to assess the level and quality of teachers' engagement in pedagogical practices showed that on average teachers would spend only 15 out of 35–40 minutes teaching time in a pedagogical activity.

Adding to the pitiable plight of the education system is the problem that in Sindh and Balochistan, over 50 per cent of primary and elementary schools lack even basic necessities and facilities. For example, approximately 24,000 schools do not provide safe drinking water, 20,000 schools are without adequate washroom facilities and 27,000 do not have functioning fans, which is particularly difficult given the extreme heat in rural Sindh.[5]

The STEP project was initiated in this context within the educational conditions depicted above.

STEP Project's Facts and Operational Context

STEP was designed and executed as a multi-faceted intervention with the goal of improving the quality and delivery of elementary education services appropriate to the poor, particularly women and children. The project aimed to enhance the capacity of teachers, head teachers, teacher educators, education managers, schools, education institutions, and district level education administration using innovative training programmes and models.[6]

The seven and a half year (2009–2016) project, funded by the Global Affairs Canada and the Aga Khan Foundation, Canada (AKF, C), worked towards the institutionalisation of a Cluster-Based Mentoring Programme (CBMP) and a Whole School Improvement Programme (WSIP) at the grass-roots level.

The project also scaled up the successful Professional Network of Teacher Development (PNTD) from its base in Karachi to other remote centres to reach more teachers in rural areas like Killa Saifullah in Balochistan, Sukkur, Khairpur, and Hyderabad in Sindh, and Hunza and Ghizar in Gilgit-Baltistan and Chitral.

The cross-cutting components of the project included the documentation of best practices, lessons learnt and the dissemination of knowledge through seminars, policy dialogues, and publications. The project had a strong focus on gender issues and aimed to work towards reducing the gender gaps and dealing with other related issues in the educational system.

Project Components

The project was sliced into three interconnected components with gender a cross-cutting theme, as explained in Figure 1. Situated within the three key components of the project, several capacity building and school improvement activities were undertaken during the seven and a half years of the project.

As mentioned in Chapter 2, reflecting on past experiences from reform projects and programmes and considering the ground realities, the STEP project adopted some specific models of professional development and institutional capacity building. The models, their processes, and outcomes are briefly described in the following section.

Figure 1: Three Components of the STEP Project

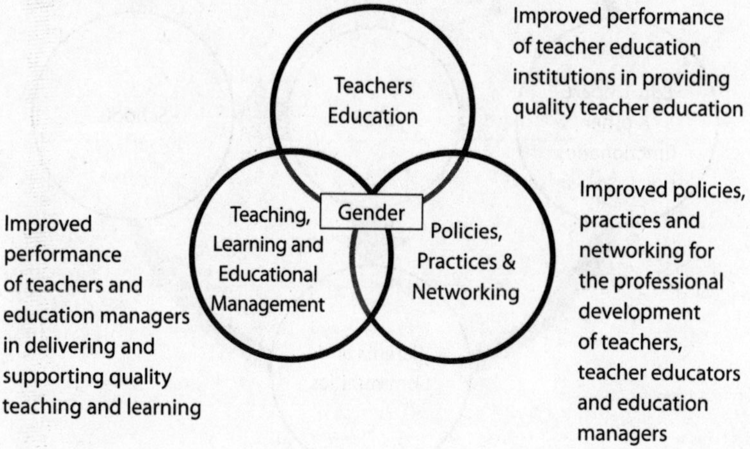

Each of the above components and a gender cross-cutting theme subsumed a wide-range of interventions. These interventions within and across components were interwoven in such a way that they inevitably complemented and supplemented each other. This was achieved largely through adopting a change model explained in Figure 2. As shown in Figure 2, STEP ensured all-encompassing coverage of stakeholder groups. It simultaneously worked with teachers, managers, and educators as first-line actors in reform implementation.

STEP worked closely with school management committees, parents and members of the wider community in target districts to

Figure 2: STEP's Model of Change

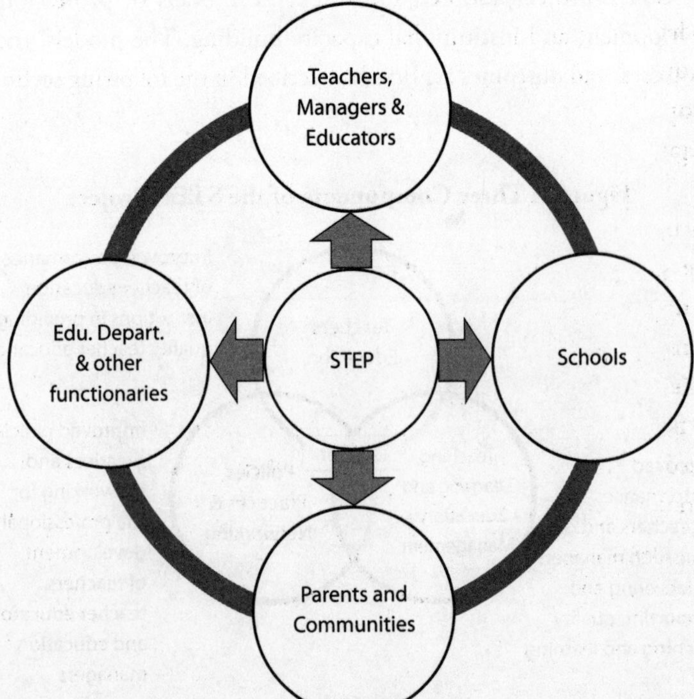

promote educational awareness and it meaningfully engaged this vitally important stakeholder group. It focused its efforts on schools as the fundamental units of change. STEP also engaged provincial departments and other apex institutions, functionaries, and regulatory bodies such as bureaus of curriculum (BoCs), Provincial Institutes of Teacher Education (PITEs), Policy, Planning and Implementation Unit (PPIU) of Balochistan, and Reform Support Unit (RSU) of Sindh. The broad representation of the stakeholders group helped generate a great deal of support and ensured the buy-in of the stakeholders.

By and large, STEP's model of change confirms to the principles of system-wide approach to educational reform widely advocated in the literature. STEP experience therefore provides a good opportunity to reflect on and learn about the interface of theory and practice of educational reform.

The Cluster-Based Mentoring Programme (CBMP)

The CBMP was the flagship programme initiated by the STEP project. The model was based on four important considerations:

- First, it was intended to reach out to a greater number of teachers, particularly women in remote rural areas of Sindh and Balochistan by taking professional development opportunities to their doorsteps because teachers, particularly women, constrained by economic and socio-cultural factors, can rarely access training opportunities outside their villages, districts, or towns. The CBMP model was meant to cater to this particular contextual need.
- Second, to create a multiplier effect, the model used a cascading approach to training, which enabled the use of existing

human power and physical structures and facilities within the government system to benefit at a large scale—the maximum number of teachers.

- Third, the training activities were conducted at school sites to help teachers practice their new learning in their schools within their own classroom realities under the mentorship of both the experienced teacher mentors and their school head teachers, who also received STEP training.
- Fourth, the training programmes conducted both for teacher mentors and teacher mentees focused on primary curriculum content and standards (Students Learning Achievements) in four core curriculum areas: social studies, English language, mathematics, and general science. The training emphasised both content enhancement and the development of child-centred interactive pedagogies.
- Fifth, the model attempted to address one of the chronic challenges associated with project-based approach to in-service teacher training. Project-driven in-service training programmes in Pakistan have been devoid of having lasting impact on classroom practices because of the absence of embedded follow-up support. As a result, teachers do not use new ideas and instructional techniques and revert to their old practices. The CBMP model included provision of follow-up support by the teacher mentors and the head teacher for an extended period of time. This added a unique feature to the model, making it distinct from other field professional development models used worldwide.

Implementation of the Model

The programme began with the selection of 135 government teachers through an intensive, competitive process (test and interview). These teachers were to be trained to become teacher mentors in the above mentioned four subject areas through a tailor-made one year Advanced Diploma in Primary Education (content focused) programme.

Upon completion of the programme in 2010, the teacher mentors returned to their respective clusters to carry out the training activities at the field-level (cluster and schools). They were responsible for:

i) transforming the then 140 existing Learning Resource Centres (LRCs) created during Education Sector Reform programme implemented by AKU-IED (chapter 2) in collaboration with the government of Sindh and Balochistan) into Union Council Level Teacher Resource Centres (UC-TRCs);
ii) planning and delivering subject-based workshops on a rotational basis for four subject areas in their respective clusters; and
iii) providing mentoring and follow-up support within the classroom to teachers in their clusters.

Altogether, 135 UC-TRCs were created and equipped with necessary resources. These UC-TRCs became the hub of professional development where mentor and mentee teachers gathered for workshops and meetings. Over 1,600 primary and elementary schools were clustered under 135 UC-TRCs, each cluster having 10–12 feeder schools. Over 3,500 teachers (60 per cent female) participated in training activities (with 256 contact hours in cluster-based rotational workshops spread over a period of four years) and they received intensive and extensive mentoring support (144 contact hours over a period of four years) from their mentors and head teachers. In addition, the teachers participated in workshops on special topics such as gender, community mobilisation, assessment, and resource development conducted by the mentors, the project academic team and gender experts.

With considerable variation in the individual mentor's approach to and capacity of mentoring, the mentoring process typically involved mentors visiting their mentees (one mentor mentored 20–25 mentees), organising teaching and learning with their mentees, planning lessons, observing mentees in action, giving constructive feedback for further improvement and addressing specific issues faced by the mentees in their efforts to integrate their newly learnt knowledge and skills (more details in chapters 6).

Reflection on the CBM Model: Processes and Outcomes

Our experiences suggest that the CBM model has certain advantages over other models of teacher in-service training used in Pakistan and internationally. It is effective in terms of accessing and training a large number of teachers, mainly in remote rural contexts within a specific period of time and using existing physical infrastructure. The model proved to be user-friendly and cost effective in the sense that teachers, particularly women with competing social responsibilities and socio-cultural inhibitions received professional development within their schools, villages, or districts.

Moreover, the training and mentoring took place in schools within the school realities, allowing teachers to relate theory to practice. Also school improvement, teaching and learning improvement and teacher development activities were carried out hand-in-hand.

Furthermore, the follow-up component, built into the STEP model of mentoring, brought an added value to the quality, relevance and effectiveness of the programme. Though the follow-up was an expensive exercise because STEP had to provide some allowance to the teacher mentors to compensate their travel expense, yet it proved its worth. From a sustainability point of view, the activity and the model itself is replicable because STEP trained mentors, head teachers and supervisors have been appointed as Tehsil Education Officers (TEOs), whose main responsibility is to visit schools and provide academic or pedagogical support to teachers. In fact, the Balochistan government has already started scaling up the cluster-based model led by the Provincial Institute of Teacher Education (PITE) at Quetta.

While implementing the CBM model, the project team confronted some challenges which were not necessarily related to the model but were either embedded in the socio-cultural context in which the programme was implemented or linked with the modus operandi of the programme. For example, some of these challenges involved the mentoring capacity of some of the mentors, mentors having to balance their time and schedule, the impoverished physical environment in some schools, the unwarranted posting, and transfer of teachers and head teachers of UC-TRCs[7].

Some of the mentors had difficulty in conducting content-based workshops, and mentoring teachers in all four subjects because of their own limited content knowledge in those subjects. With the passage of time, the mentors' skills, content knowledge, and teaching practices improved significantly. Through the AKU-IED based reinforcement sessions, training programmes, and the follow-ups conducted by STEP team members in the field, the mentors had various opportunities to develop their capacities as teachers. After returning to their schools, they were able to implement new items from their acquired training, they were able to reflect and identify areas of weaknesses for potential improvement, and then work towards further strengthening their capacities.

Initially, male and female mentors encountered some difficulty in working with the opposite sex, due to socio-cultural factors or personal comfort. The situation was more difficult for female mentors because either they themselves lacked confidence to work with male teachers or they encountered acceptance issues.

But gradually many male and female mentors overcame these challenges and developed the confidence to work with opposite sex participants. The success of the mentoring process largely depended on the mentor-mentee relationship. By conducting regular follow-up visits at the feeder schools, the mentors were able to help the mentee teachers formulate strategies and teaching techniques in response to the specific needs of each school's teachers and students[8]. The project's academic team members (Teaching Associates), STEP district coordinators and the monitoring and evaluation team also regularly visited schools to provide required academic and logistical support to mentors and teachers.

The teacher mentors were primary, elementary, or secondary school teachers. Some worked as supervisors or head teachers. They had to perform their normal duties along with the STEP project's work. Mentors committed 50 per cent of their time to the project and 50 per cent to their routine duties in their schools. It was difficult for them to maintain this balance. It was also difficult for schools to arrange alternate/substitute teachers to teach when mentors were out of their classroom for STEP work, particularly during their visits to schools. The mentors were encouraged to conduct workshops in the afternoon. This worked for some mentors but not for all because of the distance they had to travel to training centres. To cope with this situation, STEP encouraged and facilitated the mentors and teachers to engage in training activities during summer vacations. This strategy worked well; a good number of planned workshops were conducted during the summer break in Sindh and during the long winter breaks in Balochistan.

Table 1: Summary of Direct Beneficiaries[9]

Beneficiaries	Male	Female	Total
Education Managers	250	119	369
MEd Graduates	29	14	43
Teacher Educators and Trainers	479	209	688
Head Teachers	145	80	225
Teachers	2752	2937	5689
School Management Committees (members)	1996	972	2968
Community Members	13612	11942	25554
Training about Gender Mainstreaming	101	205	306
Policy Seminars/Dialogues Participants	317	156	473
Schools	1273	377	1650
Sub Total (Training Participants)	20954	17010	37964
Students Enrolled in Target Schools	186000	114000	300000
Grand Total	205681	130633	336314
Schools and Provision of Educational Resources			
Target Schools	1273	377	1650
UC-TRCs	35	100	135
Model Learning Resource Centres	10	10	30
Teacher Guide and Teaching Kit for Multi-Grade Schools	95	155	250
Provision of Computers and Library Resource	58	22	80

Programme Outcomes

The mentoring model has been found effective in terms of enhancing teachers' capacity to undertake effective school improvement-related activities. Empirical evidence about the effectiveness of the model has been gathered through systematic studies (more empirical evidence in chapter 6). Through on-going monitoring of the programme, numerous success stories, anecdotal accounts and reflections have been gathered which together illuminate positive changes in classrooms.

A succinct summary of some significant changes stimulated by CBMP intervention observed in classrooms is as follows:

Certain UC-TRCs and feeder schools that have demonstrated exceptional improvement have been hailed by government officials as 'Model Schools' in two of the project districts. In such schools, teachers maintain student portfolios, and collect students' monthly test records, attendance records and parent meeting records. These are positive signs of schools getting on the path to improvement. Other schools need to emulate them and learn from their experiences. This process has already begun. For instance, in Hyderabad district, the Additional Director Schools, has initiated a model called ASK (Attitude, Skills, and Knowledge) which is based on the STEP intervention. She aims to inculcate a collaborative teaching and learning culture across public schools in her district and has empowered supervisors to continue as mentors for STEP as well as non-STEP schools. Similarly, the DEO in Khairpur district has assigned TEOs in his district to transform at least one school in their charge into a model school based on the CBMP model[10]. This reflects the commitment and inspiration that STEP has generated in the government officials. This also demonstrates the potential for sustainability, carrying forward the learning from the STEP intervention in selected schools and replicating it in other schools as well.

Government officials have observed the significant and clearly evident improvements in schools. In this regard, the DEO (Elementary) from Hyderabad[11] remarked, for example:

> The environment in STEP intervention schools is entirely different than other government schools' environment, in term of teaching, student motivation and involvement, displays, cleanliness and the attitude of mentee teachers and the head teacher. I wish to see such an environment in all other government schools.

Another DEO[12] in one of the project districts in Sindh commented:

> I visit workshops and follow-ups to see mentors' and teachers' work, encourage them and assure them of my support. I get inspired every time when I visit a school and see teachers in action and students engrossed in learning. I highly appreciate the work of the STEP project; it has proved that it can bring real change in any context with the support of the administration and strong community participation.

The results are visible upon entering a CBMP nucleus or feeder school. Prior to STEP's activities, the walls were generally bare and devoid of any displays. Now, schools are fully decorated with pictures, drawings, posters, children's handicrafts, displays, and other low-cost decoration materials created by teachers and students. The improvements in the physical environment of the classroom are important changes. Cultivating a child-friendly and girl-friendly environment where students are encouraged to think creatively, to use their imagination, and explore is resulting in significant changes in students' attitudes and behaviour.

Furthermore, when parents, government officials, and community members visit the school and observe the visible transformation of the school into a vibrant, colourful centre of learning, they are more inclined to offer additional support to their children and invest more in education. These visual displays—charts, diagrams, maps—also function as teaching tools and aids. Students can consult these displays for learning more about various subject topics, such as diagrams of organs in the human body, on which each component of the organ is labelled with its corresponding function.

Whole School Improvement Programme (WSIP)

The notion of school improvement remains at the centre of the contemporary discourse on educational reform and research worldwide. As a result, an impressive body of literature on school improvement has come into existence. A wide variety of school improvement programmes, projects, and models have been implemented in schools in various parts of the world. School improvement programmes undertaken in different educational settings vary in their focus, scope, as well as the realities within which they are implemented. School improvement thus has been understood as a multi-faceted and multi-layered effort that combines people, resources, ideas, structures, cultures, systems, contexts, values, beliefs, strategies, and activities (Fullan, 1992; Stoll, 1999).

The lessons learnt from the experiences of educational reform in Pakistan and elsewhere in the world, stress the importance of considering the school as a unit of change caused by establishing supportive conditions for improvement and change at multiple levels including the teacher level, the group level and the whole school level (Hopkins & West, 1994). Whole school improvement is a comprehensive reform strategy that meets the needs of all students by improving all school structures that target students' learning. It is a collaborative process that leads to measurable outcomes applying rigorous processes (Harris, 2000). This approach is based on the theory supported by research evidence which shows that efforts towards improvement at multiple levels together can have greater impact on school improvement than focusing on one aspect on its own (Anderson & Stiegelbauer, 2004; Fullan 2001; Hopkins et al. 1994).

While designing the programme, attention was paid to the fact that various school improvement models developed and used in Pakistan or elsewhere may not match well to the unique needs of the project schools without necessary modification and adaptation (Ali, 2012). Thus, attempts were made to make the programme more responsive to the unique improvement needs of these schools.

The need for the contextualization of the model entailed greater emphasis on certain areas which together provided a framework for the programme. As shown in Figure 3, STEP implemented a hexagonal model of WSIP that concurrently focused on six key outcomes:

i) Improved capacity of the lead teacher and the head teacher;
ii) School-based professional development of teachers;
iii) Enhanced community participation;
iv) Improved availability and utilisation of resources;
v) Improved implementation of the curriculum; and
vi) Continuous monitoring and evaluation.

Improvement in all these areas (shown in Figure 3) was geared towards improvement in teaching and learning in the classroom. A gender perspective was integrated within and throughout all the components.

The programme was implemented in 20 centrally located primary/elementary schools, two in each of the 10 target districts of the project. Clustered with each of the main schools were four-to-five neighbouring schools within a radius of four-to-five kilometres; 95 neighbouring schools participated in the WSIP. As stated above, WSIP was developed as a multi-dimensional model, which simultaneously and synchronously dealt with multiple aspects of schools with a focus on improving the quality of teaching and learning through overall capacity of the school to initiate and sustain change, and engage in continued improvement. The selected WSI schools developed 'school development plans' (SDPs) with a gender-perspective for a common vision for school improvement.

Figure 3: Framework for the Whole School Improvement Programme

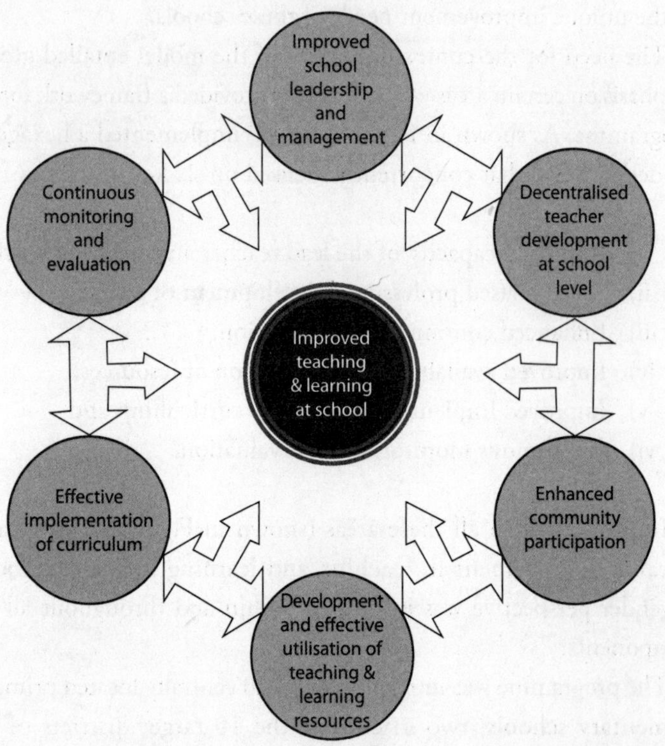

Before the implementation of the WSIP in schools, a critical mass of change agents was developed for each of the 20 nucleus WSIP schools. One experienced and capable teacher from each school was identified and developed as a lead teacher through a tailor-made one-year Advanced Diploma Programme conducted at AKU-IED, with a strong field-based component. This allowed the participants to learn about theories and strategies of school improvement and use these theories in a real context using project-based and action research methods. An inquiry into the impact of the training on the participants' knowledge, skills, and attitude reported a visible positive influence of the programme on the participants' capacity to perform as leaders and change agents in their schools (Ali, 2013).

Moreover, the head teachers of the 20 target schools also received training at AKU-IED through a customised certificate programme extended over 6 months, including face-to-face training sessions and field-based activities. The lead teachers and the head teachers received more opportunities to participate in refresher workshops and reflective meetings at the university and at their districts throughout the programme. These workshops and reflective meetings not only refreshed their knowledge and skills but also helped sustain their level of motivation and commitment towards the programme and its intended outcomes.

Furthermore, the nucleus WSIP schools were provided with educational resources, including books for children and teachers, audio visual aids, computers and a multimedia projector. Some of the resource centres, created at WSIP schools, were transformed into model Learning Resource Centres (LRCs) with the provision of more resources. These model LRCs have been developed with the idea that the government can replicate them in other schools.

The STEP trained head teachers, lead teachers and other teachers together with a project designated focal person developed School Development Plans (SDPs) which reflected the developmental or improvement needs of the school. These were identified through a systematic and thorough needs assessment along with the available opportunities and resources. These SDPs among other targets included in-house professional development for teachers, enhancement of school-parents and community relationships as well as the creation of co-curricular and other opportunities for students to learn and gain experience outside textbook knowledge.

The WSIP activities were extended to selected neighbouring schools two years after the implementation of WSIP in the main schools. The main schools had by this time gained the confidence to support other schools and were able to showcase their achievements so that the neighbouring school could also learn from their practices and achievements. A limited number of teachers (2–4) from neighbouring schools participated in workshops conducted by the lead teachers in the main schools over a period of four years. The lead teachers also visited the neighbouring schools to do a follow-up of the training and help these schools with the development and execution of SDPs. The Project M & E team and academic staff (Teaching Associates) conducted regular visits to the target schools to monitor the programme and provide required support to the schools in their efforts to bring about change in accordance with the agreed upon SDPs.

Programme Outcomes

The schools in the WSI programme have made significant strides in terms of more effective and interactive teaching and learning, improvements in the physical environment of the school, use of teaching resources and most importantly, in student learning outcomes. The teachers claim that they have become aware of gender-insensitive practices in their teaching, and are now taking the necessary steps to ensure that male and female students receive equal attention and treatment. Teachers, head teachers, and lead teachers communicate frequently with parents, who are encouraged to get involved in their children's education. Since girl students tend to drop out of school at higher rates and earlier than boys, head teachers are taking particular proactive steps to promote girls' education within the school and the larger community. Such activities include more effective teaching within the classroom, but also activities, recreational events, and celebrations with influential community members. Celebrations such as Quiz Competitions in mathematics, science and other subjects draw much needed attention to the importance of girls' education. This is because participating in such competitions for many girls is a unique opportunity to engage in friendly competition, demonstrate their academic skills, and instil in them the confidence and self-esteem to sustain their interest in education[13].

In light of the data collected through M&E tools, the outcomes of the WSIP could be observed in terms of the following indicators[14]:

- School Development Plans: There have been noticeable improvements in all SDP dimensions, including: leadership/ management, curriculum implementation, monitoring and evaluation, professional development, the use of teaching resources, community participation, and the integration of gender sensitivity in school activities and functions.
- Curriculum Implementation: The head teachers coordinate with all teachers to ensure that lesson plans are in accordance with the national curriculum standards and benchmarks for all subjects. Monitoring mechanisms have been implemented to link learning activities to students' learning outcomes.
- Management of teaching and learning: The head teachers and lead teachers are responsible for engaging their teachers through mentoring and peer coaching activities for further professional development. The head teachers of WSI schools conducted review meetings with teachers to evaluate the progress on teaching, learning, and student performance.
- Continuous monitoring and evaluation: Schools have implemented their own M&E plans to track the progress on School Development Plans. Schools are maintaining records of assessment results and students' work samples. Mechanisms have been implemented to monitor and ensure proper student enrolment and attendance.
- Resources, facilitation, and environment: There have been observable improvements in schools' cleanliness and hygiene

at school facilities. Washrooms are now functional and well maintained (albeit with some exceptions).

- Children have been observed participating in artistic and creative group activities utilising material resources provided to the schools. The students are now actively discussing and sharing their ideas with each other, and teachers are displaying the students' artwork in the classroom and school hallways.
- Teachers are taking their own initiative to apply new skills and pedagogical techniques and are making more effective use of available resources in their daily activities. Seating in many classrooms has been rearranged to promote more interaction, and students are being given equal opportunities to participate in classroom discussions. In some schools, where there were shortages of chairs and desks, community members and teachers have intervened to provide these.
- School infrastructure: In some WSIP schools, additional classrooms have been constructed to accommodate the full student body either with the help of the local community or with funds from philanthropists and contribution by parents and teachers. This is an indicator of positive community engagement engendered by the STEP project.
- Relationship with the community: Most of the WSIP schools now have functional and active school development committees to improve the quality of education and school facilities. There is an increasing interest from parents in school improvement issues. School Management Committee (SMC) meetings are regularly conducted. Teachers are motivating local communities in their area to work towards the improvement of schools.
- As a result of increased community participation in school activities, student attendance and punctuality is steadily increasing and parents are ensuring that their children regularly attend school[15]. This is a highly significant result. It is

particularly imperative that parents understand the importance of educating their daughters, given the stark gender disparities observed in these districts.

STEP had planned to provide school-based professional development opportunities to a limited number of teachers from the main (3–4 from each) and neighbouring schools (1–2 from each), corresponding to the budget allocated to the programme. But the number increased to nearly 500 teachers by the culmination of the programme because of the demands of schools and teachers. The activity became a good demonstrable example of a 'demand-driven' initiative, as emphasised in Chapter 1. Schools and teachers found value in it. Of the 460 teachers, only 200 received financial compensation for their participation in workshops. The remaining 260 participated in the programme voluntarily; the majority of them lived in close proximity of the main school and were self-motivated to attend the workshops. In fact, the teachers, who had initially not registered in the programme, eagerly requested that STEP should expand WSIP so more schools and teachers could benefit from it. In some primary or elementary schools, which were later upgraded to secondary schools as a result, the number of teachers increased. It became evident that the whole school could not be developed without the full participation of the majority of teachers.

Teachers have acquired a better understanding of how all six themes of WSIP are interlinked. Teachers are motivated to work towards improving and enhancing teaching and learning in all areas. With the assistance of STEP, teachers have developed a variety of teaching methods to use in their classes, some of which are: brainstorming, cooperative learning, discussions and role playing[16]. Gender-sensitive school development plans focused on key areas such as curriculum implementation, the use of teaching resources, professional development, leadership and management, monitoring and evaluation and community participation. The purpose of the gender-focused initiatives was to ensure that school/classroom practices and environments promote gender equality.

The following example from case studies of WSIP schools illustrates the breadth and depth of impact in terms of change and improvement not just in infrastructure and teaching but also in terms of ideas and perceptions.

Government Boys High School, Shah-e-Mardan Shah, Khairpur

This school is a good example of improvement in quality influencing change at many levels. Since the STEP intervention has been introduced at the school, changes in perception have taken place. Under the head teacher's leadership, the school has introduced various quality improvement measures from improving infrastructure to making the environment more student friendly and the teaching more child-centric to engaging the community. The head teacher explains:

> I used to come to school to merely ensure that teachers show up and leave on time. That was me before the STEP project started. The democratic person in me was awoken by the project. I started listening to the teachers and students. My learning from trainings and my interaction with IED faculty and other head teachers during the training programme changed my world view. Classroom teaching and quality is given priority. No classrooms are kept vacant. Teachers make regular lesson plans and organise activities to supplement classroom learning. As a result, confidence and creativity of the students has increased and parents are more involved seeing these significant changes in their children. Enrolment has reached over 800 and the school now has to turn people away due to overcrowding issues. Some children walk up to four kilometers to commute to school.

Highlighting the successes, the head teacher reports the active participation of the School Management Committee (SMC) in school improvement activities. The SMC recently donated water coolers as well as 40 fans to the school. These very visible results also develop a sense of trust within the community which is a key to increasing girls' enrolment. Giving equal opportunities to girls and boys as well as ensuring that dropout rates are reduced for girls is a priority in their SDP. The school has developed such a level of trust that girls from families that observe strict purdah (veil) come to this school which is a co-educational school, noted one of the members of the SMC.

Broad-Based Community Mobilisation (BBM)

Community mobilisation for school development was not embedded initially in the CBMP and WSIP models. But as CBMP and WSIP activities progressed, it became apparent to the project management and other stakeholders that sustainable school improvement could not be achieved without the active involvement of parents and the wider community. The findings of the Mid-Term Review of the project reaffirmed the assertion that improving schools inevitably required community involvement. Henceforth, it was decided to expand community engagement from school's or project team's interaction with school management committees to broad-based community mobilisation[17].

The STEP team comprised community mobilisers, teaching associates, a gender equality team (gender focal person) and district coordinators, who worked closely with both WSI and schools to motivate community members and the school management team to ensure implementation of school improvement plans. The STEP team members conducted regular meetings with WSIP schools to discuss community-related issues and followed up on school improvement plans.

The specific community engagement strategies used by STEP included building capacity for the members of school management committees, organising events such as parents' days, other special educational events such as International Women's Day, Literacy Day, Environmental Day and Pakistan Day where parents, community members, mainly women, and community leaders participated in large numbers. Also, special awareness sessions were conducted for mothers and women at different school sites. These activities helped a great deal in promoting awareness among local communities about the importance of education and pressing issues facing schools and parents such as high dropout rates, low enrolment, high trend of student absenteeism, lack of basic resources and facilities in schools, health and hygiene issues and gender-related issues facing children in homes and at schools. In a net shell, STEP community engagement strategy achieved the following outcomes:

- Organised Parents' Committees/School Management Committees and created mechanisms for continuous coordination with them;
- Developed capacity of PTSMCs/SMCs by organising training for their members on their roles and responsibilities;
- Updated community about STEP interventions and sensitised parents and community members towards majors issues facing schools;
- Created awareness about the importance of education in general and girls' education in particular among the community members;
- Generated community support in achieving some of the goals set for school development plans;
- Organised community mobilisation sessions for selected

members of the community in order to sensitise them about issues related to school enrolment, dropout rates and pervasive gender discrimination in school and family environments; and

- Conducted seminars to highlight the importance of girls' education and dealing with gender disparity, gender stereotypes and discriminatory practices within classrooms, schools, homes and the society at large.
- The community mobiliser assisted in organising public theatrical events that promoted gender awareness and encouraged open discussions on gender equality. In some communities, several women were appointed as honourary SMC members to support community activities.

Model Learning Resource Centres (LRCs)

Two key areas of STEP's WSIP model were the development and effective utilisation of teaching and learning resources. To further strengthen these areas and also to present them to the government as an exemplary practice, STEP set up 30 model Learning Resource Centres (LRCs) in selected STEP schools (three LRCs on average in each target district) equipped with necessary resources to support quality teaching, learning, and professional development activities in schools. These resources included library resources (books for children and teachers in Urdu, English, and Sindhi languages), instructional material (audio-visual aids and lab material), equipment (a desktop computer, a multimedia projector), and other material (chairs, shelves, tables, and white boards) to facilitate on-going professional development. Associated with the computers and the multimedia projector, the schools also received other resources or services, including a school management information system; national curriculum theme page development and hyperlinks to relevant internet based resources for student and teacher use; linkages to online children and other digital libraries for more resources; and off-link softcopies of the national curriculum documents; accessioning, classification and cataloguing of library books, and access to MS Office, endnote software, MIS Software, library software and school intranet facilities.

The information management system software was developed and provided to the schools to enable them to maintain digital records of student attendance, enrolment, examination results, contact information, and basic background information for each student. Similarly, through the software, schools could maintain a database on teacher information including teacher attendance, educational background and qualifications, and information on the teacher's class within the school. The software also had a unique feature that generated reports linking student exam results with each teacher. This feature could potentially address a major structural weakness in the public educational sector which is the decoupling of student performance and achievement with teacher performance. Linking student achievement with teacher performance will allow educational managers to identify which teachers are performing poorly and are in need of further teacher development and those teachers who are demonstrating high levels of teaching competence.

Some of the schools located in urban areas i.e. Hyderabad, Quetta, Sukkur, and Khairpur have intranet service, which enabled schools to access links to internet-based resources of the National Curriculum, links to interactive online videos, learning activities, online exercises, visual displays, and other online content (e.g. Khan Academy) to enrich the teaching and learning experience.

The project also conducted a week long capacity building course for the people (teachers designated as Library Resource Person) responsible for managing LRCs in schools. It was important that the key people who were responsible for making these resources accessible to other teachers and students were conversant with the ways of effective utilisation of library and ICT resources, and their integration in classroom activities. Moreover, helping and encouraging students and teachers to go beyond the textbook and using library and ICT resources to enrich their learning was equally important.

The newly adopted technological approach to school information and resource management was initiated on a pilot basis. STEP made efforts to convince the government to expand and replicate the Model LRCs in more schools. Government officials were invited and given an orientation of the facilities and resources provided in the LRCs and the purpose underlying this initiative. STEP tried to get across the message that if the government is serious about improving the quality of education in schools it needs to provide a minimum level of required resources and facilities to schools. Improvement in the quality of teaching and learning processes in government schools will never take place in a vacuum it rather needs an environment that provides better working conditions for teachers and students. Efforts were made to convince the government to allocate resources in every fiscal year for the establishment of at least two LRCs in each district of Sindh and Balochistan. The worth and success of this initiative could be seen in the happiness and motivation expressed by children from deprived families having the opportunity to read a picture story book or watch an educational video.

Network for Teacher Professional Development (PNTD)

The concept of professional learning communities (PLCs) has gained currency in the recent literature on educational reform and professional development. According to Stoll (2006, p. 223), a PLC is 'a group of people sharing and critically interrogating their practice in an on-going, reflective, collaborative, inclusive, learning-oriented, growth-promoting way.'

PLC is about cultivating a collaborative culture in an organisation. In fact, it is said that for an institution to be a PLC it must have a culture in which learning by all is valued, encouraged, and supported (Olivier, 2009). Thus, a PLC may be described as a platform through which teachers are provided with opportunities to share and reflect upon their professional teaching and learning practices.

This concept, which has originated from the literature on teachers' networks, mostly refers to a common understanding that traditional approaches of professional development have proved to be less or ineffective. Teacher networks are overwhelmingly encouraged for collective learning, whereby they come together to improve their professional expertise. Teacher network is defined as '…groups of teachers organised for purposes related to teacher learning, inquiry, support, or school improvement' (Niesz, 2007, p. 605). The advocates of teacher networks often consider this type of learning approach as an example of communities of practice which offer a distinct social theory of learning. However, the context in which various teachers' networks operate may vary from one society to another.

With this understanding, in 1997, a Professional Network was created by the alumnae of AKU-IED with support from the faculty members (more details in chapter 2). It was then named Pakistan Teacher Association Network (PTAN) but later on to make the title more acceptable to the government system, it was renamed Professional Network for Teacher Development (PNTD).

PNTD operated from AKU-IED, Karachi. Due to the devotion of the network's founding members and the volunteers, the network achieved huge success; as a result, its membership and activities expanded. Under STEP project funding, it was decided to expand PNTD to five other geographical locations. Thus, seven new chapters were opened in different locations including three in Sindh (Hyderabad, Khairpur, and Sukkur), one each in Ghizar and Hunza districts in Gilgit-Baltistan, one chapter in the Chitral district of KPK and a seventh chapter in the Killa Saifullah district in Balochistan. However, teacher culture (e.g. lack of volunteerisms and intrinsic motivation and the induced effect of travel and per diem) within public sector and communication challenges in Gilgit-Baltistan, Chitral, and Balochistan pose greater threat to the long-term sustainability of the PNDT initiative.

In a context like Pakistan, where collaborative learning in schools and other educational institutions usually does not occur, professional network like PNDT seems to be a safe sanctuary for the teachers and head teachers who are intrinsically motivated towards their continued profession. This was an important lesson learnt in the research study undertaken in STEP project to determine the impact of PNDT and CMBM models in creating and sustaining PLCs in schools.

Cascading Approach to Training about Multi-grade Teaching

The multi-grade school context, where children of two or more different grade-levels sit together in one classroom, is common all across the country. Findings from the Annual Status of Education Report[18] state that in the provinces of Sindh and Balochistan, 65.4 per cent and 48.5 per cent of schools, respectively, are in fact multi-grade schools. Altogether, 44.4 per cent of schools in the country are multi-grade schools. Because of the high prevalence of multi-grade schools, multi-grade teaching is therefore considered an inevitable option for Pakistan. More importantly, effective multi-grade teaching is considered a useful strategy for increasing enrolment rates and maximising optimal use of limited financial and human resources. Moreover, in rural and remote areas where a tiered schooling system is neither financially feasible nor practical, multi-grade schooling (and the corresponding multi-grade teaching) allows children of varying age groups in one locality to attend school together.

Having discovered the fact that in schools in Sindh and Balochistan, the teaching and learning process in multi-grade schools is inadequate, due to situations created by resource and space constraints coupled with teachers' capacity issues (teachers are not trained in and oriented towards handling situations in multi-grade schools), STEP, as a demonstration initiative, designed programmes for master trainers and teachers around multi-grade teaching. Altogether 140 master trainers and 270 teachers from multi-grade schools were trained through a meticulously planned programme to cater to the unique needs of 250 schools. STEP designed a 'Teacher Guide' on multi-grade teaching and provided copies to 250 schools. The Teacher Guide includes teaching tips, and space and classroom management strategies.

A programme of multi-grade was conducted towards the closing phase of the project; it was not possible to collect any data on the impact of the programme. However, anecdotal data gathered through district reports showed an encouraging response of the teachers to the programme.

Integrated Approach to Gender Mainstreaming

STEP aimed to promote gender equality in and through the teaching and learning process in the targeted districts of Sindh, Balochistan, and Gilgit-Baltistan. This was a cross-cutting theme in the project and was embedded in all core project activities.

Recent reports from international organisations indicate that Pakistan is far from achieving gender equality by any measurement. One such recent report from the World Economic Forum rated Pakistan as the second worst in the world in terms of gender equality and equitable division of resources and opportunities for males and females. In terms of equitable access to educational services, Pakistan ranks as the eighth worst in the world.[19]

The lack of law and order makes life especially difficult for women and girls. The increase in honour killings, incidents of rape, domestic violence and acid attacks all indicate that the difficulties women and girls must contend with on a daily basis are, in some regards, getting worse each year. News reports daily cite stories of young girls and even children being raped, killed, beaten, or being subject to other forms of violence within and outside the household.

The harsh realities for women in terms of access to education and in society more broadly compel an integrative and comprehensive approach towards promoting gender equality. In this regard, gender was used as a cross-cutting theme across the STEP project. In all STEP programmatic activities, particular attention was given to female beneficiaries, including students, teachers and education managers, to ensure equal female participation and engagement.

The project developed and engaged a strong Gender Team led by a highly experienced and senior university faculty member having grounded experience and a specialisation in gender studies. The Gender Team got involved in all AKU-IED-based conferences, seminars and capacity-building workshops, delivering lessons and specialised sessions to sensitise participants to gender issues and concerns. The Gender Team recognised that promoting gender equality and challenging gender biases and discrimination is a continuous process. Therefore, the team regularly conducted reinforcement and follow-up sessions at AKU-IED and in the field. These were designed to refresh and review gender concepts, to discuss gender-related challenges with female beneficiaries, and to formulate strategies for managing and overcoming gender discrimination. A few examples from the reflections from programme beneficiaries may serve to illustrate the claims above more concretely. One female participant of the MEd programme reflected[20] on STEP's gender initiatives:

> My experience with STEP at IED gave me another lens to look at my daily routine and life and see all the gender inequalities in my life and around me. I developed my Master's thesis on gender leadership and professional development programmes. After returning to my context, I faced all the challenges of gender discrimination, but I persisted and now my colleagues listen to me and respect my ideas. I have new confidence because of my Master's Degree, and I am committed to helping other females in my area.

STEP aimed to not only facilitate participation of female beneficiaries and course participants, but also strived to change the attitudes and perceptions of male beneficiaries as well.

The Gender Team learned that men—fathers, brothers, and sons—are important stakeholders in promoting gender equality. The encouragement and support of male family members and friends is crucial for transforming society. One course participant shared[21]:

> Before this programme, I did not think girls' education was that important since men are the main earners for the family. But now I realise that everyone should be educated. So I have now also enrolled my daughters and younger sisters in school, and I will personally make sure that they get a full education.

STEP strived to improve gender equality for all students, teachers, and administrators in the Pakistan education sector. Besides providing gender awareness sessions and seminars during the project, the gender team also reviewed all programme content and material developed and disseminated by STEP. The gender team reviewed monitoring and evaluation frameworks and tools so that the tools and frameworks identified and captured gender-related inequities in student learning processes. For example, in the tools evaluating the Learning Resource Centres, the Gender Team added questions to evaluate whether male and female students had equal access and opportunities to use the material provided.

The project took special initiatives to ensure equal participation of males and females in all STEP programmatic activities. With regards to the MEd and other residential programmes, STEP adopted a case-by-case approach, providing additional and special support to female students when necessary. This, inter alia, involved approaching families (parents, husband, and brothers) of participants to get support for female course participation. Provision was arranged for the special allowance for female students from Gilgit-Baltistan and Sindh to keep their children with them during their studies.

In a nutshell, by exposing the participants of various training programmes to alternate perspectives on issues related to gender within school, family and societal environment, and engaging them in discussions, evoking their self-critique and making them critically reflect upon their beliefs and practices, the STEP team was able to help the participants deconstruct the understanding and demystify the perceptions they brought to gender. In some cases, it was observed that a change in the teachers' and managers' beliefs about gender was reflected in a change in the practices of these people. From this experience, we learnt that stereotypical beliefs, biases, and negative perceptions people bring to gender can be altered, and in some situations, completely transformed, if we work on them using appropriate strategies. Hence, educating the new generation about the myths and cultivating in them a positive attitude towards gender through education is the only sustainable and effective way to address issues that arise from gender-based inequalities and discriminations in the society.

Summary

Educational development projects like STEP are a beacon of hope for a country where educational challenges are innumerable and often times seem insurmountable. STEP reached out to over 37,964 direct beneficiaries through quality professional capacity programmes and nearly 300,000 students benefited from the project through the training programmes and activities conducted for various educational stakeholders. This has been enhanced with the distribution of resources provided to schools. Both have impacted teaching and learning processes in classrooms.

STEP has demonstrated how, in the context of a large-scale reform, dots are connected to depict a holistic picture of change. It does not claim to have transformed education in the provinces, districts, or institutions it has worked in. Nonetheless, it has benefited the most deprived segment of communities, their schools and children. It has ignited a ray of hope of change in the face of despair and sometimes in what seems insurmountable difficulty. The phenomenal increase in student enrolment, the notable decrease in student dropout, marked improvement in student attendance delineate how the modest but genuine efforts on the part of the project have influenced students' and their parents' perceptions and motivation towards education. Private school students leaving their schools and getting enroled in government schools is in fact a demonstration of the renewed confidence of parents in the change in government schools precipitated by STEP efforts.

The STEP project seems to have stirred motivation and determination in teachers, educators, head teachers, managers, parents, and communities towards bringing about improvement in their practice, and translating these practices into opportunities for optimizing students' learning. Nonetheless, the facts cannot be denied that the 'child' by and large remains marginalised in the public sector education system. STEP underscored the need to bring the child to the centre of what is done in education. STEP was a small, yet an important step towards giving centrality to the child in education.

From the above experience we can draw a few simple but very important lessons having far-reaching implications for educational reform and development in Pakistan. Real and lasting change at the school and classroom level in difficult circumstances comes through a complex, highly politicised, highly fragile, deadly slow and painful process, but change is always possible. The only way to overcome resistance to change in schools is persistence on the part of change agents. There is a real potential that, with little management support, teachers and head teachers in public schools can achieve a great deal of success for their schools and students. There is no dearth of able, committed, and creative teachers and head teachers in public schools. These people can be mobilised, energised, and supported through acknowledging their sincere efforts, hard work, and achievements; and by ensuring provision of equitable justice in the system.

The narrative widely present in public discourse in our country that parents and community members' lack interest in education may be partially true in some situations, but the majority of parents in rural communities are aware, willing and motivated towards getting involved in their children's education despite their socio-economic backgrounds and stereotypes attributed to them.

The changes in teaching practices and schools' performance are evident. Shifts in teachers' attitudes, the re-conceptualisation of their roles as professional educators, integration of gender sensitivity in educational practices, and initiatives to stimulate creativity and to provoke the intellectual curiosity of children are some observed and noted changes. Other developments include improvements in the overall physical environment of the schools. Classrooms need to be clean, orderly, and decorated with colourful displays, charts, and paintings. A vibrant classroom environment coupled with effective teaching, as STEP's experience suggests, provokes a young student's imagination, and inspires a child to think more creatively, innovatively, and analytically.

Though teachers are the main beneficiaries of the STEP project, children are always ultimately the end beneficiaries of any such initiative, and STEP's guiding philosophy was that all efforts should ultimately be directed towards enhancing opportunities for student learning. There is an observed change in students' level of confidence, self-esteem, and attitude towards learning. The most significant indicator is a marked increase in student enrolment in the project's schools. Across all districts, reports and analyses indicate a significant improvement in students' analytical skills, conceptual understanding of the subject matter, and an overall increase in test scores/examination results.

STEP's primary focus was teachers and schools. However, as our experience suggests, schools are gateways for transforming communities. Providing better learning opportunities for the children of Pakistan and by improving the education sector, we hope that the project's impact will endure and its humble contributions will serve to improve the quality of education for future generations as well.

On a final note, many of the challenges the project has encountered in the field are highly complex and contextual, and arise from deeply entrenched cultural and religious beliefs, such as those beliefs that discourage female education. STEP discovered that improving schools and training teachers is not sufficient without engaging families and parents to encourage and support their children in school.

References

Ali. T., 'Developing teacher leadership: A multifaceted approach to bringing about improvement in rural elementary schools in Pakistan'. *Professional Development in Education,* 40/3, (2013).

Ali, T., 'The importance of context in school improvement', in A. Bashiruddin,

Z. Bana & A.K. Afridi, eds. *Education in Pakistan: Learning from Research Partnerships* (Karachi: Oxford University Press, 2012), 59–88.

Anderson, S.E., and Stielgebauer, S., 'Institutionalization and Renewal in Restructured Secondary School', *School Organization,* 14/3 (1994), 279–293.

Fullan, M., *The New Meaning of Educational Change* (3rd ed, Toronto: Irwin Publishing Ltd., 2001).

Fullan, M., *Successful School Improvement* (Buckingham: Open University Press, 1992).

Hargreaves, A., 'Rethinking educational change: Going deeper and wider in the quest for success', in A. Hargreaves, eds. *Year Book: Rethinking Educational Change with Heart and Mind* (Alexandria, Virginia: ASCD, 1997), 1–27.

Harris, H., 'What works in school improvement? Lessons from the field and future directions', *Educational Research,* 42/1, (2000), 1–11.

Hopkins, D., Ainsco, M. & West, M., *School Improvement in an Era of Change* (London: Cassell, 1994).

Hopkins, D., & West, M., 'Teacher development and school improvement: An account of improving the quality of education for all (IQEA) project', in R. Wallings, eds., *Teacher as leaders: Perspectives on the Professional development of Teachers* (Bloomington, IN: Phi Delta Kappa Educational Foundation, 1994), 179–199.

Niesz, T., 'Why Teacher Networks (Can) Work', *the Phi Delta Kappa International, 88*(8), (2007), 605–610.

Olivier, D.F., *Assessing Schools as Professional Learning Communities Symposium* (Lafayettee: Louisiana Education Research Association, 2009).

Stoll, L., 'Realizing our potential: Understanding and developing capacity for lasting Improvement', *School Effectiveness and School Improvement,* 10/4, (1999), 503–532.

Stoll, L, et al., 'Creating and Sustaining an Effective Professional Learning Community'. Source Material: Booklet 2 'Familiarization and deepening understanding', National College of School Leadership (Nottingham, and DfES Innovation Unit, London, 2006).

Notes

1. ASER, Pakistan (2016). Annual Status of Education 2010–2015. (Idara-e-Taleem-o-Aaggahi, Lahore, Pakistan. <www.aserpakistan.org>accessed 10 May 2016. (ASER—The Annual Status of Education Report is the largest citizen-

led household based initiative that aims to provide reliable estimates on the schooling status of children aged 3–16 years residing in all rural and few urban districts of Pakistan). Alif Ailaan (2016). Pakistan district education ranking 2016. <www.alifailaan.pk> accessed 10 May 2016. (Alif Ailaan is a Pakistan-based NGO working for Education; every year it collects data from selected districts from all over Pakistan and does a comparative analysis of student achievement across sampled districts).

2. The Aga Khan University-Institute for Educational Development (2010). STEP Project baseline report.
3. 'Ghost teacher' or 'visa teacher' are two popular concepts interchangeably used in Pakistan to describe teachers who do not perform their duty in schools but receive a salary and other benefits from the government.
4. http://x.dawn.com/2013/07/02/khuhro-deplores-lack-of-facilities-in-govt-schools/
5. The Aga Khan Foundation, Canada (2007). Programme Proposal: The Strengthening Teacher Education in Pakistan.
6. The Aga Khan University-Institute for Educational Development (2012), 'STEP Annual Narrative Report–2012'.
7. Ibid.
8. The Aga Khan University-Institute for Educational Development (2016), 'STEP Final Narrative Report–2016'.
9. The Aga Khan University-Institute for Educational Development (2014), 'STEP Annual Narrative Report–2014'.
10. The Aga Khan University-Institute for Educational Development (2013), 'STEP Annual Narrative Report–2013'.
11. Ibid.
12. The Aga Khan University-Institute for Educational Development (2014), 'STEP Annual Narrative Report–2014'.
13. The Aga Khan University-Institute for Educational Development (20132), 'STEP Annual Narrative Report–2013'.
14. The Aga Khan University-Institute for Educational Development (2013), 'STEP Annual Narrative Report–2013'.
15. Ibid.
16. The Aga Khan University-Institute for Educational Development (2012), 'STEP Mid-Term Review Report 2012'.
17. http://www.aserpakistan.org/document/aser_policy_briefs/2011/Multigrade.pdf
18. http://www.dawn.com/news/1051796/pakistan-second-worst-country-in-gender-equality-wef
19. The Aga Khan University-Institute for Educational Development (2013), 'STEP Annual Narrative Report–2013'.
20. Ibid.
21. Ibid.

4

Leadership Capacity Building: A Pathway to Enduring Educational Change

Takbir Ali

Introduction

As a result of researchers' and educational theorists' growing interest in understanding the myths and mysteries of educational change, an impressive body of knowledge has come into existence. In the literature on education change there is a broader consensus about the factors that predominantly contribute to bringing about change in educational practices and outcomes. In the existing scholarship on educational change, 'human' factor has been identified as the most crucial element in the equation of educational change (Fullan 2001; Glewwe et al., 2012; Hargreaves, 1994; Stoll, 1999). This means that people are more important than structural and material resources in bringing about positive changes in educational processes, practices and its outcomes at school and classroom levels.

With this understanding, the development of human resource capacity through professional development and other means becomes an essential pathway to institutional capacity building—the sin quo non for enduring change and improvement. This chapter discusses why and how the STEP project used 'leadership capacity building' as an approach to institutional capacity building. The chapter briefly describes and analyses some major capacity building training programmes that STEP organised under its three key components for various educational stakeholder groups responsible for school and educational management and leadership.

Teacher Education Institutions

The STEP project was primarily concerned with the improvement of the quality of delivery of service of teacher education institutions (GECEs, GCEs, PITEs, and BoCs). To achieve this outcome, the project conducted customised capacity building programmes for the administrators (principals, vice principal, directors) and teacher educators (faculty members, researchers) of teacher training institutions (TTIs) in Sindh, Balochistan, and Gilgit-Baltistan.

Development of Quality Human Resource through Two-Year MEd Programme

Having recognised that there is no alternative to providing quality human resource in institutions to achieve better results, in Pakistan there is a dearth of capable and well-trained educators in teacher training institutions in the public sector to deliver high quality teacher education and professional development programmes. Realising this need, STEP aimed to sponsor 45 practicing or prospective teacher educators from Sindh, Balochistan, and Gilgit-Baltistan to undergo a two-year international-standard MEd programme at AKU-IED. It provided 43 scholarships to candidates (male and female), elementary to high school teachers. Finding appropriate candidates was difficult because the majority of prospective candidates either did not meet the university admission criteria or did not get through the competitive selection process that involved an English language test and interviews. However, efforts including organising intensive preparatory programmes (focused on achieving English language proficiency) for potential applicants before the entry test, helped to increase the number of qualified candidates.

Forty-three MEd graduates (2010–2015) completed their degree and are now back in the field, working at their institutions and implementing their learning. STEP worked with government authorities to ensure the proper placement of graduates in the contexts where they could make a positive impact. The MEd graduates had been prepared to work as teacher educators, having specialisation in teacher education and educational leadership and management. This entailed having the project authorities ensure that the graduating students were placed appropriately and were given the opportunity to utilise the knowledge and skills they had learned to improve the education sector. Not getting the required number of practicing educators from teacher training institutions (TTIs), STEP provided scholarships to school teachers who met the university admission selection criteria and passed the entry test.

In fact, upon graduation, a few graduates (school teachers) got placed at TTIs as teacher educators but the majority returned to their own schools. The teachers continued working with the hope that they would also get an opportunity to work with TTIs in order to be able to use their expertise. Existing policies and structures are not favourable to accommodating such changes. TTIs are mainly staffed with people who are not necessarily trained as educators. School teachers and people working at management positions become faculty of TTIs through personal efforts or connections. Not giving the 'right job to the right people' is perhaps one of the biggest challenges to educational improvement in Pakistan.

The evidence collected from schools suggests that many graduates are not only incorporating innovative teaching methodologies in their own classrooms but are also building capacity and disseminating their learning to other teachers and educators as well. The graduates also contributed to the field-based activities of the STEP project conducted under CBMP, WSIP, PNTD, and community mobilisation. In addition, these graduates have expanded their sphere of influence beyond their institution by getting involved in other social and volunteer activities in their communities (more details in chapters 7 and 8).

The project regularly monitored and evaluated the progress of graduates' work and performance to ensure that they implemented their knowledge and skills within their work environment. The following examples reflect the contribution of selected MEd graduates who have returned to the field. They illustrate the changes that the graduates have implemented and the impact of their work as well as their effort in sustaining this change. Chapters 7 and 8 in this volume provide more insights into the impact of MEd graduates.

Strengthening Capacities of the Bureau of Curriculum and Allied Institutions

The passing of the 18th Amendment of the Constitution has devolved curriculum development, planning, and policy to the provincial governments. Previously, curriculum development and policy were the responsibility of the Federal Curriculum Wing. With the abolition of the Federal Wing, the responsibility of setting up the Curriculum has fallen entirely upon the provinces. Although, the provincial bureaus of curriculum were part of the Curriculum Wing in terms of developing curriculum and textbook reviewing, they were hardly able to manage the task. Owing to this, the provincial bureaus of curriculum and allied institutions are lacking the capacity needed to manage the curriculum development that, inter alia, includes availability of: customised manuals, guides, and standard operating procedures; knowledge resources; and proficient human resource to perform the task.

As a response to the above background, the STEP Project created a capacity building opportunity for two Bureaus of Curriculum and allied institutions in Sindh and Balochistan through engaging two highly experienced Pakistani professionals who worked directly with the Bureaus and other apex educational institutions like Policy Planning and Implementation Unit (PPIU-Balochistan), Reform Support Unit (RSU-Sindh), Text Book Boards (Sindh and Balochistan), Provincial Institute for Teacher Education (PITE in Sindh and Balochistan, Provincial Education Assessment Cell (PEAC in Sindh and Balochistan).

This 10 week modular in-service programme began with studying the contexts through a well thought-out training needs assessment. In addition, interviews of some strategic people at different institutions were held to gauge the real needs of the constituencies and then provide face-to-face as well as field-based sessions for selected participants. These interventions were designed to help build staff capacity in the areas mentioned above.

However, the provincial Bureaus of Curriculum lacked the capacity needed to manage curriculum development. The programme was customised to the specific pressing needs of the institutions identified and prioritised through capacity gap analyses.

The series of workshops[1] conducted in the programmes focused on different themes and outcomes. In the first round of workshops the participants familiarised themselves with new curriculum approaches, frameworks and the impact they had on instructional materials, assessment, teaching, and learning. This awareness made the participants reflect and they realised that they needed to go deeper into each curriculum document while reviewing the textbooks and the assessment tasks. They also realised that all institutions would have to collaborate to achieve the targets of quality books and quality teaching, learning, and assessment. In the follow-up workshop which was delivered while teaching at a school, they were able to see the gap between the espoused curriculum, and the received curriculum. The outcome of this workshop was to observe the sites where the curriculum was being implemented. They felt that children on the whole had the intelligence to do more. If teachers were well prepared they could teach well. This made the participants realise the necessity of bureaus' testing departments, teacher training departments, and instructional material development departments talking to each other and collectively ensuring the curriculum reform initiatives. As and where possible, duplication of effort had to be avoided and streamlined.

The outcome of the second round of workshops[2] was the intellectualisation of the concept of curriculum: to demonstrate that while curriculum orientations are available in academia, research informs us that none of the orientations are complete and useful but generally curricula are based on eclectic orientations and the best of each interpretation is adapted to make a robust curriculum.

The follow-up workshops[3] focused on reviewing and creating specific instructional materials. This helped the participants think outside the box and look around for unexploited resources that could help in making children get clarity of concepts and give relevance to whatever is being learned. The most important outcome of these sessions was forging the understanding that there is no one textbook that is complete in nature and the coverage of content. The participants got an opportunity to review tools and understand how the Piaget theory of conserving different concepts in mathematics and science works. The learning outcomes of these sessions were that participants realised that people drew upon resources available in different contexts to develop manuals and they then drew upon that knowledge to prepare a manual themselves. The participants were motivated to work on the documents post the training programme.

Responding to the needs identified in the capacity gap analysis, the third round of workshops was designed to focus on the initiation of the strategic planning process for BoCs and their allied institutions. The outcomes of the workshop were: enhanced understanding of strategic planning and the processes to develop a strategic plan; improved stakeholder analysis for the BoC; and reviewed mission, vision and values statements of the BoC.

The fourth round of workshops helped develop the participants' reflective and analytical thinking skills. The experts who designed and delivered the capacity building programme were cognisant of the fact that 'reflective thinking is not one quick learning event for many people, but rather a habit which grows over time'[4]. The participants demonstrated willingness to keep the skills of 'reflection' as a part of their continued growth and development. In the last round of the workshops the participants collectively developed a vision and mission statement for their organisations. Some of the specific outcomes[5] of the programme included the fact that the participants:

- discussed and learnt about different templates for the manuals to be used by STBB, BoC, and PITE;
- compared the National Curriculum 2006 with the text books of 2002 to establish changes proposed in the new standard-based curriculum with the help of a template;
- presented the subject-wise constructed template of a curriculum matrix in four subject areas, English, math, science, and social studies, aligning standards, benchmarks and SLOs;
- engaged in different activities that promoted their understanding of curriculum design, models, and orientations;
- engaged in deliberations about the critical needs for improving relevant structures, processes, policies, and systems to support

the work of curriculum planning, development, implementation, review, and evaluation;
- discussed and agreed on guidelines for a manual for curriculum writers for developing textbooks and instructional materials, and teacher training;
- held discussions on the complexity of issues and how they impacted the current and future working of the organisation; and
- discussed the use of two different tools and their effectiveness in designing the strategic plans.

This was a timely initiative. Immediately after the programme, the Sindh and Balochistan governments undertook a review of curriculum and textbooks. The leadership and academic staff (subject specialists) who received training on curriculum and textbook development got involved in the curriculum review and textbook development process and were able to influence the decisions leading to improved quality of textbooks. The new textbooks present a balanced view of gender and history.

The development of curriculum and curricular material is a highly technically demanding and politically sensitive task. The BoCs and allied institutions have to go a long way to develop a pool of people with the expertise required for curriculum planning, development, and implementation. The capacity building training described above in no way claims that the staff members of the BoCs and allied institutions are now competent enough to shoulder the above mentioned responsibilities. Nevertheless, the training stirred motivation in them to take more responsible positions and play a more constructive role in the curriculum planning process at their institutions. The participants not only enhanced their understanding of new standard-based curriculum but were able to develop alignment frameworks in four subject areas (math, science, english, and social studies). Although the plan was to help them develop mid-term and long-terms strategic plans, we were only able to help them critically review their roles and think futuristically about their organisations' vision and mission statements. They were able to use scientific tools to analyse their current situation. In view of all this, it can be safely claimed that the participants are now better prepared to undertake the new curriculum review (curriculum review initiated by the government of Sindh) and development of the instructional material (textbook review and development initiated by the government of Balochistan) aligning the standards, benchmarks, and student learning outcomes.

While responding to the identified needs of the institutions, the programme seems to have made notable contribution to enhancing the overall capacity of the BoCs and their allied institutions to work towards producing quality curriculum and instructional material. Human resource development should be a regular feature at the department level, rather than relying on people from the private sector to do the job. BoCs need to encourage the subject specialists to do curriculum work rather than engaging in teacher training. The BoCs also need to enhance the capacities of their Deputy Directors through sabbaticals to attend courses about curriculum Teaching Learning and Assessment (CTLA) at AKU-IED or any other credible institutions inside or outside Pakistan.

Professional Development for Head Teacher

The STEP model of change discussed in Chapter 3, used school leadership development as an important strategy towards improving target schools and impacting teaching and learning processes and practices within classrooms. Initially STEP did not have a plan to train school leaders (head teachers, deputy/in-charge head teachers) of the intervention schools. But a year after the execution of the project it was realised that without building the professional capacity of the school leaders and engaging them in CBMP and WSIP activities, the dream of deep and lasting change in schools would not be materialised.

STEP decided to develop and conduct customised training for head teachers and in-charge teachers (senior teachers having the responsibility of managing the school until a regular head teacher was appointed). The overall aim of the programme was to engage head teachers to support school improvement activities and make them a vanguard of school improvement efforts in their schools. Through this programme, a good number of the head teachers successfully achieved the following[6]:

- developed a more comprehensive understanding of the CBMP and WSIP models and the role of the school head teacher in the programme;
- critically analysed teaching practices and identified alternatives for improving STEP initiatives in their schools;
- developed the professional knowledge, skills and competencies for taking action towards gender equality;
- enhanced their understanding about the concepts of change, change processes, and leading and managing change with specific reference to school improvement;
- identified key strategies to facilitate CBMP and action plans as school leader;
- enhanced their professional knowledge, skills and competencies to initiate and support the school improvement process; and
- developed an understanding of and positive attitude towards parental and community involvement and effectively communicate and coordinate with the STEP team and other stakeholders.

The programme emphasised[7] the need for sensitisation of the participants towards gender. The Project Gender Team conducted a full-day workshop on gender and education, including sessions on gender sensitisation, challenging existing practices of head teachers through the gender lens, understanding the concept of gender, sex, and gender discrimination, and exploring strategies for addressing gender disparities in schools. The participants found the sessions on gender and education particularly useful. The sessions gave them an opportunity to reflect on their teaching practices and identify gender-discriminatory practices within their local contexts. One activity, which entailed reflecting on 'sayings' in local languages about women and women's position in society, allowed participants to understand the deeply rooted biases against women that were embedded not only in practice, actions, but also in the manner in which one speaks and conceptualises the world around oneself. These sessions seem to have left strong impressions on participants' beliefs about gender. A participant, for example, shared her reflection[8]:

> It was an eye opening session for me. I had several misconceptions about gender. I was of the opinion that gender means rights of women; this concept is against our religious education. I got clarity of such misconceptions. I can say now confidently that if we want to improve our society we need to work for gender equality.

The impact seen through this raised awareness is transformational. The schools part of the STEP project have seen increased girls enrolment as well as more willingness from rural conservative communities to send their daughters to school. This has been made possible by the evidence of quality that the schools have been able to provide as well as the trust they have been able to develop. Students' confidence has also improved, as a result of the equitable opportunities provided by schools under the leadership of the trained head teachers. A student in one of the government girls' elementary school in Balochistan said[9]:

> My teachers persuaded my parents to send me to school. This is a backward area and the only way my parents would let me go to school is if they see any actual benefit and safety. I am the only girl in my family who is getting an education. This school and the way the teachers teach have given me hopes and dreams of becoming a doctor. My parents might not agree but I often argue that we look for lady doctors to take our women to. How can we find lady doctors if there are not any around?

Each project intervention school developed a School Development Plan (SDP) and implemented it under the leadership of the head teacher. Monitoring and follow-up indicated that these plans were visible in the schools and teachers were aware and took measures to bring about holistic change in these schools. The scheme of work as well as timetables were displayed and adhered to. Head teachers led the way for other stakeholders in the school including teachers, students, and parents to take ownership of the school's improvement. Many schools also worked on increasing enrolment and ran regular campaigns for the same, in addition to working on reducing dropout rates by engaging the community. Schools got support from SMCs/PTMCs that supported not just the infrastructure and facilities but also engaged with teachers and students with respect to curriculum, teaching, and assessment.

As a result of training and support for community mobilisation over the life of the project, the engagement of schools with the community strengthened. Follow-up and monitoring indicated a deep sense of engagement and visible commitment from SMCs to the schools. For instance, at the Government Boys' High School in one of the districts of Balochistan, the head teacher worked very closely with the community. The school worked with a local hospital to raise awareness among children as well as in the community about health issues. In addition, a community hall was built on the school premise which was used by the school as well as the wider community. This resulted in many more community members coming to the school and engaging in school's activities. A strong sense of trust and collaboration became evident. The community increasingly got involved in decision-making at the school and was instrumental in supporting the change of the medium of instruction to English as well as the introduction of students' uniforms that the school was able to implement as its own initiative. These initiatives by the school remained successful, and as a result, the provincial government, following the example of the school, decided to change the medium of instruction from Urdu to English in selected schools in other districts.

Capacity Building for District Management

STEP learnt over a period of time that the ownership of teacher professional development and school improvement activities was indispensable for securing required level of support and assistance from the district managers and enhancing the impact of interventions. STEP endeavoured to strengthen the capacity of the district education management through customised courses, refresher workshops, reflective follow-up meetings, and policy seminars/dialogues. Almost all management and supervisory staff of project districts including, District Education Officers (DEOs), Directors, Deputy District Education Officials (DDEOs), Assistant District Education Officials (ADEOs renamed as TEOs), Supervisors, Learning Coordinators, as well as divisional-level education officials such as Directors and Assistant Directors Schools attended various educational activities organised by the project.

The project placed high emphasis on the need for widespread representation and involvement of stakeholders, including senior government officials throughout the span of the project. This led to an increased level of awareness among district and divisional-level officials about the project's intervention strategies. The district officials and supervisory staff increasingly got involved in supervision with optimism and positive attitudes. Visiting schools and seeing change in the classrooms for themselves, they began to develop and nurture a hope for change in government schools operating within difficult working conditions.

The results of the training of government officials are evident in the field. Government officials now regularly meet with the teachers and head teachers of schools, providing assistance when necessary, and communicating challenges schools encounter to the higher tiers of governance for appropriate action. The collaboration between the district government and schools enhances trust in the public education sector and provides incentives to communities and parents to invest more in their children's education. Through these training programmes and refresher courses, the district management staff learned how to: re-conceptualise their roles and responsibilities as educational managers; provide support as leaders to improve the existing teaching and learning process, the school structures, resources, and facilities; reflect on the current supervisory practices and use innovative practices; develop action plans for their field work to make it systematic; conduct observation of teaching and learning and give constructive feedback to teachers and head teachers; involve parents in their children's education; and engage the local community to mobilise resources and support for school improvement activities.

STEP District Coordinators (DCs) held quarterly workshops/meetings in the field for district officials. The purposes of the meetings were to ensure the continued monitoring of ADOEs'/Supervisors' work and to review their plans for their on-going contribution to

CBMP and WSIP activities in schools. The Teaching Associates (TAs) from STEP also regularly attended the meetings to provide support and to help government officials develop and improvise strategies for overcoming challenges encountered in the field. Challenges and lessons learnt related to teacher absenteeism and punctuality, student absenteeism, student enrolment and dropouts, teacher shortages, school resources and facilities, parental and community involvement, effective utilisation of the instructional resources provided by the project; these were some of the topics discussed. ADOEs and Supervisors/Learning Coordinators (LCs) were also asked to increase the frequency of their follow-up visits in CBMP/WSIP schools to evaluate and provide support for school improvement.

STEP's District Coordinators also arranged quarterly meetings with ADOEs and Supervisors to share findings and to discuss issues related to school supervision and monitoring. Male and female workshop participants both reported a significant change in their views regarding their roles as educational managers. Several supervisory staff took initiatives within their district to address educational challenges such as teacher attendance, assessment practices, and the provision and utilisation of educational resources. Reports were completed after each visit and submitted to the district office when necessary.

Moreover, the project team worked closely with education managers to use a standard school supervision tool which took into account the local context. Frequent transfers, demotions and promotions on political grounds of senior education managers, ADOEs and supervisors were serious issues affecting the school monitoring work negatively. Sometimes abrupt changes in the management team caused difficulties for reform initiatives and posed a serious threat to the sustainability of change. STEP intervened in postings and transfers to stop any undesirable transfer of either district supervisory staff or head teachers trained by the project. In some situations the intervention worked but in other cases the project was not able to leverage any influence on decisions regarding transfer of district supervisory staff or head teachers. Overall, education managers significantly enhanced the monitoring and supervision systems within their districts. DEOs, ADOEs, and supervisors engaged in classroom observations, and held meetings and sessions to provide mentees with feedback and criticism. ADOEs trained by STEP became more actively involved in project activities, often taking a lead role in mobilising human resources at the tehsil level. These meetings allowed ADOEs to receive updates regarding schools within their area.

The following selected examples can serve to develop a more concrete understanding of the situation described above:

- In one of the districts of Sindh, the DOE (Elementary) distributed appreciation letters to mentee teachers. Such a simple act of recognition and appreciation is particularly noteworthy in the context of Pakistan, where teachers often feel demoralised and unmotivated to work due to the perceived widespread neglect of the government sectors in responding to the needs of the people, particularly those in poor and rural areas. Moreover, such an act fosters a positive environment of coordination and collaboration. The formal official and the informal relationships between teachers and the management, developed as a result of these efforts, set the groundwork for further synergies in the future. Moreover, because of STEP's interventions, teachers report that for the first time, government officials are taking an active interest in school performance and student learning outcomes and taking responsibility for it.
- In another district, the government officials developed Taluka-wise committees which consisted of TEOs, head teachers, mentors, and teachers. These committees worked collaboratively towards monitoring, evaluating, and improving STEP programmatic activities in their district. Though district

coordinators facilitated and encouraged the formation of these committees, the district government officials spearheaded these activities. More importantly, since lack of coordination amongst various tiers of educational governance is a recurring challenge in education development of this 'task force' is a major change, marking not only a shift in terms of management, leadership, and coordination but also self-motivation to assume responsibility and ownership over educational outcomes in their districts. These district government officials regularly and willingly attended AKU-IED based conferences and seminars to further enhance their knowledge and training, and communicated regularly with project management. STEP solidified and formalised connections so that the initiatives undertaken continue.

The experiences and reflections discussed above, clearly explain that wide-spread involvement of stakeholders and capacity building of district management helped create better conditions for changes to occur and be sustained in schools and classrooms.

Policy Advocacy

Under the third component of the project, a series of policy dialogues/seminars were conducted throughout the project, where a large audience from all walks of life, ranging from teachers to politicians, gathered and engaged in discussions around policy relevant issues and topics. The policy dialogues/seminars were aimed at disseminating lessons learnt in the project and at sensitising stakeholders about ways to help create an environment for the project that would be conducive to impacting the education system in a positive way. These activities provided the university with an opportunity to work closely with government institutions to ensure their ownership of the project initiatives and to advocate for sustainability of reform. Some of the policy dialogues/seminars that generated critical discussion about important issues in education in Pakistan are briefly discussed below.

Dissemination of Baseline Study's Findings

STEP conducted a comprehensive baseline study using a robust and systematic data collection methodology. The study yielded important findings, having important implications for decision-making related to educational governance and management. A policy dialogue session was organised to widely share the results of the baseline study and its implications.

The first policy seminar was held on November 22, 2011. A wide range of government officials from the Sindh Province, principals, and GAC representatives from Islamabad were in attendance at the policy seminar. The findings of the seminar received wide attention and dissemination in the national print and electronic media. For instance, the *Dawn*[10] newspaper, one of the most popular and reliable national dailies, reported the findings as below:

> Public-sector education in Pakistan, particularly at the primary level, is adrift and rudderless. Although the country is in the midst of an 'education emergency', it appears the state is doing very little to rectify matters. Though the alarm has been sounded in the past, yet another reminder of the grim state of affairs has come in the form of a baseline study conducted by the Aga Khan University`s Institute for Educational Development under the Strengthening Teacher Education in Pakistan project. The study, which covered nearly 200 schools in seven districts of Sindh, found that around 70 per cent of teachers teach for only 15 minutes in a 35–minute period. Ten per cent teach for less than five minutes. The study also indicates that

the surveyed schools suffered from high rates of truancy (only 56 per cent of students attended classes regularly) while pass percentages were largely abysmal. Gender bias in schools was also a major concern. The study may have been limited to specific districts, but it would not be wrong to assume the situation is similar across Sindh.

Though millions of school-age children are out of school in Pakistan, the project`s coordinator pointed out that the children that are enrolled are not being educated. This depressing reality should shake the state out of its slumber. Simply enrolling children to fulfil statistical obligations is not enough; once in school efforts must be made to actually educate these young minds. The state is not fulfilling its constitutional obligation by turning a blind eye to the woeful standards of public schools. The study offers numerous solutions—enhancing teachers` morale, improving the capabilities of head teachers, etc. Yet these and other policy prescriptions cannot deliver until the state demonstrates it has the political will to do what is needed to stem the rot in education.

Governance of Education

Through the 18th Constitutional Amendment in Pakistan, education was devolved to the provinces; however, issues such as good governance, access, equity, and quality are still unresolved. The Pakistan Education Task Force consisting of members from the federal and provincial governments, NGOs, and the private sector also painted a dismal picture of education as it is facing an 'educational emergency' which has badly affected the country's socioeconomic development.

To deliberate on the specific issue of 'governance of education' in Sindh, STEP project and Sindh Education Foundation (SEF) organised a policy dialogue. The event brought together a number of eminent social scientists, educationists, policy-makers, professionals, government officials, intellectuals, and other stakeholders. The deliberations were covered through the national print and electronic media. The dialogue allowed the participants to openly share their views and experiences, ask critical questions and forge a consensus about key recommendations which were highly appreciated by the participants, panellists, moderators, and observers. The participants also liked the idea of a joint initiative between the Government of Sindh and AKU-IED (STEP project) which added an element of critical thinking and intellectual discourse. The participants thought that this dialogue helped them unpack the notion of 'governance' and understand the complexity of 'governance of education'.

The panellists stated that the 18th amendment should not be viewed as a challenge but as a great opportunity. They agreed that the crucial issue was not financing but governance and in that regard the province of Sindh had a lot of room for improvement. The need for the government to work with NGOs and the private sector was emphasised in order to help improve the situation by delegating the management of the schools to them. The panellists felt that there was a dire need to have the capacity to plan, implement, monitor, and evaluate at the local level, the lack thereof being primarily the reason we are not doing well in the field of education. They emphasised the necessity of the government's role in undertaking significant measures in order to achieve the goal of education for all children as set under the 18th amendment.

Some of the key deliberations and ensuing recommendations[11] were as follows:

- Education in Pakistan has never been a national priority. Efforts at the governmental level have never gone beyond rhetoric; education has received lip service by successive governments in terms of lofty promises and baseless claims about increase in education budget etc.

- 'Political will' and 'education ordinance' are required to provide free compulsory education to each and every child up to Grade 10 as per Article 25-A of the Constitution.
- There is a strong need to link education to improving literacy and alleviating poverty for sustainable development.
- Provincial governments have a severe capacity building issue, which has been further aggravated by the 18th Constitutional Amendment. Hence, the Sindh Education Department should be restructured to respond to the 18th Constitutional Amendment's implications/challenges.
- The 18th Constitutional Amendment brings opportunities as well as challenges. The Sindh provincial government needs to develop cohesive and focused strategies to capitalise on opportunities and cope with the challenges.
- Lack of financial resources should not be considered as the primary reason for the poor performance of the education system; the main reason contributing to poor performance of public education sectors is ineffective use of available resources.
- Per child education cost in the public sector is higher as compared to the private sector but the quality of education imparted by a public system is deplorably low.
- Improvement in the public sector schools is only possible if corruption is eliminated through good governance. A phenomenon of ghost schools, teacher absenteeism, teachers' sub-contracting their jobs, malpractice in assessment, political interference in the recruitment and transfer of teachers and others has to be controlled.
- There is a need to introduce national education standards for student learning outcomes as well as for provision of education facilities and resources. The majority of schools are without basic facilities and an environment conducive to learning.
- School improvement initiatives are highly dependent on good

governance. Those individuals /organisations who are adopting public sector schools for better education quality should be fully empowered and be given full powers for hiring and firing. Thus, a policy for 'adoption of schools' is needed.

- In the past, the successive governments have made more investment in 'brick and mortar' than in 'human capital' which should be given top priority.
- Corruption should be stopped through an ordinance and all recruitments should be merit-based. 'The right people for the right job' principle should be strictly followed. Those who violate the law should be punished.
- Research should be given due importance in improving governance of the education system. Hence, an academy of educational planning, research, and governance should be established at the provincial level.
- Academics should have a more active role in improving education and its governance. At the provincial level, a cadre of 'educational advisors' should be introduced; these advisors should be experienced and well qualified educationists and should assist the bureaucracy in education policy matters.
- A Think-Tank on education should be formed to advise the provincial education department on strategic and policy matters.
- Teachers are the linchpin of the education system. Presently, the education system badly lacks 'best' teachers; hence there is a need to attract the best graduates and prepare them as the best teachers through powerful teacher education programmes. Teachers licensing and accreditation of teacher education programmes should be given top priority.
- Handing over the public sector schools to NGOs is not the only solution. There is a need to link school budget to school performance. Non-performing schools should be dealt with by different approaches through better monitoring and inspection.

School Supervision

Supervision being the core of quality assurance in education must be paid special attention to in any educational system. STEP held a policy dialogue to tackle this important subject. The main objectives of this dialogue were:

- To examine the historical background of school supervision in the subcontinent and its trajectory in order to understand the process of development in school supervision in the context of Pakistan.
- To evaluate and understand the current situation of elementary school supervision in Pakistan, in order to analyse its advantages and challenges.

The participants of the seminar included senior officials from BoC (Balochistan), DEOs and ADOs from Sindh as well as Balochistan, from the STEP intervention districts in Sindh and Balochistan and the Project Director, CIDA Debt Swap Project from Balochistan.

The seminar provided the participants, mainly the people involved in school supervision, with an opportunity to thresh out ideas about effective school supervision aimed at improved educational outcomes of schools and students. Most importantly, some of the major challenges were identified and strategies proposed during the panel and group discussions. Some of the key challenges and recommendations were highlighted as the following[12]:

(a) Absence of Job Description

There are no job descriptions or terms of references (ToRs) available for supervisors and Assistant District Officer (ADOs). ToRs were developed and revised in 1999 but never got implemented. ToRs are highly important. In their absence it would not only be difficult to make supervisors accountable for what they do in their supervisory role, but would also make it impossible to evaluate the performance of the persons responsible for supervision and monitoring of the work of schools.

(b) Absence of Pre- and In-service Training

There are no institutional arrangements for the pre- and in-service professional training of the supervisors. Supervisors at various levels of the career ladder require specific training to meet the requirement of effective and efficient supervision. In the absence of institutionalised training, it is very difficult to expect quality performance according to the criteria established by the relevant education departments.

(c) Absence of Transparent Appointments and Promotions

One of the major issues is the sabotaging of merit and the absence of defined criteria in the appointment of people at the supervisory and ADO level. Currently, teachers from colleges are being appointed as ADOs. This creates frustration among the deserving and meritorious candidates, who are being deprived of deserved promotions and professional development opportunities.

(d) Inconsistent Transfers

Supervisors are frequently transferred on a short notice and to places where it is practically difficult for them to perform their duties due to geographical location and contextual challenges. These logistical issues often create a lack of consistency in the implementation of procedures and operational plans as well as frustration and lack of ownership among the supervisors, who wish to improve the quality of the education system.

(e) Lack of Action on Supervisors' Feedback

Supervisors often face the issue of little or no action regarding the suggestions or feedback they provide to their seniors for improvement of conditions that impact the quality of teaching and learning in schools or inside classrooms. This discourages the supervisors from taking new initiatives and being assertive and innovative in their supervisory practices.

(f) Political Influence

Interference of political figures in school affairs or undue exertion of influence and nepotism on the part of influential personage make supervisors' work more complex. The rampant political influence in the appointments, transfers, and promotions, coupled with pressure from Teachers' Unions, severely damage the integrity and quality of effective and efficient supervision in school education.

(g) Lack of Appropriate Funding and Transportation Facilities

Public education in Pakistan continues to remain as one of the most underfunded sectors. Unavailability of adequate funds required for supervisors' in-service training and other supervisory activities such as transportation for school visits, and compensatory allowances adversely affect the quality and the outcome of supervision. The absence of transportation facility hampers females as in the given social, cultural, and security situation, it becomes difficult for them to travel on public transport for long distances.

(h) Safety and Security

Safety and security are considered to be one of the major concerns of supervisors and ADOs. Supervisory staff is threatened by teachers with political backing in cases where any disciplinary action is taken against absenteeism or not fulfilling their duties. There is little or no security assurance from the government or the education department in such cases where supervisory staff needs to enforce the accountability of teachers.

(i) Repetition of Paper Work

Supervisors and ADOs are responsible for reporting to and providing the district education department with data about school demographics as well as performance of head teachers and teachers. However, generally there exists a poor data management system at the administration level. The supervisory staff members are asked multiple times to provide the same information, which is a waste of time and resources.

(j) Control of Education by Civil Bureaucrats

The education system is governed by bureaucrats who often do not have the required qualification, training, and experience to lead and manage the education system. These bureaucrats not only lack an understanding of the system of education but also succumb to expediencies. This creates erosion in the supervisory practices from top-to-bottom.

Policy Recommendations

In the light of the above mentioned issues and challenges, the following policy recommendations were put forward:[13]

- Transparency in Appointments through the Sindh Civil Service Commission: The participants of the meeting highly recommended that the appointment of ADOs and supervisors, learning coordinators as well as all other administrative positions at a higher level be carried out on a merit basis in a transparent and systematic way. It has been suggested that the appointment of administrative positions should be made through the Sindh Civil Service Commission (SCSC) conducting competitive exams from among the interested candidates of the education department for the various administrative positions. This process will ensure the appointment of only meritorious candidates for these positions, and will also phenomenally reduce political interference.
- Training in School Supervision: In general, currently teachers are appointed as supervisors without any training in school supervision and monitoring. Therefore, they lack the required knowledge, skills, and tools of effective supervision and monitoring of the schools. It is highly important to train supervisors, ADOs and other administrative officers in the area of supervision, monitoring and leadership skills so as to be effective and efficient on modern lines.
- Developing Independent Monitoring and Evaluation System: It is highly important to develop an independent school monitoring and evaluation system at the provincial and district level to ensure smooth functioning of schools. To ensure transparency and validity of the process, it is important to ensure

that there is no interference of the education department or political forces in the monitoring and evaluation system.

- Shift in Attitude from Administrative Control to Academic and Community Support: In the current situation, supervisors spend 68 per cent of their time in administrative activities whereas they spend only three per cent time in community relationships and 32 per cent time in academic support. It is highly important to reorient supervisors/learning coordinators towards provision of academic support so as to maintain a productive balance between administrative and academic matters.
- Subject Support Coordinator: Considering the current level of high engagement of the supervisors in the administrative activities, it is desirable to develop a cadre of subject specialists as mentors at the Union Council (UC) level who could provide on-going academic support to teachers in the area of their subject specialisation. These mentors/subject specialists will concentrate only on the academic development of teachers in schools, which could be very beneficial in terms of improved teaching and learning at the school level.

It may be pointed out that, in conformity with the above recommendations, Sindh government in 2014 introduced a new cadre of supervisory staff-Taloqua Education Officers (TEOs) though a competitive selection/recruitment process. STEP organised a short training programme for the newly recruited TEOs in order to orient them to the supervisory and monitoring practices STEP had introduced in the project schools. The reports received through STE District Coordinator about the performance of TEOs are very positive.

Gender Mainstreaming in Education

Gender, being the cross-cutting theme of the STEP project, received special attention in terms of conducting policy dialogues/seminars on issues emanating from gender inequalities. One of the first policy dialogues about gender conducted by STEP project focused on 'gender mainstreaming in education'.

The panellists included prominent educators, social scientist, and civil society activists. The panellists spoke about a wide range of issues faced by women in contemporary Pakistani society. The main focus of the dialogue, however, was on the establishment of policy frameworks that guide gender mainstreaming in education. While deliberating through policy recommendations, the panellists and audience agreed on the following key points:

- Attainment of the Millennium Development Goals (MDGs) must be stressed.
- Gender perspective should be integrated into pre-service and in-service teacher education.
- Work needs to be done at all levels in order to cultivate the importance of female education and eliminate gendered messages from educational discourse.
- Every member of the community must be taken along in order to move forward towards an educated society.

In order to integrate awareness of gender mainstreaming in education, schools, parents, family, religious leaders, and the community need to work in tandem.

Summary

The STEP project's extensive and intensive engagement with capacity building activities at different levels with different educational institutions and stakeholders ranging from teachers to curriculum developers has provided important lessons.

The first important lesson is that people in disadvantaged contexts need opportunities to enhance their professional knowledge, update or acquire new skills and undergo attitudinal change before they become part of a change process within their institutions and in the system at large. People are willing to learn and are motivated to use their learning to make a difference in what they do and how they do it on a day-to-day basis, if they are provided with relevant opportunities.

Second, it is obvious that lasting and systematic change in the realm of education can be brought about through strengthening institutions rather than individuals. This suggests that human resource development at the leadership level needs to be approached in a way that it contributes to institutional strengthening. It therefore may be argued that quality human resources in educational institutions are a precondition for institutional capacity building.

In education, institutional capacity building would mean building the capacity of schools and other institutions responsible for the provision of support service to schools so as to enable them to accept and initiate change, sustain it and build upon it. Capacity of schools and other institutions that are in the frontline to support schools, including teacher training institutions, institutions responsible for making curriculum and curricular material and district education departments, necessarily involve professional development of teachers, school leaders (head teachers), teacher educators, administrators and district mangers. With this understanding in mind, the STEP project focused on the training of each of these primary stakeholders groups. As a result, at least school level institutional capacity building was achieved for a good member of schools.

This is gradually getting translated into improvement in areas such as teaching and learning, student and teacher attendance, and improvement in the physical environment of the schools. The capacity of teachers, head teachers, and managers in terms of enhanced skills and knowledge alone cannot help, attitudinal change is more important. The long duration of STEP project helped bring about positive change in the attitude and disposition and ethical orientation of the people.

Sustainability is central to the long-term success of the STEP project. These reflections provide evidence to how participants have acquired the ability to take their own initiatives to further carry out programmes and activities as needed. This, at a basic level, ensures sustainability in that the lessons and skills learnt will be continuously implemented and disseminated widely.

Having said all this, it may be pointed out that capacity building is not a linear process; capacity building of human resource does not necessarily equate institutional capacity building. Institutional capacity building is not a quick fix, to be achieved merely through training of staff. There are numerous other factors involved in getting human resource capacity building translated into enhanced institutional capacity. It is an on-going practice which is done through internal motivation, institutional development programmes for their human resource, challenging tasks with supportive scaffolding, and matching human resources with structural and material resources, and strong policy support.

References

Fullan, M., *The New Meaning of Educational Change* (3rd ed, Toronto: Irwin Publishing Ltd., 2001).

Glewwe, P., Hanushek, E., Humpage, S. & Ravina, R., '*School resources and educational outcomes in developing countries: A review of the literature from 1990 to 2010* (Centre for International Food and Agricultural Policy University of Minnesota, Department of Applied Economics, 2012).

Hargreaves, A., Changing *Teachers, Changing Times: Teachers' Work and Culture in The Postmodern Age* (New York: Teachers College Press, 1994).

Stoll, L., 'Realising our potential: Understanding and developing capacity for lasting Improvement', *School Effectiveness and School Improvement*, 10/4, (1999), 503–532.

Notes

1. The Aga Khan University-Institute for Educational Development (2014), 'Programme completion report 2014'.
2. Ibid.
3. Ibid.
4. Ibid.
5. Ibid.
6. The Aga Khan University-Institute for Educational Development (2015), 'STEP Annual Narrative Report–2015'.
7. Ibid.
8. Ibid.
9. Ibid.
10. http://www.dawn.com/2011/11/25/education-collapse.html
11. Sindh Education Foundation and Aga Khan University-Institute for Educational Development (2012). Report on the Policy Dialogues on Educational Governance in Sindh.
12. The Aga Khan University-Institute for Educational Development (2011), 'Report of STEP Policy Seminar on School Supervision'.
13. Ibid.

5

Educational Development and Improvement Programme (EDIP): An Innovative School Improvement Model Implemented in Gilgit-Baltistan

Mola Dad Shafa, Sharifullah Baig, and *Zeenat Shah*

Introduction

During the last two decades several small and large-scale projects[1] have been implemented across Gilgit-Baltistan to improve education system in public and private sector. As mentioned in Chapter 2, more recently a large-scale multi-faceted reform project known as 'Education Development and Improvement Programme' (EDIP) was implemented in all seven districts of Gilgit-Baltistan. The Department of Foreign Affairs and Trade (DFAT), Australia provided financial resources and the Aga Khan Development Network (AKDN) managed EDIP. The programme was designed with the purpose to increase children's access to improved quality of education in Gilgit-Baltistan, Pakistan. EDIP aimed to augment the Department of Education, Gilgit-Baltistan's (DoE GB) capacities to ensure the sustainability of the project initiatives, on the one hand, and to help the department meet the growing demands from its clientele on the other. This chapter presents a comprehensive overview of the EDIP and its achievements. The chapter is organised in three main sections.

The first section introduces the socio-cultural and religious context of the programme and sheds light on the contribution of the Aga Khan Development Network (AKDN) to social and educational development of Gilgit-Baltistan. The second section discusses EDIP's context, beneficiaries and key features (interventions and outcomes). The third section describes EDIP's expansion to Diamer district; it highlights key programmatic interventions, outcomes, impact and important lessons learnt from EDIP's experience of undertaking a pioneering work in the district. The chapter ends with a summary.

The Socio-Cultural and Religious Context

Gilgit-Baltistan (GB), the northeastern-most administrative unit of Pakistan, spans an area of 72,490 square kilometres and consists of ten administrative units, called districts namely Hunza, Nagar, Gilgit, Ghizar, Skardu, Shigar, Kharmang, Ghanche, Astore, and Diamer. The recent estimates suggest that the population of Gilgit-Baltistan is 1.25 million (Pakistan Education Statistics, 2013–2014), holding a literacy rate of 44 per cent which is lower than the 61.5 per cent national literacy rate (Government of Pakistan, 2014–2015).

With an increasing population and meagre economic prospects in the region, an overwhelming majority of the people in Gilgit-Baltistan live below the poverty line. Agriculture is the major means of subsistence for the people of Gilgit-Baltistan. However, the severe climatic conditions, the uneven landscape, and merely two to three per cent arable land available for crops make agriculture a very challenging occupation. The other sources of income include rearing livestock and limited employment opportunities mainly associated with the Pakistan Army, health and education departments and other service providing agencies in the public and private sectors.

A description of the economic situation in Gilgit-Baltistan would remain incomplete without mention of the contributions of both the Karakorum Highway (KKH) and the initiatives of the Aga Khan Development Network (AKDN) institutions.[2] The KKH connects Pakistan and China. When it became operational in 1978, Gilgit-Baltistan, until then an isolated region, became accessible to and connected with the major urban centres of China and Pakistan. This opportunity helped in diversifying the conventional sources of income. As a result, tourism emerged as a new venue for socioeconomic development.

By religion, the people of Gilgit-Baltistan are Muslims attached to one of the four different sects of Islam, each following a different school of jurisprudence. These sects are known as the *Sunni* Muslims, the *Shia Ithna Ashari* Muslims, the *Shia Ismaili* Muslims, and the *Noor-Bakhshi* Muslims. Despite their religious differences, the people have always believed in co-existence, tolerance, and peace, as they had been living together peacefully in Gilgit-Baltistan for centuries. However, from 1980s onward several sectarian conflicts have created tensions, more so in some areas than others, which jeopardised peace and harmony in the region. While these communal conflicts have brought people adhering to the same faith closer to each other, on the one hand, they have created a gulf amongst people following different interpretations of faith. A sectarian conflict that erupted between local *Sunnis* and *Shias Ithna Ashari M*uslims during 1988, and which was considered to be the worst in the history of Gilgit-Baltistan, resulted in the loss of many lives and destruction of much property on both sides. The years following this unfortunate event witnessed increasing tensions, intermittent communal clashes and resulting widespread sectarian hatred having severe repercussions for the socio-economic development of the region.

AKDN: A Partner of Choice in Gilgit-Baltistan

The Aga Khan Development Network (AKDN) brings together, under one coherent aegis, institutions and programmes whose shared mandate is to help society overcome the issues hindering social development. Over the last several decades, AKDN, partnering with local stakeholders including the government, has made tangible contributions to the socioeconomic development in Gilgit-Baltistan. Its development endeavours have spanned rural and community development, primary and community health, education and educational development, built environment and physical planning, water, housing improvement and sanitation, micro-finance and regular banking services, and disaster preparedness and mitigation.

AKDN's ethical framework is characterised by its inclusive and compassionate approach towards social development. Its developmental philosophy is rooted in increasing people's access to knowledge and research to enable them to become self-reliant and to honour the invaluable divine gifts of life and health. The ethical framework enjoins the development partners to demonstrate their sensitivity and commitment to ensuring a sustained physical, social, and cultural environment for the future generations. In addition, it attaches the highest premium with maintaining transparency and accountability in engagements ranging from day-to-day routine activities to high profile roles in achieving the goals of social development.

EDIP: An Introduction

EDIP focused on both infrastructure development and human resource capacity building of government schools. The key focus areas of EDIP included improving the physical environment of project schools, upgrading teachers' and head teachers' skills and students' learning outcomes. Therefore, the project sought the involvement of the public sector, local communities, NGOs, civil society, and the private sector in the implementation of the programme. Originally, EDIP was designed as a three-year project (i.e. July 2010–June 2013), however, it was given a no-cost extension (NCE) for two more years and hence it concluded in June 2015. The 109 target schools in all seven districts of Gilgit-Baltistan, DoE GB, along with its district education offices benefited the most from EDIP support.

Programme Goal and Objectives

The overall goal of EDIP had its focus on 'enhancing access, equity and quality of education with increased gender parity, participation and sustainability of community participation in targeted districts of Gilgit-Baltistan'. More specifically, the project aimed at:

- Increased enrolment and retention in schools, and improved participation of communities in the management and general life of the schools;
- Enhanced professionalism of head teachers and teachers and improved quality of the physical learning environment and resources in cluster schools; and
- Enhanced leadership capacity of the DoE GB to improve governance and sustain the reforms initiated by the project.

Commenced in July 2010, EDIP was implemented in 98 schools in GB of which 48 government schools were AKU-IED/PDCN-managed whereas the rest were AKESP-managed project schools. However, 11 schools in Diamer district were added from January 2013 to the PDCN-managed project schools bringing the total number of

EDIP schools in GB to 109. Of the total schools, 27 (24 per cent) were boys' schools, 26 (24 per cent were girls' schools and more than half (51 per cent) were co-education schools[3]. Each cluster consisted of a learning resource school (LRS) and three feeding schools, with a learning resource centre (LRC) established in each LRS. The LRS was a secondary school while the feeding schools included either primary, middle or, in certain cases, secondary schools. An AKU-IED's MEd graduate, having his/her specialty in teacher education and school improvement, was placed at the LRS to lead the school improvement initiative in each cluster; these cluster-based facilitators were called professional development teachers (PDTs). The share of the government and AKESP schools in the total EDIP project was 76 per cent and 24 per cent, respectively.

The EDIP Cluster Model

The practice of clustering schools and creating networks among them for school improvement purposes is gaining momentum in different parts of the world (Street & Temperley, 2005). As mentioned in Chapter 2, AKU-IED, Pakistan has used the cluster-based mentoring approach to upgrade teachers' capacities in the provinces of Sindh and Balochistan since 1990s which heralded the introduction of a new approach for school improvement in Pakistan. AKU-IED used the learning from the Cluster-Based Mentoring (CBM) Model in designing and implementing WSIP through PDCN in Gilgit-Baltistan.

The EDIP model of school improvement involved a cluster-based approach where schools located in the close vicinity of a centrally located secondary school formed one cluster. The centrally located high school, also called the learning resource school (LRS), was used as a hub of school improvement activities. The LRS was expected to emerge as a showcase of success for the other feeding schools, as well as for the other schools in the area to emulate.

The EDIP model emerged as the most comprehensive model ever implemented in GB. It was designed on the principles of multi-input area development (MIAD) in that a consortium of seven AKDN specialist organisations worked in tandem and brought in their particular inputs for the overall success of the project. This is aligned with the insights emerging from the literature highlighting the importance of multi-level intervention to promote school improvement (Harris, 2002). In fact, the EDIP cluster model sought inspiration from the research-based knowledge which emphasises that there is little teacher development without school development (Hopkins, 1996) and that the effectiveness is enhanced if schools and the newly trained individuals are able to move forward at the same pace (Hargreaves, 1994; Stoll & Fink, 1995). It particularly recommends looking at the processes of school improvement and the links between processes and outcomes (Gray et al., 1999). The EDIP cluster model, therefore, recommends working with four schools simultaneously to rally the inside-school and outside-school stakeholders behind the well-defined and achievable school improvement goals.

The extensive networking and multi-layered partnerships distinguished EDIP from the other educational development programmes implemented in the context of Gilgit-Baltistan. Under the leadership of AKF (P), the implementing partners including AKU-IED/PDCN, Department of Education GB, Aga Khan Education Service, Pakistan (AKESP), Aga Khan Planning and Building Services (AKPBS), FOCUS Humanitarian Assistance, Network of Organisations Working with People with Disabilities, Pakistan (NOWPDP), Civil Society Resource Center (CSRC) and Aga Khan University-Human Development Programme (AKU-HDP) were threaded into a seamless partnership and a web of networking. The specialised inputs from each partner made EDIP an exemplary cooperative endeavour reflecting a consortium-based model of educational development.

The Consortium-Based Model

EDIP was a comprehensive, integrated, and consortium-based school development approach consisting of the following seven AKDN agencies to contribute to the project through their respective expertise and experiences:

Table 1: EDIP Implementing Partners and their Areas of Expertise

S. No.	Partner	Nature of Contribution	Nature of Partnership
1.	AKU-IED/PDCN	Access, Quality, Professional Development, and Facilitation to all other Partners	Implementing Partner
2.	Aga Khan Education Service, Pakistan (AKESP)	Access, Quality, Professional Development, Adult Literacy	Implementing Partner
3.	Aga Khan Planning and Building Service, Pakistan (AKPBSP)	School Construction and Retrofitting	Implementing Partner
4.	Civil Society Resource Centre (CSRC)	Participation of Parents and Communities	Auxiliary Partner

S. No.	Partner	Nature of Contribution	Nature of Partnership
5.	Network of Organisations Working with People with Disability in Pakistan (NOWPDP)	Disability and Inclusive Education	Auxiliary Partner
6.	AKU-Human Development Programme (AKU-HDP)	Early Childhood Education and Disability	Auxiliary Partner
7.	FOCUS Humanitarian Assistance	Disaster Risk Reduction	Auxiliary Partner

As the consortium partners, AKU-IED/PDCN and AKESP, building upon and maximising their earlier experiences of using the whole school improvement (WSI) approach in GB, attended to the various issues having a bearing on the change initiatives in schools. Considering an entire school as a unit of change and improvement, and with the sustainability question in mind, they focused on improving various dimensions of the school through multi-layered and multi-level inputs.

The Aga Khan Planning and Building Services, Pakistan (AKPBSP) introduced the most recent technologies in construction and strengthening of the existing infrastructures; they used thermal-efficient as well as inclusive approaches to help buildings become seismic-resistant and to curtail the harshness of the climatic conditions; and also to facilitate moderately-disabled children to attend schools. The Network of Organisations Working with People with Disability in Pakistan (NOWPDP) introduced teachers and parents to different inclusive approaches to take care of the children with mild-to-moderate disabilities. Interestingly, parents and teachers got the knowledge for the first time that children with mild disabilities can be made part of mainstream education. Their understanding improved on how the various issues related to children's disability can be taken care of. The Civil Society Resource Centre (CSRC) augmented school committees' leadership for community mobilisation to narrow down the gap between schools and the wider school communities. The Aga Khan University's Human Development Programme (AKU-HDP) contributed its expertise in strengthening the initiative of early years' education and disability and, more importantly, conducted research in these areas to generate context-specific knowledge related to EDIP. The FOCUS International Humanitarian Assistance brought into the project their expertise on disaster risk reduction and management and introduced parents, teachers, and students to various techniques on how to ensure safety and security of human life and property and to minimise the risk related to various natural disasters such as earthquakes, floods, landslides, and/or fire.

The monitoring and supervision mechanism required the EDIP partners to report to AKFP as the chief executing agency on all contractual, grant management, and strategic matters. Although AKFP established its provincial coordination office in Gilgit to coordinate with each of the seven implementing partners in Gilgit-Baltistan, each partner, however, reported progress related to programme activities to AKFP through the individual organisational management and governance structures.

AKU-IED/PDCN worked as a hub of EDIP implementing activities and, in addition to implementing its own programmatic activities, it also extended on-going logistical and administrative support to AKFP and the secondary partners. The EDIP cluster model of school improvement was implemented by PDCN in 59 public sector schools with 14 learning resource centres (LRCs) equipped with valuable books and advanced computers with internet facility and solar power provision. PDCN enjoyed a very healthy and cooperative professional relationship with the DoE GB and encouraged their involvement at all levels which helped the Department develop a sense of ownership of the project.

At the strategic level, a multi-stakeholder EDIP Steering Committee (SC) was formed to monitor the overall progress of the EDIP project. The SC was co-chaired by the Secretary Education, GB and the CEO of AKFP. In addition, at the operational level, an Advisory Committee (AC) was established to closely monitor and supervise the day-to-day operations including the achievements and challenges of EDIP implementation. This was chaired by the Director Education (Academics) Gilgit. The AC consisted of representatives from the government of GB, AKES Pakistan, and AKF Pakistan. However, for various reasons both these strategic committees could not hold their progress review meetings more than once throughout the project life. A majority of the staff in the district offices of education, PDTs and Advanced Diploma in Education-Educational Leadership and Management (ADE-ELM) graduates attended the needs assessment and technical workshops. They identified needs for capacity building of district management staff and improving infrastructure. They also highlighted the way forward for sustainability and replicability of the project initiatives. AKF and PDCN conducted sessions for district offices on different needs identified such as developing PC–1, computer skills and report writing.

Establishing/Revitalizing the Local Level Institutions and Community Involvement

Different types of Local Level Institutions (LLIs) such as school management committees (SMCs) and mother support groups (MSGs) were formed and engaged for community mobilisation. Although they remained dormant in most previous cases, the concept of school management committees (SMCs) was not new in the public sector schools in GB; SMCs existed, albeit on paper, and many of them were dysfunctional. EDIP established, where needed, and activated the existing SMCs in the EDIP schools. The concept of mother support groups (MSGs) was introduced for the first time in most of the project schools. All implementing partners worked with and through these LLIs to sensitise the local community on issues including girls education, school safety, disaster risk reduction and management, child-friendly environment at schools, health and hygiene, inclusive education, and overall school improvement. Besides sharing concepts on the need and significance of voluntarism, responsibilities of LLIs', civil society's role in community development and school development plans, exposure visits were also organised for the LLIs to learn from the best practices in schools. During the project life, 992 community members participated in field-based and PDCN-based capacity building workshops while 1,900 parents, including 750 mothers, attended the LRS-based seminars on EDIP.

The impact of PDCN-initiated capacity building sessions for LLIs was multifarious. Some of the LLIs-initiated community awareness campaigns and contributed their time to school monitoring and support which took place in close coordination with the school head teachers. Some other LLIs started monitoring morning assemblies to ensure punctuality and regularity of students and teachers. Schools shared the data of late arrivals and absenteeism with the LLIs and they visited students' homes and discussed these issues with their parents. Moreover, the LLIs became active in developing close linkages with the DoE GB, particularly with the district offices, and shared with them their school issues regularly. Moreover, they monitored the EDIP-initiated as well as the regular construction activities and immensely contributed to the improvement of schools' physical environment. In certain cases, i.e. at LRS Karimabad, Hunza and LRS Chilas in Diamer, the LLIs helped in starting regular computer classes in the computer laboratory established by the EDIP project. In some cases, LLIs mobilised the community for resource generation for classroom construction and other school improvement needs. Since access to school with gender parity including children with disabilities was the first objective of EDIP, the LLIs remained instrumental in raising awareness of parents and communities to promote girls' education and also to educate their children with mild disabilities. Consequently, the enrolment of 7,884 students noted in the baseline in 2010 increased to 12,061 in 2015, reflecting the net increase of 4,177 students in EDIP schools. The new admissions also included 267 children with disabilities and 386 dropouts.

EDIP Beneficiaries

EDIP supported the government and communities of Gilgit-Baltistan to provide quality education to children, a majority of whom were attending public sector schools. Furthermore, it provided the DoE GB senior leadership training opportunities and exposure to the best practices, both country-based and abroad, to build their capacity to achieve the goal of improving the quality of institutional services to meet the increasing community demands.

The 59 PDCN-managed EDIP schools included 12,061 students, 3, 231 teachers and head teachers, 992 LLI members and 70 DoE GB officials as the direct beneficiaries of the project. In addition to the professional development opportunities for the school and DoE GB-based staff, the project schools were physically assessed in a holistic way to identify the seismic resistance needs, general rehabilitation needs, the requirements related to children having moderate disability and the thermal efficiency of schools to cope with the extreme climate of GB. The 14 LRSs were provided with a number of facilities such as LRCs connected with internet, while 12 of these LRSs were also provided solar energy to ascertain uninterrupted supply of electricity to use computers. Moreover, all project schools received furniture, learning materials such as stationery, reference books, textbooks, dictionaries and other books with book shelves, retrofitting of rooms, construction of new rooms, provision of learning materials and electronic hardware for teaching purposes. Table 2 illustrates the direct beneficiaries of the EDIP project:

Table 2: The Direct Beneficiaries of the EDIP Project

Beneficiaries	Gilgit-Baltistan
EDIP Project Schools	Total: 59 schools including 13 secondary schools and 46 primary/elementary schools
Local Level Institutions	59 school management committees and 16 MSGs (992 members)
Project School Parents	7051
Total Students in Schools	12061 (Pre-primary to secondary school children)
Number of Teachers	3231 teachers

AKU-IED/PDCN also contributed to the technical capacity of the Gilgit-Baltistan Education Department to review and upgrade the Gilgit-Baltistan Education Strategy into a viable policy document under the current political and economic scenario. PDCN provided the venue and technical and logistic support for the working group meetings which led to the reviewing and upgrading of the Gilgit-Baltistan Education Strategy (GBES: 2015–2030). Following these efforts, the GBES has been formally ratified by the Gilgit-Baltistan Legislative Assembly (GBLA); hence, the GBES has become the government-validated roadmap for education in GB for the next 15 years.

EDIP Features

Amongst the several school improvement models and the teacher development initiatives experimented over the last decades by AKDN and the government in GB, EDIP stands out as the most comprehensive, integrated and consortium-based model ever implemented in the context of Gilgit-Baltistan. For instance, it characterised the field-based nature of the Field-Based Teacher Professional Development Programme (FBDTP[4]), the feature of active community involvement of the UNICEF-sponsored Child-Friendly School (CFS) project, and pedagogical and content knowledge (PCK) focus of the AKESP-initiated 'Mathematics and Science Improvement Programme' (MASIP). The following are some of the key features of the EDIP project which distinguished it from many other school improvement models implemented in GB and beyond.

Whole School Improvement Programme (WSIP)[5]

Teachers trained away from their schools and having no professional support mechanisms put in place in their work places often get immersed in the conventional cultures forcing them to revert to old ways of doing business. Our experiences have repeatedly shown that expecting a teacher who availed an out-of-school professional development opportunity to replace the existing deep-rooted school culture to bring improvement in schools is often a far-fetched and an unrealistic idea. Therefore, considering the school as the unit of change (Hopkins, 2002), rather than working with individual teachers, gave birth to the idea of 'whole school improvement' (WSI) which encourages investment of time, resources and efforts to improve teachers' pedagogical content knowledge (PCK), governance and management-related practices, including accountability, team work, student assessment, resource generation and utilisation, and community participation in schools.

Contrary to the traditional top-down approach in education delivery, the WSI philosophy advocates for increasing involvement of heads, teachers, students and school community in the school decisions. 'The assumption underpinning the policy is that a decentralised education system is more responsive to local needs, and nurtures a culture of ownership, partnership and commitment' (Akyeampong, 2004).

EDIP was a synthesis of the Whole School Improvement Programme (WSIP) implemented by PDCN since 1999 in Gilgit-Baltistan (Shafa, 2014). The WSIP implemented in Gilgit-Baltistan during 2010–2015 was a school-based training programme, designed to improve the quality of teaching and learning and to develop the school as a learning organisation. It aimed to improve students' learning outcomes and build local capacity to address the school improvement issues on an on-going basis. In this programme, WSIP was initiated with an intensive needs analysis and base-line followed by an orientation to the heads of the project schools. During orientation, the heads were facilitated to develop school development plans (SDPs) for their schools so that they had a sense of ownership for school improvement right from the beginning of the project. Where possible, teachers from these schools were then brought to PDCN for an orientation; otherwise, orientations for teachers were held in their schools.

In the process of bringing about change and improvement in schools, WSIP facilitates teachers to employ a holistic approach to help students develop the different dimensions of their personalities. The following structure reflects the six important elements for WSIP:

WSIP Framework

The six key elements of WSIP guiding and shaping the EDIP initiatives in the project schools are as follows:

Table 3: The Six Focus Areas of WSIP

The Key Aspects of WSIP	Specific Goals
Quality of Teaching and Learning	Teachers have high expectations of pupils' achievements. Teachers have clear objectives, lesson plans and evaluation procedures. Teachers use appropriate textbooks, displays and resources for teaching and learning. Children are active learners and do sustained work. They are highly motivated, eager to learn and show initiative. They take risks and are not afraid to make mistakes.
Curriculum Enrichment and Staff Development	National Curriculum is enriched by the use of relevant resources and information. The curriculum is broad, balanced, relevant and matched to children's needs and experiences. It is challenging. Head teacher and teachers organise regular in-service training. They constantly endeavour to improve their knowledge and skills.
Leadership, Management and Administration	Head teacher has a clear vision for the school and high expectations. Head teacher communicates effectively, demonstrates instructional leadership, supports teachers and visits them in class, shares responsibility, provides for staff development, manages finance, plans ahead and keeps good records, works collaboratively with parents and community.

The Key Aspects of WSIP	Specific Goals
Building, Accommodation and Resources	School environment is well maintained, inviting and attractive. It is effectively used. Resources, including the library, are adequate and easily accessible. There are good displays of children's work and other materials. Children and teachers take pride in their environment and maintain high standards.
Community Involvement	Parents and community are involved in the work of the school. They co-operate and collaborate with head teacher and teaching staff. Parents are involved in their children's learning, and policymaking. Parents and community share their skills with teachers and children. School organises regular meetings and classes for the community.
Students' Social and Moral Development and Health Education	Standards of students' behaviour and discipline are exemplary. Students are well behaved, cooperative and keen to take responsibility. Students and teachers collaborate, and show respect towards each other and all members of the school community.

The Two-Tiered Approach of Professional Development

EDIP's professional development model focused on development and on-going mentoring of teachers and staff in the project schools. A number of short-term, medium-term and long-term professional development courses were conducted for teachers. These courses benefited 3,413 stakeholders including teachers, head teachers, AEOs and LLIs members. The training and professional development activities were reinforced through provision of rigorous and systematic follow-up support to the schools and teachers by the LRS-based Professional Development Teachers. These inputs into teacher learning and school improvement enhanced the overall impact of the programme on teaching and learning processes and its outcomes. The professional development initiatives at PDCN and in schools primarily aimed to improve teachers' pedagogical content knowledge (PCK) including their sense of professionalism. They were facilitated to reflect on their own knowledge, attitude, values, skills and practices and take initiatives for improvement in their day-to-day teaching. The concepts such as how children learn, use of various teaching and learning styles, tailoring teaching to meet individual learning needs, use of appropriate instructional resources and the assessment of learning were used as the overarching themes in the capacity building courses. Moreover, teachers also learnt how to organise and manage a more inclusive learning-friendly environment that values what children bring to school and has high and clear expectations of their achievements.

The head teachers were engaged in school improvement as key agents of change in the project. They were provided with the opportunities to learn new strategies and techniques to create conditions for and strengthen the efforts towards enhancing outputs from students, teachers and parents. The head teachers and teachers were also provided the opportunity to attend certified courses such as the AKU-IED MEd, Advanced Diploma in Educational Leadership and Management, Certificate in Early Childhood Education and Development and Certificate in Primary Education to enhance their professional knowledge and skills in the area of teaching and learning.

The EDIP contributions also included the capacity building of 60 head teachers and deputy head teachers from the DoE GB schools through the one-year Advanced Diploma in Education: Educational Leadership and Management (ADELM) at PDCN. These participants were trained in the areas of leadership and management, monitoring and evaluation and school-based action research. These head teachers are presently working at critical positions in different schools helping to sustain the EDIP initiatives.

Sustainability of the Project Gains

PDCN believes that an appropriately qualified educator plays a central role in sustaining the learning environment in schools. Hence, a teacher from each LRS, who demonstrated his/her commitment to bring about positive change and met the admission criteria, was selected and developed through AKU-IED's two-year MEd programme. These graduates, i.e. the EDIP scholarship beneficiaries, upon completion of their studies, returned to their schools and took the lead role in school improvement in the school. This was a long-term strategy to develop institutional capacity of the public sector schools as the MEd graduates were seen as valuable resources to sustain the innovations in the project schools and to provide professional support to teachers in their own as well as in the neighbouring schools, even after the project life. Altogether EDIP sponsored 25 teachers for MEd studies at AKU-IED. Furthermore, EDIP built the capacity of head teachers and district education office personnel through different courses; they were expected to sustain the project gains in their schools and districts. These graduates have already started proving themselves as invaluable assets of the government education system in GB.

Multi-Layered Monitoring and Supervision of the Project

The EDIP project adopted a multi-layered monitoring and supervision plan to ascertain timely delivery and quality of programmatic inputs. PDCN employed a comprehensive data collection and report submission mechanism using the Project Monitoring Framework. The implementing partners were responsible for the assurance of programme content and field delivery. PDCN as the lead partner was responsible to implement a large chunk of the programmatic activities and to provide logistical/administrative support to AKFP and the secondary partners. The secondary partners were responsible for specific activities within a thematic and/or component context. All partners reported to AKFP as the chief executing agency on all contractual, grant management, and strategic matters. AKFP worked with both tiers to ensure clear communications and smooth operations within the programme. Each partner reported programmatic activities through the individual organisational management and governance structures. Furthermore, the DoE GB and its line departments were involved to provide policy support and adequate human resources to ensure that the programmes' outcomes were achieved.

Inclusive Approach to Educational Change

Under the inclusive education initiative, the programme conducted a needs assessment survey of beneficiary/feeder communities of EDIP schools to gain an understanding of their attitudes towards perceptions about disability. These were used to develop community-oriented training programmes to inform and raise awareness regarding physical disabilities. The objective was to develop relevant training materials regarding disability sensitisation amongst the school communities. In this regard, 117 teachers were trained and 19 master trainers were developed and as a result of these efforts 267 students with mild-to-moderate disability were enrolled and mainstreamed into formal education.

EDIP Extension to Diamer District

Diamer district was part of the Northern Pakistan Education Project (1998–2003) funded by the World Bank and implemented by the Department of Education, Gilgit-Baltistan (DoE-GB). It also remained part of the government's mainstream initiatives for socioeconomic development in GB. However, despite these efforts,

Diamer remained as one of the most backward districts in GB in terms of its literacy as well as its human resource development indicators. A host of challenges, including those related to extremism and terrorism, violation of human rights and lack of motivation on the part of local communities to partake in the development processes severely restricted the process of social development including school improvement in Diamer district. In fact, it was during NPEP that several girls' schools in the District were damaged by anti-girl-education elements which shook the confidence and motivation of the development partners to venture into going to the district and contribute to the cause of education in Diamer.

EDIP did not include Diamer as a site for intervention right from the beginning (July 2010) due largely to the challenges emanating from the volatile and deteriorating law-and-order situation in the district. The intermittent terrorist incidents that took place in or around Diamer tarnished the image of the district all over the world as an abode of extremists. These incidences of terrorism unfortunately coincided with the commencement and early implementation of EDIP, thereby dimming the hope to extend EDIP in Diamer. Further, AKDN was advised to refrain from taking EDIP to Diamer.

Although sporadic efforts were made to include teachers from Diamer in the EDIP-sponsored PDCN-based professional development programmes, the project was not implemented in its entirety in the district for the obvious reasons of security and demotivation of local communities. However, despite the fact that Diamer was not formally part of the EDIP project, by December 2012, 116 teachers participated in the PDCN-based courses who, on their return, seemed to have played a significant role in convincing teachers and community members on the importance of the EDIP project and the quality learning opportunities offered at PDCN. At a later time, these PDCN graduates became instrumental in addressing apprehensions and misconceptions about PDCN and its EDIP project among their communities in the district.

The Tripartite Partnership among AKDN, DoE GB, and the Police Department

The stalemate of avoiding AKDN's physical presence in Diamer district took a new turn as a result of the tripartite partnership signed by the Department of Education, Gilgit-Baltistan (DoE, GB), the Police Department of GB and AKDN (PDCN and AKF) towards the end of 2012. Repeated requests from the PD-GB to AKFP to support the seven Police-run home-based girls' schools in Diamer[6] provided the impetus to form the tripartite partnership. Agreeing to facilitate the Police-managed schools in Diamer, AKFP convened a series of meetings with the leadership of the Police Department of GB and DoE-GB in Gilgit and Islamabad. An MoU, highlighting the key roles of the three partners, was signed by the then Inspector General of Police (IGP), the Principal Secretary to the Chief Minister of GB and the CEO, of AKF, P. The MoU included the following roles to be played by the government and the AKDN:

- The Police Department, GB would provide security to the implementing partners in Diamer district.
- The DoE, GB would contribute essential logistical support for EDIP in Diamer.
- The AKDN (AKFP and PDCN) would provide financial and technical support to improve the teaching and learning conditions in the project schools in Diamer through EDIP.

As part of the formal extension of EDIP to Diamer from January 1, 2013, briefings were conducted for schools to understand the nature of the project and show their willingness through applications seeking approval regarding their participation in the project. In consultation with the authorities of the district education department, four schools located at Chilas (district headquarter) town were selected to be developed through EDIP. In addition seven police-run girls' schools were brought into the fold of the EDIP project.

The EDIP input to the project school teachers in Diamer included the school-, LRS-, and PDCN-based professional development sessions for the teachers. Material resources including stationery were provided to schools as well as to individual teachers to facilitate them in achieving the school improvement goals. A computer laboratory including twelve computers, with internet connectivity, was established at the LRS while two computers each were provided to the three feeding schools of the LRS Chilas.

In addition, the EDIP contributions to Diamer also included the AKU-IED MEd scholarships for teachers to develop them as academic leaders and change facilitators for the district. While allocating district-wise EDIP scholarships for MEd at AKU-IED, Diamer was given the biggest share, i.e. five scholarships, in consideration of its unique needs.

Key Achievements of the EDIP Project in Diamer

The EDIP implementation in Diamer yielded numerous tangible and intangible benefits. These benefits range from improvement in educational conditions in schools, to enhanced awareness among local communities about the need and importance of education, to upgrading the infrastructure, to provision of educational resources to school. These outcomes are briefly discussed hereafter.

Increased Children's Access to Schools

The current enrolment (2,913) in the eleven EDIP intervention schools in Diamer, when compared with the baseline statistics (2,475), clearly shows that there has been a significant increase in the number of children who have started attending schools. The support in terms of provision of textbooks, uniforms, notebooks, health and hygiene kits, and furniture extended to the schools was instrumental in attracting increasing numbers of children to these schools. In fact, in some of these EDIP project schools the space to accommodate children has emerged as a challenge because of the swelling number of children in these schools.

Increasing Acceptability for Donor Contribution in Diamer

Due largely to various socio-political reasons, Diamer has long remained as a highly 'resistant-to-change' district. The anti-development campaigns by the local 'power-wielders' for many decades clouded the thinking and vision of the local communities, forcing them to develop extremely narrow worldviews and perspectives about themselves and others. Consequently, the local populace remained highly suspicious of the development agencies willing to make interventions in the district. The development agenda of 'women empowerment' and/or 'female education' particularly raised eyebrows of the local people who feared that these initiatives might spread indecency among people causing damage to the local culture characterised by women strictly observing 'purdah' (veil) and confining themselves to their homes. It could be due to this sort of fear and apprehensions that more than a dozen girls' schools were dynamited over the last decade or so in Diamer. Resultantly, only a few NGOs dared to go to Diamer with a development agenda and so was the case for AKDN.

However, PDCN's careful and calculated efforts to reach out to these long-ignored communities and successfully working with eleven government schools and the local communities paved the way for the donor community to contribute to the cause of social development in Diamer. The story of change narrated here presents us with a unique opportunity to analyse the lessons learnt regarding the strategies towards spreading social and educational awareness among the communities which are normally portrayed as ignorant, extremist and backward in the discourse around social development and change.

Increased Community Involvement and Interest in Education

The EDIP project in Diamer, over 25 months, reached out to the school community including the school management committees (SMCs) and fathers of the school children. On a limited scale, the single female teacher educator engaged by EDIP interacted with the mothers. These interactions with school parents played a vital role in enhancing their understanding of the importance of educating their children. The increased enrolment (of both boys and girls) in schools, improved cleanliness of children and the improved regularity and punctuality of the children and teachers in the schools, are some of the evidences of the impact of the initiatives undertaken by EDIP.

Improved Students Learning Achievement

There is tangible evidence of improved students learning achievements in the EDIP intervention schools in Diamer. This improvement relates to both the quantitative and qualitative aspects of students' learning achievements. For instance, in the Annual Examination 2014, three students from Government Primary School Takia (an EDIP feeding school of LRS Chilas) bagged the top three positions at the district level. Likewise, there is anecdotal evidence of how the EDIP project motivated children in schools to work harder in their studies. The Director Education Gilgit and the Head of PDCN were pleasantly surprised to hear a Grade 2 student in a Police-managed school in Tangir (a Tehsil in Diamer) counting numbers up to 100 in English. A student in another police-managed school in Tangir impressed the visitors by asking them questions, which clearly reflected confidence, motivation, and the ability of the student. The monthly reports from the schools showed that there was visible improvement in teachers' classroom punctuality and regularity, and in their content and pedagogical knowledge which, in turn, contributed to improving students' learning achievements. In the EDIP end line report, the evaluators awarded the Government Primary School Painkote A+ grade for its improved teaching and learning conditions.

Making School Management Committees Functional

As part of its initiatives, EDIP established school management committees (SMCs) and conducted programmes for their capacity building. These SMCs were provided with opportunities to participate in the awareness-raising sessions in Chilas and at PDCN. However, an exposure visit organised for these SMCs to show them the best practices in Hunza and Ghizar districts (areas where AKDN has a long history of intervention) proved to be highly powerful in increasing their level of motivation and awareness, and contributing to their ability to play a productive role in making the SMCs functional. They also played a positive and effective role in the advocacy for and generating political support for EDIP in the district. There is compelling evidence of PDCN interventions having an impact on increasing the effectiveness of SMCs in the Diamer district. The following excerpt from the EDIP Final 2015 Evaluation report[7] adequately endorses the assertion about the project's impact on education in the district: 'The most dramatic change was experienced in Diamer, where SMCs either did not exist or were mostly dormant. The project played a key role in creating or resuscitating SMCs in the district' (p.16). In the same report, a quote from an SMC member illustrates this: 'PDCN has opened our eyes. We have replaced the gun with the pen'.

Key Insights Gained from the EDIP Experience in Diamer

Despite the numerous daunting challenges faced in the process, the experiences gained through the implementation of EDIP in Diamer provided us with valuable learning about and rich insights into the sociology of educational change. These insights certainly inform our overall understanding of and knowledge-base about planning and executing development initiatives in a highly challenging geographical and sociocultural context, replete with security and other risks and uncertainties. Some of the key insights emanating from this exciting and fulfilling experience in Diamer are briefly discussed in the following paragraphs:

Respect for Cultural Values

In our day-to-day interactions with teachers, heads, parents, and community members from Diamer, be it in Diamer and/or at PDCN, we remained highly sensitive to and cautious about the behaviours displayed by individual participants. We cared about and respected the values and perceptions they brought with them. While visiting Diamer, we dressed like them, ate like them, and tried to speak in their local language, where possible. This assimilation into the nuances of the local culture helped us a great deal to generate acceptance and created space for us. Often, accepting invitations to their homes, we sat, ate, and drank like them.[8] These small and yet powerful gestures contributed to enhancing our acceptability and augmented personal relationships with people in the district. Understandably, this approach yielded tangible returns in the form of their respect and acceptance for us and for our contributions and professional inputs (i.e. knowledge, skills, and resources) to improve their education system. We learnt that it is highly significant to respect the cultural values to win the hearts and minds of the local people. So, we can safely say that change is the business of hearts, minds, and hands; a combination of all three can produce results not short of miracles.

The EDIP experience also provided us with the insight that it is wiser not to touch the sensitive issues such as 'girls' education' and/or 'women emancipation' as an overt developmental agenda in such communities like the ones living in the Diamer district. Instead, it is desirable to take the smoother and indirect route to avoid early roadblocks. We learnt that any direct reference of an 'outsider' to women-related issues, let alone interacting with women face-to-face or taking initiatives for their emancipation, could have possibly led to insurmountable resistance from the local communities. Even women staff members would need to exercise caution for how they appeared and what they discussed with other women; a slight misunderstanding or apprehension developed amongst the local people would have caused serious damage to the credibility of the institutions and disrupted the initiatives. PDCN supported seven EDIP girls' schools in Diamer. We were lucky that these schools were seen as police-owned schools where we carefully engineered our intervention through a local female teacher educator. Hence, we successfully averted any adverse reactions from the local community.

Furthermore, the EDIP experience in Diamer showed that it is imperative to have a deeper understanding of the local, cultural, and contextual dynamics before an intervention is planned and executed in a notoriously risky area, like Diamer. We found it helpful to know the sources of power in these areas such as the political and religious leadership, the tribal chieftains, ultra-rich people and other influential persons wielding power and influence on decisions in the local communities. We also learnt that it helps in getting connected and building personal relationships with people when we are able to speak with them in their native language. For instance, one of the senior government officials from the District Education Office in Chilas could not hide his happiness from the Head of PDCN when he was spoken to in his native language. He said: 'Sir, honestly it sounds great when you speak in our local language. Having a conversation with you in our local language gives me a feeling that you are an insider and not an outsider for us'[9] (Monitoring and Evaluation Report: June 2014).

Working with the District Education Office Diamer

Recognising the importance of the government's and the community's ownership of change, EDIP decided to work closely with the government and community institutions in the district. It developed strong working relationships with the DoE, GB, the Police Department, Gilgit-Baltistan and the district education office. This helped a great deal in planning and execution of the project in the district. Each of the three partners played a pivotal role in achieving the overall goals and the intended outcomes of the project. PDCN, however, facilitated the process of forging and promoting a productive partnership by providing required financial and technical support. This helped PDCN become a linchpin in coordination, and instrumental in maintaining the momentum in the work accomplished through the tripartite partnership of institutions. Because of the high level of motivation and commitment each partner brought to the project, Diamer achieved far greater results compared with other project districts. The leadership of the DoE GB, particularly Mr Majeed Khan, the then Director Education (Academics), Gilgit extended his unflinching support to the project work in the Diamer District.

Conducting Training Needs Analysis (TNA) and Addressing the Exigency of Needs

The training needs assessment as well as our direct experiences in the eleven EDIP project schools in Diamer showed that these schools had an acute shortage of resources including furniture for children, which compelled students to sit on bare floor even during harsh weather and in unhygienic conditions. EDIP provided furniture, uniforms for students, textbooks, notebooks, health and hygiene kits, whiteboards, and constructed 14 classrooms and nine toilet blocks in the EDIP project schools. The school improvement 'package' for Diamer was richer than the material resources provided to other districts and it was considered essential in view of the particular contextual realities (ultra-poverty and the acute shortage of resources) in the district. The material contributions to the project schools made an immediate impact on the perceptions of the school community about the usefulness of EDIP resulting in increased community support to the project.

We learnt from the project that it was productive to allocate material resources to address the issues of missing facilities (the hardware of school improvement) in schools. However, it was equally important to initiate teachers', head teachers' and district management's capacity building (software of school improvement) as the second priority in the school improvement agenda.

Flexibility: A Key to EDIP Success in Diamer

Although PDCN had a well-conceived integrated school development (i.e. EDIP) model already successfully experimented elsewhere in GB, we adapted this model in view of the compelling local realities. For instance, the four Chilas-based government schools were organised as a cluster (i.e. an LRS linked with three feeding schools to be led by a PDT) whereas the seven police-run home-based schools in five valleys, and far apart from each other, were organised as another cluster to be led by a Chilas-based female master trainer. The conclusion that we drew from tailoring the EDIP model in Diamer is that we should not see the school improvement models carved in stone; rather they should be kept flexible enough and adapted to the needs and realities of the local context.

PDCN also demonstrated flexibility on various occasions in inviting teachers from Diamer to attend capacity building courses in Gilgit. People from Diamer are deeply conscious of their culture, particularly their attire. They like to dress up in *shalwar-qameez (*local dress), cap and a thin locally-made blanket which they love to put on their bodies. Also, the men grow a long beard based on their religious beliefs; hence, they are easily recognisable. Since the law-and-order situation often remained volatile in Gilgit during the project life, it was advisable not to invite large cohorts of teachers from Diamer to attend professional development courses at PDCN in Gilgit. It was part of PDCN's strategy to implement EDIP in Diamer that in consultation with the District Education Office, professional development sessions for large cohorts of teachers and head teachers were conducted in Chilas.

Moreover, PDCN's approach of creating a critical mass of graduates through different courses offered at PDCN even prior to the EDIP project yielded tangible benefits as these graduates were instrumental in spreading the EDIP message widely and effectively in the district. It was through the NPEP and EDIP courses that several teachers and head teachers were given opportunities to come and attend capacity building programmes at PDCN. These teachers and head teachers became PDCN's points of contact when we formally launched EDIP in Diamer district from January 2013.

Teachers' Sense of Ownership for the EDIP Project

As part of the consent-seeking process, PDCN visited all the potential schools identified by the district management prior to the project commencement, and briefed teachers and other stakeholders about the project's demands and promises. The teachers decided to participate in the project's activities after getting first-hand knowledge of the project activities and its implications. Some teachers did not willingly participate in the programme, implying that the buy-in of stakeholders is essential, even at the initial stage of an intervention. Super imposition does not guarantee ownership of the change by the beneficiaries.

Exposure Visits for the SMCs, Heads, and Teachers

Exposing the school committees, teachers, and head teachers to the best practices elsewhere in Gilgit-Baltistan proved to be highly productive in terms of their impact on the visitors from Diamer. Their first-hand experience of seeing EDIP contributions in government schools in Hunza and Ghizar was instrumental in influencing their attitude towards and realisation of the significance of the EDIP project. These exposure visits increased their intrinsic motivation to accept EDIP contributions in Diamer and to act as ambassadors of the EDIP project in the district.

Home-Based Support for the Police-Run School Teachers in Diamer

The complex cultural dynamics in Diamer necessitated exercising extraordinary caution in enacting change and improvement in schools in the district. The seven police-run schools operating in different valleys of Diamer are staffed by female teachers operating schools from their homes. It is due largely to the women's veil system that it is unthinkable for a male outsider to see and interact with women from Diamer. Hence, this deep-rooted cultural value required us to be innovative and creative in our efforts to reach out to the female teachers running the police-managed schools. We worked with these home-based schools through a Chilas-based female teacher educator. She was facilitated to come to PDCN with her husband and children to attend orientation sessions designed for her to become and work as a teacher educator. Moreover, she was provided on-going support from PDCN in planning sessions on basic literacy and numeracy concepts using a mobile phone. She then started working with the seven police-managed schools and provided school-based mentoring to the female teachers of these schools. This, we believe, proved to be an innovative approach to address the issue of building the capacity of female teachers running the seven home schools in the district.

EDIP Impact

The project's impact can be gauged from the overall change in the stakeholders' beliefs, behaviours, and practices. More specifically, 'impact' is measured against the objectives that a project or a programme seeks to achieve through various activities during the project life. The EDIP project aimed to achieve three objectives including (i) increased access to education with gender parity at 59 schools in underprivileged contexts of Gilgit-Baltistan, (ii) improved quality of education through improving learning conditions in project schools, and (iii) improved education governance through improved capacity of the Department of Education, Gilgit-Baltistan. EDIP was a well-conceived project and the project proposal meticulously articulated the project details through its logical framework analysis (LFA), work breakdown structure (WBS), project implementation plan (PIP), and the detailed baseline survey to collect data on each objective and activity of the project. Hence, the EDIP impact could be gauged through the baseline data and the LFA indicators. The project impact has also been illustrated in the following, providing evidence related to the goals of 'access' and 'quality' of EDIP:

Objective One: To enhance gender parity and access to and equity of education in targeted schools of Gilgit-Baltistan

Overall 5,066 participants including 3,332 teachers, 1,664 community members (including mothers) and 70 officials from the government education department received trainings on generic themes, subject contents, governance and awareness raising sessions. A total of 7,051 parents also got the opportunity to participate in awareness sessions conducted in the field.

As a result of the parents' enhanced level of awareness, their active involvement in improving learning conditions in schools and the project's various contributions, the project schools gradually emerged as schools of choice for the parents. Realising that the EDIP-managed public sector schools provided better quality free education at their doorsteps, parents started giving preference to the EDIP schools over the privately-run schools for their children's education. In certain communities, i.e. Singal in Ghizar district, the previously-run private schools closed down and/or the student enrolment in these schools drastically dropped.

The impact of EDIP initiatives to increase community involvement in schools could also be traced from the fact that parents, towards the conclusion of EDIP, demonstrated more sensitivity in sending their children to school with basic learning resources and in neat and clean uniforms. The ratio of parents' visits to schools also increased in some cases due to the apparent attitudinal change and improved communication skills in teachers and head teachers. More than before, parents including mothers started getting involved in school improvement activities including facilitation of co-curricular activities for children's holistic development, one of the key dimensions of the WSIP model.

SMCs and MSGs are now better informed about their roles and responsibilities; they have now become more responsible and functional in liaising with and addressing various issues faced by schools. They frequently visit schools to monitor morning assembly, assist teachers in executing the repair and maintenance related work and play their roles in bringing the out-of-school children to schools. There are better linkages between the district education offices and the school committees which help in resolving the emerging or pending school issues. In some cases, the community members also visit homes to address individual students' issues and raise parents' awareness about children's physical, psycho-social, and educational needs. As a result, the school environment, and teachers and students' regularity and punctuality have improved in most EDIP schools. In the case of Government Girls' Middle School (i.e. a feeding school of LRS) at Gupis in Ghizar district, the community constructed classrooms from their own resources. In certain communities, the SMCs and MSGs prepared school development plans (SDPs) with the help of the head teacher to resolve school issues on a priority basis.

Objective Two: To improve the quality and relevance of education in target districts of GB

The teacher trainings on subject knowledge from primary to secondary level improved teachers' competency in both content and teaching skills. The overall average score that teachers achieved in various trainings showed 30 per cent improvement as compared to the pre-training test scores. These trainings were planned based on teachers' professional needs identified through assessment survey. These trainings contributed to improved results in terms of students' learning outcomes measured through standardised tests or examinations conducted for Grade 5, 8, and 10 students. For example, Grade 10 average result of LRSs improved from 38.20 per cent in baseline score recorded in 2010 to 68.56 per cent in 2015. It is worth noting that this improvement became possible despite numerous odds including those related to frequent and untimely transfer of teachers and high officials and unavailability of subject teachers, especially at the secondary level. Similarly, Grades 5 and 8 average results of all project schools improved from 77.80 per cent to 86.50 per cent and from 89.60 per cent to 94.11 per cent respectively. More significantly, the students from EDIP project schools achieved distinctions in Grade 5 and 8 annual examinations at district as well as at GB levels. Moreover, the data reflects that more than 50 per cent teachers now use instructional materials to involve students in activity-based teaching to promote conceptual learning. The schools also effectively utilise the computers and science labs for supporting teaching and learning[10]. In response to all these achievements, DoE-GB declared, based on the predetermined criteria, 10 EDIP schools as the Best Schools of the year which consistently performed exceptionally well since 2013.

The teachers' sense of voluntarism and professionalism improved towards the end of the project. They are now more regular and punctual in their schools and in classrooms. They have also been noted to spare time for students' individual support after school hours. More importantly, winter and summer camps were organised for Grades 9 and 10 students to prepare them for the examinations conducted by external examination boards. The head teachers' school management skills including resource management, monitoring and evaluation have also improved as a result of their participation in the training programme conducted by EDIP at PDCN. Their vision about school improvement has been broadened to include areas like physical environment, school safety, community involvement, and teachers' professional development as a means to improving the quality of teaching and learning in schools. In some LRSs the head teachers and teachers developed assessment and teaching tools using computers and kept all the records on the computer. Some teachers, especially the teachers at LRS Karimabad and Shigar use internet to access web-based knowledge and learn about innovative teaching techniques. These teachers collected good quality images and video clips and used them in the classroom to increase students' motivation and curiosity and promote conceptual learning.

The following excerpt from an interview with a teacher in Gorikote in Astor district illustrates the impact of EDIP-initiated professional development activities:

> Now I have realised that before the EDIP intervention I was not teaching but merely reading the text to students. I never consciously thought of the objectives for my lessons nor did I try to involve students in the classroom activities. I considered myself as the final authority in the classroom. I never allowed my students to ask questions, instead, they were expected to note down all the answers that I wrote on the blackboard and memorise them. After attending various professional development sessions at PDCN and at the LRS, I became aware of the philosophical underpinnings of teaching. It shifted my teaching from teacher-centred to student centred[11].

Another teacher commented:

> This was the first time ever in my teaching career that I was given a chance to attend a professional development course. I really enjoyed the content-based sessions of biology. Our instructor was highly competent and clarified many concepts which we were not even able

to understand during our university days. This course, I must say, has helped me to revisit and correct my misconceptions[12].

Moreover, the following awards given to the schools, teachers, and students also reflect the EDIP project's impact:

- 10 EDIP project schools were awarded the best school awards from 2013 to 2015;
- 7 teachers from the project schools received the best teacher awards during 2013 and 2015;
- 44 students remained amongst the top ten position holders at district level examinations.

Summary

Education Development and Improvement Programme (EDIP) was a consortium-based, inclusive and a unique project implemented during July 2010 to June 2015 in Gilgit-Baltistan. The project aimed to improve children's access to quality education in schools. Seven AKDN agencies contributed to achieve the project goals and objectives drawing on their expertise. The programmatic inputs by different partners ranged from capacity building of stakeholders to raising community awareness of education, inclusive education, construction and retrofitting of school buildings and school safety. EDIP emerged as a unique project ever implemented in the history of Gilgit-Baltistan as it expanded its intervention from working with individual teachers and schools as units of change and reform to developing school clusters.

The project also characterised the approach of inclusive education, resuscitating the LLIs and the cluster-based placement of professional development teachers (PDTs) to provide on-going professional support to teachers, head teachers, and LLIs. The construction of 35 insulated and seismic-resistant classrooms and 28 toilets which were made accessible to the children with mild to-moderate disabilities were one of EDIP's unprecedented contributions to the landscape of education in Gilgit-Baltistan. The project helped to equip each target school with the essential learning resources including books, computers, charts, globes, maps, sports kits, stationery, dictionaries and science equipment to refurbish the laboratories. More significantly, the project established 14 learning resource centres (LRCs) with internet connection at each LRS.

The project contributed significantly to the capacity building of different stakeholders such as the DoE GB officials, teachers, head teachers, school management committees (SMCs) and mother support groups (MSGs). Parents, especially mothers were also sensitised about their roles in education and child development. The Diamer district, which is still considered by many to be a 'no-go-area' for development workers remained a key focus of EDIP and achieved some significant and historical successes related to positively influencing the 'resistant-to-change' attitudes of the local people.

The impact of EDIP on the educational landscape of Gilgit-Baltistan could be easily traced in students' improved academic attainment, specifically students of project school scoring the highest marks and getting positions in standardised examinations. Moreover, the attendance registers data revealed that teachers' and students' punctuality and regularity improved and the teachers sense of voluntarism and professionalism augmented as they were seen dedicating their time after school hours and during summer and winter vacation to provide support to students to enhance student learning outcomes. Through EDIP's support, 25 teachers completed their MEd studies from AKU-IED. The graduates returned to their schools and are making significant contributions to the cause of education in Gilgit-Baltistan.

Furthermore, EDIP also helped the DoE, GB in developing and

upgrading the Gilgit-Baltistan Education Strategy (GBES) which not only guarantees sustainability of the innovations introduced by the project but also provides a direction for the long-term efforts towards development and improvement of education in GB. In a nutshell, EDIP made various successful attempts to challenge the status-quo in terms of bringing about change in practices, beliefs and attitude of the communities, particularly in the case of the Diamer district. Based on the multi-dimensional empirical evidence, it is safe to say that EDIP broke the inertia and created awareness among parents and communities by making them revisit their assumptions, beliefs, and practices.

References

Akyeampong K., 'Aid for self-help effort developing sustainable alternative route to basic education in Northern Ghana', *Journal of International Cooperation in Education*, 7/1, (2004), 41–52.

Government of Pakistan, 'Economic Survey of Pakistan', Ministry of Finance (2007–8). <http://www.finance.gov.pk/survey/chapters/10-Education09.pdf>accessed 04January 2016.

Gray, J., Hopkins D., Reynolds D., Wilcox B., Farrell S., & Jesson D., *Improving Schools: Performance & Potential* (Buckingham: Open University Press, 1999).

Hargreaves, A., *Changing Teachers, Changing Times: Teachers' Work and Culture in the Postmodern Age* (New York: Teachers College Press, 1994).

Harris, A., *School Improvement (*London & New York: Routledge Falmer, 2002).

Hopkins, D., 'Towards a theory for school improvement', in J. Gray, D. Reynolds, C. Fitz- Gibbob & D. Jesson, eds. *Merging Traditions. The Future of School Research on School Effectiveness and School improvement* (London: Cassell, 1996), 30–50.

Hopkins, D., 'Educational innovation: generic lessons learned from (a) regional practice', eds. A. Thijs, L. de Feiter, & J. van den Akker, *International learning on educational reform: towards more effective ways of cooperation* (Amsterdam/Enschede: DECIDE, 2002).

Shafa, M., 'Initiating Reform through Whole School Improvement Programme: Aga Khan University's Experiences from Pakistan', *Journal of Education and Human Development*, 3/1, (2014), 347–368.

Stoll, L. and Fink, D., *Changing Our Schools* (Buckingham: Open University Press, 1995).

Street, H. & Temperley J., ed., *Improving Schools through Collaborative Enquiry* (London: Continuum, 2005).

Notes

1. Professional Development Centre, North (2014–15), The EDIP M&E Report, 2014–15.
2. Northern Pakistan Education Project (NPEP) (1998–2008) funded by the European Union, the Northern Areas Education Project (NAEP) funded by the World Bank, the Child-Friendly Schools Project (2005 to-date) funded by UNICEF, and the Canadian Debt for Education Conversion Project (2006 to-date) funded by GAC, are some of the recent examples of the international community's interest and generosity to improve the educational landscape in Gilgit-Baltistan.
3. The Aga Khan Development Network is a group of development agencies working in health, education, culture, and rural and economic development, primarily in Asia and Africa. His Highness Prince Karim Aga Khan, the 49th *Imam* (spiritual leader) of the Shia Ismaili Muslims, is the head of the AKDN institutions.
4. An innovative in-service donor funded teacher development programme implemented by the Aga Khan education Service, Pakistan in Gilgit-Baltistan and Chitral in the 1980s.
5. STEP project's model of WSIP has been discussed in Chapter 2; EDIP also implemented a WSIP model which resembles STEP's WSIP model in some ways and differs in other ways but the central feature common to both the models is treating 'school' as a unit of change.

6. Seven ladies from Diamer were appointed as police constables in a historically merit-based and transparent appointment process led by the inspector general of police GB himself. When these ladies declined to report at the police recruitment training centre in Gilgit for their 6-month recruitment training because of the 'purdha' (veil) issue and offered their resignations, the police chief allowed these constables to organise and run girls schools from their homes. Hence, seven police-managed girls' schools emerged in Diamer where girls' education is still seen by many as a social taboo. The police chief in a conversation with the author shared that the long-term solution to fight terrorism is to facilitate a potential terrorist to marry an educated girl. 'An educated wife and/or mother would never allow her husband and/or son to follow the route of terrorism', he added.
7. Professional Development Centre, North (2015), 'EDIP Final Evaluation Report'.
8. The people in Diamer love sitting cross-legged on the floor in their homes, eating food including rice with their hands (often licking their fingers), and holding the glass of drink with their right hand. They would ensure that the guests at their homes start eating before them. These people are well known for their hospitality.
9. Professional Development Centre, North (2014), 'EDIP Monitoring and Evaluation Report, June 2014'.
10. Professional Development Centre, North (2014), 'EDIP Monitoring and Evaluation Report 2014–15'.
11. Professional Development Centre, North (2014), 'EDIP Monitoring and Evaluation Report 2014–15.
12. Ibid.

6

Exploring the Nature and Pattern of Mentoring Practices: A Study on Mentees' Perspectives

Sadia Muzaffar Bhutta, Takbir Ali, and
Nahid Parween Anwar

Introduction

There are numerous approaches to and models of in-service professional development used worldwide for teacher in-service professional development. Mentoring is one of the models of teacher professional development being used by institutions and education systems all over the world to help novice or less-experienced teachers learn from the experiences of their experienced colleagues.

The STEP project, as discussed in the preceding chapters, designed and implemented a Field-Based Mentoring Programme (CBMP). The structure and the salient features of the programme have been discussed in detail in Chapters 3. This chapter presents results of a study, which, by employing quantitative research designed (a cross-sectional survey), explored the nature and pattern of mentoring and its effects on mentees' perspective about their classroom practices. The chapter, while drawing on the literature, first examines the concept of 'mentoring', its origin and theoretical underpinnings, and processes, practices, and challenges involved in mentoring as a pathway to professional development of in-service primary teachers. Next, it discusses the research design used in the study and the results yielded by the study and implications of the results for policy and practice. It ends with a summary of the important lessons learnt in the study.

Theoretical Underpinnings of Mentoring

A mentor is a character taken from Greek mythology, described as a wise and a trusted person who is considered as a role model for personal and professional growth (Colley, 2001). Though the concept of a mentor is very old, yet it has maintained its essence. Considering the importance of the concept and the effectiveness of the processes involved, the term is applied across a variety of professions; however, the degree of working, its impact and outcome may vary from context to context. Traditionally, mentoring is defined as a unique interpersonal relationship between two individuals. Based on a review of a variety of definitions of 'mentoring' as a process, Clutterbuck (2004) concluded that mentoring is a one-to-one relationship where the mentor is a wise, experienced and a knowledgeable individual who helps and supports people to manage their learning, develop skills, performance, and become the persons they want to be. In doing so, the mentor supports and challenges his/her mentees to work towards their goals.

Like in other professions, mentoring in education is a designed and structured activity to facilitate engagement between mentor and mentee to enhance the mentee's professional capability as an effective teacher. Experiencing the effectiveness of this combination, the process of mentoring is gaining acceptance in teacher education. A mentoring relationship is based on strong pillars of objectivity, credibility, honesty, trustworthiness, and confidentiality (Memon, Lalwani & Meher, 2006; Parsloe & Wray, 2000). Mentoring is conceptualised as a four-way practice: (i) an 'intentional process', where mentor and mentee are committed to learn; (ii) a 'nurturing process', which cares for growth and change; (iii) an 'insightful process' to acquire and apply the wisdom gained; and (iv) a 'supportive process', where the mentee gets the backing he/she needs (Vazir & Meher, 2010). In this process of support, the mentor performs several roles as facilitator, moderator, counsellor, and a critical friend (Memon, Lalwani & Meher, 2006). In any given role, the major responsibility of the mentor is to help the mentees improve their teaching ability, reflect on their own actions, and move them to a higher level of professional thinking (Jarvis, McKeon, F., Coates, D., & Vause, 2001; Tomlinson, 1995).

Over the last few decades many schools of education and developmental projects around the world have been adopting and incorporating new knowledge of teaching and learning in their curriculum both in pre-service and in-service programmes of teacher education. Within the school effectiveness research, attention is given to teacher effectiveness, where the quality of teacher-child classroom interaction is of prime importance. Preparing children to think critically and solve problems demands skilled teachers, having the knowledge of learners and teaching strategies (Zhu, Wang, Cai, & Engels, 2013). Innovative teaching and learning is dependent on an understanding of what students know and how they think (Darling-Hammond, 1995; Koster, Brekelmans, Korthagen & Wubbels, 2005; Runco, 2003).

In such a situation, with the emerging demands of teacher education, the need for teacher professional development is felt more than ever. Mentoring appears to be an effective strategy to get more experienced and knowledgeable and less-experienced and knowledgeable teachers to work closely as mentor and mentee to improve classroom teaching. This close relationship helps create new knowledge about teaching, which may lead to change by enhancing teachers' competence (Clutterbuck, 2004; Norman & Feiman-Nemser, 2005; Tang & Choi, 2005).

Mentoring Models

Usually mentoring requires a professional relationship to be developed and nurtured between mentors and mentees. This suggests that mentoring is a professional partnership between two people intended at tangible outcomes in terms of mentees improved learning and professional growth. There is no single form or a model of mentoring. Worldwide different forms, types, or models of mentoring have been developed over time, depending upon priorities, local needs, and prevailing situations. Jennie (2014), for example, mentions four types of mentoring including, one-to-one peer mentoring, group mentoring, two-by-two, and team peer mentoring. To get the most out of any model of a mentoring programme, it is imperative to raise awareness of mentor and mentee about expectations through mentoring. Mentor and mentee should share experiences, views, stories, and reflections as a part of their training. Similarly, some key factors such as: matching, mentor training, pre-mentoring expectation discussion, on-going support and evaluation, need to be considered carefully for success of a formal mentoring programme (Clutterbuck, 2004). Needless to say, the practice needs to be institutionalised by embedding mentoring in professional learning activities and networking among experienced teachers where all participants focus on learning together to make the school a dynamic and active agent of change (Long, 2009).

The Process of Mentoring

Mentoring involves a productive and professional relationship between a mentor and a mentee. A mentor's role is pivotal in making this relationship a success. Hudson (2007) highlighted five characteristics of a 'mentor's role': mentor's use of 'personal attributes' to 'model' the education 'system requirement' and 'pedagogical knowledge' for guiding the mentee's development. The mentor's role also includes, providing 'feedback' on the mentee's practices, to assist the mentee, think more critically, to perceive solutions to problems and analyse situations from different perspectives. With these characteristics, the term mentor and mentee are used to make a shift from a supervisory nature to a nurturing role to build capacities of mentee teachers (Ganser, 1996; Hudson, 2013). Similarly, mentors perceive three features of their role as, 'pragmatic (provider of feedback, observer, instructor, and role model), the inter-personal (counsellor, equal partner, and critical friend) and the managerial (assessor, quality control, and manager)' (Kwan & Lopez-Real, 2005, p. 284).

Hudson's, Usak and Savran-Gencer, (2009) overview of research on the role of the mentor in the mentoring relationship found mentor facilitating mentee in areas including pedagogical knowledge about planning, subject specific teaching strategies and its implementation, content knowledge, problem solving, time tabling, enhancing content knowledge of the mentee, and modelling exemplary teaching practice.

Zachary (2000) has identified four developmental stages within mentoring, including preparing, negotiating, enabling, and closing the relationship. The preparing phase provides an opportunity to the mentor and mentee to know each other and discuss the expectations of the relationship. In the negotiating stage, the mentor clarifies the goals established. Enabling is a very important stage as the mentor challenges the mentee towards becoming more autonomous. The final closing stage involves giving and receiving feedback to review progress and to bring this relationship to an end. Similarly, Clutterbuck and Lane (2004) mention different phases of interaction such as building rapport, setting direction, progression, winding up, and moving on. At each stage the intensity of interaction could differ. The initiating and ending phases have low learning intensity while the middle stages (progressing and winding up stages) have the highest learning intensity. Expectations are not fixed but developed during the process. However, early setting of expectations between the mentor and mentee helps avoid problems with mismatch and misunderstanding and ensure smooth progress. Once the relationship is established in this process of support, the mentor plays the role of a change agent in breaking the status quo and changing the teaching and learning environment of their mentees' classrooms (Hussain & Rahim, 2010).

Significant change in the mentees' attitude and belief is observed based on three basic principles: (i) change takes time, as it is a slow and difficult process for teachers; (ii) there is a need to monitor and encourage teachers along with providing regular and constructive feedback on the student learning process; and, (iii) regular follow-up support is very valuable (Guskey, 2002, 2000). Taking these principles into consideration, it can be argued that a major responsibility of a mentor is to help mentees improve their ability to teach, reflect on their own action, and move them to a higher level of professional thinking (Jarvis et al., 2001; Tomlinson, 1995).

In a nutshell, the process of mentoring demands sharing of information, explanation and advice, offering feedback, acting as a role model, performing a socialising role/helping to settle and acting as assessors. Furthermore, personal reflection plays an important role in the continuous improvement of mentors as well as mentees.

Challenges of Mentoring

Mentoring is not smooth sailing. The literature has cited multiple challenges which mentors and mentees may encounter during the mentoring process. Some of these include: the mentee's academic background and accountability as well as the inappropriateness of the mentor's skills and professional experience (Campbell & Kovar, 1994). Interestingly, a mentee who excels during the mentoring process may receive positive comments from colleagues which may lead to an ego problem for the mentor. Another hitch from the mentee's perspective is that over dependence on the mentor may limit the mentee's taking risks and learning through the process. The mentor's dual role as supporter and assessor may also create tension. Additionally, the assessment procedure itself is stressful; therefore, to assess teachers even for facilitation may create tension. This may lead to developing a negative experience for mentees, if not managed properly (Benton, 1990).

In a formalised mentoring programme, the onus of developing a mentee teacher lies on a mentor, who could be a trained person or selected on the basis of experience. In many cases principals call upon the experienced teacher of the school to mentor a newly inducted teacher or someone who needs further guidance. Experienced teachers are usually not formally trained. Due to low resources, at times, such mentor teachers are not released from their usual duties. That is why, experienced teachers refuse the role of a mentor as it is time consuming, takes them away from teaching (their main responsibility), provides no further incentive, and may become an enduring commitment from which they cannot escape (Long, 1997). At times, volunteer experienced teachers may not be suitable for the role of a mentor due to a variety of professional reasons (Hale, 2000). Sometimes 'generalist' mentors face difficulty in working as 'specialist' mentors for science and mathematics as they lack adequate content knowledge in these subjects (Memon, Lalwani & Meher, 2006). Summarising factors that inhibit mentoring, Long (2009) has identified mentors' limited knowledge and skills to develop adult learners. Mentors could be too imposing and strict rather than being empowering and developmentally focused.

A range of commitments is required from the trained mentor to fulfill his/her role as a facilitator. In this regards, time is often a constraint. Various spans of time are required to: interact with mentees, discuss curriculum issues and planning, lesson observation and debriefing, and discuss future planning. Therefore, effective utilisation of time is an essential aspect of mentoring (Ganser, 2002). The time commitment required of a mentor is high, particularly in case of those mentees who require more assistance than others (Longs, 1997). In addition, commuting to the mentees' school is also time-consuming. Long distances, harsh climate (in too hot or too cold regions) affect the mobility of the mentors (Memon, Lalwani & Meher, 2006). That is why, time planning in the mentor-mentee interaction is crucial so that the mentor's time is focused, specific, and productive. Moreover, managerial issues such as high turnover and transfers of education officers at the directorate and district offices affect the sustainability and working of mentors (Memon, Lalwani & Meher, 2006).

To sum up, it may be argued that mentoring holds a strong standing in the teacher professional development endeavors. Maximum benefits can only be achieved if mentoring is properly planned and executed. Otherwise, it could be a total disaster. It is a learning process for both mentor and mentee. Trust, confidentiality, openness, and honesty are the driving forces to make the combination a success.

Research Design

This chapter is part of a large mixed-method study which consists of three parts, including: a '*survey*' of the nature and pattern of mentoring practices; '*qualitative interviews*' to identify factors which contribute to mentors' and mentees' learning; and '*quasi-experiment*' to isolate the impact of STEP on pedagogical practices of mentees. Here, the focus is on the findings of the first part of the study where the authors employed a cross-sectional survey to explore the nature and patterns of the mentoring process from the mentees' perspectives in the selected districts of Sindh and Balochistan. This survey study was guided by the following research question: What are the mentees' perceptions of their mentors' support for enhancing their classroom practice during the mentoring process?

Sample and Sampling

A multistage-cluster sampling strategy was employed to recruit 1,148 mentees from randomly selected districts of the STEP project in the provinces of Sindh and Balochistan. Of the 1,148 mentees, 60 per cent were male (n=685) and 40 per cent were female (n=463). This gender ratio is representative of the mentees' population in the CBMP project (Male–62 per cent: Female–38 per cent). Table 1 depicts the academic and professional qualification profiles of the participant mentees. Evidently, a majority of the mentees in this sample hold a Bachelor degree for both academic (n=536; 47.2 per cent) and professional (n=502; 45.1 per cent) qualifications. Interestingly, academic credentials of the participants represented a better ratio at the higher end (n=453; 39.9 per cent) as compared to their professional (n=268; 24.1 per cent) credentials.

Table 1: Mentees' Academic and Professional Qualifications

Academic Qualification	
Secondary School Certificate (10 years of education)	51 (4.5 %)
Higher Secondary School Certificate (12 years of education)	95 (8.4%)
Bachelor's degree (14 years of education)	536 (47.2%)
Master's degree (16 years of education)	453 (39.9%)
Professional Qualification	
Primary Teacher Certificate & Certificate in Teaching (1 - year pre-service training after 10 and 12 years of academic education)	344 (30.9%)
BEd (one year of pre-service training after 14 years of academic education)	502 (45.1%)
MEd (one year pre-or in-service education after 14 years of academic and one year profession (BEd) training	268 (24.1%)

Data Sources

Data were collected using a 5-point scale—Mentoring for Effective Primary Teaching (MEPT) adapted from Hudson, Brooks and Skamp (2005)[1]. Scoring on Likert scale ranged from 1 (Strongly Disagree) to 5 (Strongly Agree). The original MEPT focuses on five factors of mentoring: personal attributes, pedagogical knowledge, modelling, feedback, and system requirement. In view of contextual variation, additional factors were added to the tool to gather information on two aspects, particularly relevant to the STEP-project, including: development and use of material and gender equality. The data were analysed using SPSS 20. The mentees perceptions of the mentoring practice of their mentors were summarised using averages and variations. In addition, the cumulative percentage of mentees, who either 'agreed' or 'strongly agreed' with the given MEPT statement about their mentors' mentoring practice, was used to describe their reported practices.

Results

This section presents results of the above mentioned survey, which was undertaken to explore the mentees' views on their mentoring practices during the implementation of CBMP. The section first presents an overview of the seven dimensions of mentoring practices, focused in MEPT, followed by a detailed analytical description of the mentees on each construct.

Mentoring Practice: An Overall Pattern

Table 2 encapsulates the mentees' overall perceptions on seven constructs focused in the MEPT scale. The Mean scale score on mentees' perception of their mentors' practices fell within a 0.97 range (i.e. 3.58 to 4.55). The mentees' perceived *personal attributes* (M=4.55; SD=0.49) of the mentor as the most important factor which contributes to streamlining the mentoring process by building a good relationship between mentor and mentees. Furthermore, they have appreciated their mentors' efforts towards promoting *gender equality* during workshops and follow-up visits. The mentors' efforts in improving mentees' practice through *modelling* effective strategies (M=4.33; SD=0.74), demonstrating good *pedagogical practice* (M=4.31; SD=0.58) and providing *feedback* for improvement (M=4.05; SD=0.65) were regarded positively too. Contrary to this, the mentees felt that more could have been done by their mentors in sharing knowledge about *system requirement* (M=3.58; SD=1.01).

Table 2: Mentoring Practice: An Overall Pattern

Mentoring Practices	Minimum	Maximum	Mean	Std. Deviation
Personal attributes	01	05	4.55	0.49
Pedagogical knowledge	01	05	4.31	0.58
Modelling	01	05	4.33	0.74
Feedback	01	05	4.21	0.65
System requirement	01	05	3.58	1.01
Teaching material	01	05	4.05	0.86
Gender equality	01	05	4.54	0.53

Personal Attributes

Table 3 summarises the mentees' perceptions about *personal attributes* (Mean 4.43 to 4.65; SD 0.60 to 0.74) which were perceived to be the most important factors contributing towards building a good relationship between mentor and mentee. More than 90 per cent of the mentees registered their agreement in support of all the aspects of personal attributes. According to the mentees' reports, their mentors have managed to instill a positive attitude and confidence in them for teaching in primary classrooms. In doing so, the mentors talked comfortably with their mentees and displayed a supportive gesture by listening to the mentees attentively on various teaching matters. Assisting mentees to critically reflect in order to improve their teaching was also identified as one of the important personal attributes of mentors, which helped mentees to improve their practice in primary classrooms.

Table 3: Personal Attributes for Mentoring Primary Classroom Teaching

Mentoring Practices	Minimum	Maximum	Percentage*	Mean	Std. Deviation
Comfortable in talking	01	05	97	4.65	0.60
Instilled confidence	01	05	96	4.64	0.67
Supportive	01	05	98	4.61	0.61
Listened attentively	01	05	95	4.54	0.72
Instilled positive attitude	01	05	96	4.49	0.65
Assisted in reflecting	01	05	94	4.43	0.74

*Cumulative percentage of mentees who either 'agreed' or 'strongly agreed' with given MEPT statements about their mentors' mentoring practice.

Pedagogical Knowledge

The mentors' pedagogical knowledge (mean value range 3.69 to 4.56; SD range 0.71 to 1.29) was also perceived to be one of the important factors contributing to enhancing mentees' practice in primary classrooms. Table 4 presents a summary of the mentees' views on the assistance they received from their mentors in terms of pedagogical knowledge during the mentoring practice. An overwhelming majority (> 90 per cent) of the mentees reported to be assisted by their mentors in planning lessons and preparing for teaching. Similarly, over 90 per cent of the mentees claimed that their mentors supported them at the implementation stage through assistance with classroom management and the use of various teaching strategies. Furthermore, providing viewpoints on primary teaching was also considered an area of high priority (91 per cent). Likewise, over 85 per cent of the mentees reported that their mentors supported them at the implementation stage by discussing problem solving strategies for effective teaching at primary schools, sharing various strategies for assessment, providing insights into pedagogical knowledge in primary teaching as well as discussing effective questioning skills. While the mentees were provided with adequate support on various aspects of pedagogical knowledge at the planning and implementation stages, 32 per cent of the mentees were not assisted in developing timetables for their teaching. This implies that either the timetable is set by the school management or perhaps mentors were more focused towards other aspects of pedagogical knowledge related to planning and implementation.

Table 4: 'Pedagogical Knowledge' for Mentoring Primary Classroom Teaching

Mentoring Practices	Minimum	Maximum	Percentage*	Mean	Std. Deviation
Assisted in planning	01	05	94	4.56	0.71
Assisted with teaching strategies	01	05	91	4.48	0.71

Mentoring Practices	Minimum	Maximum	Percentage*	Mean	Std. Deviation
Guided lesson preparation	01	05	93	4.45	0.75
Provided viewpoints on primary teaching	01	05	91	4.41	0.82
Assisted with classroom management	01	05	92	4.40	0.79
Discussed implementation	01	05	94	4.38	0.79
Discussed problem-solving	01	05	89	4.30	0.86
Discussed assessment	01	05	89	4.29	0.85
Discussed knowledge for teaching	01	05	89	4.29	0.82
Discussed questioning techniques	01	05	87	4.24	0.88
Assisted with timetabling	01	05	68	3.69	1.29

*Cumulative percentage of mentees who either 'agreed' or 'strongly agreed' with given MEPT statements about their mentors' mentoring practice.

Modelling

Table 5 presents a summary of the mentees' views on the assistance they received from their mentors through modelling of teaching practice. Mean item score (Mean value range 4.07 to 4.51; SD range: 0.84 to 1.04) indicated that a majority of mentors was expected to model in order to provide visual and aural demonstration of effective teaching practices in primary classrooms. The three characteristics—

modelling enthusiasm for teaching, rapport with primary students, and effective primary school teaching—were perceived by more than 90 per cent of the mentees as representative practices. Similarly, more than 85 per cent of the mentees claimed that their mentors modelled classroom teaching, and through this modelling, they demonstrated well-designed and hands-on lessons with effective classroom management. Still more than 80 per cent of the mentees agreed that their mentors used syllabus language; however, this practice appeared to be relatively less representative as compared to other aspects defined for this construct.

Table 5: 'Modelling' for Mentoring Primary Classroom Teaching

Mentoring Practices	Minimum	Maximum	Percentage*	Mean	Std. Deviation
Displayed enthusiasm	01	05	93	4.51	0.84
Modelled rapport with students	01	05	91	4.47	0.84
Modelled effective teaching	01	05	92	4.38	0.85
Modelled well-designed activities	01	05	89	4.37	0.94
Modelled classroom teaching	01	05	89	4.34	0.94
Modelled effective hands-on activities	01	05	87	4.29	0.96

Mentoring Practices	Minimum	Maximum	Percentage*	Mean	Std. Deviation
Modelled classroom management	01	05	85	4.24	0.98
Used syllabus language	01	05	81	4.07	1.04
*Cumulative percentage of mentees who either 'agreed' or 'strongly agreed' with given MEPT statements about their mentors' mentoring practice.					

Feedback

Table 6 presents a summary of the mentees' views on the feedback they received from their mentors as part of the mentoring process. It is to be argued that the feedback on the mentees' planning and teaching is one of the important elements of the mentoring process in improving teaching practice. In this study, the mean item score (Mean value range 4.45 to 3.64; SD range: 0.76 to 1.28) indicated that a majority of mentees agreed that their mentors provided feedback as part of the mentoring practices in primary school teaching. An overwhelming majority of mentees (> 90 per cent) reported that during the mentoring process, their mentors evaluated their teaching, provided oral feedback and shared expectations for further improvement in practices. Besides, review of lesson plans (85 per cent) and observation of teaching (88 per cent) were perceived to be the other two representative practices of their mentors. It is interesting to note that oral feedback was identified as one of the most prevalent practices (93 per cent), while written feedback remained at the lowest end (66 per cent). Evidently, a majority of mentors had limited themselves to providing oral feedback for improving their mentees' practice. The lack of written feedback might have been necessitated by the time or expertise the mentors had at their disposal.

Table 6: 'Feedback' for Mentoring Primary Classroom Teaching

Mentoring Practices	Minimum	Maximum	Percentage	Mean	Std. Deviation
Provided evaluation on teaching	01	05	92	4.34	0.78
Provided oral feedback	01	05	93	4.40	0.76
Provided written feedback	01	05	66	3.64	1.28
Reviewed lesson plans	01	05	85	4.16	0.98
Articulated expectations	01	05	92	4.45	0.78
Observed teaching for feedback	01	05	88	4.28	0.87

*Cumulative percentage of mentees who either 'agreed' or 'strongly agreed' with given MEPT statements about their mentors' mentoring practice.

System Requirements

The items displayed under the construct system requirement presented a different picture from the other constructs included in the MEPT scale (Mean value range 3.30 to 3.98; SD range: 1.11 to 1.38). As presented in Table 7, in this study, 47 per cent of the mentees reported that their mentors did not outline the primary curriculum documents. Similarly, 39 per cent claimed that school policies were not discussed with them. Contrary to these two aspects, a majority (81 per cent) identified 'discussing aims of teaching primary school subjects' as one of the most prevalent practice under the construct of system requirement. It is to be argued that the curriculum and the aim of teaching different subjects are equally important as the related school policies for implementing system requirement in order to provide uniformity and direction for employing education.

Table 7: 'System Requirement' for Mentoring Primary Classroom Teaching

Mentoring Practices	Minimum	Maximum	Percentage	Mean	Std. Deviation
Discussed school policies	01	05	61	3.48	1.27
Outlined curriculum	01	05	53	3.30	1.38
Discussed aims of teaching different subjects	01	05	81	3.98	1.11

*Cumulative percentage of mentees who either 'agreed' or 'strongly agreed' with given MEPT statements about their mentors' mentoring practice.

Teaching Material

Enhancing the mentees' skills in development and usage of low-cost or no-cost instructions and library resources by STEP to enrich their teaching was one of the most important undertakings of CBMP. Keeping this aspect of the project in consideration, four items were defined to gather information related to teaching material. As presented in Table 8, teaching material (mean value range 3.80 to 4.35; SD range 0.90 to 1.25) was perceived to be an important construct, which contributed to improved mentees' classroom teaching. Mentors' assistance in developing low-cost or no-cost material was perceived to be the most prevalent (90 per cent) practice during the mentoring process. Similarly, a significant majority (80 per cent) of the mentees acknowledged their mentors' efforts in modelling the use of low-cost and no-cost teaching materials as well as the instructional resources provided by STEP. It is important to mention that provision or development of material is one step, which would not bear fruit without modelling the use of this material. Interestingly, 29 per cent of the mentees were of the view that they were not encouraged to develop learning corners in classrooms. It is to be argued that a vast majority has assigned high ratings to the practices of material development and its usage. Development of learning corners could be classified as one of the uses of teaching material. Why did more than a quarter of the respondents feel that they were not encouraged to develop learning corner? There could be many reasons for a relatively lower rating on this aspect. Perhaps, limited physical space inside classrooms did not allow developing and maintaining learning corners. Anecdotally, double-shift schooling also hindered the practice as the children and staff from the 'other' shift may not necessarily value and protect this 'addition' in the classrooms. The mentors' own acquaintance with the theory and practice of learning corners may also have contributed to these patterns of practice.

Table 8: 'Teaching Material' for Mentoring Primary Classroom Teaching

Mentoring Practices	Minimum	Maximum	Percentage	Mean	Std. Deviation
Encouraged to develop learning corners	01	05	71	3.80	1.25
Facilitated to develop low cost material	01	05	90	4.35	0.90
Modelled low cost material	01	05	80	4.05	1.11

Mentoring Practices	Minimum	Maximum	Percentage	Mean	Std. Deviation
Modelled use of STEP-provided material	01	05	80	4.01	1.14
*Cumulative percentage of mentees who either 'agreed' or 'strongly agreed' with given MEPT statement about their mentors' mentoring practice.					

Gender Equality

Gender mainstreaming was treated as an important theme that cut across all components of the STEP project, including CBMP. Promoting gender equality in practice was one of the fundamental aims of CBMP; therefore, five items were added in MEPT to gather information on this aspect. That said, all items were not relevant to all respondents. For example, in some target districts of STEP, mentors conducted workshops and followed-up the mentees of the same sex. In other words, female mentors conducted workshops and provided follow-up support to female mentees and male mentors to male mentees. Cultural sensitivities did not allow otherwise. In such a situation, mentors did not need to counsel their mentees to work in mix-gender groups, to provide equal opportunities to both genders; to work with mentees of the opposite sex. Therefore, an option of *Not Applicable* was permitted on these three items. The results summarised in Table 9 reveal that on average, gender equality was considered to be an important factor of the mentoring process in developing and maintaining good relationships between mentor and mentees (mean value range 4.26 to 4.73; SD range 0.54 to 0.92). An overwhelming majority of the mentees (>95 per cent) claimed that their mentors provided them equal opportunities regardless of their gender, used gender-sensitive language during workshops and follow-up activities, and they felt comfortable working with mentors of the opposite sex. Similarly, a vast majority (≥90 per cent) acknowledged their mentors' efforts in counselling them to work in mix-gender groups and maintaining a gender-friendly environment through displaying gender impartiality in resources (e.g. similar representation of both genders in displays and text).

Table 9: 'Gender Equality' for Mentoring Primary Classroom Teaching

Mentoring Practices	Minimum	Maximum	Percentage	Mean	Std. Deviation
Counselled to work in mix-gender group	01	05	90	4.26	0.92
Provided equal opportunities for male and female mentees	01	05	98	4.71	0.54
Maintained gender-friendly environment	01	05	93	4.38	0.78
Used gender-sensitive language	01	05	98	4.73	0.55
Felt comfortable working with mentor of opposite sex	01	05	96	4.63	0.66

*Cumulative percentage of mentees who either 'agreed' or 'strongly agreed' with given MEPT statement about their mentors' mentoring practice.

Discussion and Conclusion

The results presented above show that the mean scale scores on mentees' perceptions of their mentors' practices fell between 3.58

(*system requirement*) and 4.55 (*personal attributes*). Mentees' perceived personal attributes of the mentor as the most significant factor (M=4.55; SD=0.49) towards streamlining the mentoring process by building a good relationship between mentor and mentees. Furthermore, the mentees shared positive views about their mentors' efforts towards promoting gender impartiality (M=4.54; SD=0.53) during workshop and follow-up visits. Contrary to this, the mentees felt that more could have been done by their mentors in sharing knowledge about system requirement (M=3.58; SD=1.01) with a particular focus on issues such as school policies (M=3.48; SD=1.27) and the national curriculum (M=3.30; SD=1.38). Furthermore, some aspects in the high scoring factors were highlighted by the mentees as areas for further improvement. The mentees reported that their mentors could have assisted them more rigorously in setting a timetable (M=3.69; SD=1.29), providing written feedback (M=3.64; SD=1.28) and encouraging them to develop learning corners (M=3.80; SD=1.25) in their classrooms.

The strong positive responses on various constructs indicated that the CBMP mentors were prepared to assist their mentees in developing teaching knowledge and skills; yet they required further direction on specific aspects of mentoring such as providing written feedback, timetabling, and other negatively-perceived items. These results validate the findings of other studies that also illustrate areas of perceived strengths and weaknesses in mentoring (Hudson, 2007; Hudson et al., 2009; Hudson, Spooner-Lane & Murray, 2013; Hudson, 2014). It is argued that mentors may not exhibit these particular practices, or mentoring may need to be more explicit for mentees to notice such practices. Either way, this requires further education on mentoring practices that may not be apparent to the mentees. Importantly, the mentees' perceptions of their mentors' practices may aid in determining mentoring needs.

In a nutshell, the results of the study contribute to the body of much-needed knowledge in the context of developing countries. This study provides a strong foundation for further research on a larger scale and with a more varied sample. The MEPT instrument validated for the Pakistani context as part of the study provides a way to evaluate practices in line with empirical evidence about mentoring.

Hence, the results may prove useful for professional development for the mentors and mentees through specific mentoring programmes in order to enhance teaching practices in primary classrooms in Pakistan. Based on the findings of the study, we recommend that the government systems take steps to institutionalise mentoring as a model of teachers' continued professional development. Newly inducted teachers and a large number of primary and elementary school teachers, who have not received any formal in-service training and lack knowledge and skills in and attitudes towards effective teaching of school curriculum, may be taken through the mentoring process, either within their own schools or outside. Another opportunity to use mentoring as a viable strategy in the public sector is to transform teaching practicum in pre-service programmes (Associate Degree in Education and four year BEd) into a rigorous mentoring process by increasing the duration of the activity and identifying capable teachers in schools and developing their capacity to work as mentors with trainee teachers.

References

Benton, P., ed., '*The Oxford internship scheme: Integration and partnership in initial teacher Education*' (London: Calouste Gulbenkian Foundation, 1990).

Campbell, K., and Kovar, S.K., Fitness/Exercise internships: How to ensure success', *Journal of Physical Education, Recreation and Dance*, 65/2, (1994), 69–72.

Clutterbuck, D., *Everyone Needs a Mentor* (London: Chartered Institute of Personnel and Development, 2004).

Clutterbuck, D., and Lane, G., *'The situational mentor: An International Review of Competences and capabilities in mentoring'* (Aldershot, Hants, Englan: Burlington, VT, Gower, 2004).

Colley, H., 'Righting rewritings of the myth of Mentor: A critical perspective on career guidance mentoring', *British Journal of Guidance & Counselling,* 29/2, (2001), 177–197.

Darling–Hammond, L., 'Changing conceptions of teaching and teacher development', *Teacher Education Quarterly,* 22/4, (1995), 9–26.

Ganser, T., 'How teachers compare the role of corresponding teacher and mentor', *Educational Forum,* 66/4, (2002), 380–85.

Ganser, T., 'Preparing mentors for beginning teachers: An overview for staff developers', *Journal of Staff Development,* 17/4, (1996), 8–11.

Glazer, E.M. & Hannafin, M.J., 'The collaborative apprenticeship model: situated professional development within school settings', *Teaching and Teacher Education,* 22 /2, (2006), 179–193.

Guskey, T.R., *Evaluating Professional Development* (Thousand Oaks, California: Corwin Press, 2000).

Guskey, T.R., 'Professional development and teacher change', *Teachers and Teaching: Theory and Practice,* 83/4, (2002), 381–391.

Hudson, P., 'Feedback consistencies and inconsistencies: eight mentors' observations on one pre-service teacher's lesson', *European Journal of Teacher Education,* 37/1, (2014), 63–73.

Hudson, P., Spooner-lane, R. & Murry, M., 'Making mentoring explicit: Articulating pedagogical knowledge practices', *School Leadership & Management: Formerly School Organization,* 33/3, (2013), 284–301.

Hudson, P., Usak, M. & Savran-Gencer, A., 'Employing the five factor mentoring instrument: analysing mentoring practices for teaching primary science', *European Journal of Teacher Education,* 32/1, (2009), 63–74.

Hudson, P., 'Examining mentors' practices for enhancing pre-service teachers' pedagogical development in mathematics and science', *Mentoring & Tutoring: Partnership in Learning,* 15/2, (2007), 201–17.

Hudson, P., Brooks, L., & Skamp, K., 'Development of an instrument: Mentoring for effective primary science teaching', *Science Education,* 89/4, (2005), 657–74.

Hudson, P., 'Mentoring as professional development: 'growth for both' mentor and mentee', *Professional Development in Education,* 39/5, (2013), 771–783.

Hussain, R. & Rahim, H., 'Mentoring as leadership in action', in J. Khaki & Q. Safdar, eds. *Educational Leadership in Pakistan:* (Ideals and Realities (Karachi: Oxford University Press, 2010), 209–230.

Jarvis, T., McKeon, F., Coates, D., & Vause J., 'Beyond generic mentoring: Helping trainee teachers to teach primary science', *Research in Science and Technological Education,* 19/1, (2001), 5–23.

Jennie. P., *Mentoring: Supporting and Promoting Professional Development and Learning,* The Scottish Social Services Council, UK, 2014).

Koster, B., Brekelmans, M., Korthagen, F., & Wubbels, T., 'Quality requirements for teacher educators', *Teaching and Teacher Education,* 21, (2005), 157–176.

Kwan, T. & Lopez-Real, F., 'Mentors' perceptions of their roles in mentoring students teachers', *Asia-Pacific Journal of Teacher Education, 33/*3, (2005), 275–287.

Long J., 'Assisting beginning teachers and school communities to grow through extended and collaborative mentoring experience', *Mentoring & Tutoring: Partnership in Learning,* 17/4, (2009), 317–327.

Long, J., 'The dark side of mentoring', *Australian Educational Researcher, 24/2,* (1997), 115–133.

Memon, M., Lalwani, F., & Meher, R., 'Mentoring as an alternative approach to in-service teacher education in Balochistan: Some successes and challenges', in I. Farah & B. Jowarski, eds. *Partnership in Educational Development* (Karachi: Oxford University Press, 2006).

Norman, P.J. & Feiman-Nemser, S., 'Mind activity in teaching and mentoring', *Teaching and Teacher Education,* 21, (2005), 679–97.

Parsloe, E. & Wray, M., *Coaching and mentoring* (London: Kogan Page, 2000).

Runco, M.A., 'Education for creative potential', *Scandinavian Journal of Educational Research*, 47/3, (2003), 317–324.

Tang, S.Y.F. & Choi, P.L., 'Connecting theory and practice in mentor preparation: mentoring for the improvement of teaching and learning, mentoring & tutoring', *Partnership in Learning*, 13/3, (2005), 383–401.

Tomlinson, P., *Understanding Mentoring: Reflective Strategies for School Based Teacher Preparation* (Buckingham: Open University Press, 1995).

Vazir, N., & Meher, R., 'Mentoring in teacher education: Building nurturing contexts and teaching communities for rural primary school teachers in Sindh, Pakistan', *Journal of Educational Research*, 13/1, (2010), 123–142.

Zachary, L.J., The *Mentor's Guide: Facilitating Effective Learning Relationship.* (San Francisco. CA: Jossey-Bass, 2000).

Zhu, C., Wang, D., Cai, Y., & Engels, N., 'What core competencies are related to teachers' innovative teaching?' Asia-*Pacific Journal of Teacher Education*, 41/1, (2013), 9–27.

Note

1. Tool was used after obtaining permission from the author.

7

The Nature of Experience of AKU-IED's MEd Graduates: A Phenomenological Study

Ayesha Bashiruddin and *Mir Afzal Tajik*

Introduction

As discussed in the earlier chapters, one of the key components of the 'Strengthening Teacher Education in Pakistan' (STEP) was professional development of teachers, head teachers, and teacher educators through a variety of teacher education programmes including a two-year (MEd) Programme offered by AKU-IED. To achieve 'improved performance of teacher education institutions in providing quality teacher education', the project offered scholarships to enrol around 43 teachers, principals, and teacher educators from the project districts in the MEd programme. The purpose of developing these MEd graduates was that upon completion of their degree, they would initiate and lead positive reforms in their respective schools and teacher education institutions.

At the time of conducting this study, over 32 teachers, head teachers and teacher educators from public schools and teacher education institutions in Sindh, Balochistan, and Gilgit-Baltistan had successfully graduated from the MEd programme and returned to their districts where they were actively working as agents of change.

The donor agencies and other stakeholders in the project districts were keen to know the nature of the experience these graduates had in the MEd programme, the capacity they had built, and the extent to which they had been able to apply their learning in their respective schools/institutions. The Mid-Term Review of the project conducted by independent consultants also raised a number of questions about the relevance and impact of the MEd programme.

A qualitative research study was conducted to explore the nature, relevance, rigor, and richness of the experiences of the MEd graduates. The purpose of the study was to explore the nature of the experiences of the graduates in the programme and to see how these experiences had helped them develop the understanding, technical skills, and dispositions they required to become effective teachers, teacher educators, leaders, and agents of change in their respective schools. The findings of the study provide useful insights into the graduates' self-actualization, transformation of their professional beliefs and practices, the difference they have made in their schools, and the challenges they faced. The study also provides evidence of how the implementation of this multi-stakeholder and multi-partner STEP programme led to the development of 'communities of practice' in schools. The study makes a number of recommendations for policy and practice related to teacher education programmes as well as for partnerships in education.

Theoretical Perspectives on Professional Development

The in-service training was found to be an effective method of connecting teachers to an emerging knowledge base (Ramatlapana, 2009). Such training provided teachers with opportunities to refresh their knowledge, and reflect upon their practices. More importantly it allows them to gain a critical understanding of the theories of deconstruction, and reconstruction of ideas, and conceptual frameworks that guide their approach and practices of teaching and learning (Tajik, 2004). Educational leaders and teachers are trained by means of a range of professional development training courses. There is evidence to suggest that such training brings positive change in the behaviour and practices of the trainees (Fields, 1990; Leach & Conto, 1999; Saiti & Saitis, 2006). However, the implementation of theories acquired from training in a context which may not resemble the training setting, is complex and difficult. In the process of applying theory into practice, trainees had to constantly look for answers to newly emerging questions, which often left them confused and frustrated (Lamb, 1995). For their frustrations to be minimised, trainees need to feel that their expertise is valued and respected (Pyle et al., 2011).

Some other studies have also identified factors that have helped the graduates of in-service training programmes in implementing their learning to bring about positive changes in their schools. For example, a culture of collaboration and collegiality amongst the graduates and fellow teachers alongside a greater sense of shared commitment for development result in greater possibilities for implementing course ideas (Grimmett & Crehan, 1992). The monitoring and ongoing support of the professionals help trainees to sustain the mastery of skills attained in the workshops (Fields, 1990). The individual who provides post-training performance feedback should be the person who initially conducts the training and is thus held in high regard by the participants (Leach & Conto, 1999). Therefore, in-service courses should incorporate follow-up programmes if teachers are to sustain the mastery of skills attained in the workshops (Fields, 1990; Ramatlapana, 2009)).

Studies conducted in Pakistan support research in other contexts. The research reveals issues such as the relevance of ideas to the context, consultation with the implementers and the nature of the planners' understanding of the realities of the implementers' professional environment (Mohammed & Harlech-Jones, 2008; Mohammed, 2006; Pereira, 2011). Moreover, once the graduates return to their own work environment, the administrative, professional, and emotional support they receive determines the extent to which they are able to put the acquired theory into practice (Rizvi & Elliot, 2007). Studies suggest that it is unproductive to leave teachers without support in their organisations and at the same time to expect them to be effective change agents (Mohammed, 2006). Successful examples of improved competencies among teachers, as a result of in-service courses, can be linked to the supportive structures built around the training programme (Hussain & Ali, 2010).

A number of research studies have been carried out to explore students' experiences of learning and professional development in the in-service programmes offered by AKU-IED. Other studies have focused on exploring the impact of these programmes on the personal and professional development of the graduates. For example, the study carried out by Khamis (2000) explores the impact of AKU-IED programme on its Cooperating Schools in Pakistan. It reveals that AKU-IED has made a significant educational impact through its intervention strategy which promotes teacher development activities in Cooperative Schools. Due to the active engagement of teachers and school heads in reflective practices, the teachers' application of instructive methods significantly improved. The head teachers experienced a paradigm shift in their approaches to leadership and the way they practiced it.

Another study was carried out to evaluate AKU-IED's initiatives for capacity building in Afghanistan and Syria (Tajik & Bashiruddin, 2009). Its objective was to explore how and to what extent the initiatives had contributed to the individual and institutional capacity building in these two countries. This study was grounded in the methodological framework suggested by Guskey (2002) to assess how and to what extent the capacity-building programmes' objectives and expectations were achieved. The findings revealed that the stakeholders in general and the graduates in particular were fully satisfied with the overall structure, relevance, contents, delivery, monitoring, and faculty input in the programmes. The graduates of the programmes had proved to their respective educational managers and other stakeholders that the schools in which they worked were far ahead of other schools in achieving quality in teaching and learning, higher learning outcomes, effective school management, dynamic leadership, and stronger relationships between schools and local communities. It was evident that the graduates had transformed their professional outlook and had become more supporting and empowering facilitators. They had also changed their leadership approach and professional disposition by moving from a bureaucratic and authoritarian 'boss' to a 'pedagogical leadership approach'.

Yet another impact study conducted by Halai and Anderson (2005) explored cases of school improvement in two of the AKU-IED Cooperative Schools in Karachi. The major findings revealed that a significant change had taken place at one of the Cooperative schools (Girls Secondary School) since it had begun cooperating alongside AKU-IED's professional development programmes. The impact of the programme with its focus on continuous improvement highlighted eight interrelated elements (i) dynamic vision for school development; (ii) sustained leadership commitment; (iii) strategic interaction with external resources; (iv) investment in collective professional capacity development; (v) leadership differentiation and distribution;(vi) progressive alignment of practices and structures affecting teaching and learning; (vii) constant reflection on progress in school development and student learning; and (viii) evolutionary restructuring of support for improvement. The study strongly recommended the need to continue the support for continuous improvement in cooperating schools even if they had already benefited from substantial inputs in the form of trained teachers and administrators.

A study by Shamim (2005) evaluated the impact of the 'Whole School Improvement Programme' (WSIP) offered by AKU-IED's Professional Development Centre North (PDCN) in Gilgit-Baltistan. Case studies of eight schools from the three educational systems served by PDCN, specifically the government, AKES, and the private-sector, were undertaken. The impact of WSIP-intervention was attributed mainly to its focus on capacity building of teachers, head teachers and through formal workshops for professional development and school-based support. The study made some useful recommendations:

1. School reform efforts should focus on 'maintenance' strategies along with 'development' strategies.
2. There should be a more integrated approach in all school improvement projects, similar to WSIP which would include: (a) developing shared purposes and strategies for school improvement at the pre-intervention stage; and (b) strategic planning for ongoing monitoring and support during the intervention stage, and after the completion of the project.

More studies conducted in Pakistan to trace the impact of AKU-IED's graduates have shown that the MEd programme has succeeded in driving people out of the classroom (Shamim & Halai, 2006) based on the assumption that AKU-IED graduates feel they are better qualified to serve in higher positions. Shamim and Halai (2006) have also found that the graduates report a sense of major transformation, in terms of personal and professional growth which they attribute to the teacher development programme and a supportive learning environment. This is the reason why AKU-IED graduates have been able to introduce innovations in private sector institutions where they serve. However, the same authors have also revealed:

> The PDTs from the public sector in Pakistan report that there is a general reluctance on the part of their management in using their skills even at the school level as they are often more 'knowledgeable' than their head teachers. Also many of them are young junior teachers and are seen as a threat by their senior colleagues (p.62).

All these studies provided useful insights and a framework to carry out our research study. A review of these studies helped us to develop our research questions and the methodology to conduct the research. However, none of the above mentioned studies focused on the nature of experiences of learning and success stories of the graduates who attended the AKU-IED's MEd Programme. Hence, the present study was an attempt to explore the nature of experiences of learning and development and to validate the success stories of the graduates who attended AKU-IED's MEd programme and who are now working in their different work environments.

Research Methodology

A phenomenological approach was used to investigate the question: 'What is the nature of the STEP sponsored graduates' learning experiences in the MEd programme and how have these experiences fostered their own professional development and their ability to bring about positive changes in their schools?' Phenomenology seeks, through systematic reflection, to determine the essential properties and structures of experience. It views experiences as conscious. The 'nature' in layperson's terminology, would translate into the type/s of experience/s in a given situation. For example 'what' was the experience and 'how' was it experienced. We encouraged the participants to give a full description of their experience, including their thoughts, feelings, images, sensations, and memories along with a description of the situation in which the experience occurred.

The nature of experience refers to the kind of experiences graduates had during the study and how they used these experiences. For instance, learning theoretical concepts would have been challenging for some, while for others it would have been a valuable experience. Second, from an epistemological standpoint (Creswell, 2013; Holloway, 1997; Mason, 1996), data collected for the study looked at issues which focused on the creation and dissemination of knowledge in particular areas of inquiry. Third, '…a phenomenological study describes the common meaning for several individuals of their lived experiences of a concept or a phenomenon' (Creswell, 2013, p. 76). As researchers, it allowed us to be as non-directive as possible and asked the participants to describe their 'lived experience' of a phenomenon. Fourth, phenomenology allowed us to elicit the participants' perceptions, attitudes, beliefs, and experiences. We encouraged them to give a full description of their experience, including their thoughts, feelings, images, sensations, and memories—their stream of consciousness—along with a description of the situation in which the experience occurred. As researchers, we tried to *bracket* ourselves out of the study so that the focus remained on the participants' personal experiences. Data was analysed using systematic procedures. First, significant statements were identified. From these, we developed a composite description of the essence of the experience for all the graduates. Later, broader meaning units were developed. All the data was analysed so as to present the 'essence' of the phenomenon studied.

The Participants

A purposive sample of 23 STEP-sponsored MEd graduates of

AKU-IED participated in the study. They were involved in focus group discussions. Six participants were selected, two from each of the three regions for in-depth one-to-one interviews, classroom observations, and where possible, shadowing. The following research criteria were developed for the selection of participants:

1. The participants should have at least three years' experience after their graduation so that they can narrate and reflect on their experiences;
2. From each region, two participants would be selected, one from the Teacher Education strand and one from the Educational Leadership and Management strand of the MEd programme. One male and one female would be selected from Gilgit-Baltistan. In other target regions, only male participants who are graduates of AKU-IED would be selected; and
3. The participants should be interested in the study and inclined to share the nature of experiences in detail. They should also be willing to make time for in-depth interviews.

Data Collection Procedures (Instruments and Materials)

Data for this study was collected through focus group interviews, one-to-one interviews, document analysis, observations, and shadowing. Focus group interviews were conducted with participants from each region. Out of the 23 participants, two were selected from each region for in-depth one-to-one interviews, classroom observations if they were teachers, and shadowing if they were head teachers or educational managers.

Focus Group Discussion

Focus group discussion is rarely used in phenomenological studies.

However, there are a few studies which have used focus group discussions (e.g. de Visser & Smith, 2007; Reid et al., 2005) to understand the phenomena collectively. In our study, we employed both focus group discussion and one-to-one interviews. We used a focus group discussion with the MEd graduates who belonged to one geographical context. We intended to gather what Haymes (2012, p. 143) calls 'collective memory' where groups blend memories into shared stories. Since this is a naturally occurring group, (STEP sponsored MEd graduates) who lived the experience of a particular programme because it was easy for them to understand the phenomena. Through focus group discussion, the group dynamics added rich data to the study. Some participants joined the focus group through SKYPE or via telephone because they lived far away from the central place. We made sure that all of them got equal opportunities to talk about their experiences. Three sites central to each region were selected, namely: Sukkur, Quetta, and Gilgit. The focus group discussion was conducted only once at the beginning of the study and lasted for approximately two hours.

Individual Unstructured Interviews

Phenomenological studies frequently use one-to-one interviews to get in-depth data about the phenomena being studied. This kind of study would require more than one interview with each participant (Clare, 2002). Since the intent of the phenomenological studies was to get to the core of the experience, we tried to conduct three one-to-one in-depth interviews with six participants. In some cases, reaching schools was a challenge because of geographical distance. Therefore, with some participants, we were able to only conduct two interviews. In other cases we observed classes and based our interviews around them. Through these interviews we encouraged participants to articulate stories, thoughts, emotions, and feelings about their experiences of the phenomena (Smith, 2004). The first interview was about developing rapport with the participants, which is important for acquiring detailed and comprehensive data. This step was not too cumbersome since we knew the students before hand. Although the main question became the starting point for discussion, some guiding probes were also followed. The interviews were audio-recorded and transcribed.

Document Analysis

At different points, we collected documents which included materials that participants had developed to teach, and other materials which provided evidence of their learning and professional development. One such example was the lesson plans that some of the respondents provided while we observed their classes.

Classroom Observations

We tried to observe research participants in their natural setting of the classroom. Fraenkel and Wallen (2006) define non-participant observations by stating that in non-participant observation, the researcher merely observes and records what happens as things naturally occur. These classroom observations gave us an opportunity to witness the actual application of their learning. In each region, the classroom observation varied from school to school depending on the geographical distance and time for data collection.

Shadowing

Since the sampling included non-teaching school leaders, we used the shadowing method to understand the complex nature of their work within their respective school settings. We interviewed them after shadowing. We shadowed some head teachers but there were challenges in obtaining permission from government officials in some regions.

Field Notes

We wrote field notes regularly during interviews and classroom observations, which according to Beattie (1995), are descriptions of 'the context of the study itself, consisting of participant observation, journals, interviews, letters, interpretive accounts and informal writings as a result of conversations, discussions, meetings, and planning sessions' (p. 62). Through these field notes, we were able to capture details such as the room occurrence, body language, facial expressions, our emotions and those of the teachers. Since we wanted to be as unobtrusive as possible, we did not use a tape recorder inside the classroom.

Findings

This section presents the key findings which emerged from the three focus group discussions, five individual interviews, document analysis, classroom observations, and shadowing. Five major themes were articulated as: (a) self-actualization both at the personal and professional level; (b) positive influence of the AKU-IED's culture on their attitudes; (c) their efforts to make a difference as social change agents; (d) phases of their professional development; and (e) challenges during and after AKU-IED. Each finding with detailed evidence is discussed below.

Self-Actualization

Self-actualization is usually understood as the ability to transcend levels of physiological, psychological, and social needs, to obtain fulfillment of personal needs. For the graduates, self-actualization refers to the realisation of their own worth and their motivation to fulfill their maximum potential both personally and professionally. The graduates who participated in this study unanimously acknowledged AKU-IED for providing them with an enabling and non-hierarchical environment in which they explored their potential and talents. As one graduate from a rural background stated: 'I entered AKU-IED with a low self-esteem and shaky confidence, because of my modest education and financial background, but I rediscovered myself and explored my talent when I experienced the enabling environment of AKU-IED'. Most of the graduates appreciated the fact that at AKU-IED, every student was respected, valued, and made to feel important. A group of graduates in a focused group discussion stated:

> We started believing in ourselves and in our abilities once we observed the overall culture and environment at AKU-IED; from the Director to the faculty to support staff, everyone treated us with respect. We were made to feel that every student has the talent and capacity to grow. Our contributions to discussions were highly appreciated and no student was made to feel that he/she is less intelligent or less knowledgeable than others.

Another graduate went on to describe: 'At AKU-IED' every talent is appreciated and celebrated and therefore we were encouraged to express our talents without any hesitation.' Other graduates also appreciated the status-free and enabling environment of AKU-IED that allowed them to explore and further develop their hidden potential. As one of them articulated, 'I never thought I had artistic potential and it only became noticeable when I found lots of appreciation for artistic skills at AKU-IED.' He further stated that a number of students who came from rural backgrounds were initially very shy and hesitant to express themselves or show their talents but as they got support from the faculty, they rediscovered themselves as creative writers, critical analysts, innovative presenters, good singers and dancers, and a lot more.

Other graduates also expressed that the curricular and co-curricular activities they engaged in throughout the MEd Programme provided them with opportunities for holistic development. One graduate said:

> Learning at AKU-IED was not confined to reading and writing or doing academic work only. We were engaged in a variety of activities that helped us develop holistically and I mean personally, professionally, socially and morally. It was this focus on holistic development that encouraged us to identify our potential and develop ourselves not only as good teachers and educators but also as skillful and ethical persons.

The graduates expressed with a great sense of pride that they have established a special identity and credibility in their respective institutions. 'Only after returning from AKU-IED, I have realised my self-worth and value as a person and professional', a graduate from Gilgit-Baltistan stated. She further said that not only her school management but her community leaders also have high expectations from her. She is seen as a change agent and a valuable resource in both the school and the community. Other graduates from the same regions mentioned that their market value increased since many well-reputed institutions specifically mention in their job advertisement that AKU-IED's graduates are preferred. However, the student are sometime concerned about the increasing, and at times unrealistic, expectations of teachers, school management, education authorities, and local communities.

The graduates who belonged to rural areas, where gender stereotypes and discrimination against women was rampant, found the co-education and gender inclusive culture at AKU-IED both interesting and challenging. For most of them, it was their first time studying and working with female colleagues at AKU-IED. A graduate from rural Sindh mentioned:

> Initially it was very difficult for me to sit face-to-face and interact with female students in our class but as I worked in groups with both male and female colleagues and I observed how other male students talked to female students, I started feeling comfortable in working with and talking to female students. It was a turning point for me as I came with preconceived notions of women and men.

He went on to say that he now thinks of men and women as equal in terms of rights and respect. Another graduate stated that the experience at AKU-IED totally changed his perceptions about women. 'Soon after returning from AKU-IED, I apologised to my wife, daughters and sisters for my discriminatory behaviour towards them in the past and I assured them that I would work for gender equality in our village'. Some female graduates mentioned that their attitude changed with regard to gender roles in terms of men and women having specific responsibilities. One of them stated that she came to realise that she was teaching in school, working at home, looking after the children while her husband did not assist her in any home chores. Once she graduated from AKU-IED, she developed a culture at home where everyone participated in household chores. In the beginning her husband resisted and their marriage was put in jeopardy because of this change but gradually she made him understand that they are all equal and they should take responsibility collectively. Hence, gender awareness was not only limited to their professional lives but also influenced their personal lives.

The Positive Culture of AKU-IED

Invariably, all the graduates talked about the unique and positive culture of AKU-IED. They found the culture unique for various reasons. The first prominent feature of AKU-IED was its ambience, the place itself, which according to one of the graduates, emanated the vibes of change. Another graduate stated: '…when I entered AKU-IED, I felt a new environment where people were more educated and rational'. They talked of AKU-IED as a catalyst for change because it was unique and different from many institutions that they had been students, teachers, or educational leaders in. They complimented on the cleanliness of the building and the refreshing ambience. They were impressed by the educational environment and culture and one of the graduates pointed out: '…when I entered AKU-IED it seemed to be a different kind of a place, a different kind of a setup; it had enormous resources, an environment which I had never seen or dreamt of.' It was deemed as a turning point for many of them. Some of them also pointed out that though the environment was very good it was different so adjustment posed some challenges. The graduates also commended the time management at AKU-IED. They commented on how everyone worked to meet a deadline including facilitators, course participants, administration, and how everyone contributed towards its smooth operation. The facilitators were always on time in the class.

Other important features of AKU-IED's culture, mentioned by the graduates, were its faculty, the courses, the pedagogy, and the assignments. The graduates applauded the faculty whom they deemed as role models. They thought of them as role models because of their attitude, their knowledge, experience, expertise in subject areas, and their instruction methods. They found the faculty members to be very empathetic and polite, saying that they treated them 'as human beings'. The faculty were very understanding and supported them in finishing their assignments.

Many of them commented on how the faculty influenced them in more than one way. For example, one of the graduates pointed out about the strong character of the faculty, their hard work and preparedness which was evident through their courses and teaching. They were well-prepared and their knowledge was unmatched. The graduates were astonished to see how the faculty was friendly, talked to them openly and gave them a lot of respect. One of the graduates stated that the faculty was genuinely concerned about them; they also advised them not to compromise their health and should eat, walk more, take rest, and do their assignments on time'. However, a few of them pointed out that there were some faculty members who were at times very critical and discouraging. Overall, though the majority of the graduates felt that after completing their MEd, they had become much more compassionate and had developed not only professionally but also as good human beings.

The students also commented that the learning experience they went through at the University was unique as compared to all the universities and other institutions that they had attended. Many of the graduates found the faculty members as being role models. Each faculty had expertise in specific areas and taught with passion. They were all well-prepared for the class and used various interesting pedagogies to engage them in learning. All the graduates mentioned that the faculty members were highly admired for their knowledge and their passion. The graduates also admired the type of courses that were designed for them with current readings and assignments. One of them said:

> This MEd programme is very different from other universities which mostly emphasise memorising and passing the examinations…but in MEd, which is a more holistic programme, we had to review multiple articles and textbooks. We honed our research skills and developed

> critical thinking, reading and writing skills...We were encouraged to develop our ICT skills as well. Learning about SPSS and how it operates helped me in analysing the data for my quantitative study.

The graduates felt that another distinctive feature of AKU-IED is the orientation course through which course participants are admitted in the MEd Programme. They also complimented the introduction of the 'Academic Literacy course' which helped them in writing academic English. The graduates commented on the various types of pedagogies the faculty members used in their courses. They showed amazement and admiration for these innovative methods. Several examples were recounted such as making a collage of their experiences on becoming a teacher and reflecting on it, and doing presentations of various types which included seminars, workshops, and mini-research findings.

Many of them also applauded the way assignments were designed and facilitated. They mentioned how the step-by-step processes helped them achieve their targets. They were overwhelmed with the number of assignments and readings but the faculty knew how to engage each one of them and in this way reduced the anxiety and fear of assignments.

Another very important feature which they found incredible was the status-free non-hierarchical culture at AKU-IED. They found that everyone was given an equal opportunity. One of the graduates said, '...this non-hierarchical culture really attracted and motivated me.' Another graduate also mentioned:

> In Social Area [Cafeteria] everyone queued up for lunch and the teachers would sit with us and discuss our lives and aspirations. They appreciated us and our ideas. All the staff including the administrator and director would sit with us.

One of the graduates mentioned that this environment made a major shift in his thinking. He appreciated the whole non-hierarchical system at AKU-IED. He felt that respect and a sense of ownership were witnessed at multiple levels.

Another graduate pointed out, 'I experienced a cultural shock; there was no difference between, professors, directors, programme heads… every one respected each other and they all seemed to be relaxed'. He further compared his experience to public sector universities and institutions where only authority is respected whereas at AKU-IED, everyone is given respect.' He learned the concept of equality and equity which manifested itself in the AKU-IED's environment.

Making a Difference as Change Agents

The data revealed that most graduates play multiple roles in their schools/institutions and the communities they belong to. These roles include classroom teacher, teacher educator, head-teacher, principal, education manager, researcher, and social organiser/community mobiliser. In a broader sense, most graduates work as innovators and agents of socio-educational change in their respective institutions and regions. For example, the graduates from Gilgit-Baltistan mentioned that they worked with teachers, head teachers and local education officials to bring about positive changes in schools. They also said that they worked as volunteers with civil society and community-based organisations to mobilise local communities towards education. One of them stated, 'I play my role as teacher educator/educational reformer and community developer because I believe we cannot bring about change in schools without mobilising the local communities.' Similarly, a graduate from Sindh stated:

> I teach not only my subjects at my school but also work with my fellow teachers to help them improve their practice. I also assist the principal

> in developing effective management structures and practices in the school. In my spare time, I volunteer to visit and meet local politicians, religious leaders, professionals, and social activists to create awareness about education in local communities and to generate resources for the school.

The graduates expressed that the MEd programme provided them with enriching and diverse experiences and prepared them for multiple roles. Therefore, they felt confident to take on multiple roles in their schools. They shared several stories of the difference they made in their schools/institutions and communities after their return from AKU-IED. These stories include transforming teaching and learning processes, influencing leadership and management policies and practices, creating a culture of teamwork and collegiality, mobilising and effectively utilising resources, and building stronger collaboration between schools and local communities. Some of these stories were validated through observations and discussions with the graduates' employers and school management. For example, one of the graduates from Sindh was posted in an office and asked to do secretarial tasks such as arranging meetings, filing records, and maintaining data and so on. He requested the concerned authorities to transfer him to a school or teacher education college where he could apply his learning from AKU-IED but he did not have any success. He approached higher authorities and after several attempts, he finally got transferred to a teacher education college. This institution had several issues—a decrepit building, decreasing enrolment, teachers' absenteeism lack of motivation, and scarcity of resources—all of which resulted in dismal student performance. He took it as a challenge and started with small steps which included motivating teachers, introducing new and innovative pedagogies in his own classroom and inviting other teachers to observe. He also conducted workshops for teachers, approached political leaders and philanthropists to give donations for repairing classrooms, established a computer lab, and met with local communities to create awareness about education, particularly the importance of the teaching profession. He faced many challenges and resistance in the process but never gave up. As a result, he motivated five other teachers to join him in this struggle for change. He used some of his personal resources and time to organise a number of events in the college. 'It took me a year to bring about some improvement in both the physical outlook and academic offerings at the college and once the teachers saw improvements, they joined me', the graduate explained.

The graduates from Balochistan shared that the schools they had joined had been suffering from low enrolment and lack of coordination between the schools and local parents and communities. The graduates had taken a number of initiatives to address these issues, including introduction of innovative and more interesting pedagogies, co-curricular activities, student-led committees, reactivation of Parents-Teachers Council (PTC), and admission campaigns. As a result, there was a significant increase in enrolment at these schools. 'Students from other schools have enrolled in my school because of the improved teaching and learning processes and interesting co-curricular activities we have started', a graduate stated.

Professional Development

In this section, a detailed analysis of the data is presented which explains professional development experiences of the graduates before, during, and after MEd studies at AKU-IED.

Pre AKU-IED

A significant majority of the graduates stated that before they joined AKU-IED, they were not really teaching in the true sense of the word.

Many of them became teachers after completing Intermediate, BA, or MA in various subject areas. Some changed their profession because they were inspired by their teachers. One of the graduates stated that he was basically a lawyer; his teacher inspired him to become a teacher. When he joined the teaching profession, he was asked to teach sociology.

Some graduates wanted to improve their education and took admission in higher education institutions but were not satisfied with the standard of education and left the university. Many of them did not have professional training such as BEd when they joined AKU-IED. One of them said:

> I did not have a BEd degree or any other certificate in education neither had training in teaching when I joined AKU-IED… I had been teaching in a couple of schools; I had one year of experience as a school administrator. I did not have much knowledge about the practice of teaching or the curriculum. I taught using guide books.

Some of the graduates already had BEd qualifications. One of them stated, 'I did BEd from Allama Iqbal Open University but I felt it was not enough'. Some other graduates had already attended a workshop on teacher training through a donor-funded agency but they felt that they lagged behind and needed to develop themselves further. Many of them said that though they had been teaching for quite some time, they wanted to improve their teaching. Hence they decided to join AKU-IED.

During MEd Studies

During the MEd programme, the participants were exposed to different methods of teaching and different theories of knowledge. One participant asked a series of questions:

> I have experience in teaching and school management. But I am still intrigued by many questions: What is real teaching? How does one plan the curriculum? How do the SLOs [student learning outcomes] complement the curriculum? How does the class room practice complement all these things? How does the teaching and learning take place? How is learning assessed? What are the learning outcomes?

They talked about how they were excited and amazed to know about many things that they had taken for granted. For example, one of the graduates said that in their class of Curriculum Learning Teaching and Assessment course, when the facilitator introduced the concept of curriculum, they were all amazed. Before this, most of them equated curriculum with textbooks.

During their learning at AKU-IED, their perception of learning changed. As they were all experienced teachers and educational leaders, they assumed that they were knowledgeable and had a lot of experience of teaching in the classroom and managing schools. But after entering AKU-IED they realised that they knew very little and in many ways, they knew nothing about teaching or education for that matter. One of the graduates stated that she had always thought of herself as fully knowledgeable to teach but when she joined the MEd programme, she realised that she knew very little. She also learnt about the important concept of lifelong learning and its emphasis on continuous learning. It was only at AKU-IED, stated one of the graduates, that she actually came to know the importance of knowing different teaching methods and the discipline of learning independently. One of them pointed out, '...we had to take responsibility of our own learning and give examples from our own context, relate theory to practice'. In the beginning, they found this self-directed learning very difficult since they were not used to it. In their past experiences, they worked on their own, and there was hardly any interaction with colleagues in their schools. At AKU-IED, a collegial environment was prevalent.

The faculty members were also good role models of collegiality. The students were encouraged to work in groups to develop skills of collegiality. They found it very useful because they learned from each other.

They also became computer literate. Initially some of them who had never used the computer, got a shock when on the very first day they were asked to use the computer. One of them stated, 'I only knew how to switch the computer on and off, but gradually I learned so much and this was because, we were compelled to use the computer for writing assignments, creating presentations and for research'. In their courses, they were encouraged to use technology, search the internet and look for research articles. They had no idea before coming to AKU-IED that so many resources are available on the internet. Previously they just used to go to libraries and look for books, but now the 'whole world of knowledge is open to them'.

Many of them talked specifically about the faculty who they were impressed with and from whom they had learnt a great deal. They felt that the faculty challenged them and enhanced their critical thinking which they found rather difficult to work on in the beginning but later found that it was useful for them as professionals. One of them stated, '…we came to know how our facilitators worked so hard with us, and how important our contribution to teacher education' is. They commented that the courses at AKU-IED helped them in their jobs later, in various ways. For example, one of the graduates stated that when he had to work with an Examination Board later, he was well equipped to follow what was required of him such as curriculum, assessment, and course design.

The graduates said that they actually came to know what 'learning to teach' was. Many of them commented that they had the content but they learned how to develop methods to teach the content at AKU-IED. One of them said, '…I had the content but how to deliver that content was not easy for me. I learned many ways of delivering the content, I learned how to become a reflective practitioner, and I came to know that a teacher must not go to the classroom blank; the teacher should be well prepared. I am trying my best to implement this in my teaching and I am now quite successful in implementing all that I have learnt'.

Another very important aspect that the graduates talked about was that they learned the pedagogy and content of each subject. For example, one of the graduates pointed out, '…I have been teaching science for a long time… I came to know how to teach science subjects by keeping in mind the specific content and the teaching and learning methodologies. Another graduate said that he did not know how to engage students in map or globe reading, and asked what some of the interesting and unique ways of teaching it would be in social studies. Another such example was given by a graduate about learning how to teach mathematics by using real life experiences in the context and with the help of available resources. Many of them talked about becoming good instructional leaders in their schools.

Many of the graduates talked about the change in perception about learning to teach. One of them stated that he learned about a number of concepts such as inquiry-based teaching, research-based teaching, and techniques involving students in interactive learning. He found interactive teaching an effective way of teaching students. Student, also appreciated the diverse ways of teaching and learning because each individual learns in a different way. Graduates gave several examples of teaching and learning methods such as lectures, audios, videos, books, real environment, seminars, workshops, developing action plans and teacher continuous development programmes.

The graduates also talked of the skills that they developed in their groups such as listening skills, critical and analytical skills, how to give positive feedback, and how to respect each other's views. All these skills made them better team workers and they valued collegial learning. One of them said that he was trying to create the same kind of collegial work environment at his place of work so that everyone was involved in the process of learning and decision-making.

Post MEd Experience

After the graduates returned to their respective work environments, they were motivated to apply their learning and make a difference in the education sector. They appreciated AKU-IED's efforts to work at the grass-root level. A group of graduates stated that they started helping students and teachers in areas which they found difficult. This was all a self-directed effort. One of them pointed out, 'We are promoting a vibrant culture of ownership and volunteerism.'

They pointed out that one thing that they learned at AKU-IED was that learning did not necessarily have to be in a brick and mortar setting; it was also possible to continue it outside the class. They talked about how much they learned from field trips such as the one in science class when they went out and learned in the real setting. They were also given tasks outside the class which they analysed and presented during the class. This is an example of flip classroom teaching. They have now started focusing on bringing about change by introducing new approaches to teaching that would impact student learning outcomes. They initiated many other ways of bringing about change such as dealing with colleagues and how to care about their students. One of them stated: 'We do not need to tell people about the changes we bring about, our work should speak for itself'.

They learned about virtual environment in a number of courses at AKU-IED. Some of the students developed virtual spaces on Facebook for communication. There is a gradual change observed in the regions where AKU-IED's graduates are returning to their institutions. One of the graduates talked about overcoming political interference and how all the graduates together fought their cases for promotion. Many of the graduates also complimented their senior management who were very cooperative and provide opportunities for bringing about positive change. One of them stated, '… the principal is very much cooperative. All the change that is occurring is because of him'. Another graduate also narrated how her head teacher was keen to encourage change. She encouraged the MEd graduates to help other teachers in lesson planning, asked them to observe and help other teachers in developing school scheme of studies and timetables.

The graduates were given responsible positions in their institutions so that they could lead others and bring about change. One of them said that when she left her school to do her MEd, she was a teacher and when she came back, she was appointed as an academic coordinator.

The graduates stated that their knowledge was enhanced because of going through this rigorous programme. One of them stated, 'I feel lucky that I attended the MEd programme at AKU-IED and I have come to know what constructive noise in the class means as normally we always wanted our students to remain quiet in the classroom'. One of the graduates stated, 'I feel honoured when my work is appreciated in my school and in the rest of the school communities…it was a golden chance for me [to study at AKU-IED]'.

The graduates learnt at AKU-IED, the skills of collegiality which they are now implementing in their respective contexts. They have initiated some small-scale projects through which they want to bring about change. These projects have became part of their professional growth. As discussed earlier, the graduates were much more open to engage with other colleagues. They wanted to encourage collegiality because in most of their respective contexts, everyone was working on an individual basis. Many of them were supporting their colleagues mentoring and tutoring on informal basis.

One of the examples of such initiatives is the introduction of teachers' portfolios through which graduate can reflect on their teaching, share project-based learning within the schools to generate content of different subjects, share curriculum documents with colleagues. One of the graduates shared that he initiated course planning workshops for teachers and also developed a Facebook page through which teachers could learn and communicate. Another graduate said that he first applied lesson planning in his own class and then helped other colleagues to develop their lesson plans. He said, 'Now I never go to class without a lesson plan, and I engage students through planned activities'.

Many of them felt happy to share that their teaching practices have changed. They are also a human pool resource for all the teachers. Some of them developed their libraries which was also a way of providing teachers facilities for professional development. Therefore they are gradually developing resources in their respective institutions. Another student also stated that there were many documents meant for teachers such as teachers' professional standards but were gathering dust in the library. He asked his principal to give these document to the teachers and facilitated in discussing them with his colleagues.

All the graduates mentioned how research was an important learning tool for them. They were introduced to research methods and were constantly engaged in research throughout their period of study. Once they graduated from AKU-IED, they made good use of knowledge by applying it within their contexts. One of the graduates spoke about it in this manner:

> When I returned after finishing at AKU-IED, I used the knowledge I had acquired. I worked with all the private schools voluntarily. They had no knowledge or opportunity to learn about curriculum and its link with Student Learning Outcomes (SLOs). They have learnt about teaching English, theories of learning English, methods of learning English, and ways of assessing learning.

Another graduate proclaimed that he worked in the area that most interested him, which was Environmental Education. He worked with local NGOs especially in the area of sustainability and climate change. He also contributed in disaster management related courses.

Many of the graduates were being asked to work with international agencies such as UNICEF. They stated that when they went for their first meeting with UNICEF where there were other people from different universities they were appreciated for the work that they had done and for their professional attitude. The graduates pointed out that there were many projects from different donor agencies who preferred to work with them. In this way they further developed their knowledge and competencies.

The graduates said that at the beginning they found reading very tedious but later as they read more, they developed their reading skills and also understood the content more since the readings were discussed in the class. After some time, they felt that they could easily search for articles and also used the reading material that they got in different courses at AKU-IED. They also tried to inculcate this reading habit in their colleagues and students. However, they also pointed out that at each step they met resistance but since they were all committed to their profession they made sure that they worked hard and applied everything that they learnt at AKU-IED.

Besides learning about content and pedagogy many graduates pointed out that after they graduated, they realised that they had developed a certain disposition which was required by the professionals. They became very punctual, had a lot of respect for people with different perspectives, planned their lessons well before going to class, reflected at every stage, cared for students and were ready to work with colleagues. They also pointed out that they developed not only professionally but personally also. 'We became much more tolerant and patient…our attitude towards human beings changed', the graduates mentioned during a focus group discussion. Some of the graduates said that they had many personal issues but

AKU-IED taught them how to face challenges and how to resolve them. So now '…problems do not seem to overwhelm us'.

Finding Solutions to the Challenges

The graduates mentioned that there was no reading culture in their respective institutions; hence they found it challenging to read course readings given to them. Now that they were back in their work environment they had reverted to the same culture. One of the graduates elaborated by mentioning that he had developed very good reading habits at AKU-IED, but in his work environment, he hardly got any opportunity to read. Sometimes graduates go back to their reading packs and read what they require. But they are not abreast with the latest research and readings. Some of them reported that they tried to inculcate reading habits in their classes and encouraged children to read. However, there were very few libraries and not many books for the students to read. One of the graduates said that she went to PDCN[1] sometimes to read the new books. She said that in the school that she was teaching in, the EDIP project had given them books but so far there was no mobile library. One of them suggested that, '[AKU-IED] should give us access to digital library even after we leave the institution'.

The graduates found re-adjusting to their own context rather difficult because they were holistically transformed. The graduates' experiences at AKU-IED and its non-hierarchal structure influenced the way they wanted to function in their own work places. This created ripples of discomfort in their organisations and schools. They were accused of being disrespectful to elders. One of the graduates stated, '…we had all the respect for each one of our colleagues but when we spoke with confidence, we were labelled as disrespectful, we were called the AKU-IED people'. They felt that they had to struggle to get their ideas across because their ideas were unique and were taken as threats by senior colleagues who thought of themselves as more experienced and knowledgeable teachers. They said that they went back to their work with a very positive attitude that they would make a difference and change the culture. However, they did make difference in various ways through their teaching. They changed their way of caring for their students but changing the attitudes of colleagues and students was the most challenging experience and 'sometimes impossible'. One of them said:

> In the government system, there are certain norms such as differences between seniors and juniors. We were juniors and we became empowered after graduating from AKU-IED; this was not accepted by our senior colleagues…we were often accused of talking too much, or giving suggestions.

Many of them narrated incidents where they were discouraged even to talk about their experiences at AKU-IED, and told off on several occasions. The seniors would say that they had been there for more than three decades and there had been no change, so how could they make a difference, or change things now? This created many clashes and unpleasant situations among them and their senior colleagues. One of them said, 'When I came back from AKU-IED after graduating, I was the most junior teacher in my school. I was a student of the same school, and many of my colleagues had been my teachers, but they had no concept of life-long learning, and they were not ready for any change. Hence there was a lot of resistance to what I did or said'. Some graduates said that many of their colleagues tried to demotivate them but they took small steps to bring about changes in their teaching and gradually the results of their teaching became evident. One of them pointed out that he was very lonely and felt lost since he was the only graduate in the whole of the district. He had no one to discuss his ideas with nor did he have access to the internet and library. Initially, he was very frustrated but gradually he started discussing his ideas with his colleagues and some even started working with him.

The lives of some graduates got disrupted as they were away from their families. Many of them suffered immensely as their relationships were affected because of the long distances. One of the female graduates stated, 'When I decided to join MEd, my husband clearly told me that I could study further but I had to take care of all the chores, and look after the children as he would not take any responsibility while I was studying'. She found this to be very disturbing as she did not get any support from her husband. So the demands on her multiplied. She had to bring her children and her mother along with her to Karachi to look after the children. Others also talked about such family responsibilities which they were expected to shoulder as women. Even after graduating they had to meet competing demands. They had to manage their work in schools and institutions, prepare presentations for different forums, work on time consuming projects and had to look after their families. They faced such challenges and had to learn to cope with them while living away from family. One of the female graduates said that her mother-in-law was very upset and kept on complaining that she did not spend time with her, as she was busy in school and when she came back home she was reading or planning for some event. Similarly, male graduates from rural contexts found it difficult first to adjust in the culture of AKU-IED where they had to work with female facilitators and classmates. Later when they went back to their contexts they expected the same kind of intellectual standards from their spouses. One of them made an effort to educate his spouse so that they could be compatible. Others found it hard to adjust with their family and spouses because their entire world view had changed.

They also found that in some schools it was hard to initiate anything new. For example, one of the graduates stated that it was very challenging to convince the head teachers and the teachers to plan their lessons because many of them planned as they taught. So, she took an initiative to help teachers to plan despite a lot of resistance from some teachers. One of them said, 'There is no space for people like us; there is so much politics and leg pulling that it is hard to start anything new'. Another started taking classes voluntarily. But in the beginning there were a lot of problems. They had to face a lot of negativity. In some of the schools, the graduates reported that the head teacher was like a dictator who dictated how to teach in the classes. No change was accepted by him. Some of them felt frustrated because of resistance or a lack of cooperation from the school head. One of them stated, 'AKU-IED gives us a lot of potential to progress but the environment in schools is very demotivating'. They face many taunts from seniors and colleagues. Another graduate also stated that it is '... difficult to apply knowledge at their home institute as changes are not easily accepted. Skills and knowledge learned at AKU-IED are going to waste because of negative attitude'. There is a lot of professional jealousy and the graduates are hampered in bringing about change.

Summary

There were several other challenges that the graduates faced while they were at AKU-IED. The biggest challenge was to finish and submit their assignments on time. Some of them also got stressed out and had to take advice from the student counselor and faculty. Some of them became sick because they could not cope with the workload. One of them said, 'We thought it would be like any public institution where they will have classes and we will go home, but it was very demanding and we were not used to this kind of workload and pressure'. Hence, it was suggested by some graduates that AKU-IED should bridge the gap between different institutions, initiate collaboration with public sector universities and influence the teaching and learning processes.

In many districts, according to the graduates, no one knew AKU-IED; they thought that it was an NGO and therefore did not value the contribution of graduates or even their degrees. One of them said that he was working in a government college and he had done educational leadership and management. He wanted to get transferred to a college of education but he was denied because the higher management did not recognise his qualifications.

As for the courses, the graduates felt that there should be more choices as the variety was very limited. For example, one of them pointed out that the course Curriculum, Learning, Teaching and Assessment was a very important course but it was not sufficient. These should all be separate courses. If one is working in the area of assessment there should be enough content on the subject. So these courses should be separated and expanded. One of the graduates said that in this course, only the theory of curriculum was taught which was not enough; he said that some hands-on activities should be included. As he is now developing curriculum but he has no idea of how to go about it. He said, 'There should be a specialisation in curriculum, assessment and other areas'. He added that there was a choice in elective courses but no choice in core courses which sometimes became frustrating. They also suggested that the Qualitative and Quantitative research courses should be offered separately. One of the cohorts had a course in which both were merged. This cohort found that they could not fully understand either one of them.

Many of them said that in their courses in various subject areas there should be more focus on the methods of teaching these subject areas. There is a lot of emphasis on content but how to actually deliver the content is not focused. They said that they needed more practical experience of using the pedagogy to teach specific disciplines. They also pointed out that many readings and examples in the courses were given from other contexts. There should be more readings from contexts in which they were working or similar contexts.

Another challenge that the graduates face is that they lose link with AKU-IED once they leave. They suggested that there should be regular follow-up sessions for the alumni and they should be given regular feedback on their institutional tasks. The alumni should be involved in research which AKU-IED conducts. They should also be provided feedback on the research proposals that they sometimes develop in their institutions. One graduate mentioned that he approached one of the faculty members at AKU-IED who did give him feedback on his proposal which he greatly appreciated. However, he suggested that a regular activity should be maintained. The graduates also found that the content-based courses such as English, mathematics, science and social studies should also be offered separately so that they could develop their expertise in them. They said that their students were very weak and they really did not know how to work with them. The teaching methods that they had learnt at AKU-IED were very innovative; however, implementing them at the school level where students were very weak was difficult. Another reason why they could not change the teaching and learning processes was that the students were not used to new ways of learning and other colleagues taught them in the traditional way.

Recommendations

The following recommendations are made after reviewing the findings of the study:

1. AKU-IED is a leading institution widely recognised for its strong influence on the students who attend its programmes. Its culture impacts both personal and professional lives of the

graduates. The institution should continue to further strengthen its collaboration with the public and private sector education institutions to scale up its impact on the programmes offered by other institutions;

2. This kind of research should be an on-going feature of AKU-IED. A large-scale research study should be carried out to examine the evolving nature of AKU-IED with specific focus on its graduate programmes and the graduates themselves;
3. The study provides useful insights into engaging students in reflective practice and action research for their continuing professional development and makes policy recommendations for reviewing and revising teacher education curriculum, especially for in-service teacher education programmes;
4. The study also recommends, particularly in the public sector, that the graduates who work as change agents must not be transferred frequently as staying in one school for a longer period helps bring about positive changes; and
5. The graduates in leadership roles have been quite successful in transforming their schools and therefore the concerned government authorities must empower the graduates and effectively utilise their services to improve the quality of education in their schools.

References

Beattie, M., *Constructing Professional Knowledge: A Narrative of Change and Development* (New York: Teachers College Press, 1995).

Clare, L., 'We'll fight it as long as we can: Coping with the onset of Alzheimer's disease', *Aging & Mental Health, 6*/2, (2002), 139–148.

Creswell, J., *Qualitative Inquiry and Research Design: Choosing among Five Approaches* (3rd ed, Los Angeles: SAGE Publications, 2013).

de Visser, R. & Smith, J., 'Alcohol consumption and masculine identity among young men', *Psychology & Health, 22*/5, (2007), 595–614.

Fields, B., 'Minimal intervention in-service training for teachers: An experimental study in primary classrooms', *South Pacific Journal of Teacher Education,* 18/1, (1990), 41–50.

Fraenkel, J. & Wallen, Norman E., *How to design and evaluate research in education with power web* (6th ed, New York: McGraw-Hill Higher Education, 2006).

Grimmett, P.P. & Crehan, E.P., 'The nature of collegiality in teacher development: The case of clinical supervision', in M. Fullan & A. Hargreaves, eds. *Teacher Development and Educational Change* (London; New York: Routledge Falmer, 1992), 56–85.

Guskey, T.R., 'Professional development and teachers change', *Teachers and Teaching,* 8/3, 381–391, 2002, DOI: 10.1080/13540600210000512.

Halai, A. and Anderson, S., *Case Studies of School Improvement in Pakistan.* Unpublished Research Report, Aga Khan University-Institute for Educational Development, Karachi: 2005).

Haymes, S.N., 'Memory, reality and ethnography in a Colombian war zone: Towards a social phenomenology of collective remembrance', *Philosophical Studies in Education,* 43, (2012), 138–151.

Holloway, I., *Basic Concepts for Qualitative Research* (Oxford: Blackwell Science, 1997).

Hussain, R. & Ali, S., 'Improving public school teachers in Pakistan: Challenges and opportunities', *Improving Schools,* 13/1, (2010), 70–80.

Khamis, A. 'The various impacts of the Institute for Educational Development in its co-operating schools in Pakistan'. Unpublished Doctoral Thesis, University of London, UK, 2000).

Lamb, M., 'The consequences of INSET', *ELT Journal,* 49/1, (1995), 72–80.

Leach, D. & Conto, H., 'The additional effects of process and outcome feedback following brief in-service teacher training', *Educational Psychology,* 19/4, (1999), 441–462.

Mason, J., *Qualitative Researching* (London: Sage Publications, 1996).

Mohammed, R.F., 'What hinders change in classroom practice? Lessons from the field and future directions in Pakistan', *Journal of In-Service Education,* 32/3, (2006), 375–385.

Mohammed, R. & Harlech-Jones, B., 'The fault is in ourselves: Looking at failures in implementation', *Compare: A Journal of Comparative and International Education,* 38/1, (2008), 39–51.

Pereira, F., 'In-service teacher education and scholar innovation: The semantics of action and reflection on action as a mediation device', *Australian Journal of Teacher Education,* 36/11, (2011), 33–50.

Pyle, A., Wade-Woolley, L. & Hutchinson, N.L., '"Just listen to us": The role of teacher empowerment in the implementation of responsiveness to intervention', *Alberta Journal of Educational Research,* 57/3, (2011), 258–272.

Ramatlapana, K.A., 'Provision of in-service training of mathematics and science teachers in Botswana: Teachers' perspectives', *Journal of Mathematics Teacher Education,* 12/2, (2009), 153–159.

Reid, K., Flowers, P. & Larkin, M., 'Exploring lived experience: An introduction to interpretative phenomenological analyses, *The Psychologist,* 18/1, (2005), 20–23.

Rizvi, M. & Elliott, B., 'Enhancing and sustaining teacher professionalism in Pakistan', *Teachers and Teaching,* 13/1, (2007), 5–19.

Saiti, A. & Saitis, C., 'In-service training for teachers who work in full-day schools. Evidence from Greece 1', *European Journal of Teacher Education,* 29/4, (2006), 455–470.

Shamim, F. & Halai, A., 'Developing professional development teacher', in I. Farah & B. Jaworski, eds. *Partnerships in Educational Development* (Oxford: Symposium Books, 2006), 47–68.

Shamim. F., *Impact and Sustainability of the Whole School Improvement Programme, Professional Development Centre, North.* Unpublished research report, Aga Khan University-Institute for Educational Development, Karachi, 2005.

Smith, J.A., 'Advocating pluralism: Invited commentary on 'qualitative interviews in psychology: problems and perspectives', by Jonathan Potter and Alexa Hepburn, *Qualitative Research in Psychology*, 2, (2005), 309–311.

Tajik, M.A. and Bashiruddin, A., '*Evaluation of AKU-IED's Capacity-building Initiatives in Afghanistan and Syria*'. Unpublished Research Report, Aga Khan University-Institute for Educational Development, Karachi, 2009.

Tajik, M.A., 'From Educational Reformers to Community Developers: The Changing Roles of Field Education Officers of the Aga Khan Education Service Pakistan' (Unpublished doctoral thesis, University of Toronto, Canada, 2004).

Note

1. Professional Development Centre, North.

8

Private and Social Returns of Higher Education: A Case Study of AKU-IED's MEd Graduates

Naureen Madhani

Introduction

Governments, bilateral and multilateral agencies, institutions, and individuals invest in higher education for a wide range of reasons. For those who take a human capital approach to higher education, an increase in the education and training of a nation's labour force translates into an increase in its ability to create goods and services. In their seminal paper on higher education and economic development in Africa, Bloom, Canning and Chan (2006, p. iv) found that a one-year increase in 'tertiary education stock' could raise Africa's income by five per cent in five years and about 12 per cent in the long-term. This increase in ability leads to an increase in productivity for the country and therefore its economic development.

Higher education also has significant non-market private and social returns. Graduates of quality programmes tend to lead better quality lives, experiencing increased work satisfaction and longer and healthier lives. They tend to engage in more community service than non-graduates, are more supportive of human rights, and are more informed citizens. They also tend to have better parenting skills and have fewer children than those who do not have any higher education. These private non-market benefits have a significant impact on the graduates' communities. However, there is limited research about these non-market benefits, particularly in the context of the developing world.

The purpose of this study was to contribute to the research on the benefits of higher education by investigating the non-market social returns to graduates of AKU-IED's MEd programme in Karachi, Pakistan. The study focused on indirect social benefits, such as volunteer work, family and community interactions, use of leisure and other ways in which the programme has changed the lives of graduates and their communities.

The first section of the chapter begins with a literature review, in order to set the study into its theoretical context. This is followed by a description of the purpose of the study and its research questions. The methodology section describes the case study method, the sample, data collection and method of analysis. Finally, the findings of the study are presented, followed by a discussion of the results in light of previous research. The conclusion highlights some of the policy implications from this study as well as areas for future research.

Literature Review

Market Returns

Proponents of human capital theory argue that individuals weigh the costs and benefits of investing in higher education on the basis of their level of investment. For individuals, these costs would include tuition and related costs such as textbooks, as well as the income foregone (opportunity costs), while enrolled in higher education. The financial benefits of this investment are graduates' higher earnings after degree completion. For governments, the costs of investing in higher education include the cost of subsidizing it, as well as any opportunity costs of using that money for higher education (e.g. income foregone from returns to other investment). The economic returns for the government are the contribution to economic growth that educated individuals make. Hence, at the individual, as well as the societal level, human capital theorists argue that the economic costs and benefits must be weighed in order to find optimal rates of return.

In their seminal paper on higher education's contribution to economic development in Africa, Bloom, Canning and Chan (2006, p. iii) find that higher education may 'promote faster technological catch-up' leading to an improvement in economic output. Using data from 103 countries during the period 1960–2000, the authors find that each additional year of education raises the long-run GDP per capita by 12.2 per cent.

Non-Market Returns

Non-market returns are bifurcated into private and public returns:

Private returns

In addition to higher lifetime earnings, higher education graduates are more likely to have more satisfying work environments, live healthier lives, manage their time better, have better parenting skills (and fewer children), and are more likely to be lifelong learners (Baum, Ma & Payea, 2013; Bynner et al., 2003; Perna, 2003; Psacharopoulos, 1972). They are also more likely to develop the attitudes required for the support of human rights (Bynner et al., 2003) as well as the trust, respect and social capital to bring about social change (Helliwell & Putnam, 1999).

Public or social returns

Several studies have identified the non-market societal benefits of education (Baum, Ma & Payea, 2013; McMahon, 1997). For example, as educational attainment in a society increases, crime rates fall, tax contributions to government increase and the overall health of the society increases. The quality of students in a classroom creates an environment for richer learning for all students, and graduates tend to contribute more to society by volunteering and voting as well as through their decreased dependence on welfare (McMahon, 2009). Higher education therefore contributes not only to economic development but also to social and cultural development of a society.

The 'portion of the market and non-market benefits, realised by the individual, that are due to the education of others' (McMahon, 2009), are known as 'education externalities'. For example, society benefits not only from recent graduates but also from people who graduated 20–30 years ago.

Another way in which graduates contribute to the development of a country is by contributing to university research and training. For example, as graduates go into the teaching profession, they develop other graduates and contribute to the creation of more human capital. They also are responsible for knowledge generation through their own research and therefore contribute to the development of a knowledge economy. Similarly, since they are more efficient users of technology, they make the overall economy more productive, pushing out the production frontier of a country. Countries that invest in higher education therefore not only benefit directly from the graduates' own skills but also from the contribution of these graduates to education, research and technological innovation.

Endogenous Development Theory

According to the Endogenous Development Theory developed by McMahon (2009), high economic growth leads to high levels of education, which in the long-term, leads to an accumulation of indirect effects on education. This leads to a change in the rate of development i.e. the pace of development is changed dramatically by the accumulation of education externalities. Hence, poor countries with low economic growth, invest less in basic and higher education. Therefore, not only are they deprived of the direct benefit of economic growth resulting from human capital growth but they also do not accumulate education externalities. These externalities as well as the direct economic returns to higher education are reinvested by richer countries leading to a change in the rate of development experienced by these countries.

Figure 1 summarises the above discussion on the private and social benefits of higher education.

As can be seen in Figure 1, in order to capture the totality of the returns to higher education, research has to move beyond a simplistic calculation of economic returns captured at one moment in time. Researchers need to account for the externalities of education, the accumulation of economic and social returns and the changes in the rate of growth of a society due to these complex interactions.

Purpose

The purpose of this study was to investigate the non-monetary private and social returns to higher education through a case study of AKU-IED's MEd programme in Karachi, Pakistan. The study aimed to contribute to the literature on returns to higher education in the developing world by focusing on private non-market benefits to

Figure 1: Private and social benefits to higher education[1]

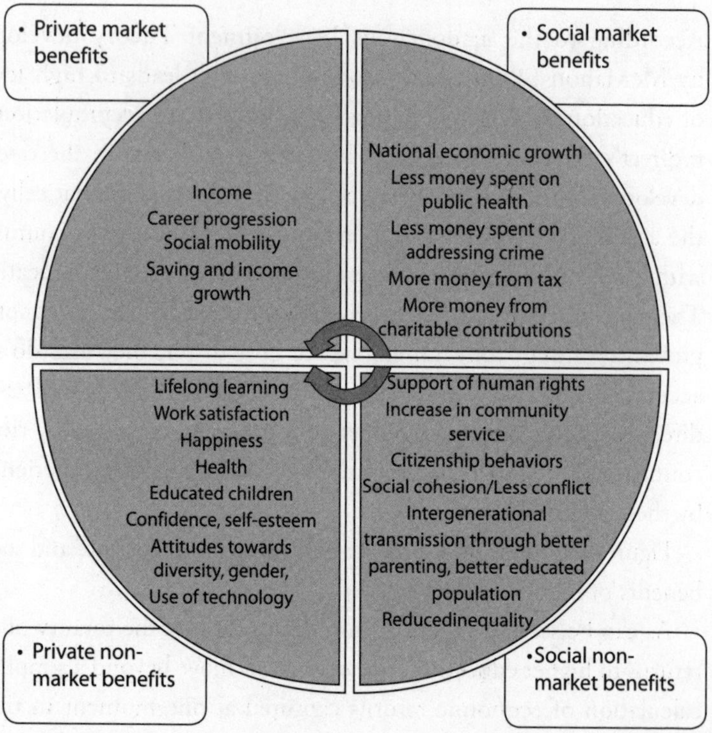

individuals, such as improved health, increased satisfaction with work environments, better use of leisure time, and the desire to continue learning over their lifetimes. It also investigated the social returns that families and communities experience due to changes in individuals' attitudes and lifestyles. The study aimed to highlight the wider impact of investments in post-secondary or higher education.

Methodology

Case Study

AKU-IED's MEd is designed to develop graduates who have a strong commitment to educational change so that the benefits of their educational achievements accrue not only to them as individuals but also to their institutions and communities. This case study of the graduates of AKU-IED's MEd programme is a useful example of the societal impact of investment in the higher education of individuals. The overall question guiding the case study was: What are the non-monetary private and social returns to AKU-IED's MEd programme?

The case study approach enables an 'intensive' focus on a large number of variables within the case, rather than the 'extensiveness' offered by studying a few variables in a large number of cases (Thomas, 2011, p.512). It sets the case into its historical, political, and social contexts (Stake, 2005). This context informs the issue for study, which in this case, are the non-market benefits of higher education. It is this overarching issue or 'object' of the study, which provides the analytical frame for the study.

Access

Aga Khan Foundation, Canada and Strengthening Teacher Education in Pakitan (STEP) project staff negotiated access to AKU-IED's MEd graduates. Potential candidates were then approached for their willingness to participate in the study. Each participant was informed of the purpose of the study and was given a written consent form. The participants who were interviewed gave their verbal consent after the consent form was read out and e-mailed to them. Those interviewed face-to-face signed the consent form (in English or Urdu as appropriate).

Sample

A purposive sample of 30 graduates was selected based on region, year of graduation, funding source, availability for interview. The Table 10 provides a profile of study participants by gender and region.

Table 10: Study Participants by Gender and Region

Gender	Gilgit-Baltistan	Sindh	Balochistan	Karachi	Total
Female	09	00	01	05	15
Male	05	06	04	00	15

Of these, 17 were funded through the STEP project and 11 were funded from other sources. All five of the Karachi participants were funded from sources other than STEP; however, two of the five were working on the STEP project team.

Data Collection and Analysis

A semi-structured interview guide was developed based on literature on the private and social benefits of higher education. The questionnaire and informed consent form were translated into Urdu. Two focus groups, lasting about an hour-and-a-half with five to seven participants each were conducted in Gilgit-Baltistan (GB). All the data collection took place during a three-week period in July–August 2014. Individual telephone interviews as well as some face-to-face interviews with participants from Balochistan and Interior Sindh were conducted in Karachi.

Sources of data for the study included extensive field notes and documents regarding the STEP project, the MEd programme and the wider social and political context of the country.

Transcribed and translated interviews were coded and analysed using Nvivo. Codes drawn from the literature served as starting points for the analysis and the researcher added to these as analysis proceeded.

Findings

Career

A majority of the participants reported more satisfying positions, better work environments, and increased financial benefits. For the most part, they stayed within the public sector. Some received promotions within their schools and some transferred to other public institutions in order to get a promotion or so that they could be assigned a relevant position. Five participants were working at AKU-IED (all non-STEP graduates), of whom two were working with the STEP project.

In interior Sindh, all four of the graduates from Sukkur were promoted and appointed to the newly established Education Department at the Institute of Business Administration, Sukkur. This is a public university, established as a 'Management University' for the community colleges planned by the Government of Sindh[2]. One of the Sukkur graduates was working as the Academic Coordinator of the Faculty of Education while the others worked as faculty.

Of the 30 participating graduates, only five did not experience change in their position or salary status. These were more recent graduates, waiting for appointments from the District Education Office.

Teaching and Learning

Graduates reported a transformation in their attitude towards teaching and learning as well as their vision of what a teacher could achieve, regardless of resources and opportunities available. A graduate reported:

> The biggest benefit was professional development. My thinking as a teacher was limited; I used to think of myself as a teacher, a very good teacher, a very big teacher because I had not gone outside my school or district. When I went outside, I discovered that teaching just inside the class is not teaching…a teacher… has to have a bigger picture with an understanding that he is a change agent.

The graduates developed skills related to using technology to enhance teaching and learning, the ability to engage students of different abilities, and the motivation to reach out to parents as needed. They emphasised the role that technology had come to play in their lives and the ways in which they were promoting its use to their families.

The graduates' journey was not limited to skill acquisition. The MEd programme had an impact on their personal lives, as well as their commitment to becoming change agents.

Bringing about Change

The graduates spoke passionately about their desire to engage with societal problems, such as lack of education and conflict between religious and ethnic communities. They facilitated workshops aimed at developing a respect for diversity and were reaching out to teachers from other schools to foster a community of learners. They saw themselves as role models for their family and community members and noted for example, how others in their communities had been inspired to pursue education. 'In my family, no one else has done his Masters. My daughter is in the 5th grade. Earlier, no girls used to go out of the home. This encouragement is from there [IED], one of the graduates reported.

The graduates described their community service in terms of helping in classrooms on a voluntary basis, and in some cases, using their skills to establish non-profit schools or NGOs. Three graduates had established NGOs aimed at addressing education in their contexts.

> My community is illiterate but people really appreciated it—before I left and after I came back—that I completed my masters. The University has a name that everyone knows. As you progress, your vision is broadened. If you have a passion for work then you can do more for your community, more than just for yourself.

The graduates also underscored the respect and status they acquired as a result of acquiring the MEd degree. They felt that they were able to influence others in their families and communities not only because of their own role-modelling but also because getting a degree from Aga Khan University gave the graduates an enhanced status and credibility.

Respect as a Lever for Change

The graduates reported that in addition to the status associated with their credentials, they also earned the respect of their communities because of the different way they lived their lives and through volunteer work, by advocating for change and by becoming role models for others in their communities. One graduate went on to say, 'People not only listen to my speech but they also act on it. They get a strong message. They also convey this message to their children by supporting, facilitating and encouraging them to pursue higher education.'

This respect has proved to be an important lever for change. Rasul (pseudonym) from GB described his work in developing quality standards for volunteer teachers, stating that it would impact 20,000 teachers in Pakistan. Similarly, Laal's (pseudonym) status as an AKU-IED's graduate, as well as his work with students in his own school, led to his neighbours seeking him out for help with their children's school work:

> [The] neighborhood kids start coming to me from morning until sunset for tuition. They learn from me and also support each other. But I do not charge fees. They think that because I am an IED graduate, I must have a treasure of knowledge. So, I am trying to transfer whatever knowledge I have learnt. There is motivation!

Thus, the graduates were serving in their communities as ambassadors for education and social change. However, the participants recognised that change was a slow process and that, in order for it to be sustainable, they had to remain committed and had to gain the trust of others:

> In order for me to bring change in my school I have to take everyone with me. But not everyone will be with you. It is a government institution. You do not have authority or power. In a private institution, it is a different environment. But here you have full security but you do not have any control, even if you want to work with another teacher, it is difficult to get them to work with you. One has to cut through a lot of political obstacles. So those are challenges. It takes time to face them or overcome them. One should not get disheartened and keep striving for change.

Although the graduates usually began with a description of how their teaching and learning practices had changed, they also talked extensively and eloquently about how the programme had impacted their personal lives.

Personal Lives

The participants described how the MEd programme had taught them to become lifelong learners and to reflect and to think critically. The women in particular reported increased levels of confidence and self-esteem: 'I think I am more confident…I speak with authority. I am more confident in my conversation with people', one of the graduates mentioned.

The graduates talked of being more patient with their family members because they had learnt to reflect on other perspectives. They highlighted the importance of remaining positive and optimistic during times of stress in order to resolve conflict in a patient and thoughtful manner:

> Before, family members used to quarrel or have discussions on irrelevant things …we were part of that discussion. Our education at AKU-IED taught us to be reflective and now we can teach our parents; we can convince them to do things differently.

Another way in which the MEd programme affected the graduates' daily lives was in terms of their awareness of healthy lifestyles and their health-seeking behaviour. The graduates noted that they were more aware of healthy eating habits and hygiene practices. Amber (pseudonym) noted that her mental health had improved and Aliya (pseudonym) talked about wanting to work with her students so that they could become 'health ambassadors' to their homes.

Appreciation of Diversity

Although Karachi is a more cosmopolitan environment with people from all parts of Pakistan and where a variety of religions and cultures are found in a small geographical area, it is still possible to remain isolated within the norms of one's own culture. This is even more prevalent in the rural areas in Pakistan, where people live and work within their own micro-cultures with limited interaction with those from outside their village. The diverse culture at AKU-IED fostered an increased respect and appreciation for other religions, cultures, and traditions: 'When I came here, I met people, from GB, Chitral and different districts of Karachi. Even one of my class-fellows belonged to Afghanistan. I came to know different things from him as well'. Similarly, another graduate stated:

> I was very conservative in my beliefs, especially as regards to Muslim and non-Muslim.... Now I feel that I have matured in my outlook and have become more aware of diversity; as human beings, we have to go beyond our biases. We need to care about each other as human beings.

Gender

The graduates also gave examples of changes in relation to gender in their communities. For example, girls were increasingly allowed to participate more fully in school and work environments. Attitudes towards women had changed over time so that they were more women-friendly. These changes began with changes in graduates' own attitudes towards gender issues. One of the graduates said:

> I stayed away from this issue. I did not have interaction with women. But at IED, the environment was such that my mind about gender changed. [I learnt that] I can learn not only from males but also from

> females and my learning is much better if I share with others… Before I used to think that women should just work at home, they do not need to work outside. But now I think that women's education is as important as men's.

Mariya (pseudonym), who came from a very conservative village in GB, emphasised the importance of persisting in the face of difficult environments and making an effort to change them. She used every social occasion in her community to raise awareness about gender issues. Dilip, who was from a rural community in Sindh, talked about the status of his family in his community and how that had enabled others to follow the family's lead in sending their girls to school.

Participants in one of the focus groups in GB provided examples of the ways in which the District Education Office had become more women friendly over the last 14 years:

> There is a lot of change in the Directorate office. A couple of years back we used to pass by this gate but we never went inside. Now look at this scene [pointing to the four women chatting comfortably with their male colleagues]. Now my colleagues and I work in the Directorate.

But the women were also realistic about what society demanded of them in terms of the roles they had to play. Although they thought that they might have influenced the ways in which their children thought about gender roles, they realised that the structural constraints that they worked in could not change dramatically; despite their increased agency, they still had to work within the gender constructs in their communities:

> What I feel is that after MEd, we have had to do all the work that we did before because that is expected from us. Even if I return at 9 o'clock at night, it does not matter. My role changes as soon as I

> return home, my role shifts to a mother and wife. I can do the chores after quarrelling or I can do them happily, but I have to do them. That is the reality, and we cannot change everyone.

Women who completed the programme also had to juggle with family opposition as well as the responsibilities of being primary caregivers to their children and to the elderly in their extended families. They described the role of STEP and AKU-IED staff in making it all possible and emphasised the importance of the community of care that they experienced at AKU-IED.

The graduates chose to enroll in the MEd despite all the challenges they faced. A majority had completed at least one graduate degree (for some, multiple degrees) before enrolling in the programme.

The next section describes what they thought was different about this MEd.

Making the Choice to Enrol in AKU-IED's MEd

The graduates were asked why they had decided to enroll in this particular programme. Every graduate interviewed answered this question by emphasising both the difference in approach to teaching and learning as well as the environment for personal growth offered by AKU-IED. They thought that AKU-IED had taught them to be reflective, to think critically and to develop a broad vision for change. Thus, the graduates were serving in their communities as ambassadors for education and social change. One of the graduates from Balochistan stated:

> In my opinion, AKU-IED does a lot for personal development in addition to professional development. If I had done it from somewhere else, perhaps I would have learnt professionally but would not have

> had personal development, especially in terms of vision, or breadth of thinking.

Likewise, another graduate reported:

> If I keep all my other education on one side and AKU-IED on the other then I see a distinct difference. Like when I came here, I understood what higher education really is; how can we look at our life in a different way; how can we critically analyse everything; and what is the actual purpose of education? I learn about it all at AKU-IED.

Discussion

In newspaper articles and in popular media around the world, getting a graduate degree is seen as the road to greater economic success for the individual and the nation. Students buy into this rhetoric by enrolling in greater numbers in programmes with higher economic returns such as business or technology. The graduates in this study knew they were not in a profession that would give a high monetary return. They were seeking the high social returns associated with the MEd degree from AKU-IED.

If these graduates had undervalued the importance of this Master's degree in Education due to poor public information about non-market private as well as social returns, then they might not have invested the time and energy in acquiring what was for most, a second or third graduate degree. Certainly,, they expected to be promoted after acquiring the MEd, and most were. But they were also seeking the benefits that were 'over and above the income effects' (McMahon, 2009, p.122) of education: personal growth; a passion for serving their communities; a deep engagement with their professions; an increase in respect and status in their families and communities; and an opportunity to continue learning.

As discussed in the literature review section of this chapter, private non-market benefits of higher education are non-monetary benefits that accrue to individuals, such as more productive use of leisure time, the ability to continue learning, improved health outcomes and greater overall satisfaction and happiness in life (McMahon, 2009). Graduates in this study used their private time to discuss the importance of education and to continue to learn. They emphasised the ways in which the MEd programme taught them to learn, to think reflectively and critically and to use technology to enhance learning not only in their classrooms but also in their own personal lives.

One of the private non-market benefits is the ability of graduates to manage their time better McMahon (2009). Women graduates in this study gave examples of how they were better time managers and were able to allocate their time between their personal and professional lives more efficiently. They also gave examples of how their own learning impacted the ways in which they supported the learning of their children, by engaging them in active learning and hands-on strategies rather than by limiting learning to rote methods.

Although this study did not directly ask graduates if they were happier after completing the programme, they talked of increased satisfaction in their personal and professional lives. Often, they used the word 'passion' to describe this increase in enjoyment:

> MEd programme also stimulated passion in us. One is job responsibility that I have to do it. But it is also commitment and passion ...with commitment, passion is also important. You need to enjoy your work. The MEd programme has ignited my passion.

Alongside passion and commitment to work, the graduates described a transformation in their attitudes, which affected them at personal, professional, and community levels. At a personal level, the graduates reported becoming more tolerant of dissenting opinions within their families and an ability to use their newly acquired problem-solving skills and confidence levels to resolve such issues. At a professional level, the graduates described resolving problems related to their classroom practices or to increasing participation and engagement of the community.

In addition to the positive benefits that classmates gain from enriching discussions within and outside the higher education classroom, the development of tolerant and respectful attitudes is the building block of human rights support (Bynner, 2003). While Sumaira (pseudonym) from Skardu and Sultan (pseudonym) from Balochistan described the activities they had undertaken to increase this tolerance in their communities, others talked about informal conversations with families and community members about the importance of respecting diverse opinions and cultures and the importance of treating all human beings as equal. These attitudes were reflected in the graduates' work in raising awareness of gender and health issues, in increasing the participation of girls in education and in discussing the importance of equal rights for both men and women in the community.

Helliwell and Putnam (1999) show that higher education is correlated with measures of social capital, such as trust building and participation in community work. Similarly, graduates in this study had earned the respect and trust of their communities, which enabled them to effectively bring about change. From Galib's (pseudonym) description of how a rural community that refused development work had begun to take an interest in its schools to Nabat's (pseudonym) story of the ways in which the District Education Office in GB had become more women-friendly; the social benefits of higher education are not limited to the graduates' own lives but extend to their communities as well.

The impact of these graduates also has the potential to have multiplier effects in the long-term. The Endogenous Development Theory (McMahon, 2009) referred to earlier proposes that high economic growth leads to high levels of education (human capital), which in turn, creates more human capital and pushes out the knowledge frontier.

As graduates of the programme continue to educate teachers and contribute to research and dissemination of new knowledge, the outcomes of their work can be felt not only in terms of economic benefits to them individually and to the country, but also by the increase in the number of teachers who have a passion for bringing about change. For example, four graduates in interior Sindh had joined the government's mission to create community colleges aimed at providing access to higher education across the province of Sindh. The graduates in the study who intended to enroll in PhD programmes also contributed to contextually relevant research.

Those working in schools and public universities also continue to generate benefits for themselves as well as for the wider society in Pakistan. A concrete example of the long-term benefits of higher education can be seen in the graduates' description of the changes in the District Education Office (DEO) in Gilgit. Over a period of 14 years, each graduate who joined the DEO's office, and each new project that was brought in, had an incremental impact on the work environment. In 2014, the work environment was a lot more woman-friendly than it had been in 2000.

The community work described by the graduates also points to changes in demand for education in the community. In a remote village in GB, Galib convinced his conservative community to allow an externally funded project to establish schools and worked at engaging the community so that they now contribute 50 per cent of the cost of running the schools. In Interior Sindh, all four of AKU-IED's graduates were snapped up by the relatively new Institute for

Business Administration. In Balochistan, Sultan established an NGO that would help establish support schools in areas that were affected by conflict. In Gilgit-Baltistan (Skardu), Sumaira also established a not-for-profit school for children with disabilities. All of these changes signal an increase in the demand for quality education, and indicate financial as well as educational benefits to the graduates' communities.

Conclusion

This study provides evidence of the beneficial effects of investments in quality higher education for individuals and societies. Stories of individuals from rural Balochistan, Gilgit-Baltistan, and Interior Sindh as well as those from the more urban city of Karachi indicate that the value of the credential does not lie only in its economic returns. It leads to an overall satisfaction and passion for bringing about change and contributing to human and social development. The graduates completed the programme, sometimes despite facing great odds, and continue to contribute to their communities after their return.

Despite their increased agency and confidence, graduates struggled with the structural constraints presented by their institutions and the educational policies of the government. Since graduates did not have the 'substantial freedoms' (Nussbaum, 2011, p.19) to bring about sustained change, they were not able to fully realise their potential. The Capabilities Approach, pioneered by Amartia Sen (1999), a development economist, argues that the capabilities that an individual has (i.e. the ability to do or to be), depends on the 'nature of social arrangements' (p. 263). Sen argues that this 'freedom to be' is central to development because a nation's development can only be determined by the individual's freedom that individuals enjoy. It is because of this freedom that individuals can further engage in their own and their country's development.

A concrete example of the institutional constraints faced by the graduates was the policy of frequent transfers of teachers. Graduates also identified the need for greater support from head teachers and educational managers for educational reforms; as Imran from Balochistan pointed out, the graduates do not have the authority or power to take others with them in the change process. Policy-makers in Pakistan could resolve these structural constraints by involving teachers and AKU-IED's MEd graduates in identifying the institutional support and policies needed to bring about sustained improvement in the quality of education.

The results of this study underline the importance of educating potential students and their families about the private and public non-market returns to higher education so that they do not underestimate the returns to an investment in higher education. This would also help potential female students to gain the support of their families to enroll in AKU-IED's programmes, thus reducing another structural constraint faced by these students.

The study could also be used to inform policies about the benefits of investment in higher education. Disseminating it at the local, regional, and national levels could enable policy-makers and funding agencies to understand the widespread returns on investments in quality higher education.

Future research could include longitudinal studies of the graduates and their communities, in order to understand the long-term impact of the programme as well as factors that affect the graduates' abilities to bring about change. A research study estimating the non-market private and social benefits may contribute quantitative evidence of these returns.

References

Baum, S., Ma, J., & Payea, K., *Education Pays 2013: The Benefits of Higher Education for Individuals and Society.* (College Board<https://trends.collegeboard.org/sites/default/files/education-pays-2013-full-report.pdf> accessed September 9, 2014).

Bloom, D.E., Canning, D. & Chan, K., *Higher Education and Economic Development in Africa* (Washington, DC: World Bank, 2006).

Bynner, J., Dolton, P., Feinstein, L., Makepeace, G., Malmberg, L. & Woods, L., *Revisiting the Benefits of Higher Education* (London: Bedford Group for Life Course Statistical Studies, Institute of Education, University of London, 2003).

Helliwell, J.F. & Putnam, R.D., Education *and Social Capital* (Working Paper No. 7121) (New York: National Bureau of Economic Research, 1999).

McMahon, W.W., 'Recent advances in measuring the social and individual benefits of education', *International Journal of Educational Research,* 27/6, (1997), 449–531.

McMahon, W.W., *Higher Learning, Greater Good: The Private and Social Benefits of Higher Education* (Baltimore: Johns Hopkins University Press, 2009).

Nussbaum, M., *Creating Capabilities* (Cambridge, MA: Harvard University Press, 2011).

Perna, L.H., 'The private benefits of higher education: An examination of the earnings premium', *Research in Higher Education,* 44/4, (2003), 451–472.

Psacharopoulos, G., 'The economic returns to higher education in twenty-five countries', *Higher Education,* 1/2, (1972), 141–158.

Sen, A., *Development as Freedom* (Oxford, UK: Oxford University Press, 1999).

Stake, R.E., 'Qualitative case studies' in Denzin and Lincoln, eds. *The Sage Handbook of Qualitative Research,* (3rd Edition, Thousand Oaks: California, 2005).

Thomas, G., 'A typology for the case study in social science following a review of definition, discourse and structure', *Qualitative Inquiry, 17/6,* (2011), 511–521.

Notes

1. Adapted from McMahon, W. W. (2009). *Higher learning, greater good. The private and social benefits of higher education*. Baltimore: Johns Hopkins University Press. Figure 4.1, p. 129.
2. http://www.iba-suk.edu.pk/ibasuk/community/wpaboutC.C.aspx

PART III:
UNDERSTANDING ISSUES IN EDUCATIONAL GOVERNANCE

9

Educational Governance Conundrum: Decision-Making Structure, Processes, and Outcomes

Takbir Ali and *Dilshad Ashraf*

Introduction

Pakistan is the sixth most populous country in the world with a population of nearly 200 million people. The country is facing critical development challenges with some of the lowest development indicators in the world. In particular, the education system faces a myriad of problems such as access and student achievement across primary and secondary levels. Inequalities in access, quality, and educational outcomes persist across gender, across income, between urban and rural schools, and among the country's four provinces which can explain the country's low performance in achieving its universal primary education targets by 2015 (Aziz et al., 2014). Besides inadequate teacher preparation and teacher attendance at schools, deficient processes and structures of educational governance stand out as a major challenge hampering education reform initiatives in the country (Aziz et al., 2014). Millions of out-of-school boys and girls and poor learning outcomes of schooling further accentuate prompt action and reform towards governance related bottlenecks and challenges to improve the provision of quality education in the country.

Implementation of the large-scale, multi-faceted Strengthening Teacher Education in Pakistan (STEP) project required us to interact with a wide variety of educational stakeholders ranging from top level bureaucracy to bottom level beneficiaries, including teachers, communities, and children. This interaction brought us face-to-face with complex situations related to educational governance and management at different levels. It was evident that the complexity of educational governance and its structures had a bearing on the functioning of education systems and the children they serve. Use and abuse of power and authority within educational governance called for critical examination of educational governance, structures, and processes.

This chapter reports on a large-scale study that explored educational governance with a focus on decision-making processes, structures, and outcomes in and around schools in Pakistan. It is organised in four sections. The first section explains the background with specific reference to issues of educational governance and examines relevant literature. The second section describes the research questions and the methodology employed for the study. The third section presents research findings which illustrate relationships and the power struggle between different groups in the decision-making processes, and outcomes in educational governance. The last section details key conclusions derived from the findings and its implications for policy and practice. A set of recommendations with regards to improvement of educational governance concludes the chapter.

Literature Review

Defining Governance

Good governance is an elusive term, but one simple definition of governance is the 'process of decision-making and the process by which decisions are implemented (or not implemented)' (UNESCAP, 2000). Governance also refers to the set of norms, values, and rules of the game through which public affairs are managed in a manner that is transparent, participatory, inclusive, and responsive to the needs of society. By extension, 'good' governance is further defined by characteristics such as political accountability, bureaucratic transparency, exercise of legitimate power, freedom of association and participation, freedom of information and expression, sound fiscal accountability, respect for human rights, and respect for the rule of law (Hope, 2009). Reflecting on these definitions, this paper maintains that educational governance constitutes the decision-making processes involving competing, conflicting, cooperative interests amongst various education stakeholders (Hufty, 2011).

It is uncertain whether governance is a necessary prerequisite, an outcome, or a process of growth and development. Shepherd (2000) challenges the notion of a 'one-best-way-model' of governance that leads to development. Rather he argues that such a model fails to account for multiple pathways to and states of development. The research reported in this chapter did not delve into governance from developmental theory perspective; rather it examined how educational governance in the context of Pakistan is structured and influenced by existing socio-political structures, distribution and access to power and resources, the relationships between groups who do and do not have access to power and resources, and the processes that sustain, reinforce, create, or transform these relationships.

Educational Governance in Pakistan

Educational governance has undergone major structural changes over a period of time. Expansion in the governance system i.e. the establishment of new institutions, departments, functionaries, management structure created at central, provincial, district, and tehsil levels, and the huge workforce engaged in governance, corresponding to demographic realties, explains the structural evolution of educational governance in the country. Nevertheless, the system of educational governance at all levels, despite all the structural changes, has either suffered from stagnation or even deteriorated in terms of its outcomes. Reforms in educational governance envisaged in successive education policies never got materialised. The question that arises here is why the structural changes, resources, and efforts invested in governance reform from time to time do not get translated into improved outcomes?

Examining the history and evolution of local government reforms in Pakistan, from the British rule to the present, Cheema et al., (2005) suggest that such reforms in Pakistan have been promoted to centralise the power of a non-representative centre. For example, the responsibilities delegated to the district governments are merely nominal; the district government officials lack the power and autonomy to exercise authority.

Review of educational reform history indicates that major structural reforms were introduced in 2001 under the Devolution of Power Plan, 2001 purportedly to empower local governments. Four reasons are generally cited for the establishment and use of local governance: to depoliticise governance; to create a new group of political elite at the lower level; to legitimise political authority in the face of international scrutiny; and to undermine federalism by bypassing the provincial political, administrative, and fiscal powers (International Crisis Group, 2004).

It is widely accepted that decentralisation in Pakistan has not succeeded in empowering people at the local level. Decentralisation, when imposed from top-down in the context of weak formal institutions of governance, can produce new forms of patron-clientelism and informal governance at the local level. The newly created political officials (at the lower tiers) are then provided the resources to build clientelistic networks resulting in new variations of 'elite capture' (Eaton et al., 2011). Research on governance structures in Pakistan strongly suggests a reinforcement of local forms of informal governance at the village level (Malik, 2009). Local notables who held positions of power in prior forms of informal governance then also acquired official positions in the political system—such as postings at the district-level government—as a result of the Devolution Plan. Thus, traditional personalised forms of governance have neither been dismantled nor displaced due to devolution; rather these forms have acquired official sanction.

Educational Governance and Decision-Making in Pakistan

The literature on educational governance and decision-making in Pakistan is sparse. Studies on the educational sector explore governance and bureaucratic structures, and the resulting outcomes in terms of student learning achievements, and literacy levels. However, there have been relatively few studies undertaken on how decisions are made within educational governance, particularly at the lower tiers—including the school and the district level.

Malik (2007) examined the decision-making systems for the delivery of primary educational services after the 2001 Devolution of Power Plan. Though he incorporated models and theories of political science and political economy within his analysis, Malik (2007) did not comprehensively and fully explore the power relations that mediate decision-making, especially at the lower (district, tehsil, and school) tiers of governance. His research did not further delve into how decision-making processes disenfranchise or marginalise groups according to race, ethnicity, caste, or gender.

This situation described above calls for investigation into the decision-making patterns of educational governance including the role of important stakeholders, dynamics of local, national, and international agents and their impact on teachers, schools, and communities. Another important factor that needs immediate attention is the effect of gender, ethnicity, religion, and caste on the access and quality of education.

Research Questions and Methodology

In order to investigate and understand decision-making processes and structures in educational governance, the study was guided by the following questions:

1. Who are the dominant actors (or groups of actors) in decision-making? Who makes the decisions?
2. How do the groups interact? What are the forms of these interactions? How do the interactions affect educational outcomes?
3. What decision-making structures affect school governance relationships within and between the provincial, district, and school levels?
   a. How do external actors (IFIs or externally-funded projects, such as STEP) impact the local dynamics of school governance?

b. How do the existing decision-making patterns impact the lives of teachers, students and the community?
c. How are decisions made within schools?

4. a. What knowledge and whose knowledge is valued during the decision-making processes in educational governance?
b. How do gender, class, language, ethnicity, or caste effect decision-making in educational governance?

The focus of the study i.e. examining decision making processes within education governance in a complex socio-political context warranted the use of critical ethnography research method. However, limited time for the field work and researchers' fewer possible visits to the field challenged the prospects of collecting rich and thick data—a distinctive characteristic of ethnographic study. Nevertheless, to maintain a stance of ethnographic research, the study used a quasi-ethnographic approach, which enabled the study to explore the respondents' experiences from a deeper level. The focal site of our research was the school, around which we examined decision-making processes and governance. We engaged key stakeholders as research participants to explore their perceptions for developing a richer and more holistic understanding of the processes, structures and the key actors involved in decision-making in educational governance.

The primary sources of data included semi-structured focus group discussions and interviews of teachers, parents, students, head teachers, government district officials, local notables and influential members of each village/community. From each school, the head teacher, five teachers, five to six students, four to six parents, at least two to three government officials, and several local notables were selected either for an interview or for participation in a focus group discussion.

The secondary sources of data included documents such as government education policies, official curriculum documents, electronic and print news media, school policies, school attendance and enrolment records, school development plans, school meeting minutes, school organisation charts, and other official school records. Collecting data from documentary sources allowed the researchers to evaluate the data to increase the validity and credibility of the findings.

Geographic Location and Sampling

The study was carried out in thirteen districts from the provinces of Sindh, Balochistan, and Gilgit-Baltistan. The primary data collection sites were the primary schools located within each district and the corresponding district government offices (for interviews with government stakeholders). In total, there were thirteen primary schools (five boys' primary schools; eight girls' primary schools) from the three provinces. While selecting the schools, special consideration was given to maintaining gender, regional and urban/rural balance. Where possible, preference was given to schools which had a student population with diverse language, ethnic, and socio-economic backgrounds.

By using a purposive sampling approach, the sample was carefully selected to understand agencies and tensions that participants experience in their daily lives, in terms of decision-making processes in educational governance. The research participants were selected based on the various layers of decision-making levels that influence decision-making patterns in and around schools, including provincial education secretaries, district education administration, teachers, head teachers, community members, parents, and students. Table 1 presents a summary of the research sample.

Table 1: Number of Respondents Participating in the Research Study

Type of respondent	Constituencies and Number of Respondents														
	Education Departments			Teacher Education Institutions			Schools			Community			Other		
	M	F	Total	M	F	Total	M	F	Total	M	F	Total	M	F	Total
Directors	07	02	09	02		02	-	-	-	-	-	-	-	-	-
DEOs	11		11	-	-	-	-	-	-	-	-	-	-	-	-
ADOs & Supervisors	10	11	21	-	-	-	-	-	-	-	-	-	-	-	-
Administrators/Principals	-	-	-	01		01	-	-	-	-	-	-	-	-	-
Head teachers	-	-	-	-	-	-	05	08	13	-	-	-	-	-	-
Teachers	-	-	-	01	02	03	24	35	59	-	-	-	-	-	-
Students	-	-	-	-	-	-	27	42	69	-	-	-	-	-	-
SMC members	-	-	-	-	-	-	-	-	-	20	30	50	-	-	-
Parents	-	-	-	-	-	-	-	-	-	34	48	82	-	-	-
Teacher Union representatives	-	-	-	-	-	-	-	-	-	-	-	-	02		02
Politicians	-	-	-	-	-	-	-	-	-	-	-	-	04		04
Notables	-	-	-	-	-	-	-	-	-	-	-	-	04		04
Total	**28**	**13**	**41**	**04**	**02**	**06**	**56**	**85**	**141**	**54**	**78**	**132**	**10**		**10**

Findings and Discussion

Data analysis helped in recognising several recurring themes. Key insights from the study present a holistic account of educational governance by assessing decision-making processes, structures, and outcomes.

A cursory perusal of decision-making processes suggests that actors at all levels tend to either make decisions arbitrarily, erratically, or under political duress. This chapter maintains the definition of a decision as a 'specific commitment to action' (Mintzberg, Raisinghani & Theoret, 1976, p. 246). Unstructured decision-making processes are defined as 'decision processes that have not been encountered in quite the same form and for which no predetermined and explicit set of ordered responses exists in the organisation' (ibid). The study's findings indicate the prevalence of 'unstructured', arbitrary decision-making practice across all tiers of governance. Furthermore, the absence of proper communication apparently has made the unstructured decision-making process circular and self-reproducing. The study reveals that the arbitrary and unstructured decision-making processes reinforce existing social structures and marginalisation of certain communities in the education sector.

Power Bases in Decision-Making in Education

The data analysis indicated the presence of four discernible and distinct social groups within the sphere of educational governance. Each of these groups has access to power and resources, albeit in varying degree, from which they derive the authority and ability to make and implement decisions. However, the relationships and interactions between these groups are unstable and indecisive; they simultaneously compete and collude. The dynamics between these groups produce decision-making processes and decision outcomes. In the ensuing section, we will examine each power group, the extent/expanse of its domain, the constituent elements of each group, the internal dynamics within and amongst the groups, how each of the power group individually exerts influence on decision-making process and decision outcomes in educational governance, and the nexus between and among the four groups that determines how decisions are made and the outcomes of these decisions.

Bureaucracy

Bureaucracy[1] as a strong power base is constituted by the bureaucrats sitting at the helm of educational affairs. Decision-making authority within bureaucracy and implementation is meant to proceed from the top to the lower levels of management. The evidence gleaned in the study suggests that the bureaucratic power group overwhelmingly and disproportionately maintains a firm stranglehold on authority and power in making-decisions with regards to teachers and head teachers recruitment, education and development, deployment, promotion, and accountability (reward and punishment); utilisation and appropriation of financial resources; procurement and supply of materials and equipment; curriculum and textbook development and revision; and student assessment and promotions, and donor-funded reform programmes or projects. These are some important areas around which decision-making and enforcement regularly occurs in educational governance.

Politicians and Community Notables/Elites

Though politically-oriented wealthy and local community elites[2] constitute a miniscule fraction of the country's total population, they yield disproportionate power and control over most resources. By virtue of these politicians' and community notables' active engagement in politics and power play within the political system of the country, their influence extends to decision-making processes around schools and educational governance.

The data analysis suggests that the community elites or leaders derive their power from the privileged history of the families, tribes, caste, religious, and ethnic backgrounds to which they belong, their inherited wealth, and their social and cultural capital. These individuals command a great deal of respect in the community which allows them to leverage their authority and power on decision-making in educational governance and other spheres of life. They influence decisions in governance in education through manipulations of situations and using various overt or covert coercive tactics. The various influences, many of them necessarily linked with the socio-cultural and religious norms of the community, are used to make the whole community acquiescent to their demands; members of the community will blindly follow their chief or leader.

In fact, politicians and local community elites hold multiple identities which are fluid and which change with circumstances. More often than not, the community elites and their family members actively participate in politics, contest polls, and easily win seats in the National and Provincial Assemblies of Pakistan and the Senate. Their success in politics is due to the unconditional and unwavering support elites receive from their followers. As a result, community elites also become ministers, advisors, chairman/chairperson of various Standing Committees and Commissions in the National and Provincial Assemblies and the Senate. There is not a single area in education governance which is impervious from their undue influences and interventions. In many cases, the community elites/notables claim ownership of the school buildings because they have either leased or sold out or donated the land to the government on which school building has been built.

Throughout the interviews and focus group discussions across thirteen districts, recurring reference to 'political interference' was made in the contexts of teacher appointment and transfer, manipulation of material resources, including 'school specific budgets' and overall deteriorating quality of education. Except for a few anecdotes about the positive role played by the politicians and community elites in improving education for their communities, the participants, including teachers, head teachers, supervisors, educators, administrators, and senior bureaucrats generally reported these individuals' negative influence on education development. The root cause for many problems such as violation of a merit system, appointments of 'ghost' (or non-existent) teachers, the establishment of 'ghost schools' (non-existent or non-functional schools), nepotism, favoritism, widespread corruption (misuse of resources and authority), are attributed to influences exerted by political and community elites.

Examples of positive patronage of educational endeavours by the community elite surfaced during extensive data collection visits. Such an example from a district of Sindh province here illustrates constructive engagement of community leaders in expanding an equitable provision of education for a rural community.

Mahmood Shah (pseudonym) is an aged, highly respected figure of his tribe. His father had founded the village where there are around 1,500 households today. Mahmood Shah established a small school (initially only for boys) in the village in the outskirts of the district. He himself taught in the school and later on appointed a female teacher who resided in the main town. However, because there were not any roads or transport facilities, it was difficult for her to commute to the school. He arranged a *tanga* (horse carriage) for the teacher's daily commute. He also donated a piece of land, and with the support of the then Education Secretary, he got the school building constructed. He met this secretary during his travel to Mecca (Saudi Arabia) for Hajj (pilgrimage). During this travel he informed the secretary about dedicating a piece of land for the school building. The secretary readily approved the construction of the building and also appointed a teacher. Mahmood Shah said that he made his villagers believe that education was necessary for both boys and girls. They started sending their daughters to the school. Responding to a question, 'Why did you feel that girls' education is important?' he said, 'I have been a teacher myself, therefore, I am aware of the importance of girls' education. If a girl is educated, she would be a better daughter, sister, wife, and mother. So she can have a lasting impact on generations'. Currently in this school, there are 200 students (Grade 1–5), 10 per cent of which are girls, and one teacher works in the school. Mahmood Shah said that he was willing to give more land for the school building if the authorities cooperate and upgrade the school up to the middle level.

Another example here from the data will elucidate how the community elites with different identities can positively ensure education for the community. Mr Rehmat Ali (pseudonym), a senior political leader with a long political career, and a member of a family that ruled the area for centuries, was elected as a member of the Gilgit-Baltistan Legislative Assembly. Also working as a minister he reported his positive role in expansion of education for his people by opening eighteen new schools. As a proponent of merit-based appointment of teachers, he made sure that the process of assessing these teachers' candidacy included tests and interviews. Despite all these good intentions, Mr Rehmat Ali reported his inability to resolve the issue of teacher shortage. Many teachers, according to him, remained absent soon after their appointment as teachers. He explained:

> A teacher newly appointed disappeared [remained absent] three months after joining the school. If he is not interested then he should resign so that I can appoint another teacher in his place, but he neither gives his resignation nor does he come to school. I cannot take action but the authorities despite being aware of the situation continue to ignore it.

He stated that he raised the teacher absenteeism issue in the Assembly, but the Speaker of the Assembly silenced any discussion on the issue, knowing that many teachers in his and other members' constituencies were not performing their duties properly. Raising the issues in the Assembly potentially would have provoked and angered those teachers and their supporters. As a result, any discussion on teacher absenteeism was essentially censored. Mr Rehmat Ali persistently followed the issue, and as a result, most of the teachers returned to their schools.

Bureaucracy and Politicians: Competing and Colluding

For the political representatives and influential personages in the community there is a strong (self-perceived) justification for their interference and involvement in educational decisions and governance at the management levels. In fact, the dynamics of the relationship between community leaders and people within the bureaucratic structure appear to be complex. On the one hand, when their interests converge or they find an opportunity to agree on a mutually beneficial agenda, they collude. The data contains stories shared by various respondents groups that explain how bureaucrats and community leaders collude in embezzlement of public funds. On the other hand, there seems to be a huge trust deficit between government bureaucrats and the community leadership. The bureaucrats believe that the politicians and other influential individuals in the community neither have the right to directly intervene in the day-to-day business of the education system nor are they trained to make decisions in matters pertaining to teachers' and managers' recruitment, placement, transfer and development, examination or assessment, which is exclusively the domain of the bureaucrats. On the other hand, the politicians and the community leadership think they are better aware of the needs of their people and have the mandate to solve their problems. An excerpt from the interview with a local community leader, who also chairs the local School Management Committee in one of the districts in Sindh, explains the process:

> The power of the public is greater than the power [of decision-making] possessed by the directors. If the directors realise the power of the public and work accordingly it is good for them as well as for the public. We better understand our problems and their solutions. The director and his subordinates are nothing but government servants. I

> am selected [or elected] and empowered by the public. When I raise my voice no bureaucrat in the system can afford to ignore it.

Contrary to the above views, a senior bureaucrat in Balochistan expressed his anger over the political interference in the education system. 'You know very well that in the entire country the Waderas (landlords) and Nawabs (ruling elites) and their agents become members of national and provincial assemblies and they will not think about improvement of the education system. We train the teachers and they come and transfer them to dysfunctional schools for their political gains'. He discussed this further:

> Now after one month we will have elections in Pakistan and again the same people will come into power and occupy assemblies. The stories of corruption in teacher appointment and other areas of governance will begin to resurface. This is why we recruited and trained two thousands teachers before these newly elected political people come to power. My director and I together made this decision. We prepared simple tests focusing on prospective teachers' competence in English language and mathematics. To avoid political pressure, nepotism and favoritism in teacher recruitment, on the same day we marked the tests and prepared the merit list, and displayed the list of selected candidates on the office notice board.

Teacher Unions/Associations

The third power group, though ostensibly peripheral to decision-making in educational governance, is made up of Teacher Unions/Associations, which exerts undue influence on issues related to educational governance through their elected/selected representatives. Teacher Unions/Associations exist and operate at the national, provincial, and district levels. These bodies are not formally recognised as legitimate authorities in day-to-day decision-making in educational governance. However, motivated by their own vested interests, they have been able to create a space for themselves as a strong pressure or lobbying group. They influence not only major educational policy level decisions, but also interfere directly in matters relating to teachers' recruitment, transfer, deployment, and promotion. Generally there prevails a negative perception about the activities and the influences of Teacher Unions/Associations. Their efforts are primarily focused on advancing their own interests, such as raising teacher salaries and benefits, acquiring compensatory allowances, and promoting teachers based on seniority rather than on performance.

Nevertheless, the Teachers Union leaders, interviewed in this study, claimed that their primary mission was to contribute to educational improvement, and their secondary goal was to protect teachers' 'rights' and raise voices against many injustices done to teachers by the bureaucracy or education managers. As described by the association representatives, they get involved in resolving issues arising from such situations as unjustified posting and transfer, delayed promotions, low salaries, professional allowances and annual increments, pension benefits, selection for in-service training, school facilities, and a variety of issues faced by individual teachers on a day-to-day basis. Given the social and institutional structures, policies and practices, individually, teachers cannot protect their rights; rather they have to rely on Teacher Unions/Associations as a collective force to fight against injustices meted out to them by the bureaucracy. The Teacher Association Leaders shared numerous examples to prove how their struggles from their union platform helped protect their legitimate rights as well as address issues faced by them at individual or at teaching community level. One of such examples tends to support the association leaders' viewpoint.

During data collection in this study, the Government Secondary Teachers Association (GSTA) Sindh organised a protest march in front of the Chief Minster's Office at Karachi. The content (translated from Urdu into English) of some of the posters distributed among the participants of the protest read: 'A peaceful and historical protest against the heartless attitude of the Finance and the Education Department of Sindh towards teachers…All courageous secondary school teachers from Sindh are requested to participate in the protest'. The poster contained demands, including: time-scale to junior school teachers; provision of teaching allowances; provision of 25 per cent employment quota for the children of teachers; running scale to untrained teachers; provision of jobs under the condition of death quota for the children of those teachers who expired during their duty; and releasing salaries of newly appointed teachers, to mention a few.

It is obvious that all of the demands revolve around the teachers' personal interest; there is not a single demand for the benefit of children or betterment of the education system. Nevertheless, if some of these demands are justified within the provisions of agreed policy then why are they not fulfilled unless the teachers get out into the streets? This makes the situation more complex if the teachers' demonstration is part of their struggle for achieving their legitimate rights, or tactics used by a vested interest groups to weaken the chain of accountability through the protection of their members.

International Funding and Development Agencies

The fourth power group in educational governance includes NGOs, INGOs, international funding institutions (IFIs) and agencies, and the private sector. Pakistan has heavily relied on external funding from international funding/donor agencies for delivering basic education and improving the quality of educational services. Through or in partnership with these agencies, Pakistan has been able to provide training for teachers and other education stakeholders, build schools, improve facilities, improve curricular materials, develop assessment systems, and engage in overall reform of governance structures. The variety of international funding/donor agencies, which have a long history of and an enduring commitment to supporting education in Pakistan, do exert a leverage on educational policy and practice in the country. In fact, the history of educational reform has been dominated by the efforts on the part of international funding/donor agencies in Pakistan. Without the resources (both financial and technical expertise) provided by the INGOs and funding agencies, Pakistan would not have shown any success in pursuing efforts intended at educational reform and development in the country.

International funding/donor agencies have been influencing educational decisions both at the macro and micro levels. The INGOs and funding/donor agencies and local partners seem to influence decision-making in education significantly in areas related to budget allocation for education, and adopting development strategies. Their initiatives are also aimed at reforming programmes and approaches to improving literacy rates, enhancing the quality of basic education, and restructuring the management to catalyse educational change. There are a long list of donor and aid agencies involved in the educational reform and development in Pakistan. Some of the international financial organisations, such as the World Bank, the Asian Development Bank (ADP), and the International Monitory Fund (IMF), USAID, DFID, DAFATD, GTZ, and UNICEF have wielded greater influence than others. These institutions have their own philosophy of and approach to international development. They have been instrumental in bringing about change in the local bureaucracy's thinking about development or reform in the education sector, and have also persuaded the government to accept a greater role for the private sector in education (regardless of the outcomes).

There are doubts about the World Bank and the IMF to be promoter of neoliberal ideas and ideals rather than development partners or supporters. The efforts and policies, orchestrated by these agencies, have led the federal and provincial governments to launch a campaign to privatise education under the guise of 'public-private partnership' (PPP). A school adaptation campaign in Sindh province currently underway, supported by the World Bank, is an example of how external influences are uncritically translated into education policy and practice at the local level. Subsidies on educational and other social services are rapidly being withdrawn by the federal and provincial governments. One interpretation of privatisation suggests that the government intends to absolve itself from the responsibility of providing education to the citizens, or is using privatisation as an excuse to 'run away' from the challenges of an education system that is plagued by many complex problems and in dire need of reform and repair. Privatising education means that people of the middle and lower middle are forced to expend their meager resources for basic education.

Despite the criticism about the international funding agencies' approach to development or educational reform, generally there is a positive impression about their contribution. For example, The National Curriculum 2006 and materials developed by the Provincial Textbook Boards in Sindh and Balochistan with the support of international funding institutions reflect a notable improvement in areas including gender, diversity, democracy, and local contexts. One of the senior administrators of an institute responsible for curriculum development and implementation reports that his institution is increasingly developing its capacity in designing and producing curricular material which are free of gender and religious biases and which celebrate religious and cultural diversity. For this reason, for the first time ever in the history of the province, a private textbook publisher was recently authorised to develop textbooks for several subjects. He further elaborated on this:

> We guide the authors regarding the way of presenting content in order to make it more inclusive in terms of gender and religion.

The content needs to be presented in a manner that it does not hurt the feelings of minorities. Efforts are being made to make textbooks and other curricular materials free of gender bias, particularly in such subject areas as social studies or languages. It has been observed that in illustrations or images women have been shown mostly as housewives or working in fields, or as teachers, nurses, or doctors, while men have been shown as engineers, athletes, or farmers, etc. These images potentially can have negative imprints on children's minds.

Arenas of Decision-Making in Schools and Educational Governance

The dynamics and relationships between the four power groups seemingly produce a lack of accountability in educational governance, thereby resulting in marginalisation of grass-roots level beneficiaries from decision making structures and processes. There are several key areas which the resulting fractured decision-making processes are severely impacting. Some of these areas where decision-making occurs emphasised in the research data include the following:

Curriculum and Teaching and Learning Processes

The process of curriculum development is unstructured and unsystematic. There is an evident lack of collaboration, cooperation, and linkages between key stakeholders, including curriculum policy makers, content developers, education administration, academics, teachers, students, and communities. The result is ambiguity and frustration amongst stakeholders, adversely affecting the provision and quality of education.

An analysis of Pakistan's education policies since the country's founding, reveals a historical interplay between local and global dynamics around international commitments, religious ideologies, rigid social gendered norms, and politico-social agendas (Ashraf & Kopweh, 2012; Farah & Shera, 2007; Nayar & Salim, 2004). The tension between global, national, and local actors has played a major role in the decision-making processes of curriculum development and determination of language policy. These influences are vividly visible in curriculum development, implementation, and representation. An analysis of the latest National Curriculum (2006) shows that the views and understanding of various stakeholders and debate around the curriculum of primary schools is unclear regarding legitimacy and authority of the state, knowledge and the position of the knower and knowledge seeker. One of the main contested areas of the curriculum is its lack of responsiveness and receptiveness to the diversity of the learners' religious, ethnic, linguistic, and gender backgrounds.

In line with Burton's (1998) lens of implicit and explicit forms of curriculum and with reference to Cuban's (1995) view of multilayer curriculum, this theme takes a critical analysis of pedagogical components of teaching and the textbook contents, student and teacher engagement and language used in the classroom. Morning assembly rituals, displays, seating arrangements, co-curricular activities, and classroom and school environment will also be examined to highlight an interaction between implicit and explicit forms of taught and learnt curriculum. An important focus of this theme will also be to unpack the question, what knowledge and whose knowledge is counted in the process of making and teaching curriculum in the remote districts of Sindh, Balochistan, and Gilgit-Baltistan, three provinces where the study was carried out.

It is important to note that in general there exists a very bleak understanding of curriculum both at the school level and educational management in the districts which makes it difficult even to gather data on specific areas of the curriculum. Most often the respondents' response to curriculum related questions would include 'no' or 'yes' or 'we do not know' but efforts were made to further probe the reasons behind these very brief answers.

The data analysis indicates a consensus among various stakeholders that curriculum development is a state responsibility. Very little awareness, however, was known to these stakeholders within district education governance including teachers about the consequential impact on their role in curriculum development after the 18th Amendment in the Constitution in which the portfolio of education has become a provincial subject. This view is commonly found across the various stakeholders from teachers to district education officers. Analysis also reveals nominal awareness of some middle level management officials about the shifting responsibility of curriculum development from federal to provincial governments. However, what is entailed in curriculum development with this constitutional change has not dawned on the district governance team as yet. In one of the districts the District Education Officer (DEO) stated, 'The development of the curriculum was the responsibility of the federal government. Now this responsibility has shifted to the provincial government but I have no idea how and who are involved in the process of curriculum development'. In another district a head teacher expressed his concerns for his lack of understanding of the curriculum in these words:

> I feel that at every level of education structure including teachers and educational manager curriculum is an obscure subject. We face issues in the understanding of curriculum as there is no any channel of dissemination of the curriculum content and information.

At times implications for a stagnant curriculum surfaced as a key concern about quality and relevance of education. The quote also raises another concern about lack of communication around the 'what' and 'how' of the curriculum. The data analysis, therefore, suggests a varying nature of understanding of curriculum among the district education management and at the grass-roots level in the schools. For the majority of teachers curriculum is merely a textbook which is provided to the children by the education department. These textbooks are considered the only source of knowledge and hence teaching and learning all revolves around a textbook. The absence of these textbooks badly constrains the teaching-learning process in the classroom. During the research, the late arrival of textbooks was shared as one of the major concerns by some teachers. Teachers' interpretation of curriculum and curriculum implementation is quite obvious in the quote from a male teacher's interview, 'Yes, we follow curriculum as we are trying to teach all the content given in the textbooks. We are supposed to cover all the content provided in the textbooks to prepare students for the exam.' Another teacher in the same school stated:

> No, I have not seen any other document but textbooks and I only use books to teach.... Sometimes I bring leaves and small plants to teach students science but it is hard to do so for other subjects as many concepts and ideas are very different from the rural life and the environment.

The finding of the data shows that the process of curriculum development is flimsy. It lacks a synergistic approach of linking the key stakeholders, which includes curriculum policy makers, content developers, education administration, academics, teachers, students, and the community. The complexity of the curriculum development process and lack of proper communication may also be associated with the post 18th Amendment enhanced responsibility with insufficient capacity for the provinces to develop curriculum development processes.

Critical observation of the schooling process during the study identified manifestations of what Burton (1998) has viewed as implicit and explicit forms of curriculum and what Cuban (1995) has referred to as multi-layer curriculum. The research team's day-long presence in the focused schools explains the complications and influences implicit in the curriculum development process. Analysis of this rich data reveals the complexity of curriculum development in the schools which is heavily influenced by political interests, historical legacies, and dominant ideologies. Importantly, the demographic data of all schools in the study indicate ever persistent gender, ethnic, religious and linguistic diversity. This diversity, while it can be regarded as a strength, but lack of required preparedness of schools, teachers and district-based management staff to use this forte seemed to create a state of confusion. This challenge is more observable in the schools which have a significant number of students from religious minorities. In some schools, these 'non-Muslims' including Hindu and Christian students are in the majority. Regardless of significant diversity in school demographics, the morning assembly begins with verses from the Holy Qur'an and the subject 'Islamiyat' (subject about Islam) is taught across the schools. In the schools in Umerkot of Sindh where approximately 98 per cent students are Hindu, the morning assembly is conducted on the usual pattern with the recitation of the Holy Qur'an. An explanation for this by the head teacher was all about conformity to the officially approved norms of the morning assembly. A deviation, according to some respondents, could call for strong resentment. The issues of competing interests of state and non-state parties, as well as their agreement on other issues have created a rupture between the school community and the educational apparatus of the state. When the same issue was raised with the District Education Officer (DEO) he responded:

> I understand that there should be equal opportunities for all religious communities to practice their faith on the basis of equity. But in the

> schools under my jurisdiction I cannot allow Hindu majority schools to recite Gita in the assembly in public. If I will allow, the Moulvi (religious cleric) of the neighbouring Mosque will issue a decree against me of being a heretic and my survival both in terms of job and life will be difficult.

The sphere of authority of the district official management, as explained in the quote above, is surely curtailed when it comes to decisions around changing morning assembly rituals and school norms. A greater challenge would be around presenting some curricular alternatives to the students from religious minorities. The secondary school curriculum allows students with other religious backgrounds to study 'ethics' as a subject, an alternative to studying Islamiyat. This option is absent in the primary school curriculum where every student regardless of his/her religious background has to study Islamiyat. None of the respondents from the district-based governance hierarchy were able to offer an explanation about this matter. Some responded by equating the study of Islamiyat by students from Hindu and Christian communities with studying any other subject. A critical analysis of the stakeholders' perspective on this issue reveals a general 'pretense of ignorance' with little attempt to recognise the inherent incongruities and complexities of the situation. It was also observed that school cultures encouraged these students' participation in Muslim religious ceremonies related events in the school.

Discussions with students and other respondent also reveal a deliberate attempt for integration in the dominant majority's norms through convergence of their respective religious identities into one homogenous group as 'non-Muslim'. In one school, Hindu girls happily reported their ability to participate in such events. The teachers also expressed their appreciation for such attempts. Nonetheless, the data analysis reveals far-reaching consequences of not according due diligence to the issue around recognition of religious diversity in both explicit and implicit forms of curriculum. In their discussion, a group of all Muslim girls shared their preferential practice of not befriending 'non-Muslim' girls. Some of them also shared that they would not like to share edibles with them. A mother, during a focus group discussion, also acknowledged her daughter's approach towards exclusive friendship with Muslim girls and also explained how she counseled her for adopting an attitude of respect towards her classmates with different religious backgrounds. This exclusion and marginalisation, however, calls for an in-depth inquiry.

An example of a school with a huge dropout of Hindu girls at the transition from primary to lower secondary classes can be explained as one implication of the situation. In another instance, the school reported an instruction of an 'Apa' (an expression of respect for a big sister), non-state benefactor/patron, of admitting only Muslim girls to school. Such dropouts and selective admission rules indeed contradict with Article 25 A of the constitution which requires the state to guarantee education to all its citizens. At the grass-roots level stakeholders including teachers, community, students, and parents perceive ideological and religious perspectives of the curriculum as infringing on the personal beliefs of diverse ethnic, religious, and gender-based groups, particularly trespassing on the identity and agency of minorities.

Another important field of inquiry into the policy and practices around religious diversity also emerged from the confusion prevailing among the school and parent community. The state of confusion can be associated with no visible state policy to respond to the needs of a diverse population. A parent's perspective on diversity is an example of confusion and illusion around schools' practices and unwritten policies about the diversity:

> They [religious minorities] are living here; hence they [Christians] should have some knowledge about the local religion [Islam]. Other than that, parents should make them aware about their own religious beliefs in their home. Hence, there is no need for a separate syllabus for religious subjects.

The expectation of adherence to the majority remains a visible perspective among the teacher community as well. It is also worth noting that the teachers held a view that not providing an option to study another subject for non-Muslim student, was a way of promoting inclusion and minimising differences amongst students. One of the teachers stated, 'If there is a separate book and curriculum for them [religious minorities], then this will create problems. There will have to be a separate class for them and it would create religious differences among the students.'

To follow one standardised curriculum by all diverse religious groups is being perceived as an effective means of religious harmony and tolerance. In other words, suppressing the unique ethnic, religious or linguistic identities of various social groups provides greater unity, in this view, as compared to allowing each group to articulate their identity freely. However, the minority groups reluctantly shared their frustration and helplessness to follow the given textbooks and curriculum. One of the parents said:

> We are poor people as well as we are in the minority in the village. We have to follow and send our children to school as there is not any other option. We have never been asked about what our children should be taught and neither have we expressed our disagreement as it would create problems for our community.

Another parent belonging to the Hindu community stated:

> There is a separate subject of 'Ethics' for higher classes at matric level for non-Muslims as a substitute for Islamiyat, but there is no such option for primary students, therefore our children are compelled to study Islamiyat, otherwise they will lose 100 marks in the final exams.

The data analysis indicates that developing a curriculum which should address the plurality and diversity of society is being compromised both at the stage of development and its implementation at the school level. It seems that in the absence of a strong formal structure for decision-making at the state level the informal non-state regional and local social-religious strikers impose their will both at the district and school levels. In this scenario, the majority groups try to assimilate the minority groups into a wider communal structure by playing down the independent identities of minority groups under the notions of 'social harmony' and 'peaceful coexistence'.

This indicates that the overall socio-political, economic, ideological, and historical legacies influence the curriculum development and teaching in the context of the study. This also shows that the individuals and minority groups in the current context of Pakistan are fearful in negotiating and implementing their agency where curriculum and textbook content differ from their basic social, cultural, and religious beliefs and values. The study with its limited scope has highlighted the complexity of the curriculum related issue in the local context which also warrants another research study into how these issues affect communities at large.

Students' Enrolment, Absenteeism, and Dropouts

Schools, district government officials, and teachers do not have any systematic and structured procedures for maintaining and managing records of student enrolment, absenteeism, and dropouts. The absence of proper school management is a problem for monitoring and accountability in the education sector. Ambiguous, disorganised documentation and records obscure the issue of students' participation and attendance in schools. Such unstructured management impedes the development of a monitoring system that holds teachers accountable for performance of students and the quality of teaching.

Our field-research reveals significant and frequent discrepancies between official (recorded) enrolment, official (recorded) student attendance, and observed attendance rates. Firstly, student attendance is inconsistent; secondly, teachers' strategies for recording attendance are highly unstructured. The misrepresentation of already irregular patterns obfuscates the issue of student enrolment and attendance. Increasing enrolment and attendance is a primary concern for policy-makers, politicians, development practitioners and researchers, and a fundamental quantitative indicator of good educational governance. However, our findings suggest that in assessing and calculating net enrolment and attendance rate, what local Pakistani teachers would classify as enrolment and attendance does not meet the standard definitions for these two indicators.[3]

Through interviews with students, teachers, and parents, we gathered data on student enrolment and attendance in schools. During the days of the field visits, we observed that attendance was approximately 50 per cent of the total enrolment in all the schools; moreover, the observed attendance did not correspond with the numbers teachers had recorded in attendance records.

Enrolled students attend school with high irregularity; for example, some students attend on average one day every week; others will attend for two weeks, and then leave school for another two weeks; this pattern will continue repetitively. These students are receiving an incomplete education, though they satisfy the criteria of enrolment and attendance according to officially recognised definitions.

The causes for absenteeism and student dropouts have been well documented; general reasons are poverty, child labour, gender restrictions on mobility, illness and disease, lack of transportation, and parental neglect. This study did not assess which factors in these schools were predominant. However, for analytical and conceptual clarity, this research study proposes the following sub-categories for understanding student enrolment and attendance:

1. *Out of school children*: These students are not attending schools, are therefore not enrolled, and are entirely outside the purview of the educational system.
2. *Enrolled but not attending, irregularly attending, or dropped out*: This category can be further subdivided into three subcategories: (i) students who are officially registered in documents, but do not attend regularly or consistently; (ii) students who are enrolled, but only attend for examinations/assessments: (iii) students who have entirely discontinued their education, but whose names are not expunged from the school records.
3. *Multiple registrations and enrolment:* These students are registered in various schools simultaneously, thus giving a misrepresentation of net-enrolment rates. This is oftentimes done intentionally, under false pretenses, to expand artificially the student body size in order to misappropriate more funds towards the school. This pattern may also result as an unintended consequence when parents shift location frequently and consistently due to employment insecurities, natural disasters (floods), or militancy and terrorism.

Teachers and head teachers, within and across schools, have varying approaches towards recording student attendance. Some record the student attendance of students each day, whereas others record attendance once a week, bi-weekly, or once a month. In the case of the latter, for example, teachers will record attendance on one day of the week and re-use that same number for the entire week rather than re-calculating attendance every day.

Each teacher has a different set of procedures for how and when to remove a student's registration from enrolment records. One head teacher stated that after three months of a student's absence, she would erase the student's enrolment; the student would therefore be classified as a dropout. Some teachers wait an entire year. Other teachers will never change a child's enrolment status; in such cases, students who have not attended for ten months (or longer) are still counted officially as enrolled. In general, head teachers and teachers lack established procedures for managing and tracking student participation and engagement. Procedures vary within and across schools.

The district government supervisors have minimal awareness of how teachers maintain student records. Though supervisors' main responsibility as government officials is visiting, supervising, monitoring, and reporting on school activities. They are not enforcing the maintenance of systematic procedures and policies. Several interviewed supervisors mentioned that they were aware that school attendance is a primary concern; however, they were unable to implement any procedure to streamline the process of monitoring and tracking student attendance.

Two supervisors further shared that during their visits, certain teachers would present them with several thick notebooks of information detailing student enrolment of the past several years or even a decade. The supervisors were unable to make sense of the unwieldy collection of unorganised and superfluous information. One supervisor stated, 'I was not able to figure anything out. I do not have time to go through all these notebooks on students who were enrolled 10 years ago.' In a separate conversation, the corresponding teacher shared that the presentation of miscellaneous documents allowed her to evade further questioning while maintaining the appearance of proper record management.

Lastly, those teachers who did maintain records of student attendance, albeit in a rudimentary form, only calculated total number of students rather than examining attendance for each individual student. Therefore, a teacher could estimate the number of students present, but could not identify which specific students were coming to school and which were absent.

In the target districts of this research study, there are neither formal institutions (in terms of enforced governmental regulations) nor informal institutions (in terms of social norms) that compel parents and community members to monitor affairs within schools. Since social norms are self-enforcing, sustainable, and accrue minimal costs, there are clear benefits of informal institutions in educational governance.

Firstly, analysing the data reveals that schools, district government officials, and teachers do not have any formal or informal structures for maintaining and managing records of student enrolment, absenteeism, and dropouts. Even if any teachers properly made such calculations, the data would still be misleading because of the irregularity and inconsistency in student attendance. The result is inconsistency within schools and throughout the school system more broadly.

The large discrepancy between officially recorded, actual, and verbally testified accounts of student enrolment and attendance complicates the question of student participation in schooling. Moreover, the ambiguity is partially intended, accuracy being obscured through multiple forms of superfluous documentation. Teachers state that they present stacks of notebooks, papers, and files with incomplete or inaccurate information to government officials, oftentimes to impart the false impression that the information has been compiled and documented. The findings yield insights into the decision-making processes around such question: how teachers and head teachers produce, utilise, and interpret records in school management? Such an examination builds upon a burgeoning body of anthropological literature examining the various roles of paper materials (documents and files) in mediating social relations in bureaucratic and management structures (Hull, 2010). In this case, the surplus of documentary evidence was used as a means to evade questioning and to satisfy the requests of government officials.

Parental Perceptions and School Selection

There is an observed lack of parental and community interest and engagement in school performance, and an absence of formalised procedures for parents to measure school quality, teacher quality, and student learning outcomes. Parents therefore have limited or no information for evaluating whether their children are attaining even minimal levels of education.

Though parents cited distance as the primary factor in selecting a school for their child, the majority of parents stated they were willing to compromise if a more remote school clearly demonstrated superior performance. According to some interviewed parents, a school was considered 'good quality' if the teachers were likewise of 'good quality'. In this case, the quality of teachers was assessed by teachers' punctuality, regularity of attendance, and commitment to teaching. However, not a single interviewed parent had visited the school in the past year more than three times. Some stated that the visit to meet the field researchers (for the interview in the school) was the first time they were entering the school premises. Other parents also assessed teacher commitment and teacher quality based on the satisfaction of the child with his or her day at school; some stated that the religiosity of the teacher was the primary indicator of quality teaching. The majority stated that before the interview, they had not ever thought about what differentiates a good teacher/school from a poor one.

Those parents, who displayed greater awareness about the importance of quality education but could not afford private education, would generally respond to the question regarding their school choice by saying that their children (in some situation only 'girls') go to a government school because being a student of a government school is better than making them set idle at home and doing nothing. 'I cannot afford private schools. In a public school at least they get the opportunity to interact with other children and get socialised', a father said. There was a general perception amongst parents that private schools perform better and that public schools do not really serve any purpose other than allowing their children to idly pass the time.

Though in small communities, parents and community members can easily observe and measure teacher punctuality and teacher attendance, they rarely exercise any such monitoring strategy. There is an apparent lack of parental and community interest and engagement in school performance. The schools had not yet established means of communication with parents, who were not receiving information on student examination results or information on school celebrations and activities; parents were entirely unaware whether their child was performing well or poorly in class. Informal institutions such as those based on social norms had not created the incentive structures to compel parents to participate in their child's education.

A corollary to the previous argument is that there is an absence of formalised procedures for parents to measure school quality, teacher quality, and student learning outcomes. Parents, therefore, have limited or no information for evaluating whether their children are attaining even minimal levels of education. Moreover, there is a lack of consideration or concern on what children are learning within the classroom. Even parents living within a five minute walking distance of the school stated that they rarely if ever visited the school to speak with teachers or check up on the performance of their children. The lack of active parental involvement in their children's education is a twofold issue. Parents are not engaged in school affairs, and teachers do not initiate strategies for parental inclusion. As aforementioned, there was an observable absence of social norms and rules to compel parental involvement.

Kinship Groups and Social Structures

Ethnicity, caste, religion, tribe, and related social factors in turn influence how power and resources are distributed amongst various actors in the education sector. Kinship groups are an important social structure in patriarchal Pakistani society, and therefore are critical when examining governance and decision-making processes around schools. For example, interviewees consistently stated their tribal, caste, or ethnic affiliation when introducing themselves; moreover, each student's *zaat* [ethnicity, clan, or caste] was listed in the enrolment records.[4,5] The importance of caste or *zaat* for the respondents was noticeable in the demographic homogeneity in all the schools, with the exception of the schools in Gilgit-Baltistan. The student body in the schools in Skardu and Gilgit was highly heterogeneous, comprising up to eight different ethno-linguistic and ethnic groupings.

In one school, the parents stated that they had sent their daughter to the school because of a pre-existing relationship with the headmistress. The pre-existing relationship had formed because the parents and the headmistress were from the same *zaat* and therefore there was regular social interaction outside the school. Out of 30 randomly selected children from the school, 15 stated they bore a familial relationship (of varying degrees) with one of the teachers in the school. Those students from the immediate family of the head teacher, due to their close relationship, were promoted to the status of Head Girl and/or Monitor, a position considered quite prestigious amongst the students. The teachers and students shared that such nepotism was a common practice. Students without any familial connection were given noticeably less attention.

In several of the other examined schools, the student body and the teaching faculty were all of the same religion and caste, even though the immediate neighbourhood consisted of diverse social and religious groups. However, in several instances, the children attended the schools where the teaching staff was of the same social and religious background. In other instances, the teaching staff, the school management committee, and organisational boards consisted of prominent (male) members of the community.

The prominence of kinship grouping was most evident when the research team observed a group of Hindu children living next-door watching us from their house gate. When the Hindu mother of the children was asked why she was not sending her daughters to the school, she explained that she had not considered the option because she could not afford the cost of education. The headmistress of the school shared that she was unaware of young girls living next door and not attending her school. The Hindu family existed outside the kinship groups of the school, and therefore a link had not been formed between the two. It was apparent that in spite of living next door to the school, the Hindu family was entirely unaware that public education was free.

The above findings suggests that ethnicity, caste, tribal affiliation, *biraderi* (clan) and the related social and kinship structures constitute the informal connections between people that in turn determine how decisions are made and who is included in the decision-making process. A student's caste, class, tribal affiliation, and/or ethnicity can serve as barriers to entry in school or alternatively result in the social marginalisation of certain social groups, which can result in limited or no access to education.

School Management Committees (SMCs)

Landlords (*wadera*) and local notables have a significant influence in shaping and determining decision-making processes in SMCs. In fact, in Sindh the role of local notables in SCMs and their influence have been institutionalised through government policy. The Department of Education, Sindh has established formal bodies—School Management Committees (SMCs)—comprising parents, community members, and teachers to promote strong community participation in school affairs. However, the policy specifies that two of the members be 'notables'[6]. The government's statutory inclusion of notables in the committee is highly problematic. These notables demonstrate disproportionate amounts of power and influence in decision-making processes, and may or may not be sincerely committed towards advancing educational causes and working for school improvement. The effect of the Devolution Plan on educational governance is a complex issue. Past research and this research study argue that Devolution has further reinforced the predominance of informal governance and institutions at the local level; in particular, the influence of the local notables in school management has notably expanded.

In one particular village, the local landlord was responsible for donating the plot for the school premises, providing the needed funds for the school buildings' construction, and for submitting the official application requesting the governments' approval for the school. However, this landlord also continued to use the school land for storing his personal property, holding private sessions, meetings and gatherings within the school premises. For example, he used the roof of the school building to dry and store his wheat from the fields. In some extreme cases, the interviewed members shared that the *wadera* (landlord) or other notable confiscated the entire school property for his personal use. The proliferation of ghost schools and non-functional schools, as the local media has reported, is partially attributed to the local notables misappropriating school funds and confiscating school premises (Ali, 2013).

In the scenario described above, the parents, community members, and school headmistress acquiesce to the demands and requests of the landlord. The headmistress stated that she is unable to make any decision regarding the school without first attaining the landlord's consent. Even regarding the enrolment of students of migrant workers, she must first consult him. However, the landlord remains the primary decision-maker for school affairs. The headmistress of the school explained, 'The SMC members say that the school belongs to the *wadera* [landlord], because he owns the land and he has built the school. In other schools, the local notables formally take a seat within the SMC. Interviewed members of the SMC stated that elections for the committee were not democratic; rather, seats were allocated according to seniority within the community.

In a few of the remaining 13 schools, the SMCs existed on paper but the members rarely met; in other cases, the SMCs were operational but ineffective. In one case, where the SMC had not yet been established, the teachers stated they were aware of the concept and purpose of an SMC, but the process for forming the committee had not yet been initiated. The parents, on the other hand, had little understanding that an institutionalised framework for community participation in school affairs had been developed, though several parents expressed interest in school involvement. In the second case, the initial groundwork for the SMC had been completed; the members and chairperson had been selected. However, neither meetings nor discussions were held. In the last case, the committee members, expressed interest, but either lacked the social and economic capital or the means otherwise to effectively make and implement a decision. In such a case, the influence of local politicians and notables impeded committee operations. For example, though each committee was allocated a fixed amount of funds for school affairs, a local notable or politician would misappropriate the funds for his or her personal use, or temporarily freeze the accounts at the bank. One SMC chairperson stated, 'The SMC is only in name right now since it does not have any funding. I only managed to get this school renovated because of my personal relations with the political leader (MPA) of the area.'

In most cases, the entry of the local notables into the School Management has further legitimised the hold of power of local landowners. Though in several cases the notable's influence was benign and he wielded his influence and power to raise funds and act for educational development, it is uncertain whether the potential of leveraging power in the interests of the community is worth compromising on democratic participation, equal participation, and equality.

Appointment, Transfer, and Promotion of Teachers

Teachers are appointed, transferred, and promoted without any criteria or set of conditions. The decisions made within this arena are haphazard, dubious, unsystematic, and often done under political duress. Political interferences and frequent teacher transfers severely impede the ability of teachers to fulfill their teaching duties. In several instances, more teachers than necessary are appointed within one school; in other cases, a school is in dire need of additional teachers. The result is a simultaneous excess and shortage of teachers.

Teacher recruitment is the most problematic area in educational governance. Consequentially, decision-making practices in this area seem to have far reaching, lasting and disastrous effects on the credibility, functionality and efficiency of the education system. Citing one of many examples collected as data evidence in the study is enough to explicate the gravity of the situation about teacher recruitment. During the course of data collection in this study a scandalous scam about teachers' recruitment surfaced in one of the provinces and got wide public and media attention. Either on the intervention of the Court or the Provincial Legislative Assembly, an inquiry committee was constituted to probe into the allegedly illegal recruitment of primary and elementary school teachers. The committee investigated the scam and found that out of 461 disputed appointments, 298 were illegal on various grounds i.e. appointments on non-existent positions, or teachers being ineligible/unfit[7] for the position (Pay Scale 7–14). Consequently, the Provincial Department of Education de-notified the recruitment of 298 teachers. The notification reads:

> … [The] committees after checking documents (Academic/professional qualification) found the following teachers/officials [list annexed with the notification] ineligible/unfit for the posts as mentioned against each, therefore the competent authority has been pleased to withdraw their initial appointment orders with immediate effect (Department of Education, Gilgit-Baltistan, 2012[8]).

It was during these days that an article appeared in one of the leading English daily newspapers to shed light on the situation.

> Although corruption is rampant in almost every government department of Gilgit-Baltistan, the education department is the worst affected. Hundreds of thousands of teachers have been inducted illegally during this period. A majority of them have either fake degrees or they are underage or overage. It is a matter of grave concern for senior officials that not even a single test or interview has been carried out for years to induct teachers. Most of the beneficiaries are said to be the near and dear ones of provincial political figures, local bureaucrats, religious leaders and other influential personalities of Gilgit-Baltistan. The majority of newly inducted teachers has been upgraded to BPS–14 and BPS–16 [basic pay scale] within no time by violating merit, while

> some senior teachers have been waiting for their turn of promotion for the last several years. It is unfortunate that the most respectable profession of society is so treacherously polluted (Shigri, 2014, in press).

A teacher is considered to be the backbone of the education system. From the governance point of view, the precondition for strengthening the backbone of the education system is teacher recruitment based on a transparent process. Unfortunately, the above example demonstrates how ruthlessly the rules, regulations, and principles have been violated or compromised by the responsible authorities. In fact, the perception among educational stakeholders is widely shared that decisions pertaining to teachers' recruitment, placement, transfer, and promotions originate from corrupt practices ranging from nepotism to bribery. A teacher expressed his grievance:

> There are many teachers who have gotten a job by bribing politicians and officials; for one teaching job these people receive three to four lac rupees [$3,000–$4,000]. Among them, a few are going to school; others are sitting at home, doing nothing. You can imagine the condition of education in such circumstances. They [politicians and education officials] have done injustice to their society.

Similarly, within schools, head teachers were selected and appointment on a highly subjective and arbitrary basis. Oftentimes the head teacher is selected from the cohort of teachers based on seniority rather than competency and qualifications. The head teacher generally does not receive any specific leadership/management training or ToRs (Terms of Reference) when appointed. Those head teachers, who have received ToRs, disregard them after the initial day of work. The head teachers then learn their duties and responsibilities from having observed their predecessor or by improvising when necessary. If the teachers are from the same kinship community, then the senior-most member of the community is oftentimes appointed as the head teacher, regardless of his or her qualifications and experience. For example, in one school in interior Sindh, the head teacher was the daughter of the local feudal lord. When asked how they understood the appointment, one of the other teachers responded, 'What can we say? She is the daughter of the Saheb [local notable]'. Her appointment as head teacher was conferred to her because of the political influence held by her father.

Corruption, negligence, and inefficiency permeate deeply and widely the entire governance system in education, having a trickle-down effect from province, district, school, teacher, students, parents and community. One case of a government girls' school, which the research team visited, clearly illustrates the systematic lack of accountability in the education system. The school is well-known in the community and has a long history of imparting education to boys and girls. There are 75 women teachers drawing salaries from the school of which eight teachers have never shown up since the new head teacher took over the charge of the school a year ago. Excluding these eight teachers, the remaining 67 teachers, as reported by the head teacher, come to school to teach but teacher attendance, on the average in a month time, is below 60 per cent. On the day of the visit of the research team of this study to the school, out of 75 teachers, 54 teachers were present. Student enrolment according to school record was 541 students enrolled in Grade 1–8, but that day only 251 students were present in the school. More than 50 per cent of students were absent. The head teacher described the situation as a regular feature of the school. If one considers the gross student enrolment, the teacher-student ratio may be calculated as 1:7 but considering the average actual students' attendance in a typical day this ratio becomes 1:3. This means that to teach three students, one teacher is receiving a salary and other fringe benefits from the education department. In spite of the school's proximity to a district education office, the entire scenario of poor student attendance and teacher attendance was unfolding without any intervention or notice by the district government.

This is not a unique case of a single school or a situation in a school but most of the schools from where data in the study was collected more or less present a similar picture. For example, a similar situation existed in a school in another province where there were 39 teachers deployed in the school but the school's record showed that only 18 teachers attended the school on a regular basis; the remaining 21 teachers did not attend the school but were drawing their salaries from the school. During a focus group discussion a group of teachers registered their complaint:

> We try to teach our students to the best of our abilities. However, increasingly we are losing hope because teachers in our school outnumber students. But the dilemma is that most of the time classes are without teachers due to frequent and high rate of teacher absenteeism. There are 50 teachers to teach 150 students. We have been trying to convey our concern to the competent authorities but in vain, as if we are speaking to deaf ears.

This scenario illustrates the extraordinary amount of financial and human resources that are used ineffectively or entirely wasted in the primary school system. As one of the top level education managers in of the provinces stated:

Unfortunately neither at the personal level we are committed to our duties nor do we hold ourselves accountable for our actions and behaviours. Everywhere and at all levels we can see corruption. Poor performance of our department [education department] is not an issue of capacity; rather it is attributable to corruption pervading the system.

> When teachers receive opportunities to move from school to school, they are in fact much more likely to move from a better performing school to a poor performing or a non-functional school. Such transfers occur so that teachers can avoid attending school every day.

The appointment, transfer, and promotion of primary level schoolteachers are the responsibility of the District Education Officer (EDO) at the district level. However, interviewed officials were unable to provide any criteria or set of conditions upon which they decided to transfer, promote, or appoint a government schoolteacher. Almost all respondents stated that the majority of appointments were done on a political basis, and charged complaints against nepotism and corruption within the government education sector. In fact, in each of the thirteen districts, respondents cited the influence of politics and corruption on teacher appointment and transfer as one of the primary concerns and obstacles to educational reform. Teachers with political backing could not be transferred or dismissed, regardless of their performance. For example, the General Secretary of the Teachers Union from one district stated:

> I can tell you that the influential and political people play a powerfull role here in the transfer and appointment of teachers… They [government officers] mostly listen to and accept the orders of influential people… the system has been hijacked by these corrupt people. Teachers do not even come on duty, but still take their salary.

Another DEO (Executive District Officer) stated:

> Politicians and all the powerful people appoint and transfer those teachers with whom they have a good relationship. Or if you have money, you can bribe the people in charge. But you need to have some good relationship with the people in power. There is this one teacher

who is a cousin of the MPA. He can be posted wherever he wants because he is part of the family.

The above are perspectives shared by the respondents. During the course of the study we came across even more concrete, eye opening evidence about how teachers' appointments are manipulated by power groups.

In conclusion, teachers are appointed, transferred, and promoted without any criteria or set of conditions; the decisions made around this issue are haphazard, unsystematic, and often done under political duress. Political interferences and frequent teacher transfers severely impede the ability of teachers to fulfill their teaching duties. In several instances, more teachers than necessary are appointed within one school; in other cases, a school is in dire need of additional teachers. The result is a simultaneous excess and shortage of teachers.

Information Governance: Knowledge for All?

Good educational governance is characterised by transparency and open systems, which in turn requires full disclosure, dissemination, and access to the necessary information for educational stakeholders to make informed decisions at every level of governance. The evidence suggests that in educational governance, the policies, procedures, and mechanism for managing and distributing information are either weak or non-existent. There is general and an apparent ambiguity amongst stakeholders of how, when, where, and why decisions around almost all education matters are made. Moreover, the majority of respondents had little awareness or knowledge of occurrences, developments, and initiatives undertaken within the public education sector, though they all operate within it. There are information gaps at every stage—within and between schools, between schools and district offices, between schools and communities, and between district and higher level government officials. Information asymmetries create imbalances of power, where certain individuals have more access to information and therefore more authority than others. Moreover, information, as has been frequently theorised, can constitute a base of power and of decision-making authority.

Where Does the Buck Stop? A Circular Blame Game

As far as accountability in the context of educational governance is concerned, there appears to be a trend and a tradition of blaming others for one's own wrong doings, mishaps, failures, and poor performance. Nobody, starting from a classroom teacher to an Education Minister, was ready to accept responsibility for what happens inside schools or in institutions that are entrusted with the task of imparting education to the younger generations. The concept of self-accountability was almost nonexistent, with a few exceptions. Individuals, at their convenience, shifted blame to others in an effort to escape from self-accountability. There was an observed vicious circle of passing on blame to the next person in command—teachers to head teachers to supervisors, to district officers, to directors to secretaries, to minster to primary minster to public, etc. Ultimately the 'buck stops nowhere'. When asked how to end this 'blame game', one senior manager in Gilgit-Baltistan succinctly summarised the situation:

> Whenever two teachers meet they will start talking and complaining about the head teacher. They are least concerned about how honestly they perform their own duties. Similarly, two District Education Officials will talk against the Directors and the Directors will blame the Secretary and this continues. When we stop backstabbing others and concern ourselves with our own duties and develop the courage to admit our own mistakes and shortcomings, things can improve considerably. We need to correct our own beliefs and actions first,

and then we can intervene to correct others' mistakes. So the process of change can begin from self-renewal. Collective decision-making is a process. We are habitually depending on others instead of doing the right things by ourselves. This is why we do not have a single institution that stands for quality and encourages merit. We have lost our hope for having better performing government institutions.

Conclusion

The overarching conclusion of the findings is that education governance and its constituent structures do not function to serve its intended beneficiaries—the students. Rather the malformed structures and institutions of educational governance strictly function to serve the interests of four distinct power groups—the bureaucrats; politicians and community elites; local, teachers' associations; and national and international development agencies. These groups act largely as independent entities, but their common interest to manipulate the education sector for personal gains streamlines their actions in a manner that the young student is rendered invisible and is completely overlooked in the decision-making process.

The dynamics and relationships between the four power groups result in instances of informal institutions and personalised forms of governance and power, which in turn produce social inequities in terms of access to and delivery of quality public educational services at the primary school level. Children who are not attending school are not accounted for, thus made invisible in the public education sector domain. The efforts of teachers and district government officials who do not yield political influence are hampered due to their ethnic, socio-linguistic, or religious backgrounds. Schools oftentimes function as sites for the reproduction of social structures that produce socio-economic inequities. The analysis also revealed that the decentralisation of governance structures through the Devolution of Power Plan in 2001 has further entrenched existing informal governance at the district level. Rather than decision-making being devolved to the populace, a new group of local elites has emerged; these district-level elites maintain a stranglehold over power and misappropriate political and financial resources for their own personal gains. Local notables exercise a highly personalised form of power that largely aims to fulfill the objectives of the wielder rather that the community he or she is meant to serve.

These decision-making processes are embedded in and operate through informal relationships, structures, and institutions. As a result, children, particularly those of a minority status, who are otherwise already socially marginalised, are further distanced from the education sector and the state's hegemonic apparatus such as curriculum. Though the dynamics and interactions between the power groups vary according to the local context, the consequences are the same: poor educational governance resulting in poor educational outcomes.

In conclusion, educational governance in Pakistan has essentially made the child irrelevant, inconsequential, and even unnecessary. The child and his or her fundamental, human right to education are shrouded and forgotten in the nebulous workings of a dysfunctional, malformed education sector. Bringing forward the child, front and centre as the focal point, the ultimate and most crucial beneficiary, is a prerequisite for strengthening educational governance.

It is crystal clear from the findings of this research that without improving policy, structures, practices, processes, and outcomes in educational governance any reform of any scale in any context initiated by the government, private sector through IFIs and donors cannot produce lasting impacts on educational services intended at enhanced access and improved students' learning outcomes.

Recommendations

The findings and conclusions discussed above have important implications for the policy and practice of the government and donors and International Financial Institutions (IFIs). We propose the following recommendations to rectify issues and strengthen education governance in Pakistan:

1. *Bring forward the child* front and centre—as the ultimate beneficiary—of all policies, decision-making processes, and government actions.
2. Mechanisms for ensuring *accountability should be embedded within and throughout all tiers of educational governance*. Good governance starts from the topmost tiers of governance and emanates downwards; therefore, *a zero tolerance policy for misconduct* should be enforced at all levels, with particular emphasis on the higher tiers of governance.
3. Limited access to information hinders the ability of teachers, communities, and education managers to make appropriate and structured decisions. Rules and responsibilities, curriculum documents, Terms of Reference (ToRs), policy and budgetary related *documents should be clearly detailed, specified, and disclosed to all stakeholders in the education sector*. Furthermore, this information should be made publicly available through the appropriate mediums for transparency and easy access.
4. *Communication*: Policies, policy decisions, and the decision-making process need to be communicated to the lower tiers of governance, and particularly to teachers and lower level district education managers. Beneficiaries should have a clear understanding of changes, developments, and reforms within the education sector; a lack of awareness and understanding

amongst (uninformed) key beneficiaries hinders and weakens their ability to deliver quality education.

5. The private-public partnership model for school improvement urgently requires a critical review. Policy makers and educators must *question the viability of private-public partnership* and its ability to produce quality education and enhance student learning outcomes.
6. Communities should be educated through *a broad-based and inclusive community engagement platform*. The roles and responsibilities of various community members, particularly (female) parents, should be clearly outlined. Simple concrete steps to work towards school improvement should be detailed for all community members.
7. The district office should be made responsible for *establishing and enforcing academic and ethical standards during supervisory activities*. School supervision should aim to effectively implement such standards, closely monitoring teacher performance and appropriately reprimanding misconduct.
8. Head teachers should be *empowered and supported with the required resources* to effectively make and implement decisions within their schools. A capable and effective head teacher is a key determinant of quality education.
9. The involvement of local notables in micro-managing affairs relating to educational governance and school performance, often to the detriment of the education sector, is extensive and entrenched. The *influence of local notables at the village, tehsil, or district levels needs to be properly identified, recognised, and counteracted.*
10. Policy makers and government officials need to earnestly and forcefully *investigate and identify the extent and scope to which educational processes are politicised.*
11. *A long-term vision and planning should be embedded within*

and through all educational policy and decision-making processes. Frequent transfers, reappointments and dismissals of senior educational managers destabilise educational governance and severely disrupt initiatives towards implementing and sustaining change at the grass-roots level.

12. Though local notables can sometimes play a benign role in the committees (such as by providing the school additional funds and resources) the government should nonetheless institute mechanisms to limit the influence of the local notable, thus ensuring that parents' have a greater responsibility and role in school affairs. In some cases, the entry of a local notable into the SMC has further entrenched and legitimised local notables' stranglehold on power.
13. Private sector and INFIs also need to review their priorities of and approaches to working with government systems. This would require them to revisit and rectify some of their own policies and practices in order to bring more transparency, objectivity and logic in their own decision-making processes.

References

Ali, I., 'Law enforcers, Waderas back in schools for the wrong reasons', *The News* (2013) <http://www.thenews.com.pk/Todays-News-4-159711-Law-enforcers-Waderas-back-in-schools-for-the-wrong-reasons>accessed 13 February, 2013.

Ashraf, M. & Kopweh, P., 'Globalization and education policy in Pakistan: The challenges of access and equity in education (2012) <http://www.periglobal.org/role-state/document/document-globalisation-and-education-policy-pakistan-challenges-access-and-equit>accessed 2012.

Aziz, M., Bloom, E.D., Humair, S., Jimenez, E., Rosenberg, L. & Sathar,

Z., 'Education System Reform in Pakistan: Why, When, and How?' *IZA Policy Paper No. 76*, Institute for the Study of Labour, Germany (2014).

Burton, L.H., *An explicit or implicit curriculum: What is better for young children?* Education Resource Information Center (ERIC) (1998). <files. eric.ed.gov./full text/Ed437554.pdf,> accessed on 11th October 2014.

Cheema, A., Khawaja, A.I., & Qadir, A., *Decentralization in Pakistan: Context, content and causes*. Cambridge, Mass: John F. Kennedy School of Government, Harvard University, (2005).

Cuban, L., 'The hidden variable: How organisations influence teacher responses to secondary science curriculum reform', *Theory into Practice,* 34/1, (1995), 4–11. '25 million children out of school in Pakistan', *Dawn Newspaper* (2012). <http://beta.dawn.com/news/747895/25m-children-out-of-school-in-pakistan>accessed 8 September, 2012.

Eaton, K., Kaiser, K.A. & Smoke, P.J., *The Political Economy of Decentralization Reforms: Implications for Aid Effectiveness* (Washington, D.C: World Bank, 2011).

Farah, I. & Shera, S., 'Female education in Pakistan: A review', in R. Qureshi, & Rarieya, eds. *Gender in Education* (Karachi: Oxford university press, 2007).

Hope, K.R., 'Capacity development for good governance in developing societies: lessons from the field', *Development in Practice,* 19/1 (2009), 79–86.

Hufty, M., 'Governance: Exploring four approaches and their relevance to research. Research for Sustainable Development: Foundations, Experiences, and Perspectives', Geographica Bernensia. (2011)<http://ssrn.com/abstract=2019013>accessed 13 May2012.

Hull, M.S., *Government of Paper: The Materiality of Bureaucracy in Urban Pakistan* (Berkeley: University of California Press, 2012).

International Crisis Group, '*Devolution in Pakistan: Reform or regression*', (Islamabad: International Crisis Group, 2004).

Malik, M.R., Rand Graduate School & Rand Corporation., *Improving*

Decision-Making Systems for Decentralized Primary Education Delivery in Pakistan (Santa Monica, CA: RAND, 2007).

Malik, N., 'The modern face of traditional agrarian rule: Local government in Pakistan', *Development in Practice,* 19/8 (2009), 997–1008.

Mintzberg, H., Raisinghani, D., & Theoret, A., 'The structure of "unstructured" decision processes', Administrative *Science Quarterly,* 21/2 (1976), 249–275.

Nayyar A.H. and Salim, A., ed., *The Subtle Subversion: The State of Curriculum and Textbooks in Pakistan* (Sustainable Policy Development Institute, Islamabad, 2003)<unesco.org/pk/education/teacher education/reports/rp22.pdf> accessed on 18th December 2015.

Shepherd, A. Governance, good government and poverty reduction. *International Review of Administrative Science,* 66/2, (2000), 269-284.

Shigri, M. Khan., 'Recruiting GB teachers', *Dawn Newspaper* (2007). <http://www.dawn.com/news/1086183/recruiting-gb-teachers>accessed 11 February 2014).

United Nations Economic and Social Commission for Asia and Specific. What is good governance? <http://punescap.org/sites/default/files/good governece.pdf>accessed 25 May 2014

Notes

1. Secretaries, directors, head of department/functionaries, and managers/ administrators), their subordinates and other collaborators and other officials in the chain of command.
2. Members of the National Assembly, Members of Provincial Assemblies, Members of the Senate, Ministers, Advisors, Tribal chieftains, Landlords/Waderas, Pirs/ religious figures, Lords/Nawabs, businessmen, industrialists, etc.
3. UNICEF has three different quantitative indicators: 1) Gross primary school enrolment rate—the number of children enrolled in a level, regardless of age, divided by the population of the age group that officially corresponds to the same level; 2) Net primary school enrolment rate—the number of children enrolled in primary school that belong to the age group that officially corresponds to

primary schooling, divided by the total population of the same age group; 3) Net primary school attendance—percentage of children in the age group that officially corresponds to primary school who attend primary school. These data come from national household surveys.

4. Though interviewees used both the English term 'caste' and the term *zaat* interchangeably, at other times however, they said 'caste' refers to one's religious identification. There seemed inconsistency in the interviewees' use of caste and religion. Non-Hindus would classify Hinduism and Christianity as a caste, yet in that same view, being Muslim did not correspond with any particular caste. The 'non-Muslim', religious identity had become the primary and sole identity marker, which superseded all other potential identity choices. Moreover, it is worth noting that Muslims refused to acknowledge those of Christian and Hindu faith by the appropriate terms designating their religion, i.e. as Christians and Hindus. Rather the Muslim teacher would insist that the (Hindu) teacher was 'non-Muslim' and further explaining this label was more polite than referring to the latter as a Hindu.
5. In this chapter, we do not equate caste with *zaat* because of the differentiations the respondents maintained between the two categories. For a more detailed discussion on the terms, definitions, and how to characterise systems of social stratification, please see Farina Mir, *The Social Space of Language: Vernacular Culture in British Colonial Punjab,* (Berkeley: University of California Press, 2010): 127.
6. www.rsu-Sindh.gov.pk/home/accessed 11 May 2013.
7. Not explained, what does unfit mean, perhaps due to lack of academic/ professional qualification or being over or under aged.
8. <www.gilgitbaltistan.gove.edu.pk> accessed 12 December 2012.

PART IV:

CAPACITY BUILDING FOR TEACHER EDUCATION THROUGH STEP PROJECT

10

Professional Development Initiatives: Imperatives for Maximum Returns on Investment

Kulsoom Jaffer, *Zubeda Bana*, and *Khushal Khan*

Introduction

Continuing professional development (CPD) is an essential element in improving professional practices of organisational leaders. CPD not only adds to an individual's repertoire of knowledge and skills, but also helps to increase the institutional capacity as a whole, by way of improved human resource. However, continuing professional development is a resource intensive exercise as it requires careful planning, finances, time, and human resource with relevant expertise. It is therefore important that CPD is conceptualised, organised, and implemented well so as to get the maximum returns on the investment. Another important factor is positioning of the graduates of the programmes at the right place, and providing an environment conducive for the graduates to utilise their newly acquired learning to the maximum.

Research in continuing professional development confirms that CPD plays a key role in helping the institutional heads/managers to hone their skills and gain updated knowledge required for effectively managing their institutions, and enhancing their understanding about their own practices. Nevertheless, it is equally essential that the aspiring leaders and managers should first go through a robust pre-service programme to prepare them to take up the challenges of the role they are expected to play as leaders and managers. However, as has been a general practice in Pakistan, with enough evidence[1] that generally for government service, including the education sector, the individuals are considered for leadership positions on the basis of their seniority. Hence, there are normally internal transfers from the same Basic Pay Scale (BPS)/grade or transfers due to promotion or direct appointment through the Public Service Commission. In addition, in most cases, these education managers at school, district, and directorate levels (school heads, principals, District Officers Education, ADOEs, and Directors) have little or no management experience, as management and teaching posts are interchangeable. This means that a faculty in the Teacher Training Institute (TTI) could very well be appointed or transferred on the basis of seniority to another college, as the head of the institution (e.g. Principal or Vice Principal), but hardly with any management training or management/leadership experience. Research in education and educational management, however suggests that any educational institution's success depends on its leadership; and that there is a close correlation between the quality of teaching and the achievement of the students, and between the quality of leadership and the quality of teaching (Teacher Training Agency, UK, 1998). The heads of the educational institutions have a key decision-making role in education. In order to be able to perform their task well, heads have to have sound management, leadership, decision-making, and supervisory skills, so that they are able to support and guide the work of their staff. The Government of Pakistan's (2006) report on Government Service Reforms also recommends the development of institutional heads as educational leaders.

In the absence of a pre-service or preparatory programme for educational leaders and managers, the public sector education managers in Pakistan mainly depend on continuing professional education courses which are at times tailor-made for specific geographical contexts, but mostly are generic in nature.

Since a few decades, there have been many interventions in Pakistan, under donor-funded projects[2] to respond to the capacity development needs of the institutional heads in the government sector. Almost all the projects worked for capacity development at various levels from teachers, school heads, principals, and faculty of teacher education colleges/institutions. The strengthening Teacher Education in Pakistan (STEP) Project is one such project, which had as its key component, capacity development of public-sector teacher education college principals.

This chapter presents the findings of the research which was conducted to study the effect of a CPD course on the graduates' knowledge, skills and disposition, and whether and how it helped them to improve their work-related practices.

Context and Background

The context of the study was the Government Elementary Colleges of Education (GECEs) and Government Colleges of Education (GCEs) in Sindh, Balochistan, and Gilgit-Baltistan. These colleges offer a range of pre-service teacher education programmes including Primary Teaching Certificate course, Certificate in Teaching, one-year BEd programme, Junior Drawing Master (JMD) course, Senior Master Drawing (SMD) course, Art Teaching Certificate (ATC), Oriental Teaching Certificate (OTC), Associate Degree in Education (ADE) and four-year BEd (Honors) programme. All the research sites had purpose-built buildings with classrooms, space for the drawing programme, computer lab, library, faculty offices, and administration offices.

The CPE course under study was an approximately 140 hour tailor-made course in Educational Leadership and Management with both face-to-face and field components, wherein the participants were required to conduct assigned tasks. In addition, the project academic staff also visited the graduates at their workplaces for post programme follow-up.

The course aimed to contribute to course participants' personal and professional development and to institutional improvement. Thus, the course included topics such as leadership and management competencies to facilitate organisational culture that fosters learning; reconceptualisation of principals' role as transformational leaders; skills and knowledge to manage human, material, financial, and physical resources; the notion of educational change with specific reference to changing policies and reforms in teacher education and teacher preparation (e.g. the introduction of a two-year Associate Degree in Education programme); developing and implementing small-scale education projects and institutional development plans.

It also aimed to facilitate principals to change from top-down supervisors to facilitators, so that the staff is inspired and motivated to perform to their optimal capacity. It supported the human resource management philosophy that 'leadership is getting things done through people…all managers, are by definition, leaders in that they can only do what they have to do with the support of their teams, who must be inspired to follow them' (Armstrong, 1994, p. 84).

The professional development programme thus included the idea of bringing change in the knowledge and skills of the individuals who lead the institutions, and through them change the way in which the institution and the human resource within it was to be managed. The improvement of the institution through the management of HR requires leadership that could be trusted in their judgments and decisions. According to Branson (2010), in order to become trustworthy, leaders have to allow their followers to have some form of meaningful input into the decision-making process. This requires the leader-follower nexus to move from 'me-them' perspective to an 'us' perspective. This study thus sought to understand both the programme and its effect on understanding and application of the knowledge through facilitative leadership (Cufaude, 2005).

Conceptual Framework and Methodology

The purpose of the research was to understand how the professional development programme under the STEP project had helped develop graduates' understanding of their role as managers in developing their repertoire of management skills, and in influencing institutional development.

The framework used for evaluating the course was Guskey's (2000) five critical levels of programme evaluation:

1. Participants' reaction to the programme
2. Participants' learning
3. Organisational support and change
4. Participants' use of new knowledge and skills
5. Influence on the teaching and learning processes in their institutions

This framework clearly shows that the course offering itself is but one variable and that a contextual variable such as the graduates' work-place culture is equally important for implementation of new learning, and to have any significant impact on the practices. It also helps nurture the leadership style required to manage in the given context. According to Branson (2010), there is no one style or leadership approach that could enable educational change to happen more constructively, productively, amicably, and successfully.

For this research, the case study method under qualitative paradigm was used. With reference to the effect of the CPD programme, the graduates' context was taken as a case to understand the level, 2–5 of Guskey's framework:

- Participants' learning: Did the participants acquire the intended knowledge and skills?
- Organisational support and change: Was there a change in the organisational culture, decision making and management?
- Participants' use of new knowledge and skills: Did the participants effectively apply the new knowledge and skills?
- Influence on the teaching and learning process in their institutions: How did the participants facilitate and influence the teaching and learning practices?

In qualitative paradigm, the researcher aims to understand multiple realities, and the focus is on the research participants' experiences and perceptions (Merriam, 1988; Fraenkel & Wallen, 1990 citied in Creswell, 1994). Here, the idea of creation of knowledge takes full cognizance of the investigator, and its interaction with the 'known' (Hamilton, 1998 as cited in Jaffer, 2007).

Guided by the Guskey's programme evaluation framework, the research questions were about participants' satisfaction with the quality of the content and its delivery, the faculty's performance, whether the learning goals were achieved, and about the quality of physical facilities and material. Yin (1994)[3] supports multiple data collection methods for developing case studies. According to Bassey (1999, p. 81), these methods are asking questions (and listening intently to the answers), observing events (and noting carefully what happens), and reading documents. For this study however, the predominant data collection methods were individual interviews and focus group discussions. In addition, the researchers' own reflective notes were utilised in the data triangulation and analysis. The documents (institutional development plans and project reports) were rarely available. Six colleges were selected for the study. At each college a semi-structured interview was conducted with each principal respondent (the course graduates), who was either the principal or a senior faculty. Individual interviews were also conducted with the principals of the colleges where the graduates were other than the principals. In addition, one focus group discussion with a group of senior faculty was also held. Over all, seven individual interviews and four focus group discussions were conducted in the sampled colleges.

As the programme graduates belonged to different geographical contexts (Sindh, Balochistan, and Gilgit-Baltistan), therefore multiple case study research design was used to respond to the research questions. The units of analysis in this study were the colleges where the graduates of the programme were based, the way the professional development programme influenced their practices, how those practices helped bring about positive changes in their respective institutions, and the challenges they faced, if any, in implementing change initiatives.

Forty-seven participants, representing 28 colleges from Sindh, Balochistan, and Gilgit-Baltistan, attended the professional development programme. To be able to gather credible evidence on the impact of the professional development programme, 22 graduates were selected as respondents for this study from six colleges (one from Gilgit-Baltistan, two from Balochistan, and three from Sindh).

Key Findings

This section first presents the context of the study, followed by findings drawn from the six case studies. There are two sets of findings: those presented according to the themes in the Guskey's framework and others as general findings.

Although a representative sample was carefully selected to get rich data, however, the research team faced the following situations once data collection started in the field. These situations clearly not only impacted the sample and the data, but more importantly, the data collected also showed the implications this had for graduates' work in their context.

- In Balochistan, only one case study could be developed. The other graduate selected from Makran Division for case two was not accessible due to the security situation. Although the team identified another graduate for the second case study, however it was learnt that he or she was transferred to another institution immediately after the course.
- In Sindh, the graduate selected from the college in lower Sindh had retired. Therefore, a graduate from Karachi was added. For central and upper Sindh, two colleges with five graduates from each site were selected.
- In Gilgit-Baltistan, only one college was represented in the course; hence that college (with two graduates) was selected for the study. However, the volatile security situation did not allow the research team to physically visit the college. Therefore, telephonic interview was conducted with the graduate. However, it is important to note here that both graduates from GB had attended two CPE courses consecutively; therefore, any change in the practice could not entirely be attributed to the course conducted under the STEP project. It was also clear from the responses that the graduate was quite confused between the two courses and was mixing the content and the experiences, and finally as there was only one interview to bank on, the research team was of the view that this case did not give credible

information about the course and its influence, therefore this case study was dropped.

Profile of the Respondents

Another noteworthy point in this research was the profile of the research respondents. The leadership and management course under consideration was for the principals and vice principals of the teacher training colleges, hence the purpose of the research was to study the influence of the course on the understanding and ensuing practices of the graduates. However, as is evident from the case study data, in some instances the principals and vice principals were not part of the programme, and in the instances where the principals attended the programme they were either transferred or retired immediately after the completion of the course.

As the research team started identifying the principal respondents (the graduates of the programme) during the negotiation process, it became clear from the onset that: (i) two graduates (principals) identified for this research were on the verge of retirement at the time of attending the course, in fact they retired immediately after completing the course; (ii) one graduate was transferred from the college after the programme to another institution to a non-management position, hence he or she could only use the learning for his or her personal management and growth; and (iii) five graduates were actually from among the faculty, a majority with five and more years of teaching experience in the college they represented. None of them had a management position but due to their leadership qualities and disposition they were given some management responsibilities. As these faculty members were nominated by the institution responsible for nomination therefore their principals had no choice but to release them for the training.

This section presents findings according to five levels of Guskey's framework for programme evaluation:

Discrepancy in Nominations Criteria

Foremost, perhaps one of the most important findings is that although this Continuing Professional Education (CPE) course was designed for the principals and vice principals of the teacher training colleges, however the data suggests that: (i) not all course participants held management positions, nor were they in the seniority list, but because they were nominated by name (i.e. the college principals or vice principals were not nominated) the principals of the colleges selected for the programme had to comply and relieve their faculty for the course; (ii) three principals were on the verge of retirement when they entered the course; hence they retired immediately after the course; and (iii) three course graduates were transferred to non-management position after the course.

All this had threefold implications: (i) the graduates who retired did not have time to apply their learning, and obviously could not make any difference in their work place; (ii) the graduates who were transferred to other institutions and positions could only use the acquired knowledge and skills in their own personal/limited sphere, and could not make much difference institutionally, especially given that, they were not in management positions nor did they have leadership dispositions; and (iii) the graduates who had only teaching responsibility acknowledged that they could not relate to many management related knowledge, skills, and practices during the course. Hence, their role in the institution-wide change was not visible. They could only make a difference in their area of influence i.e. teaching.

In view of the implications mentioned above, it is vital for the government to nominate the right people for the professional development programme, and for the course organisers to make sure that the admission criteria are strictly met, as this not only has implications for the classroom dynamics but also for the application and intended outcomes of the professional development programme.

Having said that, it was also clear from two (out of five) case studies, that although the graduates were not in management positions, yet they were able to contribute to institutional development, and influence some change. This was because these graduates had a leadership disposition (innate ability to lead). They were open to sharing their knowledge, and were forthcoming in providing support and advice to the management. As one of the respondents said:

> We have learnt a lot from Amina (pseudonym) regarding our role and responsibilities. Now we have realised that the principal is a key person to any change. If we will not allow our staff to bring about change then they cannot take even a single step at the college. I encourage my staff and support them at every step. I provide them each and every available resource for the betterment of the college (interview September 24, 2014).

Another important factor was that their principals were supportive of their interventions and provided appropriate resources for the overall benefit of the institution. One of the programme graduates (who was not a principal) reported:

> Although he [the principal] has many schools under him but still he provides support, gives advice and also deputes faculty whenever we need it....no challenges... as I came back, the principal provided me with a platform to share my learning with others; the principal always supported me. When the principal was not in the college then I would fill in for him. Then finally, I was appointed a DDO [Drawing and Disbursement Officer] (interview, September 23, 2014*).*

Participants' Reaction to the Programme

This included data on the content and its delivery, the programme faculty performance, whether the learning outcomes were achieved, and how the course influenced the graduates' understanding about leadership and management and helped them reconceptualise their role as educational leaders and managers, as well as what aspects of the course played as motivators to bring about change in their institutions.

All the graduates (the primary respondents) spoke highly of the quality of the programme offered including the quality of instruction, approaches, learning materials, and physical facilities:

> In my opinion, the key things related to learning environment are physical facilities, cognitive facilities, and pedagogical facilities. These three were also according to my concept and learning from AKU-IED. Further, we build environment [culture] of our own to develop co-ordination and flexibility. Co-ordination will help resolve issues in management and in administration [of the institution]. Sincerity is the key element in our organisation. If we are sincere [then] the environment [the culture] will be built automatically and the vehicle [the institution] will run [move] forward... we learned and saw all these at AKU-IED (interview, September 23, 2014).

The other things that also influenced the graduates were the implementation and organisation of the CPE course itself, the approaches used by the faculty, and the use of resources.

Another aspect that influenced the graduates was the environment and the attitude of the staff at AKU-IED towards the course participants, the management of time, and that everyone, whether the director, faculty, students, or the support staff, was treated equally, whether it was in cafeteria or at any event. According to one of the respondents:

> ...there was no difference among professors, director, students and supporting staff in the campus, whether it was lunch break or any other event, everywhere equality existed and the concept of superiority and inferiority was discouraged. That was a source of motivation and inspiration for me (interview, September 20, 2014).

A majority of the graduates said that this motivated and inspired them to replicate these practices in their own workplaces. More than the course, it was the culture that helped bring about attitudinal change among the course participants.

Participants' Learning

This included the knowledge and skills acquired during the course, and how it helped them to make a positive change in their institution. The graduates who held management positions such as the principals, the vice principals, and the head of the lab school[4] shared that the acquired knowledge and skills were relevant to their responsibilities as managers, and helped them perform their work effectively. Some of the themes that these graduates learnt and appreciated were team work, decentralisation of roles and responsibilities, building a collaborative environment, and working towards developing a shared vision. They also learnt about the notion of professional development, and about their role in facilitating and providing professional development opportunities for their staff. In addition, they learnt how to identify professional development needs of the faculty, and assign them tasks according to their ability and interest, and to place the right people in the right place: A lab school head, for example, reported:

> ...now I am confident enough to adjust the right person in the right place at the right time. I identify the required skills and understanding of teachers and then assign them a task according to their ability and

> interest. I have found this concept very productive and meaningful. This concept was developed at AKU-IED during the ELM programme. Now I believe that the principal is a gatekeeper of change and if he or she welcomes the positive change in the college then no one can stop it (interview Lab School Head, September 24, 2014).

The course also helped the participants to reconceptualise their understanding about human resource management, especially how to behave with the staff (both academic and non-academic). One graduate said that prior to the course he considered his relationship vis-à-vis his teachers as that of a boss always giving orders to his subordinates. But from the course he learnt that the manager has to be a co-worker and a facilitator.

For the rest of the respondents, although the course was not directly relevant to their teaching responsibility, nevertheless there were elements in the course such as reflective practice, the notion of professional learning communities (PLCs) and trends in teacher education which were relevant to them as faculty. The rest of the content on management practices including financial management was a new learning experience and helped them in self-management, and provided know-how of inter-personal skills. However, contrary to their belief that the principals did not have much to do except sit in their offices and issue orders, they learnt that a principal has many responsibilities such as human and other resource management. One graduate said that the course also helped her reconceptualise the notion and effectiveness of faculty meetings:

> Previously we considered these faculty meetings as a formality and did not know about how to conduct meetings. But from the course attended at AKU-IED we came to know that there are some set rules for conducting meetings. For example, before conducting a meeting the agenda should be properly defined and meeting minutes should be

> properly noted down in black and white mentioning the action points and these should be shared with the staff. Now we do the same at our college (interview, September 24, 2014).

Other learning was about planning and implementing small-scale institutional development projects. As part of the assignment, the participants were required to develop and implement a small-scale institutional development project, such as establishing and developing college library, providing clean drinking water, establishing computer labs, and improving documentation and record keeping. According to the data, this not only helped the participants to think systematically with a system-wide approach, it also encouraged collaboration and teamwork among the faculty, the government departments, and the community, as all these stakeholders were brought together to make the project possible and successful.

Participants' Use of New Knowledge and Skills and Organisational Support

This included a change in the organisational culture and contextual challenges, if any, hindered while making positive changes in the institutions.

The principals, vice principals, and the head of the lab school shared that the course helped them to develop their people management skills such as to manage their time better; it encouraged team building, and they became better in conflict management and decision-making; they were able to develop collaboration among faculty members and also managed to implement some change initiatives of their own choosing. The graduates on the management positions were able to continue facilitating the projects that they had started during the course as part of their assignment. Some of the projects that were still running were provision of clean drinking water, the computer lab in the school, and the library project.

It was evident from the data that those graduates who were principals (in charge), were able to take initiatives and could mobilise resources because they saw value in these interventions. One research respondent said:

> I was able to improve classroom management and co-curricular activities. Also we learnt about developing a project. I had developed a project on establishing a computer lab, which I implemented during the field episode. Another initiative was that we were able to establish a library for our school (interview, September 23, 2015).

The principals, whose faculty had attended the course, were appreciative of the graduates' contribution. One principal said that the graduates with their changed attitude and disposition had influenced her so much that she also started sharing plans for faculty feedback, and providing platforms for collaboration and team work (Principal's interview, September 24, 2014).

The head of the lab school said that he was able to implement change and innovative ideas due to the support of his teaching staff, and also of the college principal in providing resources and advice.

The graduates who did not have management responsibilities were obviously not in a position to initiate any institution-wide change. During the course, these participants chose projects which were mostly classroom-based, mainly related to developing teaching resources. Thus, these graduates, inspired by the teaching and organisation of the CPE course itself, were able to make a difference in their own classroom teaching. Some senior faculty, who had leadership qualities and who had very supportive management, said that in addition to making changes in their own area of work, they also gave ideas to the principal and supported the management in any change initiative. For example, one of the participants (not in a management position), revealed:

> After the training of ELM, I planned to introduce multimedia in my class. After coming back, I started my assignment given during the Course at AKU-IED with the faculty. I asked my principal regarding introducing multimedia in the class; he was glad and allowed me to start this work (interview, September 24, 2014).

Influence on the Teaching and Learning Processes

This included: How did the participants facilitate and influence the teaching and learning practices? Most of the graduates said that their own classroom management, approaches and preparation were impacted positively. Although this was a management course, yet the way this course was organised and the approaches used by the faculty were very inspiring. Various teaching skills and approaches, for example, use of videos, classroom management, seating arrangement, time management, resource mobilisation and organisation, and display of students' work were some of the ideas that helped them in organising their own classroom teaching better. Yet another participant reflected:

> We learnt various teaching skills and approaches and use of videos. The faculty was very supportive. Classroom management, seating arrangement, time management, in short, the entire system of delivery of teaching were very well organised—more specifically, we came to know how to mobilise and organise resources for the computer lab. I was able to improve classroom management skills and manage co-curricular activities. These newly learned skills, knowledge, and behaviours helped us to organise our own teaching better (interview, September 23, 2014).

In addition, the graduates in management position also facilitated the teaching faculty by providing them classroom teaching and learning resources, helping in photocopying of the materials, updating computer lab and facilitating access for faculty and staff. As the newly introduced, two-year Associate Degree in Education (ADE) and the four-year BEd (Hons.)[5] Programmes do not have prescribed texts; therefore, the faculty is required to use the library extensively. The principals supported library development and ensured provision of reference materials for the faculty and the students.

Recommendations for Improving the Course

The recommendations for improvement of the course included exposure visits during the course, visiting the course participants during the field component to follow-up and provide support on the assignments, and post programme follow-up visit(s) to facilitate application and implementation of the learning from the course.

Another noteworthy recommendation from the respondents was about the admission criteria and giving importance to merit. There was a general feeling that the criteria for the programme should be modified, and only those principals should be invited to attend who have served at least three years in the management position, and preferably in the same institution. Some also recommended that perhaps, in the leadership and management courses, in addition to the principals and vice principals, those senior faculty members should also be invited who would have even longer to stay in the institution, and who could make a positive impact. The idea was to provide professional development opportunities for the senior faculty for grooming them as future leaders for succession planning.

Some respondents also suggested that there should be professional development opportunities for all the staff:

> ...besides principal or vice principal, other senior faculty should also be encouraged to participate in continuing professional development programmes. Teacher educators should be given training in leadership and management because eventually they will get promotion and become principal or vice principal (FGD September, 23, 2014).

It was also recommended that the training and development department should use merit as a criterion for admission to the training programme; and the data base should be so accurate and robust that the same individual does not get to attend professional development opportunities one after another. There has to be adequate time for those who avail the CPD opportunity to apply the acquired learning in the field, and learn from the process and results of the application of the new ideas to identify further CPD needs before availing another opportunity.

Discussion and Conclusion

Although this was a study of the effects of one short course, yet it gives insights into and confirms the practices in management of professional development in public sector, and shows how adherence to policy makes a difference in getting maximum returns on investment.

It was evident from the data that the changes were visible in the colleges where heads/principals or vice principals themselves attended the course. The graduates were able to mobilise and/or allocate resources, initiate change and pool-in human resource. In short, the graduates were able to implement learning from the course and bring about positive changes for institutional improvement. Then there were examples of the graduates who were not in management positions, yet due to their leadership disposition and also the support of the principal they were able to share their learning and innovative ideas, and bring about change in at least classroom teaching and learning processes and approaches.

The graduates on management positions, when transferred to other institutions, could not make much difference institutionally, as someone else was in charge there. If these graduates had leadership qualities or disposition then they would have made a difference by being a role model for their colleagues. Instead, they were waiting to get a management position to be able to make a difference.

The nomination process for the professional development programmes needs to be streamlined so that the same person does not attend multiple professional development programmes (GB as a case in point). This not only demotivates those who rarely get such opportunities, but also those who attend one programme after another and do not get enough time and space to apply the acquired knowledge and skills. In addition, the college has to pay opportunity cost due to their absence without any noticeable benefit to the institution.

Taking the point further about adhering to the programme criteria, it is important to consider the candidates' experience and their prior knowledge so that the participants are able to make most of the opportunity, such as engaging better in classroom discussions, and building on their existing knowledge. It is also important to consider essential conditions on the ground to enable the programme graduates to implement their newly acquired knowledge and skills.

In addition to the efficacy of the course, and the processes and approaches to nominating individuals for professional development programmes, there are also policy implications for the appointment of the principals, their transfers on seniority, and preparatory and continuing professional development strategy for educational leaders and managers.

Finally, the findings also suggest implications for the leadership discourse and practices. For example: Who do we call a leader? What characteristics should be considered in appointing people in management positions? Are appointments on leadership positions based on trait theory of leadership that there are specific personality traits that distinguish leaders from non-leaders, or are individuals considered leaders by virtue of their position? This report thus leaves the reader with food for thought, and also identifies areas for further research.

In conclusion, the data from this study suggests that for a real impact and for influencing change, the following combination would work for a leader or a manager: Seniority in terms of number of years in a service alone does not prepare individuals for management, hence experience in the deputy position along with continuous professional development opportunities would prepare the incumbent for the leadership position. The appointments should consider all three; the professional development opportunities, seniority, and position related rich experience as these together would enhance an individual's leadership capabilities. However, if an individual has innate leadership qualities and disposition, then with training an ordinary leader will become an extraordinary leader.

References

Armstrong, M., *Improving Organizational Effectiveness* (London: Kogan Page Limited, 1994).

Bassey, M., *Case Study Research in Educational Setting* (Buckingham: Open University Press, 1999).

Branson, C.M., *Leading Educational Change Wisely* (The Netherlands: Sense Publishers, 2010).

Creswell, J.W., *Research Design: Qualitative and Quantitative Approaches* (London: Sage Publications, 1994).

Cufaude, J. The Art of Facilitative Leadership: Maximising others' contributions, (Systems Thinker, 15, 1-5, 2005).

Government of Pakistan, *The National Commission of Government Service Reforms*, Islamabad, 2006.

Guskey, T.R., *Evaluating Professional Development* (London: Sage Publications Ltd., 2000).

Jaffer, K., '*An Analysis of the School Inspection System in Sindh, Pakistan*', Thesis submitted as partial requirement of the Doctor in Education Programme at the Institute of Education, University of London, 2007.

Lincoln, Y.S. & Guba, E.G. *Naturalistic Inquirey* (Baverly Hills, CA: Sage, 1985).

Merriam, S.B., *Case Study Research in Education: A Qualitative Approach* (San Francisco: Jossey-Bass Publishers, 1988).

Teacher Training Agency UK, '*National Standards for Headteachers*', London, 1998.

Yin, K.R. *Case Study research: Design and Methods* (Newbury Park, CA: Sage Publications, 1994)

Notes

1. Findings from the study conducted by AKU-IED (2011) on 'Developing Job Descriptions, Performance Standards and Identifying Training Needs of Teacher Managers and Teacher Education Managers under Pre-Service Teacher Education Programme (Pre-STEP).
2. Education Sector Reform Assistance (RTI-ESRA), Education-Links Project both under USAID funding for Sindh and Balochistan; CIDA Debt Swap, Canada-Pakistan Basic Education (CPBEP) Project for Punjab, AusAid funded EDIP Project for Gilgit-Baltistan, to name a few.
3. Available at http://www.sagepub.com/upm-data/41407_1.pdf. Last accessed:

April 2014. The author noted that: This chapter was written expressly for this book but draws from three previous summaries of the case study method (YIN, 2006, 2009b, and 2011a)

4. Lab School: School within the premises of the GECE (M) for teaching practice.
5. The 2-year Associate Degree in Education (ADE) and 4-year BEd (Honors) programme were introduced by the HEC as essential teacher preparation programmes with USAID support under Pre-Service Teacher Education in Pakistan (Pre-STEP) Project.

11

Action Research for Capacity Building of Teacher-Educators

Nusrat Fatima Rizvi

Introduction

Over the years, action research has earned credibility as a classroom/school-based research approach, as well as a professional development strategy. For that reason, in many countries, action research is an integral part of teacher education programmes. In Pakistan, some private in-service teacher education institutes, for example, The Aga Khan University-Institute for Educational Development (AKU-IED) and Norte Dame Institute of Education (NDI) have included action research in their teacher education programmes. However, in the government sector, action research was only made part of the curricula in recent years; it has been now included in the revised BEd programme. In this scenario, it is very important to develop the capacity of teacher education institutes in the public sector as regards to initiating action research and supervising their students' action research projects.

The Strengthening Teacher Education in Pakistan (STEP) project conducted a professional development programme focusing on action research method for the faculty members and researchers of teacher education institutions from Sindh, Balochistan, and Gilgit-Baltistan. The 12-day long short course on action research aimed at improving the capacity of faculty members of teacher education institutions from Sindh, Balochistan, and Gilgit-Baltistan to conduct research using the action research method in order to generate contextual understanding about educational issues pertaining to the quality of teaching and learning at teacher training institutions in the public sector.

Altogether, 140 faculty members from teacher education colleges and Provincial Institutes for Teacher Education (PITEs) attended the course and conducted action research on different topics under the supervision of the course tutors. The course participants of the first cohort were introduced to action research at AKU-IED. They then conducted action research in their chosen content areas in their respective contexts. At the end of the course, the tutors did a follow-up with the participants and asked them to share the research findings in a seminar. Based on the feedback received from the participants of the first cohort, the course tutors added a component of field support in the course designed for the second and third cohorts.

Out of 140 expected action research reports (one from each CP), only 68 reports from the CPs of three cohorts were available in the record maintained by the STEP office, which included 54 reports written in English and eight in Urdu. There were 33 action research reports from Sindh, 27 from Balochistan, and eight from GB.

The CPs selected different subject areas for their research studies based on their expertise in those areas. There were 12 studies in science education, 13 in Urdu or English language education, eight in computer studies or mathematics, three in Pakistan studies or social studies, two in Islamiat (Islamic studies), and 30 action research reports focusing on generic issues of teaching and learning (as shown in Table 1).

Table 1: Subject-Wise Distribution of Action Research Reports

Sindh	Science	Language: Urdu/Eng.	Generic	Pakistan studies	Maths.	Islamiat	Total
	07	05	15	00	4+1	01	33
Balochistan	Science	Language: Urdu/Eng.	Generic	Social studies	Maths.	Islamiat	Total
	04	06	13	01	02	01	27
Gilgit-Baltistan	Science	Language: Urdu/Eng.	Generic	Pakistan studies	Maths.	Islamiat	Total
	01	02	02	02	01	00	08
Grand Total	12	13	30	03	7+1	02	68

These studies presumably provide rich data, as they are situated in their own contexts, on some of the issues the CPs highlighted and also the description of the processes and outcomes of the actions, which CPs took to address these issues. These reports are also liable to provide evidence of the participants' changing understanding and skills which were developed in the process of carrying out their action research projects. However, because of the limited scope, a single action research is usually not able to generate knowledge, which can inform other researches or teaching in the broader context. This provides a rationale for doing a meta-analysis on action research reports in particular contexts or content areas in order to generate new knowledge by juxtaposing smaller bits of information obtained from individual studies in similar content areas or conducted in similar geographical regions. Therefore, STEP conducted a meta-analysis of the available action research reports and explored experiences of the teacher educators who produced those reports during and after the action research course.

This chapter presents the outcome of the meta-analysis of the action research studies. It also discusses the experiences of teacher educators during and after the action research course as to how they improved their practices in the areas which were the focus of their action research during the course at the AKU-IED.

The focus of the meta-analysis was to get an insight into a set of important questions including: What problems/issues teacher educators chose as an area of their action research in different contexts? Was there any convergence or divergence across contexts/curriculum areas? What could be the possible reasons behind choosing these problems/issues as highlighted in the reports? What strategies did they use to address the problem/issues and what challenges did they face in addressing the problems?

Next, the chapter discusses teacher-educators' experiences during the course and how they used the action research findings in their practices. The 'experiences' of teacher-educators were gauged through their reflective accounts in their action research reports, and 'retrospective' interviews with them, and their tutors, regarding their participation during the course. This provided the baseline data in relation to their experiences after the course, as they explained in face-to-face interviews with the STEP research team and presented teaching learning artifacts during field visits.

Literature Review and Theoretical Framework

Action research is a research method which integrates action and reflection. Elliot (1991) defines action research as 'The study of a social situation with a view to improving the quality of action within it' (p. 690).

Action research draws its theoretical underpinning from Dewey's philosophy of pragmatism (Argyris, 1997), which suggests that theory is extracted from practice and in turn it helps improve practice. Action research deals with self-exploration of people regarding their actions in new challenging situations and learning from their experiences (Argyris, 1997). People design their actions to achieve a preset goal while operating under a certain organisational set-up and policy structure.

Action research brings forth understanding about how policy and organisational set-ups are treated in designing actions. It not only provides the opportunity to perform actions to achieve the preset goals but also to inquire how to transform the organisational culture and inform policies. Argyris (2004) differentiates experimental research from action research. In experimental research, researchers control the environmental variables. In action research, researchers manipulate the environmental variables to carry out an action to achieve a preset goal. Knowledge generation through action research is directly related to the issues being studied with the aim to improve pedagogy. Forey, Firkins and Sengupta (2012) note:

> [T]he validity and value of the research finding are tested *in situ* within actual practice and can directly impact on systematic change. It [action research] is typically designed and conducted by practitioners who methodically collect and analyse data to improve their practice and to enrich an area of identified pedagogical concern (p. 70).

In the education sector, action research has been popular for many decades. The Association for Supervision and Curriculum Development[1](ASCD) Yearbook (1956) states:

> The procedure, however, known as 'action research' does have so much to commend it that one might well hope to see a time when school staff members would spend a part of each school day in that kind of activity as a regularly scheduled phase of school work (p. 221).

The popularity of action research firstly lies in the fact that the practitioners research their own practices; thus, they are the real beneficiaries of the research (Stephen, 1952). Also, they have a high stake in the action research. From the perspective of knowledge generation, action research has the potential to blur the boundaries between theoretical knowledge ('discovered, written and published') by university scholars and practical knowledge ('intuitively understood by teachers'). Action research gives 'voice' to teachers who have traditionally been excluded from educational research and the production of knowledge about their own profession and it makes them equal partners in the search for knowledge about teaching and learning (Altrichter et al., 1993; Winter, 1998). It helps in changing the role of a classroom teacher from that of a technician and transmitter of knowledge to a knower and agent (Cochran-Smith & Lytle, 1999). It makes an important contribution to the generation of knowledge about teaching at all levels: the individual teacher, the curriculum, the teaching profession and academic knowledge (Altrichter et al., 1993). Educational change has little chance of success unless it actively involves teachers in the change process (Valli, 2000).

Secondly, action research is based on real issues which are studied and addressed in real situations. As issues in a school faced by one teacher are usually experienced by other teachers in other schools, the nature of action research is usually collaborative. In most cases, the issues faced by the teachers are linked with school policies and the governance structure. Thus, the process of action research has the potential to influence the whole structure of an organisation (Grundy, 1994; Harold, 1957).

There are reasons to consider action research as a promising approach to engage practitioners in the generation of knowledge, situated in their own context (Delong, 2013), which will inform their practices. However, there has also been a concern that because of its limited scope, a single action research study usually is not able to generate knowledge which can inform further research or bring an improvement in practices (Brown & Jones, 2001; Halai, 2011; Sandelwoski & Barroso, 2007). At the epistemological level, action researchers perceive that the theoretical knowledge about teaching exists outside the classroom and schools, which is different from practical knowledge generated through action research (Fenstermacher, 1994). The critique suggests that knowledge cannot be generated unless the same epistemological principles are applied to it (Harold, 1957). One of the principles is consideration of convergence and divergence among the community of practitioners/action researchers within a context or across the contexts (Campbell, 2013).

This provides a rationale for doing meta-analysis of action research reports in particular contexts or content areas to generate new knowledge by juxtaposing smaller bits of information obtained from individual studies in similar content areas or conducted in similar geographical regions (Au, 2007; Halai, 2011; Jensen & Allen, 1996).

For the same reasons, faculty members of AKU-IED have conducted a meta-analysis of action research reports, produced by the course participants of the MEd programme. Halai (2011) conducted a meta-analysis of action research studies in science education. She highlighted the complexity of the situation in which teachers work as inquirers and change initiators but prepare students for examinations at the same time, focusing on rote-memorisation of textbook content. This might be one of the reasons that action research in many contexts was much more successful in the lower grades than in the senior high school (Zembylas, 2003).

Halai (2006) conducted a meta-analysis of action research studies in mathematics and highlighted the tension in the perceived role of student teachers as researchers and mentors during their field work in schools. The student teachers constructed their identity as teacher educators in a general sense and assumed the responsibility of mentoring the school teachers whereas in schools, the perception of a mentor as a subject specialist dominated. These examples show how meta-analysis brings the broader issues to the surface from the individual action research studies.

The second point of concern is related to the follow-up of an action research such as what happens to a teacher after the action research results have been incorporated into their practices. Do teachers ignore the new professional understanding and practices considering it as research-based knowledge, or do they carry out further exploration and reflection on it? Research into teaching is always contextual, so the expectation from action research training is that the practitioner will continue reflecting on their practices and there is no end to the action research process. The notion of change as an ongoing process envisages that action researchers develop a disposition towards being instrumental in a change process and also develop a lifelong habit of developing an inquiring mind. Action research assumes that practices are embedded in context, and change with time and socio-cultural and political circumstances (Grundy, 1994; Reason & Bradbury, 2001).

In this way, action research conceives a more active role for teachers; they are agents of change, rather than the objects of change. This research paradigm empowers teachers as knowledge-workers who engage in construction, reconstruction, transformation, and application of knowledge. Action research enables teachers to transform their identity from teachers as knowledge exporters to one of researchers (Britzman, 2012). For example, Campbell (2003) reported that teachers with one-to-five years of experience, who did teacher research as part of their pre-service teacher education, used the data collection procedures afterwards to construct five categories of knowledge: knowledge of classroom structure; knowledge of self as a teacher; knowledge of students; knowledge of curriculum and instruction; and knowledge of theory of classroom practices.

To sum up, this study deals with the suitability of action research as an approach for teachers and researchers alike. The chapter also takes into consideration certain concerns regarding action research's effectiveness in informing teachers' practices

Methodology

The study employed a qualitative meta-analysis of the available action research reports/papers which teacher educators (CPs) developed as deliverables at the end of action research cycles. The meta-analysis was an attempt to conduct a rigorous secondary analysis of the primary findings. In this study, the meta-analysis of different action research studies provided: (i) a comprehensive description of relationships among different phenomena studied by the course participants in a target geographical region, and identified key or overarching phenomena as they emerged from the comparison of the studies; (ii) description of participants' changed/improved practices through action research, as they are reported in their reports vis-à-vis the key phenomenon which led to a synthesis of the overall improvement in schools/organisations where action research studies were conducted; and (iii) the analysis of the challenges the CPs studied in relation to bringing about change in their practices through action research studies and documentation of key or overarching challenges as they emerged from the comparison of the studies.

The second part of the study was to explore teacher educators' experiences during and after the course. For that, we shortlisted some of the action research reports which provided us with a comparatively better understanding of the CPs' initial concerns about educational practices in their organisation, which made them conduct the action research, what strategies they used to improve the practice, and what were their successes. Initially, we thought of using the assessment criteria for selection of reports which is used in examining graduate students' research reports at AKU-IED, as the said criteria have a detailed set of rubrics on the different components of the research. However, after reviewing the action research reports during meta-analysis, we found it difficult to use such a stringent set of criteria for short-listing the reports. Also, our purpose was not to evaluate the studies, rather it was to identify the basic elements of action research in the reports to start with. Therefore, altogether, 34 studies were selected for the next step of the study, which were slightly more than 50 per cent of the total available reports.

After the selection of the research reports, the research team once again reviewed each report in detail to get the perspectives of individual teacher educators. Also, the research team conducted interviews of the tutors of the action research course in order to get insights into CPs' engagement with their action research projects as they proceeded through its different stages. The information from these two data sets provided a reference point to understand the interview and observation data gathered from the teacher educators, whose reports had been shortlisted. The purpose of the interviews and field visits was to glean evidence from multiple sources using multiple data collection tools (interviews, observations, document analysis which included lesson plans and pieces of their written reflection) about their development in areas which they had selected for their action, and also their progress in carrying out or promoting classroom based enquiry and reflection.

Data Analysis and Findings

Problems that the Action Research Studies Attempted to Address

The focus of many action research studies was to bring about improvement in teaching of school subjects including: science, mathematics, English language, Urdu language, social studies, and Islamiat through improving the practices of student teachers (students of Bachelor of Education and Advanced Diploma in Education programmes). Some of them even focused on and highlighted specific issues in teaching particular content of school subjects, for example, improving teaching of the concept of 'photosynthesis' or 'formation of day and night' in science; 'fractions' or 'place value' in mathematics; and 'pronunciation' in English or Urdu language. Findings from the reconnaissance phase indicate that the classroom environment generally in their contexts is teacher centred. Students only receive information from teachers' talk or textbooks. There is no group work or activity-based teaching. Teaching aids, specifically Audio-Visual aids are rarely used in teaching. Science teaching is usually done without any practical or scientific experimentation. Grammar-translation method is commonly used in English language teaching where the communicative aspect of English language teaching is usually ignored. In Urdu language teaching, there is no attempt to improve students' pronunciation. Therefore, the influence of local dialects is usually very prominent in students' and teachers' pronunciation in Urdu.

A couple of studies focused on improving the practicum of teacher education programmes. They highlighted that the teacher educators did not make lesson plans and did not give feedback on the lesson plans made by their student teachers. In the context of teacher development, student teachers were not provided with opportunities to develop their IT skills, oral presentations skills, and writing skills.

There are some studies which explored how students or trainee teachers were encouraged to attend the classes regularly and punctually; do their lesson planning; improve their practices of giving feedback; and use creativity in teaching. One of the studies explored why teachers were not able to apply in their own teaching some of the concepts which they had learnt in their teacher education programmes. The study reports that the teachers did not even have a vague idea of the concept of problem-based learning. Although they had been taught these approaches during their BEd and MEd courses, they never applied them as instructional strategies because they did not know how to apply and relate these different approaches to their daily life experiences.

The review of some of the reports highlighted issues which are beyond the researchers' control. For example, they did research on why trainee teachers came late to the classes. The focus of these studies was to explore the reasons behind the inappropriate behaviour of students or student teachers. It seems that these studies could not capture the essence of action research where improving self-practices is as much emphasised as knowledge generation during the process.

As such, there is no obvious pattern identified in the topics of action research in each region but a pattern can be seen in the topics selected by the teacher educators and by those who are not directly involved in teaching and learning. The latter are more generic. The former identify an issue related to teaching and learning.

Some of the studies reveal that these studies were actually conducted by the fellow teachers or student-teachers, as all the interventions were planned and implemented by them, and the researchers only produced an account of those interventions from the perspectives of those who implemented the intervention.

Possible Reasons for the Highlighted Problems

There is little description on the researchers' understanding of the root causes of the educational problems which they selected for their studies. However, some studies talked about issues of accountability and monitoring in schools and other educational institutions. They also talked about lack of resources and teachers' professional development. Some researchers reported that they joined teaching jobs after completing professional qualifications but they soon realised that the things they had learnt in teacher preparation programmes could not always be used in their jobs. The major issues these studies highlighted were associated with lack of motivation among students and teachers towards learning as they felt that students were more interested in the paper qualification rather than in the actual learning. The same was true with teachers, as studies reported that many student teachers or teachers were not intrinsically motivated to teach.

Strategies Used to Address the Problems

To address issues of teacher-centred pedagogies in the classroom teaching and learning, most of the studies engaged student teachers or teachers to implement group-work where students did a task in a group and then presented their work. These studies attempted to encourage interaction among students and between students and teachers. However, little change was noted in the tasks and activities the teachers designed for engaging students in group work. It was evident through the lesson plans that though teachers-made changes in the classroom dynamics, yet it remained beyond their realm of work to change the content of the instruction.

Several reports highlighted the importance of eliciting learners' previous knowledge. Therefore, brain-storming was the first activity in most of the lessons in the intervention stage of the action research. However, it was not clear how the teachers used this information in their teaching.

In many studies, the importance of Audio visual (AV) aids was highlighted and there was a description of how teachers developed low-cost material for teaching. In some studies, teachers used multimedia and other digital means to display information in the class.

Many studies focused on helping student teachers or teachers to develop lesson plans, considering SMART (Specific, Measureable, Attainable, and Timely) objectives. It was observed that the description of the implementation of these lessons in the class was missing in several studies.

A couple of studies focused on questioning skills. They identified attributes of good questions and effective questioning skills and implemented them in their teaching. The focus of some studies was on multi-grade teaching. In this context, peer-tutoring was considered a rescue strategy.

There were some studies which explored reasons for student teachers' and students' malpractices, found a variety of societal factors that shape students' actions and behaviours.

Successes and Challenges in Addressing the Problems

Synthesis of the findings of selected action research studies revealed that the studies, though diverse in nature, generally, brought improvement in teaching and learning. The students were more engaged in learning and expressed more interest in learning and group presentation as a result of well-thought out planning and implementation of action research cycle. However, in many studies, this improvement was more prominent in the female students as compared to the male students.

Several studies highlighted that the action research cycles helped the students explore new information by using resources outside the classrooms, such as the Internet, textbooks of other grades, newspapers, and magazines. In some studies, successes in terms of strengthening collaboration among staff members were also highlighted.

The overarching issues the studies highlighted were related to lack of a culture of research and enquiry in schools. Most of the studies were conducted in the school environment where the participants faced challenges in helping stakeholders understand that these studies were for learning and development rather than for finding faults. There were also other managerial issues such as: less time being allocated for the teaching period, large class-size, seating arrangement in classes, unavailability of teachers to work with researchers as co-researchers or critical friends. The teachers and teacher educators felt that it was quite difficult to arrange cooperative learning strategies and problem-based learning in crowded classrooms of 35-minute time periods where half the classroom time was spent in handling classroom management issues. There were also tensions of syllabus completion and examination preparation which barred the teachers from implementing innovation or change in the classrooms. Also, the mindset of the fellow teacher educators and heads of institutions was a major issue in implementing a changed pedagogy. A teacher educator reported that she asked her student teachers to prepare brief presentations on the topics on which she would give lectures. The teacher educator reported that their fellow teachers considered it as a way of not fulfilling her own responsibility of teaching, and of putting her burden on her students. The fellow student teachers considered it unfair with the students, as they come to the college to 'gain' knowledge and felt that it was the responsibility of the teacher educator to 'deliver' knowledge.

The other area of inquiry focused on the experiences of teacher educators during the course. How did the CPs further apply their learning from their action research studies in their practices/contexts?

Participants' Experiences during the Course

The CPs' 'experiences' were gauged through analysing their action research reports, course evaluation, CPs' and their tutors' retrospective accounts of their experiences during the course through using evidence and examples.

In the post-course evaluation, the CPs generally highlighted that the course helped them develop an understanding of and appreciation for action research. The following quote illustrates the views of several course participants:

> The action research concept is new for me, although I have some knowledge of research and research methods. This action research provided me with the opportunity to get involved as a researcher, so I took action for improvement. After this whole process, now I can identify many connected issues and we can solve various classroom-related problems.

Another participant from the same context shared his view as: 'I feel very privileged and honoured that I attended the action research course at AKU-IED. The proper guidance and high-quality facilitation helped me develop as a researcher.'

Many CPs also appreciated the documentation processes of the action research. They said that they adopted several good practices in their teaching, but they seldom kept an account of it. However, during the process of action research, they kept records of their learning or their students' learning as they were supposed to share it with other course participants in the seminar which the tutors organised at the end of the course. In relation to the teacher educators' experience during the course, the tutors reported that although the course was designed for the teacher educators, the profiles of most of the participants enrolled in the course did not match with the course expectations. It was thought that the course would help participants improve their classroom practices and inquiry skills. However, the tutors realised that many participants enrolled in the course had in fact been deployed in education offices, BoCs of curriculum and PITEs. These course participants did not engage in regular teaching practice and were disconnected with real classroom environments. Therefore, they struggled a lot in identifying genuine issues in teaching and learning which they could address through their action research projects. As one of the tutors reported:

> Despite the CPs' academic and professional qualifications in education, they had a very narrow understanding of teacher education and teacher development process. … They were unable to identify issues from their own practices but were interested in identifying issues to improve their colleagues' practices.

Some participants who belonged to colleges of Education offering PTC (Primary Certificate of Teaching) and CT (Certificate of Teaching) were unable to conduct their action research plans, as their colleges were no longer offering these programmes due to the recent reform efforts in pre-service education in the country. During the action research implementation period, these course participants either had no teaching opportunity at their colleges or were responsible for non-academic work e.g. record keeping and resource management. This mismatch between course participants' current role and the demands of the course presented them with a challenge to identify research questions and conduct research in real situations and they eventually lost interest in the course. This is reflected in the following quote from one of the participants who worked for PITE Quetta, Balochistan.

> We actually work on an ad hoc basis when there is any project we teach. Even in that we cannot teach what we want, rather we teach according to the demands of the project. Our focus changes as the source of our funding changes.

Another participant from the same region further elaborated in response to the interviewer's queries regarding issues they faced in implementation of the action research plan which they developed during the course at AKU-IED.

> Although we are teacher educators, we usually do not have regular teaching activities in our offices. There is no annual or weekly action plan. If we make our own plan, we cannot implement it as there is no money. We are usually sitting in our office waiting for an external project to come.

The tutors also reported that some of the CPs were near retirement and had no interest in working towards change and improvement. The CPs had informed the course tutors that they were in the course because they had not gotten such an opportunity in their career before; hence, the higher officials consider it as a last chance for them to avail the opportunity to undergo a training in a 'well-reputed international university in the country.' Some of them even fell ill during the session and missed some important sessions, which created a gap in their understanding.

The tutors also highlighted that many participants did not have any experience of research supervision or carrying out research. The short 12-day action research course was not enough to develop their research capabilities. The issue became more complicated when the tutors realised that the course participants had limited academic skills and experience of reading and writing in English and for them it was difficult to follow verbal or written instructions. Obviously, it was difficult for them to develop research plans. Eight participants wrote their reports in Urdu because of their inadequate English language proficiency, while other participants could not complete the task nor they attended research seminars because of their limited language skills.

The tutors also reported that the CPs were provided sessions on research ethics and academic integrity but there were several incidences where the CPs bypassed certain procedural demands or ethical considerations. The tutors reported, 'It has major implications for research ethics as well as reliability of research data.'

The tutors had serious doubts whether some of the participants would get the research studies done or if they did, the tutors felt that the reports had probably been written by their colleagues or some experts in their context. However, in the absence of any tangible evidence, the CPs did not face any repercussions. The tutors viewed participants' malpractices as a reflection of deep rooted practice, especially in the rural districts of the country where people unduly utilised their official authority and used personal relationships to get professional perks.

There was also a natural disaster of flood in the province of Sindh due to which some CPs could not implement their action research plan. Some of them and their families were relocated as they lost their homes in the flood and others reported that they were assigned duties in the relief camps during the time when they were supposed to do action research in the field.

The CPs reported that initially they were a little apprehensive about how they could learn about action research in just a few days at AKU-IED, as this was entirely a new concept for many of them. However, they eventually gained confidence when they were introduced to the structure of courses as it provided them opportunities to apply their learning in the field by conducting an action research project in their own context.

Considering the focus of the STEP project on gender issues, the CPs found the sessions on gender quite useful in helping them understand the gender parity index and its implications for teaching and learning.

Generally, the CPs also appreciated the role of tutors in the course to provide timely and individual guidelines for their research project. However, at times, there were some tensions when the CPs did not come up to the tutors' expectations. The following comment from one of the participants reflects the tension: 'The faculty was sometimes very strict; we are human beings, we have different responsibilities but they wanted us to give priority to the tasks they assigned to us.'

How the Participants Apply their Learning from Action Research in their Practices

The participants generally reported that engaging in action research was a valuable teaching and learning process which positively impacted their teaching. The whole process of defining the research questions, writing the literature review, developing and writing the methodology, and organising and writing the findings was a very difficult task for the respondents but it made them aware of their teaching practices and their students' needs. The participants also mentioned that the action research process made them more aware of new strategies and gave them confidence to try them. They reported that action research could empower teacher educators/teachers to change by pushing them out of their comfort-zone. However, the data shows that for many participants action research study was a one-time activity which helped them develop some research skills and try out some innovation in the class. However, they did not find the time, resources, and support to carry out any other study. Many of them thought that action research was the agenda of the university or donor agency. They anticipated that the AKU-IED faculty would again engage them in a similar activity. The following quote from a participant from Quetta, Balochistan, reflects the views of many participants across the sample:

> We wonder if AKU-IED asked us to do action research only to keep the reports on the bookshelves. It has been more than two years and no one from AKU-IED did the follow-up to see what we are doing after the course.

Some participants argued that it was not feasible to promote action research as there was no collaborative culture in their institutes. They said that a single teacher without any co-researcher or critical friend could not conduct action research, as teaching and researching were two very involved tasks which could not be managed single-handedly.

Discussion

One of the purposes of this study was to conduct a meta-analysis of action research studies produced by participants of an action research course conducted under the STEP project at AKU-IED. The meta-analysis was done to understand the problems the participants had identified; how they identified them; what they did to address the problems and finally what they learnt through the process. As the intention was not to evaluate the action research studies, we tried not to give any evaluative comments on the reports. However, the quality of the data for this part of the study was closely dependent on the quality of the write-up the participants produced. Therefore, it became necessary to highlight what conclusions we could or could not draw from the reports.

Although the reports provided information about the issues which the participants had tried to address through their action research, yet the reports did not provide much information as to how the participants identified the problems. For example, if they thought that their student teachers should adopt a particular approach, for example activity-based teaching, what benefits of such teaching would they anticipate? How did they develop their own understanding of activity-based teaching? On what grounds would they design their intervention? One reason why the action research reports did not include such information could be the lack of theoretical grounding of these studies, as there were only a couple of studies, which included a section on literature review.

It is true that some teacher researchers believed that a literature review was not essential for the teacher researcher as many published classroom researches did not include literature review (Poel, 2006). However, a good literature review can help novice teacher researchers to refine their research questions, develop their research methodology and plan their interventions and data collection procedures. A literature review can also be useful for interpreting the findings and drawing conclusions. However, as it has been noted that the participants had limited academic literacy skills, it would have been unrealistic to expect them to make use of educational literature.

Many reports have given details of their intervention in the form of lesson plans and some descriptions of how those plans were executed in classrooms. However, the process and outcome of data collection were missing in most of the studies. This reflects the participants' general inability to develop a reflective account of the actions they took in the classrooms. In Pakistan, teacher education programmes traditionally have been based on the technical approach as the teacher educators are provided some ready-made techniques to apply in their teaching. The concept of reflective teaching or reflective practice is not well established in Pakistan (Khan, Fazal & Amin, 2014). The problem becomes even more complicated when the teachers or teacher educators have limited language skills.

This study shows that the CPs were provided with a general understanding of action research which helped them develop their research plans. However, they were not provided with much support in the field during the time when they were implementing their plans. Considering the profile of the CPs, it is hard to expect that they would develop a critical stance towards their own actions when they were alone in their fields. As the core business of action research is to improve practices through self-analysis of their own actions, this meta-analysis revealed that most of the action research reports did not serve the purpose.

It is also evident that the selection of participants of the course was not appropriate as many of them, especially from Balochistan, were from BoC or PITE. These people do not engage in regular teaching. For doing action research, they went to schools as a guest or an expert to conduct action research with practicing teachers. So it was difficult for them to get any insights into the process of change and be part of it in the unique institutional context.

The meta-analysis revealed that the CPs tended to identify problems which were external to them but they presented, as they were taught, to present them in a personal way, for example:

- How can I encourage a student teacher to be punctual and regular in the class?
- How can I encourage a student teacher to incorporate activity-based teaching approaches in their lessons?

The actions they took to address the issue at hand seemed to change their own attitude towards teaching and learning, but in most of the cases, there were external factors. These action research studies were not designed to enable teachers or teacher educators to challenge contexts beyond their own classrooms. This is true with many action research studies. Carr and Kemmis (1986) have noted that action research is not seen to be critical to the systems and structures of the organisations, but it is found to be supportive in generating improvements within the established framework. In this sense, these action researches were not liberating the teacher educators from their existing frames of mind.

The meta-analysis identified that the most common problem which teacher educators identified was the lack of motivation among teachers to prepare themselves for teaching for active learning, inquiry and innovation, as they thought that these would not be helpful for them in their jobs as public school teachers. Most of the teacher educators' efforts to engage teachers to use active learning approaches in teaching were not successful to a large extent, as the general mindset did not favour these approaches. However, in some cases, the teacher educators played a vital role in improving the capacity of teachers to design inquiry-based instruction and bring innovation in their teaching. Also, in these cases, teacher educators themselves were able to continuously engage in their own professional development through collaborative learning, which played a vital role to improve their practices.

It is argued that, to change the inherent practices, action researchers need to demonstrate a high level of autonomy, capability of taking initiatives and a constructivist view of knowledge. Kemmis and McTaggart (1988) argue that action research is carried out as a collaborative process by those who have a shared concern. It is a form of collective reflective enquiry which professionals carry out in real contexts in order to improve the 'rationality and justice' (Kemmis & McTaggart, p. 6) of their own practices, as well as their understanding of these practices, and the situations in which these practices are carried out. If these are the virtues of the education system, then action research can bring about a desirable change. Although action research is generally understood as a 'grass-roots movement', this study suggests that action research can lead to a desirable change where the change process, in the upper stratum of educational system, has already started. The study recommends that to bring about sustainable change in the teaching and learning process in these regions, it is important to target those key people who have the authority in social systems to control the structure and discourse, while engaging with change at the grass-roots level.

The significance of the reported study is two-fold. First, STEP was a donor-funded project for developing the capacity of teacher education in Pakistan. It was important to explore and document how the project's intervention brought about a change in teacher educators' understanding and skills in relation to action research in Pakistan. Action research is a well-established component of teacher education programmes around the world. The findings of the study would enrich the existing scholarship on action research as a tool for improving practices in teacher education.

Conclusion

First, this study enhanced our understanding of action research as a viable professional development strategy in teacher education in Pakistan. Second, the study also provided the research participants with an opportunity to reflect on their experiences of conducting action research and consider implications for incorporating it in their future professional development plan and teaching. The field visits served a purpose to reconnect them with their action research project.

Limitation and Challenges

There was an inherent limitation in employing retrospective interviews from the CPs and their tutors about their experiences in carrying out action research as part of the course at the AKU-IED. In the absence of the base-line data, we relied on the retrospective interviews. We understand the limitation of human memory, we also understand that when people recall information they in fact reconstruct it, and their present circumstances play a significant role in the reconstruction of the past event. We expect the readers of this study to consider the professional development of CPs through conducting an action research as a self-assessment of their past and present experiences. We drew knowledge about their experiences as they ascertained their learning through examples and evidence and showcased their best practices. For the said reasons, we did not develop an interview protocol; rather we left it to them as to how they would frame their stories of understanding and conducting action research.

Due to limited academic literacy skills, the CPs did not present their research studies in a clear and concise way. Also, there were eight research reports written in Urdu. Although the research team had enough expertise to understand written Urdu, they did not have the experience of reading academic writing in Urdu, which posed a challenge. Therefore, considering the language of the research reports as an issue for us, we contacted the concerned CPs when we faced difficulties in interpreting the language of the research reports.

References

Altrichter, H., Posch, P. & Somekh, B., *Teachers Investigate their Work: An Introduction to the Methods of Action Research* (London: Routledge, 1993).

Argyris, C., *Reasons and Rationalizations: The Limits to Organizational Knowledge* (Oxford: Oxford University Press, 2004).

Argyris, C., 'Learning and teaching: A theory of action perspective', *Journal of Management Education*, 21/1, (1997), 9–27.

Au, W., 'High-stakes testing and curricular control: A qualitative meta-synthesis', *Educational Researcher,* 36/5, (2007), 258–67.

Britzman, D.P., *Practice Makes Practice: A Critical Study of Learning to Teach* (Revised edition, SUNY Press: New York, 2012).

Brown, T. & Jones, L., *Action Research and Postmodernism: Congruence and Critique* (Buckingham: Open University Press, 2001).

Campbell A., 'Teachers' research and professional development in England: Some questions, issues and concerns', *Journal of In-Service Education*, 29/3, (2003), 375–388.

Campbell, E., 'The virtuous, wise and knowledgeable teacher: Living the good life as a professional practitioner', *Educational Theory*, 63/4, (2013), 413–430.

Carr, W. & Kemmis, S., *Becoming Critical: Education, Knowledge and Action Research* (London: Falmer, 1986).

Cochran-Smith, M. & Lytle, S.L., 'Relationships of knowledge and practice: Teacher learning in communities', *Review of Research in Education*, 24, (1999), 249–305.

Delong, J., 'Action research in a culture of inquiry: Transforming teaching and learning through living-theory', *Educational Journal of Living Theories,* 6/2, (2013), 25–44.

Elliott, J., *Action Research for Educational Change* (Open University Press: UK, 1991).

Fenstermacher, G.D., 'The knower and the known: The nature of knowledge in research on teaching', *Review of Research in Education,* 20, (1994), 3–56.

Forey, G., Firkins, A., & Sengupta, S., 'Full circle: Stakeholders' evaluation of a collaborative enquiry action research literacy project', *English Teaching: Practice and Critique*, 11/ 4, (2012), 70–87.

Grundy, S., 'Curriculum and Teaching', in E. Hatton, eds. *Understanding Teaching: Curriculum and the Social Context of Schooling* (Sydney: Harcourt Brace, 1994), 28–39.

Halai, A., 'Mentoring in-service teachers: Issues of role diversity', *Teaching and Teacher Education,* 22/6, (2006), 700–710.

Halai, N., 'How teachers become action researchers in Pakistan: emerging patterns from a qualitative meta-synthesis', *Educational Action Research,* 19/2, (2011), 20–214.

Harold, L., 'Action research-A critique', *Journal of Educational Sociology,* 31/4, (1957) 137–153.

Jensen, L.A. and M.N. Allen., 'Meta-synthesis of qualitative findings', *Qualitative Health Research,* 6/4, (1996), 553–60.

Kemmis, S. & McTaggart, R., *The Action Research Reader* (3rd ed., Geelong, Australia, 1988).

Khan, M.I., Fazal, S. & Amin, M., 'Reflection in teacher education programmes in Pakistan and the UK: A comparison', *Journal of Research and Reflections in Education,* 8/2, (2014), 132–138.

Poel, E. & Dietrich, C., 'Action research in teacher preparation: An inclusive seminar', *A Journal of College Teaching & Learning,* 3/12, (2006), 1–4.

Reason, P. & H. Bradbury, *Handbook of Action Research* (London: Sage, 2001).

Sandelowski, M. & J. Barroso, *Handbook for synthesizing qualitative research* (New York: Springer, 2007).

Stephen, C., *Action Research, Fundamental Research, and Education Practices* (London: Simon & Schuster, 1952).

Valli, L., 'Connecting teacher development and school improvement: Ironic consequences of a pre-service action research course', *Teaching and Teacher Education,* 16/7, (2000), 715–730.

Winter, R., 'Managers, spectators and citizens: Where does 'theory' come from in action research?', *Educational Action Research,* 6/3, (1998), 361–376.

Zembylas, M., 'Emotions and teacher identity: A post-structural perspective', *Teachers and Teaching*, 9/3, (2003), 213–238.

Note

1. Association for Supervision and Curriculum Development, What Shall the High Schools Teach? (Washington, 1956).

12

Institutional Strengthening: Case Studies of Government Elementary Colleges of Education

Sadia Muzaffar Bhutta, Zubeda Bana, and *Kulsoom Jaffer*

Introduction

Having worked with the principal and selected faculty members of Government Elementary Colleges of Education (GECEs), STEP decided to work in a more focused and deliberate manner to strengthen the capacity of selected teacher training institutions to better support quality teacher education and to provide some case study examples that could be rolled out to other institutions. This included partnering with three GECEs, two from Sindh, and one each from Balochistan and Gilgit-Baltistan to strengthen their capacity to deliver better quality teacher education.

This chapter provides analytical reflections on the framework, the processes and the outcomes of the programme, which paves the way for efforts towards rolling out the model intervention to other institutions in each province.

Working with teacher training institutions' administrators and faculty over the past few years, in 2012 STEP recognised the capacity of institutions as a critical element of a strong education system. While the initial project framework included capacity development for faculty of teacher training institutions, it did not take into account a more holistic and targeted approach to institutional strengthening of teacher training institutions, and other relevant bodies. STEP designed an institutional strengthening programme for the three GECEs with the aim of working with the institution in a focused and participative manner with the purpose: (i) to strengthen the institution's capacity in effective delivery of the newly initiated Associate Degree in Education[1] (ADE) programme; and (ii) to develop their capacity in grounded approaches that could be rolled out to other institutions in similar contexts in these areas.

This chapter presents institutional capacity building initiatives, and their successes and challenges at GECEs in Quetta, Gilgit-Baltistan, and Sindh provinces.

Purpose of the Programme

This programme was undertaken with the purpose that after completion of this programme, the four institutions would serve as case study exemplars of approaches for strengthening teacher education institutions. The programme began with entry negotiations with the management of GECEs. The purpose of these initial negotiations was to understand the real needs of the institution and to provide critical strategic and technical support in enabling the process of programmatic change in the institution; to build ownership and consensus of the institutional leadership and the faculty in developing and implementing institutional strengthening programmes; and to coordinate with the respective provincial departments of education for providing alternate resources required to support infrastructural development and change in the institution as identified in the needs analysis dialogues.

Senior faculty members from AKU-IED and the project team,

prior to designing the programme, comprehensively assessed the professional development needs of the faculty members of the GECEs and then developed a programme tailored to the specific needs of each individual institution. The capacity gap analysis included interviews with the principals and faculty members at the target GECEs. In addition, classroom teaching was observed. Discussion and observation revealed that the major and urgent need of the faculty was orientation in various pedagogical strategies to enhance students' engagement in learning in order to improve their learning outcomes. Keeping in consideration the identified needs, an implementation plan was developed and implemented in three phases over a period of two years.

Theoretical Framework

Institutional Capacity Building (ICB) is an approach towards improving both hard and soft capabilities of an institution for sustainable change and reforms. Hard or tangible capabilities include asset building, infrastructure, legal framework and policies, whereas soft or non-tangible capabilities include social and intellectual capital development of the institution, including the faculty and institutional leadership, promoting a collaborative learning culture, valuing collective knowledge generation and dissemination, and improving the quality of teaching and learning at educational institutions. Fullan (2006) defines capacity building as a strategy that increases the collective effectiveness of a group or an institution to raise the bar and close the gap in student learning. It is a multi-faceted approach helping institutions to develop individual and collective knowledge and competencies, resources and motivation which are often ignored or underestimated (Langaas, Odeck & Bjorvig, 2007).

Defined in this way, institutional capacity building mostly refers to asset building of the human capital of the institution. There are different approaches to institutional capacity building: (i) a top-down approach which might begin with changing policies or structures (ii) a bottom-up approach which invests in skills development of staff, (iii) a partnership development approach which invests in strengthening the relationship between or among organisations and (iv) a community organising approach which engages communities into building new organisational set-ups for sustainable change and improvement (Crisp, Swerissen & Duckett, 2000). Although each of these approaches in the literature are referred to as capacity building approaches, they focus on one or the other sphere of asset building rather than on bringing the social reality of the entire institution into focus, by engaging key stakeholders in the process of change and reform.

Contemporary literature on institutional capacity building argues that capacity building in any social system is not stable, enduring and 'out there'. It occurs as a result of socio-rationalist archetype (Bushe & Coetzer, 1995) when people in the organisation mutually construct meaning in their interaction, ideas and actions to make sustained commitments and ownership at the entire organisational level (Mitchell & Sackney, 2000). These new ways of thinking about organisations consider educational institutions as living organisms, where the quality of life in the organisation is valued by human interactions and effective planning, which engage the hearts and minds of people who create the day-to-day life of the organisation.

Programme Implementation at GECE Quetta

Implementation of the programme began with an analysis of the professional development needs of the faculty members of the college. The needs analysis at the outset of the project helped us tailor the content and delivery of the workshops as per the needs of the college. As discussed earlier, classroom observations and discussions with faculty members and the principals revealed that honing faculty members' skills in using learner-centred approaches was one of the urgent needs.

Classroom observations of two teachers for two different courses (i.e. teaching of mathematics and content of social studies) concurred with the reported data that 'teacher-centred' pedagogy was found to be the predominant mode of teaching. In the 'teaching of mathematics' course the facilitator taught 'graphical representation of data' with a specific focus on pie-charts. The content delivered was mostly accurate; however, the predominant mode was 'chalk and talk' with intermittent questioning to engage student teachers or check their understanding. In a 'teaching methods' class one would expect to help student teacher extend their repertoire of pedagogical skills—a fundamentally important aspect which was almost missing in the observed teaching. The other facilitator (who was more experienced) did use 'group-work' to engage student teachers; however, they were made to sit in groups to copy text which was provided to them. While discussing the need for professional development, the principal of the college clearly articulated, 'I have some young and passionate teachers…they come with degrees in their academic area such as chemistry and mathematics; however, they need help in teaching methods'.

The other area, which was prioritised by the college principal and faculty, was practicum. Analysis of ADE (Associate Degree in Education) course handbooks demonstrated that the nature and pattern of ADE-practicum was different from CT and PTC courses. The former is more demanding in terms of skills which supervisors and school mentors need to develop to help student teachers become good practitioners. Both experienced and newly inducted facilitators required assistance to improve their practicum which is considered the 'back-bone of teacher education courses'. A two-phase training was planned according to the needs communicated during the needs-analysis. It helped to get acceptance from most of the audience which was evident from their gestures and participation.

Need-based training was the first step to 'attract' the audience; however, sustaining their interest would not have been possible without their willingness to learn. Having said that, it is important to mention that the participants could be classified into three groups based on their willingness to learn:

- ***Eager to learn:*** almost 50% of the audience seemed to have started with some scepticism but they gained momentum as the sessions progressed. This half of the faculty members were continuously engaged in intellectual discussions by 'bringing their real-classroom issues on the table for discussion', 'posing practical questions', and 'helping others by responding to their questions'. One of them commented, 'Training workshops helped us to maintain our enthusiasm as we were engaged in different [relevant] tasks'.
- ***Learning by force:*** almost 40% of the audience participated at a 'moderate to good level'. They shared ideas during the session but they did not demonstrate 'seriousness' in evaluating the workshop content and delivery for their own practice.
- ***Tired and retired:*** the rest of the 10% could be classified as the 'tired and retired' group who were the least interested in what was going on around them. They were there because they 'had to be there'. Some of them 'bunked' some of the sessions too!

It can be argued that the 'eager to learn' group is an asset for the college whose skills can be augmented further by engaging them in continuous professional development activities. They can also play an active role in encouraging and engaging the 'learning by force' group. However, the 'tired and retired' group needs further attention. Why are they not interested in their work? Is it difficult for them to accept change? If yes, what alternative strategies (if at all) can be used to encourage them?

Augmenting Participants' Pedagogical Knowledge and Skills

As mentioned earlier, 'honing pedagogical skills for classroom teaching and supervision skills for the practicum' were identified as urgent needs for professional development. Both episodes of the training workshop focused on enhancing faculty members' skills as practitioners. Four active methods of teaching were selected as part of the first phase: story-telling, role-play, discussion, and Directed Activity Related to Text (DART). Workshop participants appreciated the facilitators' input and getting opportunities for planning and translating their knowledge into practice through teaching in a real classroom. At the outset of the second phase of intervention, they were asked to reflect on the implementation of the strategies they had learnt in the first phase.

It was encouraging to know that a majority of them managed to incorporate various strategies in the assigned disciplines. Some examples are cited here:

- I used 'picture story' in language/history lessons.
- I used 'role-play' to teach 'how to manage over-crowded' classes as part of the 'school management' lesson.
- I used 'role-play' in a mathematics lesson.
- I used 'role play' to teach 1973-constitution as part of a social studies lesson.

- I used 'discussion' as part of a language lesson.
- I used DART to help students analyse text.

The participants' views showed that they had incorporated their learning into practice. It is evident that the most frequently used strategies were 'role-play' and 'story-telling' followed by 'discussion'. DART was reported to be used by one participant only. Perhaps, this was a new concept and participants needed more help to incorporate this vitally important pedagogical strategy in their teaching.

That said, the self-report did not ascertain the quality of pedagogical strategies used during teaching. The focus of the second phase was 'practicum'. Participants were given opportunities to use various monitoring tools by having a practice-session based on video clips (e.g. classroom teaching, feedback sessions). It is to be argued that ADE-handbooks present a battery of tools to monitor classroom practice of student teachers. This two-day workshop was like 'touching the tip of the ice-berg' with a focus on three aspects of the practicum: observation, feedback, and self-reflection. A lot is left to be desired. Arguably, a mechanism of repeated cycles of observation and feedback would have helped to assist college faculty to expand their repertoire of pedagogical and supervision skills. However, this rigorous but limited support was necessitated by time.

Translating Knowledge into Practice

The importance of rigorous built-in opportunities to translate knowledge into practice as part of professional development courses cannot be overstated. The sessions were planned in such a manner that participants got a chance to translate their knowledge into practice either as part of the session or 'stand-alone' classroom practice in a supervised environment. For phase-two, they watched video clips of classroom teaching to use monitoring tools and reflected on the structure and process of using them. It helped them to have a concrete example to 'rate' and to discuss inconsistencies in rating among colleagues. As part of the first phase, they planned lessons in four disciplines: science, mathematics, English, and social studies to teach in real ADE classrooms. These episodes of 'pseudo-practice' helped participants to identify pros and cons of using selected teaching strategies/monitoring tools. Follow-up discussions with faculty members also helped to explore opportunities and challenges for incorporating 'new' learning in their practice.

Grouping Strategies: Task-Oriented Groups

One of the questions we raised during the planning sessions for ourselves was: *How should we make groups to enhance interaction?* Grouping according to four core disciplines (e.g. science, mathematics, English language, and social studies) was one of the viable options, though not a perfect solution. Workshop participants worked in 'discipline-groups' throughout the first phase. However, in the second phase, where practicum was the main focus, grouping strategies varied to suit the needs of the expected outcomes of the assigned tasks. For example, participants were grouped randomly and assigned one monitoring tool for the session on 'observation'. Groups were named accordingly—rating scale, rubric, tally-sheet/checklist, and classroom drawing. Both strategies reaped some benefits. Common disciplines helped groups to share their expertise in one particular area and develop lesson plans for the particular discipline. Similarly, common tools helped group members to work on one particular example of a monitoring instrument to get acquainted with the structure and scoring scheme. They shared the assigned tool (e.g. structure of the tool and experience of rating the classroom watched in a video) with the rest of the class. The strategy seemed to help them gain more in the available time slot.

Reflection on Challenges

While implementing the programme, we reflected on a few challenges which are important to highlight hereafter.

Different Needs of the Faculty

The course was attended by a mixed group of teachers including experienced teachers and some newly-inducted but highly motivated teachers. Although, interactive pedagogies were selected, as per the needs identified, it was still difficult to define length and depth of the content to be covered. Taking into consideration the ADE curriculum and the different needs of the target audience, a range of activities was designed accordingly. During the first phase, sessions were designed to cater for the needs of a mixed audience by initiating sessions with some simple activities for orientation followed by more advanced content. Similarly, in the second phase, task-oriented grouping helped them have a common focus for discussion.

ADE Curriculum: Gap between Theory and Implementation

Analysis of ADE handbooks[2] revealed that the programme was planned in detail. For example, a battery of monitoring tools was presented in handbooks to help supervisors and school mentors to make guided observations. However, discussions during sessions on practicum revealed that the college supervisors' understanding did not necessarily resonate with the purpose the tools were developed for. All of them 'interpreted' the given indicators in their own ways. Interestingly, they were inclined to use rubrics and scales to assign 'high scores' to their students. While assigning a high score is important, the fundamental purpose of the whole exercise of feedback based on observations is to improve classroom practice of student teachers. Inflation of scores on *humanitarian grounds* would not take them far on the road of professional development. In fact, some of them realised during a session on 'observation' that the tools needed to be used objectively. One of the participants, at the end of the second phase, commented:

> I was inclined to assign a high score [to the classroom practice watched in a video] in the first round; however, discussion helped me to question my practice...we should not assign a high score when it is not deserved. Indicators should be read properly and understood.

It was an important comment which raised other issues: What do they mean by 'reading properly' and 'understanding'? How would they make sure that they understood the indicators? There are no quick-fixes. Repeated cycles of orientation and practice may help them to get better in using these indicators. They realised the importance of co-observation using these indicators which would help them develop at least a similar understanding—more scientifically speaking inter-ratter reliability.

During a period of two and a half years, need-based interventions were carried out to address the needs of the faculty members. The faculty members were engaged in focused activities during the session and implemented their learning in the classroom during inter-phases to see the applicability of the strategies learnt. Each phase of the intervention was connected to the previous one with distinct features of interactive sessions, guided practice, and debriefing. The programme culminated with a policy seminar to disseminate the impact of training on the professional development of the college faculty. The aim of this seminar was to provide a platform to the elementary college faculty to showcase their learning and the impact that this training created on their professional capacity as teacher educators. Different stakeholders from the Bureau of Curriculum (BoC), Provincial Institute for Teacher Education (PITE), Government Education College of Education (GECE) for male and female and Policy, Planning and Implementation Unit (PPIU) were invited to this seminar. Highlights of the day were a gallery walk to observe the faculty members' work and interact with the teachers, plus a panel discussion.

Since the college faculty members were the beneficiaries of this training, the focus of the seminar was to provide a platform to show the outcome of the programme to the audience generally and the government officers particularly. It was very encouraging to note that the teachers had maintained a record of their work. After each professional development session and during the training, teachers developed some teaching and learning materials and kept them as evidence of the intervention in their classrooms. All those materials helped them recall, recollect and relate to those exemplary teaching experiences. Major themes covered through this facilitation included: teaching pedagogies, ICT and practicum which were the aspects covered during the intervention sessions. As an outcome, four posters were developed: (i) Inquiry-based teaching: Process oriented classroom; (ii) Digital story; (iii) Practicum: Backbone of teacher education; and (iv) Role play: A communicative strategy for better learning.

Successful implementation of the capacity building was very much evident by the quality of the work exhibited by the faculty of the elementary college of education. Teachers actively participated in this activity and presented their work to the audience. The panel discussion generated some thought provoking insights about the importance and possibilities of professional development sessions for the teacher educators. The gallery walk was one of the last activities of the seminar and it captured the attention of the audience. Teacher educators from BoC, PITE, PPIU, and elementary college faculty were quite impressed by the quality of work exhibited by the teachers. Many pertinent questions were asked to see the importance of the strategy used.

The seminar concluded with the following recommendations:

- tailor-made professional development sessions should be arranged for teacher educators;
- a three-pronged methodology of professional development (i.e. interactive sessions, guided practice and debriefing) should be adopted;
- teacher education institutes should collaborate to offer quality and contextual professional development programmes;
- mainstreaming of CPD (regular episodes, equal opportunities, accountability, whole-school approach, mentoring and coaching, avenues for sharing best practice) should take place; and
- using questions such as: What is the difference between the previous model of lesson plans and the BOPPPS[3] model of planning? What different tools could be used to assess practicum? How are portfolios developed and managed by the student teachers? How could role play in the classroom be assessed and encouraged?

The participants at the seminar were also surprised to see the use of the Internet despite very low Internet connection facility in the college. Very healthy discussions between the presenters and the audience were noticed. The Principal of the Government Elementary College of Education (male) was surprised to see the level of work done by the faculty and wanted to have similar support and sessions in his college as well. He appreciated the hard work of the presenters and appreciated the well-organised facilitation extended to the student teachers during the practicum. Looking at the quality of the work done and the level of enthusiasm shown by the teachers, BoC officers promised to visit the college.

Institutional Strengthening: The Case of GECE, Skardu

Reflecting on the processes involved in programme development and implementation and its outcomes, this section presents the case of institutional capacity building (ICB) at GECE Skardu in Gilgit-Baltistan.

Drawing on the findings of the need assessment conducted with the college faculty, a tailor-made intervention was designed for the college. The capacity building programme for the faculty was premised on the theoretical framework of Appreciative Inquiry.

Appreciative Inquiry (AI) is best known as an intervention strategy for changing social systems; a method of identifying 'positive core' by looking at what is going right. It has been one of the most significant approaches towards institutional capacity building in the past two decades (Bana, 2014). The concept was first introduced by David Cooperrider (2008) of Case Western Reserve University in the mid-1980s. To understand the basis of the concept, it is important to unfold the meaning of the two words used: 'Appreciation' and 'Inquiry'. 'Appreciation' means to recognise strengths of things or people and value their contribution to add strengths for further development. 'Inquiry' is a systematic way to study, probe, analyse, synthesise, and draw informed conclusions from the entire process of change and reform. Appreciative Inquiry (AI) is considered as a paradigm shift that helps to move social systems from deficit thinking towards capacity building, by appreciating what is good and valuable in the present situation and learning about the ways to effect positive change for further improvement in organisations.

As mentioned elsewhere (Bana, 2014), the basic process of AI grounded in the 5Ds process of changing social systems mentioned herewith, is an attempt to generate a collective image of a new and better future by exploring the best of: (a) what is, (b) what might be, (c) what should be and (d) what can be. In other words the process engages the entire organisation in: (i) defining and discovering the best of; (ii) dreaming and designing what creates the best of; and (iii) developing the people and processes which best exemplify the best of. These are the core elements considered for sustainable change and improvement in organizations (Bushe, 1999).

Memon (2013) argues that in Pakistan, many times, teacher education efforts are addressed through administrative advices and top-down approaches, which remain at the surface in nature and purposes. Despite many attempts in teacher education reforms, a reflective analysis of the current state of education and its related impact, both on the quality and delivery of service in education presents imbalances, because most of the time, the focus of reforms is a 'one-off' intervention solving the problems of what is not working in these organisations (Bana, 2014). The solutions and advices are sought from the external players, who may not be able to understand the level of strengths in individual organisations, to take them from 'the state of poor to fair, to good, to great and to excellent' (McKinsey, 2007). One-size-fit-all approach cannot serve the purpose of capacity building in public sector educational organisations working at different levels in different contexts.

The ultimate goal of institutional capacity building is to help organisations identify good practices, design effective development plans and ensure implementation and sustainability of these efforts by engaging all key stakeholders in the process of reform. It is an extremely complex journey, hence, the role of an institutional leader is primarily pivotal in creating and maintaining the necessary conditions, culture and structure to lead the entire organisation towards a new and better future by exploring the best of what is and what has been. These new ways of thinking about institutional capacity building create a pull effect that generates evolution in teacher education reforms.

Programme Objectives

Building on the above mentioned theoretical framework, the ICB intervention under STEP's pilot initiative set the following objectives to work with the elementary college of education at Skardu:

- To understand the real needs of the institution and provide critical, strategic and technical support in enabling the process of programmatic change in the institution;
- To build ownership and consensus of the institutional leadership and the faculty in developing and implementing institutional capacity building programmes;
- To coordinate with the Department of Education in Baltistan for providing alternate resources required to support infrastructural development in the institution, as identified in the needs analysis dialogues.

Institutional Context

Government Elementary College of Education, located within the main town of Skardu, is operating in a splendid purpose-built building along with an attached elementary lab school and a three-storied student hostel, currently vacant. Established in 2002, the college is celebrating its first decade of success. The college building includes big classrooms, the principal's office, the staff room, the administrator's office, the library, science laboratories, the computer lab, a huge auditorium and playgrounds, and lavatories for students and the faculty. The college corridors and classrooms are full of displays pasted on the walls.

Currently, 20 faculty members, 10 females, and 10 males along with the principal are working as teaching staff. All the faculty members are qualified BEd and MEd graduates. One MEd graduate from AKU-IED joined the institution and earned a good reputation among the faculty and institutional leadership, but has been recently transferred to school in another district. Another MEd from AKU-IED is working in the elementary school in Skardu and is a useful resource for this teacher education institution. Most of the faculty members are exposed either to the Professional Development Centre Northern Areas (PDCN) or AKU-IED's short certificate courses in Action Research, Educational Leadership and Management and Teacher Education conducted under STEP project.

There are two major degree programmes offered at the college: (i) a newly introduced two-year Associate Degree in Education (ADE); and (ii) an already established BEd programme. The former, based on student-centred activities such as project work and assignments, is offered in English and is co-ed, whereas the BEd programme based on lecture method providing notes to the students is offered in Urdu as a medium of instructions and is separately conducted for male and female students. Both the programmes are affiliated with and obtain degree awards from the Karakorum International University.

The existing student enrolment in ADE is 40 (36 female and 4 male students), whereas in BEd the student enrolment is 87. There are 36 students enrolled in the class for males and 51 in the class for females. The total enrolled students in BEd programme is double compared to the students in the ADE programme, which is a matter of concern for all who believe in student-centred learning approaches in teacher education programmes.

How the Journey Started

The ICB project commenced after discussions with the faculty, staff and the Director of Education, Baltistan, and a mutual decision was reached that the pilot initiative under STEP would concentrate on the soft side of institutional development.

The ICB project used a constructive and Appreciative Inquiry approach whereby the faculty, staff and the institutional leadership came together in a workshop setting and were requested to share their experiences and insights related to their work in teacher education. The 20 participants were engaged in pairs, sharing narratives of their experiences and focusing on their work of teacher education at the elementary college of education. The workshop data was treated as qualitative data. Through content analysis, the facilitator looked for the organisation values and the factors that helped people in the organisation to excel in their work in teacher education. From this data, the organisation's vision and goals were developed. These statements were validated by organisation members on two aspects: (i) how far these statements captured the organisation's values and (ii) how much they liked the process. In this way, in fact, they were defining and discovering their positive core i.e. what they wanted to be, and how they could help each other discover their strengths, leading them to value the best of what they had in their organisation.

However, at the initial stage, the AI approach challenged many of the participants who used to concentrate on identifying problems rather than strengths of their organisation. Their major argument behind this deficit approach, as reported by them, was that without focusing on problems, how could they improve the situation in teacher education? Nevertheless, with constant dialogues and critical reflections, they were motivated to think about their key experiences in the past and discover the elements of what was working well in those situations and taking them to the next level, developing common images for their future.

Once they were able to develop their vision for the future, they were engaged in developing achievable steps to make their vision a reality. In pairs, they were able to develop small-scale AI projects in their ADE and BEd classes for improving their practice, focusing on the present and the future of teacher education.

The intent of the pilot project was to equip the faculty to reflect critically on their roles and responsibilities as teacher educators and help them build the soft assets of the organisation, for long-lasting change and development in elementary schools in the remote mountainous areas of Baltistan.

The process of re-conceptualising teacher education helped the faculty at the GECE to understand the knowledge, skills, strategies and disposition required for teacher educators to fulfill their role as effective teacher leaders and learners in their institutions, and at teaching practice schools. The evidence of their learning was reflected in their reflective journals. The exposure to AI processes helped them understand the need of investing in a strength-based approach for lasting change and improvement in teacher education. For example, one of the faculty members wrote:

> We [the faculty and the trainees] developed many new activities and used different methods to involve our students at teaching practice schools. We managed to develop one class as a model class to exemplify how to prepare low-cost/no-cost materials for active teaching-learning processes. We appreciated our trainees and students at schools for all the new steps they introduced in their classes.

Another senior male faculty stated, 'I am unable to sleep at nights as I consider that whatever I was doing in the name of teaching, was just waste of time and resources. Now I have realised that teaching is a very difficult job'. Another senior teacher educator said:

> During my 25 years of experience, it is for the first time that I have seen an entire lesson demonstrated by a teacher educator [the project faculty] with all meaningful activities. The students' high level of engagement in their learning was so obvious from their presentations. All these huge tasks were managed in an hour, which was an amazing learning experience for me.

Yet another participant reflected:

> The attitude of a teacher educator is a key towards success. If we think we can do it in limited time, we can. For that we need to stay away from misuse of time, like not going late to our classes, as the time blocked for us for teaching, should also be considered as the most precious resource like money to be valued.

In the programme, the participants were introduced to the concept of 'reflection'. They were encouraged to maintain a reflective journal. It seems that the participants found a value in practicing reflection. A participant, for example, in his reflective journal wrote:

> For the first time, I learnt the meaning and importance of reflection in teaching. I have started using this precious activity of writing reflection regularly and also try to promote it among my students. As a matter of fact, there is always room for improvement in every individual and organisation. Reflection plays a vital role in bringing improvement in our lives. I have learned a lot by applying the reflection process in my teaching. In my classroom two-to-three reflection exercises are compulsory for each student trainee on teaching and learning

processes. Moreover, I encourage the students to reflect even on their daily routine tasks.

The participants' reflections may help us understand how the journey of becoming teacher educators from the GECE impacted the faculty to explore new ways for continuing professional education. The following key themes emerged, as lessons learnt by the participants.

Lesson One: A Leader Does Not Mean an Authoritative Boss

In the context of Baltistan, where command and control is the way of life, a leader is always considered right. Before the workshop, the participants had a different concept of leadership. In this workshop, they realised that leadership means being responsible, guiding and inspiring others and motivating the subordinates. As one of the participants reflected:

> I understood this from the example of a bird that carried a drop of water in its beak to extinguish the fire in the time of Prophet Abraham and the dove brought the news of the restoration of peace, in the time of Prophet Noah. The lesson learnt from both the stories of the Prophets was that we should treat our subordinates like leaders helping them politely rather than bossing over them. Education changes our attitudes and our behaviours with others which is very important.

Lesson Two: Not Everybody Can Teach

Balti people also like poetic expressions. Therefore, in one of the sessions they were highly touched as they listened to a poem from the facilitator about the significance of the teaching profession. They felt happy because they realised that their profession was respectable and demanding but they became sad as the profession is not for everybody and it is not restricted to just teaching textbooks in the classroom. This was beyond what they used to think about. As one of the participants shared, 'There were many challenges and many responsibilities related to becoming a teacher. The lesson learnt was not everybody can teach'.

Lesson Three: Classrooms should be Vibrant and Engaging

In the public sector institutions, there is always a problem of managing large classes, nevertheless, in teacher training programmes they had never observed how to manage a large class in an adult classroom setting. During the workshop they invited the facilitator to take a class of ADE to demonstrate how to manage a large class. The topic given to the facilitator was 'Discovering Pakistan'.

ADE class of 40, both male and female, was first re-organised into six groups by the facilitator. All the faculty members of the GECE sat at the back of the class for observation. The facilitator used six strategies, one in each group. These were: (i) 5W1H activity sheet (what, why, when, where, who and how and so what); (ii) PMI (plus, minus and, interesting) activity; (iii) CAF (Consider all factors); (iv) brain-storming; (v) mind mapping; and (vi) SWOT (strengths, weaknesses, opportunities, and threats), to discover Pakistan. The activity sheets, with clear instructions, were provided to the students. Students were keenly engaged in discovering Pakistan using guided activities. Time was allocated to each group to present their work. It was an eye-opener for all the teacher educators observing the demonstration to see the rich data generated by the ADE students, far beyond the facts mentioned in their textbooks. At the end of the session, the facilitator asked one of social studies teachers to analyse the data and develop a summary of the findings to share with the students the next day.

In the debrief session with the faculty a discussion was generated with the question: Was it a large class management issue or the planning and executing instruction issue? A lot of critical responses were shared. It was learnt that teaching consisted of not only instructions but also classroom management. They took these lessons from that session and applied these in their ADE as well as in BEd classes. The students developed Fourteen Golden Rules for classroom management, which they displayed in their ADE Class. The lesson learnt was that the classroom should be vibrant and engaging, as illustrated by one of the participants:

> I applied the different teaching-learning strategies, like SWOT analysis, PMI strategies, and 5W1H and so on in my classes. These tools are helpful for me to generate ideas on a topic. We need to create vibrant and engaging classrooms.

Lesson Four: Words Have Transformative Power

In the workshop they were also exposed to the AI approach. It was interesting and eye opening for them to learn how positive or negative comments can either transform or destroy the entire learning environment. Words have transformative power, as one of the participants reflected on his self-practices:

> The entire discussion disturbed me and now I believe that there is a social science rather than pure sciences which helps teacher educators to transform education. As teachers, we need to be appreciative, we should encourage the students and support them in their growth, celebrating their successes and minimising their challenges.

Lesson Five: Respecting Different Perspectives and Opinions

Being teacher educators, they knew the importance of respecting different opinions, but to demonstrate this point the facilitator involved two teacher educators in a simple activity in which a piece of paper with the number six written on it was placed on the table. The teachers were asked to stand facing each other. It read number six for one but for the other the letter was nine and a conflict emerged. They were then requested to move from their positions together. When they saw the letter from one side, it was 9 and from the other side it was the number 6. They were both right looking from their own angles. The lesson learnt was that one should be open to see things from different perspectives and should not judge the people or situation as they see them from a particular vantage point.

In a nutshell, the real essence of education that was learnt from this workshop was that all the activities and deliberations that were shared were applicable at the classroom level. There was no need to chastise teachers if they became leaders in managing their classes. Students would enjoy and learn in class if the teacher engaged them in meaningful activities. Such capacity building workshops contribute a lot to the success of teachers' learning and should be continued, especially in the remote rural contexts.

There were many similar success stories narrated by the teacher educators in their reflective journals, which depicted their powerful learning experience, through these capacity building deliberations.

Challenges

Institutional capacity building is an immensely complex and rigorous process. Overall, the first phase of the capacity building initiative at the GECE Skardu was successful in terms of creating ripple effects in elementary schools. This was the first step in transforming teacher education in GB.

The STEP'S ICB pilot project has a distinct approach of AI, focused on changing the minds and attitudes to bring educational change that ultimately aimed to enhance teacher learning at all levels. This process demands a change from within which requires different, creative, exploratory, risk-taking, and adaptive orientations rooted in the 3As of modern learning (i.e. adaptation, anticipation, and adventure). The challenge is how to develop such teachers and teacher educators in a culture of top-down decisions taken by people outside the education sector who would like to see quick results and resist quality reforms. STEP with its rigorous efforts on both quantity and quality of elementary education reform has set only the first step; the constant follow-up and support is needed by the system to sustain the reform.

It is understandable that there are always challenges that come with new initiatives, but a few challenges can be minimised by appropriate communication and a high level of commitment from the system. The transfer of faculty members has to be minimised as it impacts the success of institutional capacity building. For example, during the life of this programme, out of 20 faculty members, five faculty members were reported to have been transferred from the college and others were in the process of getting transferred from the GECE Skardu. This had implications not only on the individual faculty members' learning, but also on the entire philosophy of institutional capacity building. Institutions are not only physical structures but these are manned by human beings. If these human resources are transferred, they also take away the institution's precious intellectual resource. If this trend of teacher transfer continues, how can the pilot project, built on capacity building of GECEs, be sustained and how can it be showcased as a successful project for other regions in Pakistan?

Unfortunately, in most transfer cases, decisions are not based on academic or professional considerations rather they are derived by personal and political motives.

Institutional Strengthening: The Case of GECE Hyderabad

This section presents the model of institutional capacity building designed for the faculty of two Government Elementary Colleges of Education (men and women) in Hyderabad, Sindh.

In Sindh, this capacity development initiative started off with the need assessment in the four GECEs, two each in urban and rural settings in Hyderabad and Thatta. One criterion that all four colleges met was offering a two-year Associate Degree in Education (ADE) programme. The need assessment was conducted through interviews with the college principals and focus group discussion with the faculty members. The intervention was thus designed based on identified needs. However, transfer of the principal of GECE Thatta and depletion of faculty disrupted the process which eventually dropped out of this initiative. Hence, the narrative below is only about the initiative in GECEs in Hyderabad.

'Institutional capacity', as explained earlier in this chapter, includes skills, knowledge, structure and ways of working (the culture) that make any organisation effective, and 'capacity development' means '…developing further each one of these—building on their existing strengths and addressing gaps.'[4] However, for this initiative under the STEP project, faculty academic capacity building was the focus i.e. the infrastructural and resource provisions were not under its purview. Therefore, the respondents, both faculty and the management were urged to identify their needs in their core business i.e. the academic needs. As both faculty and the management shared their needs, therefore the needs identified also included themes pertaining to institutional management; however the academic needs of the faculty dominated which were clearly related to teaching in the ADE and four-year BEd (Hons) programmes. These included areas such as orientation and training according to the national standards, working with the community, quality assurance, clinical supervision, the practicum module, student portfolio with specific reference to collecting evidence.

In addition to the direct question about their academic needs, the faculty and management were also asked about their understanding of professional development and what opportunities were available at the colleges for on-site professional development. It was evident from the responses that: (i) the professional development for the respondents was predominantly an opportunity to attend a short or long term course organised outside of the college, either by a government teacher education institution like PITE, or under donor-funded projects like STEP; and (ii) the idea of on-site and ongoing professional development had not been explored, hence, collaboration among faculty for planning, reflection, learning from each other was not conspicuous.

The Framework

As the purpose of this initiative was to use a holistic and targeted approach to professional development, therefore the philosophy underpinning this model was institution rather than an individual as a unit of change. However, the intervention also considered individual needs and concerns on the way. Considering this as a process of change, this intervention also took into account the importance of culture and context, and Hoban's (2002) idea of change being a non-linear process supported by framework for long-term teacher learning, as opposed to a mechanistic (linear) process which considers teacher learning as one-step approach. In addition, system thinking was also deemed important. This argument supports the idea (model) of mentoring and peer-coaching as part of and support for ongoing learning.

Hoban (2002) contests the idea of one-off 'workshops' or 'training sessions', and considers teacher learning not as a training episode but as 'change' and as a 'process'. This takes into account the contextual and social influence on learning, where prospective learners' interests, their beliefs and their work culture are important for learning to happen. Therefore, to understand the culture, the interests and the beliefs of the GECE faculty, the ongoing engagement was deemed important so that learning/professional development could happen organically. This also provided an opportunity to scaffold and work with the faculty to implement acquired knowledge in their work setting.

To introduce the idea of on-site professional development, and to provide a platform for faculty collaboration, the Professional Learning Community (PLC) framework was used for this project. The PLC elements used were 'collective focus on learning', 'collaboration', 'reflection, and 'action research'. These themes were covered in content and also as an approach to discuss portfolio and how to collect evidence, about the practicum module, and working with the community. Stoll et al., (2006) define Professional Learning Community (PLC) as:

> ...an inclusive group of people, motivated by a shared learning vision, who support and work with each other, finding ways, inside and outside of their immediate community, to enquire on their practice, and together learn new and better approaches that will enhance all pupils' learning (p. 9).

The PLC comprises five interconnected and mutually inclusive elements, such as shared norms and values, collective focus on learning, collaboration, reflective dialogue, and de-privatised practice. The proposed intervention plan included discussing and arriving at shared norms and values. It was however evident that the faculty dynamics were not conducive to arriving at shared norms and values. Therefore, the focus of this intervention was on the 'collective focus on learning, collaboration and reflective dialogue', with a hope that this would develop trust among the faculty to open up and engage in a creative dialogue required for developing shared norms and values, and encourage the faculty to learn from each other through peer observation and feedback.

Fullan (2006) emphasises on 'action theory' in each change effort. He argues that PLC is being treated as the latest innovation and when this happens then this (the intervention) could be taken as a 'flvour of the year' which means that it can be done away with once the taste wears off. In addition, those trying to 'implement it' would not be able to see its deeper meaning. For Fullan, a professional learning community is about 'establishing new collaborative cultures…that focus on building the capacity for continuous improvement…(and) meant to be a new Why of working and learning', hence developing enduring capacities, and not just 'another programme innovation' (2006: 6). PLC notion is about changing individual institutional culture and also about creating new multiple institutional cultures. In case of this initiative it applied to the GECEs as well as the cooperating schools.

The Process

The ultimate objective of the initiative was capacity (knowledge and skills) enhancement in a manner that it is ultimately passed down to the trainee teachers through the faculty members' own improved classroom teaching practices. The intervention spanned over a year, which included visits to the GECEs, sessions at AKU-IED, SKYPE meetings, and frequent exchange of work and feedback on emails. The process started off with reading, discussion and input on the notion of a professional learning community. This was with particular reference to collaboration and deliberation on the present practices where faculty collaboration and working together for reflection, research, sharing experiences, and for peer feedback was concerned. One issue highlighted was lack of formal structures at colleges for collaboration. This intervention itself provided many opportunities to the participating faculty to work and plan together through group work and reflection during the workshops and as part of their collaborative action research projects. Thus the notion was reinforced during the intervention period; however this needs to become part of professional development programme at the college.

The notion and cyclical nature of action research was discussed and two groups were formed. The areas for action research stemmed from the discussions on learning from each other and the practicum module of the ADE programme. For the entire process, from proposal development to reconnaissance and implementation, the nature of action research was followed by providing feedback and scaffolding. As stated above, the intervention also included issue based discussion sessions on practicum module, student portfolio, National standards, and working with the community.

Output and Outcome

The output of the intervention, foremost, was initiation of the collaborative culture, where the faculty started valuing each other as professionals, and as a source of learning. The faculty members started working together, and improvement in the relationship between the colleges and the schools began. The tangible output was two action research projects titled 'developing subject based PLCs among the faculty of GECEs (M & W)', and 'Developing a healthy relationship between elementary colleges and cooperating schools'.

Another outcome was the faculty members' presentations on their action research findings and their overall experience at an international conference and at a seminar, respectively.

Lessons Learnt

This intervention, first of all, helped develop appreciation for the GECE faculty and management who were working in a difficult context where indicators of capacity were concerned such as resource constraints, lack of need-based professional development opportunities and not absence of an environment conducive to learning.

Although for the participants of this intervention, professional development meant attending short and long term courses outside of the college, however their responses suggested that these opportunities were very few, and also not all faculty members had equal opportunity to attend these programme, perhaps because of the absence of a sound database. Hence, an on-site professional development strategy should be explored. This will not only provide opportunity to develop need-based programmes but also ensure application of the new learning.

The college leadership was committed to support and facilitate professional development. In fact, it was the college principals' support and facilitation that played an important role in the success of this intervention. It is therefore important that they are given due place in decisions about nominations to the professional development programmes that the government organises, as the principals will be able to nominate faculty as per the college and individual needs.

Reflection and feedback from the participating faculty and the principals confirmed the positive impact of this intervention on the ways of working, and faculty collaboration. It has improved their inter-personal skills and faculty group dynamics. Their research skills have been developed, and through development of presentation skills and reflective sessions, they have also learnt about each other's research. In addition, their time management and organisational skills have also improved.

There were, however, areas that needed to be addressed. First, as emphasised in an earlier section in this chapter, there was a general tendency to focus on 'issues', and highlight what was going 'wrong' rather than appreciating what was working and building on it. Holman and Cato (cited in Hammond, 1998) state that 'focusing on what is working and aspirations for the future achieves more and does it faster and more sustainability than solving problems. Second, there was a lack of formal structures to support collaboration and reflection. It would be important to provide faculty with time and venue to do collaborative work, learn about each other's practices, and celebrate successes so that the collaboration and learning of the faculty is sustained beyond the time-bound intervention.

Conclusion and the Way Forward

This initiative, in addition to providing opportunities to develop collaboration among the faculty as a model for professional development, encouraged relationship building at various levels, and initiated university-college-school partnership. This requires ongoing communication, and commitment. During the intervention, it was easier to build connection, communication, and bonding between the university and the college faculty, and to a greater extent inter-college collaboration, however relationships between colleges and the cooperating schools seemed rather a slow process, and so it needs continued efforts to further strengthen and sustain these bonds beyond the project. Also, the university-college connection should be independent and should go beyond the project as a process to develop a learning culture.

To institutionalise the change and improvement in the practices, the suggested way forward is to design further initiatives for improvement in other indicators of institutional capacity including, use of 'Appreciative Inquiry' and government supported mentoring programmes. But first would be the need for a systematic review of the intervention.

The interventions and the impact of the activities discussed in the chapter are a work in progress. Sustained efforts are required to strengthen the relationships for mutual benefit of all involved including the faculty across colleges and the cooperating schools. From the university's perspective intervention based research is proposed to further develop professional learning communities, and learn from the experience. Colleges and the schools have to strengthen their relationship for better practicum experiences for the trainee teachers. College leadership needs to provide system support and infrastructure by way of time, space and resources to facilitate the faculty from both colleges for meetings and interaction with the schools, and for on-site professional development, as Hoban (2002) notes that change and development are process-oriented which take into consideration individual faculty interest and pace.

References

Bana, Z., 'Navigating with trust: A proposal for transforming public sector schools towards learning organizations in Pakistan', *Journal of Research and Reflection in Education*, 8/1, (2014), 17–25.

Bushe, G.R. & Coetzer, G., 'Appreciative inquiry as a team-development intervention: A controlled experiment', *The Journal of Applied Behavioral Science*, 31/1, (1995), 13–30.

Cooperrider, D., *The Appreciative Inquiry Handbook: For Leaders of Change* (Berrett-Koehler Publishers, 2008).

Crisp, B. Swerissen, H. & Duckett, S., 'Four approaches to capacity building in health: consequences for measurement and accountability', *Health Promotion International*, 15/2, (2000), 99–107.

Fullan, M., *Change Theory: A Force for School Improvement* (Jolimont, Vic: CSE Centre for Strategic Education, 2006).

Hoban, G.F., *Teacher Learning for Educational Change* (Buckingham: Open University Press, 2002).

Langaas, M.D., Odeck, J. & Bjorvig, K., 'The Concept of Institutional Capacity Building and Review of Road Sector Projects', *In 23rd PIARC World Road Congress Paris,*(2007), 17–21.

McKinsey, '*How the World's most Improved School Systems Keep Getting Better*', (McKinsey & Company, 2007).

Memon, M., 'The Quality of Education cannot be Strained', *THE NEWS* e paper (June 23, 2013).

Mitchell, C. & Sackney, L., *Profound Improvement: Building Capacity for a Learning Community* (Lisse Netherlands: Swets & Zeitlinger, 2000).

Stoll, L., Bolam, R., McMahon, A., Thomas, S., Wallace, M., Greenwood, A., and Hawkey, K. 'Creating and Sustaining an Effective Professional Learning Community'. Source Material: Booklet 2 'Familiarization and deepening understanding', National College of School Leadership (Nottingham, and DfES Innovation Unit, London, 2006).

Notes

1. ADE is a 3-year pre-service teacher training programme initiated with technical support from USAID, which replaced the old PTC and CT courses offered at GECEs.

2. Practical handbook semester 3 for supervisor and practical handbook semester 4 for student teachers.
3. Bridge, objectives, pre-test, participatory learning, post-test summary (BOPPPS).
4. https://afrosai-e.org.za/sites/afrosai-e.org.za/files/ICBFGuideline.pdf. Last accessed 18 November 2015.

PART V:
CONCLUSION

13

Engaging the Global to Create Local Models for Educational Reform

Sarfaroz Niyozov

Introduction

In this chapter, I bring together some of the key features of the Strengthening Teacher Education in Pakistan (STEP) and Education Development and Improvement (EDIP) projects[1], highlighting what I believe are to be key insights from the projects, including questions of impact and sustainability, as well as borrowing and lending and reshaping the global to create local models. I argue that while STEP has been the largest and most ambitious programme of the Institute of Educational Development in Pakistan (AKU-IED or the Institute hereafter), and has probably made the strongest, lasting, and most relevant impact that the Institute has been able to make thus far, understanding the fuller and long-term impact of STEP, as well as its reconfigurations, will require more independent research, analysis, and publication in the future.[2] My second argument is that more critical and appreciative research needs to accompany large-scale projects like STEP and EDIP to produce local models that are of high quality and yet more sustainable and impactful.

I start by summarising the context of educational reform in Pakistan, where STEP, EDIP, and other education projects of the Aga Khan University's Institute for Educational Development (AKU-IED) have been taking place. Then, I highlight the key features and insights from the project and raise challenges and questions that emerge from placing this study in comparative, international and development education scholarship. In doing so, I raise questions and make suggestions about how a move towards locally sustainable, replicable, and impactful models can be made. I conclude with a comment on the volume's implications of the project for educational policy, research, and practice.

The Context of STEP and EDIP

For many decades now, developing countries have been a place of multiple development projects, including those in education. There is a rich and extensive scholarship that has documented these efforts. While there are islands of success, the overwhelming story is one of reform saturation, cultural and contextual irrelevance, ideological imposition and invasion, misguided approaches (e.g. top-down, outside-in, deficit-driven), limited impact, financial dependency, and lack of sustainability. Compared to the enormous investment of funding and efforts, the overall results and impact have been dismal and insignificant. The more things change the more they remain the same (Niyozov and Dastambuev, 2012).

Pakistan has been an example of few successes and many failures to the degree that Ali refers to it (in the introduction of this volume) as a 'graveyard' of development projects. The fact that educational interventions and reform projects (both local and global) have had very little impact in Pakistan is well documented, as one observes the persistent scale of illiteracy, lack of access, dysfunctional system, poor quality, broken infrastructure and rampant cynicism, especially about the public/government system. Public schools, which continue to be the largest system, continue to deteriorate. No one talks any more about Education for All's unachieved targets, and some are equally cynical about the new Sustainable Development Goals' success in the country. Cynicism and smiles abound when one talks passionately about the positive educational hopes, contextual relevance, capacity development, and teachers' commitment in the country. The public system is the target of ridicule and mockery at educational conferences, policy dialogues, round tables and in print and electronic media these days.

It is in this context in which both STEP (2009–2016) and EDIP (2010–2014) took place. Given the above history and background of failed reforms, wasted energy and funds, cynicism, and miserable realities, one has to be cautious regarding STEP and EDIP as the salvation and panacea, even though a desire for such proclamations exists and could be gleaned from the successful stories of the volume's chapters. A more pertinent question perhaps should be as follows: What makes STEP and EDIP significantly different from previous projects carried out locally and internationally, that raises a hope? Are STEP and EDIP two other development projects in this symbolic 'graveyard', or are they beacons of hope and models to replicate? While this volume reveals a lot of hope, the approach must always be a cautious optimism and a hard, self-critical stance towards making the new possibilities take root in local context and spread around within the existing resources and circumstances. Below, I will highlight some of the key features and insights from the two projects.

Key Features of and Insights from the Projects

First, STEP and EDIP were, by and large, carried out in the public system; the very system that is dubbed as hopeless in the Pakistani and international media and education literature. The change agent, however was, a private institution, the AKU-IED. To that end,

STEP and EDIP are both examples of the growing private-public partnership (PPP) approach that has become a hallmark of the recent global reforms, especially in the developing countries. While private-public partnership in education has been a matter of contestation, not all examples are bad. A lot in this partnership depends on the ethical framework and values of the partners. Within the partnerships described in this volume, the Institute, using its international reputation and network, as well as its intellectual and operational capacity (chapter 2, by Sadrudin Pardhan in this volume), developed the grant proposal and obtained a large sum of funding from the Global Affairs Canada and the Aga Khan Foundation, Canada for the STEP and from Australia's DFAT for the EDIP. The donors, in both projects, stipulated two main conditions: (i) the project would have to be implemented in the public system, and (ii) gender mainstreaming (another term for girls' access to education) would be a key focus. Both of these were in line with AKU-IED's mandate of contributing to the improvement of educational quality and access in Pakistan and the region. Subsequently, Sindh, Balochistan, and Gilgit-Baltistan Education Departments were approached as implementation sites.

Critics have highlighted that private-public partnership is a disguise for more privatisation, as it leads to further deskilling and disempowering of the public system. In my six months of living in Pakistan, I have noticed many occasions where representatives of the private or semi-private institutions and even public servants in the opposition parties endlessly bash the public/government system as moribund and propose more privatisation or private interventions in public education as the new solution.

A few studies have illustrated positive examples from such partnerships, such as those described by Silova and Steiner-Khamsi (2008) and Niyozov and Bulbulov (2017, forthcoming) about the work of the Open Society Institute in post-Soviet education contexts. In the post-Soviet contexts, such private-public partnerships have led to maintaining the collapsing systems, improving quality and introducing innovations such as disability education, gender parity, pre-primary education, and minority language education.

STEP and EDIP, as AKU-IED's major reform initiatives (AKU-IED; Shafa and Fency, 2015), reflect the positive example of the private-public partnership. They build on the local and global analysis of the situation and the need for intervention into the public system, which appears not only to be in a miserable situation, but also disempowered and impoverished. The key goal of STEP, for example, was to illustrate the possibility of making a difference in this context by improving the learning of the students, the teaching of the teachers and the conditions of students' learning and teachers' teaching, so as to recover the trust in the public system and empower communities to own and sustain change at grass-roots level.

The above realisation leads to the second insight that is the critical role of the focus on capacity development of the systems and individuals within them. Pardhan (chapter 2) sums this up well:

> STEP was, at its heart, a capacity-building initiative. As such, as illustrated in chapters 3 and 4 of this volume, it had a number of in-built strategies to improve the sustainability of interventions. Firstly, there was an inherent multiplier effect built into several of the components, including the cluster-based mentoring and whole school improvement programmes and the teacher educator training, which ensured that the benefits of project activities extended beyond the individual being directly reached to those that they, in turn, trained and mentored. Secondly, by involving cadres from different levels of the education system, particularly those that support teachers at the local level, including head teachers, district education officers, senior government cadres, and teacher educators, there was an increased chance that the 'enabling environment' for sustained change in schools and classrooms would be created (p. 70).

In other words, from the beginning of the project intervention, AKU-IED aimed at phasing itself out in a way that would leave the public system enthused, empowered and skilled so that it is able to take lead of its future reform, including the continuation of STEP and EDIP. Almost every chapter in this volume speaks of how the various capacities were developed by AKU-IED.

Ayesha Bashiruddin and Mir Afzal Tajik (chapter 7) and Naureen Madhani (chapter 8), for example, detail how the STEP programme, using the AKU-IED's Master's degree, has developed human resource for Sindh, Balochistan, and Gilgit-Baltistan human resources. In sum, 43 Master's degree graduates were prepared through the AKU-IED's MEd programme, who went back to their schools and systems to enable others and implement STEP's various activities. Their net story is that AKU-IED's programme transformed the students professionally and personally; pedagogically and managerially, technically and intellectually; and culturally and politically. The transformations enabled them to further their vision of and commitment to education, and affect changes in their classrooms, schools, families, and communities. The MEd graduates' narratives are passionate, genuine, and deeply educative: AKU-IED's graduates imply quality, commitment, and reflectivity; they are resilient, patient, and capable of bringing about change, asking deep questions, voicing their views, generating alternative ideas, taking risks, leading, negotiating and compromising. At the same time, the two chapters provide very strong lessons for how a programme like AKU-IED's MEd can be further improved: there is a need for: (i) moving reform further to schools and classrooms; (ii) grounding AKU-IED's courses and readings in the context and culture; (iii) building consortia and structured collaboration with schools; (iv) supporting AKU-IED's graduates through various means such as alumni chapters, online networks and so on; and (v) critically engaging both the global

('Western') and indigenous education ideas, and synthesising the two into a creative one.

Importantly, AKU-IED has been able to instill in its MEd graduates elements of critical-constructive educational visions and philosophies so as to envisage a different society and education. Post-AKU-IED lives of the IED graduates, as narrated by the authors of the two chapters, remind us of the story of structure and agency and individual and system: how the two dialectically interact; how structure tries to inhibit the acquired agency of the graduates who are now aware of both the power diffusion and the structure's vulnerability; how some structures and contexts are or could be made conducive and how ultimately both the AKU-IED graduates and their workplaces are socially constructed, amenable to change in both progressive and regressive terms. The structures, which the graduates face and are embedded in, are not just physical and material, such as resources and buildings; they are also symbolic and ideal, such as culture, language, religion and so on.

Lastly, these structures and individuals are no more localised: the graduates are exposed to global (western) ideas and practices; they are linked to the resources, ideas and tools that are beyond the local places. All these create enormous affordances and challenges for them to learn from, use and struggle with. The rich narratives from the study by Tajik and Bashiruddin show 'the complexity of human experience' where dichotomised and one way descriptions give way to humanised ones, where, depending on the context, the colleagues, principals, schools, spouses, parents, and community leaders simultaneously emerge as both transformational and obstructive; how progress means moving back and forth and sideways, how some of the graduates are able to achieve more than others, and how opportunities turn into challenges and vice versa. Developing capacity for engaging and using this post-modern complexity is a source for hope and success at personal and systemic levels.

The chapter by Bhutta, Bana, and Jaffer (chapter 12) adds a fascinating story of the successes and challenges of such capacity building at a government college in Skardu, Gilgit-Baltistan (GB), and at a government college in Hyderabad, Sindh where a newly designed pre-service teacher education programme, an Associate Degree in Education (ADE) is being implemented. This degree is a new provisional remedy, recently introduced in Pakistan, as part of enhancing its teacher education qualification. The stories show the joyful and at the same time transformative learning on the part of the prospective teachers at the Colleges of Education.

Three messages are at the core of this case study: first, institutional capacity building is central to the quality, sustainability and impact of any project; second, the soft dimension of the institutional building is equally, if not more central, to the task of developing educational reform capability; third, teacher trainers are eager to learn and change when the instructors treat them with respect, build on their knowledge, relate to their experience, and engage in discussions.

Similarly, chapter 10 by Jaffer, Bana, and Khan describes capacity building for organisational leaders. Fraught with challenges of proper recruitment, instruction, post-course/training follow-up, institutional support, and subsequent implementation of ideas learnt at the training centres, the course still developed leadership capacity. The authors found that apart from learning and enjoying a great deal, the participants also faced the hardships of implementing their course –based learning in their workplaces.

Jaffer, Bana, and Khan sum up six simple but critical lessons gained by the faculty of the colleges that participated in the customised capacity building training conducted through the Institutional Capacity Programme of the STEP project: (i) a leader does not mean a boss; (ii) attitude is important; (iii) not everybody can teach; (iv) classrooms should be vibrant and engaging; (v) words have transformative power; (vi) a respectful approach to engaging others' views and opinions is the key to learning and community building. The study shows how much the prospective teachers enjoyed global pedagogical techniques such as Plus, Minus, Interesting (PMI), Consider All Factors (CAF), Mind Map, Brainstorming and so on. When these techniques are used as shells and filled with the local content, they can be powerful engaging tools. A voice of a senior male faculty is worth mentioning to illustrate the degree of transformation: 'I am unable to sleep at nights as I consider that whatever I was doing in the name of teacher training was just wastage of time and resources. Now, I have realised that teaching is a very difficult job' (p. 413–414). Another senior teacher educator added:

> During my 25 years of experience, it is the first time I have seen an entire lesson demonstrated by a teacher educator (in this case the project faculty) with all meaningful activities. The students' high level of engagement in their learning was so obvious from their presentations. All these huge tasks were managed in an hour's time, which was an amazing learning experience for me (p. 414).

Nusrat Fatima Rizvi's meta-analytical chapter on Action Research (AR) projects carried out by STEP's course participants illustrates another component of STEP's capacity building of teacher educators. Action Research, as a global best practice, was promoted by the STEP's multi-programmatic intervention. AR demystifies research and empowers teachers, allows their voices to be heard and allows them to take charge of their practices. It systematises the basic human question of how can one do better and how can one solve a problem in a way that simultaneously leads to the development of one's problem solving skills and capacity. The case showed a sheer variety of approaches the participants took to resolve their problems ranging from simple pair reflection and action to using literature and the internet. The chapter, however, reveals that even such a seemingly easy approach to knowledge generation and practice improvement can pose multiple challenges to the course instructors and participants.

The study is important in representing the multiple challenges that the instructors and participants faced that stumble the acceptance, internalisation, and institutionalisation of the new practice. These challenges ranged from personal (what is in the practice for the participant in financial, social, and political terms), to structural (lack of research skills, facilities, time for doing extra work, resources), to cultural (lack of experience in systematic self-critical habits, absence of collaborative cultures, fear of sharing one's weaknesses, lack of experience of taking notes, hesitance in asking critical questions). The simple focus on individual teachers as well as classroom practice without engaging structural, cultural, religious, political, and economic forces limits the emancipatory power of Action Research. Rizvi also shows that the selection of participants of the course was not appropriate, because many of them, especially from Balochistan, were from the Bureau of Curriculum or Professional Institute for Teacher Education and not classroom teachers. As higher level educators, they do not engage in regular teaching.

Overall, the meta-analysis shows that if we need to increase the impact, much deeper attention with due time is needed for selecting the participants, instilling in them the belief that AR is useful for any practice, including management and leadership, and enabling them to critically 'read' and engage the local structural, cultural, and political-economic forces. More importantly, any intervention needs to be based on constructivist pedagogy whereby the change agents and participants need to unearth and expose the roots and possibilities of local forms of AR, compare them with the Western ones and develop a synthesised version from the two. In so doing, the participants need to feel that this new product is their product, requiring their protection, commitment, and advocacy.

In sum, local capacity development through STEP was not an

easy process. It took place in many ways, including through centre-based trainings such as MEd and Advanced Diploma programmes at AKU-IED, through mentoring, and on-site training such as at the Government Elementary Colleges of Education at Skardu, Quetta, and Hyderabad.

Looking at the results of the project, which he led, Ali suggests that STEP exposed some of the myths, such as the 'public system is unchangeable, incapable or unwilling to change', or 'marginalised and traditional communities are resistant to change and against sending their daughters to schools', or that 'these parents themselves are against secular education'. In fact, these are also some of the key insights of the EDIP project, described by Shafa, Baig, and Shah in this volume (chapter 5). Nothing could be further from the truth, when parents develop trust with reformers and schools leadership; when they do not see threat to their long held values; when parents see safe, clean schools available in their vicinity; when they see teachers present and working, when basic school facilities are around, when the curriculum is relevant and hopeful to their aspirations and when they see the school as a tool of mobility and hope for their children.

Shafa, Baig, and Shah provide a fascinating story of the Education Development and Improvement Project (EDIP) that was sponsored by DFAT Australia and carried out in Gilgit-Baltistan. The chapter positions the story of change through the socio-political context of Gilgit-Baltistan, including the story of the AKDN's extensive work in the area, as well as a list of externally-funded educational reforms. Cumulatively, these projects developed the technical capacity of the Professional Development Centre in Gilgit (PDCN), where the chapter's authors work.

The keys to the success are flexibility, openness, respect and sensitivity, using and developing local capacity, especially female educators, providing resource, reconstruction of schools, and not critiquing the participants' cultural and religious values. This study, like the STEP, deconstructs some of the myths, such as conservative or 'illiterate' communities do not accept western-funded projects, or they do not allow their girls to get education, or that they do not want to work with different Muslim communities. Trust and non-judgmental approach seem to be the key factors here. Once these communities 'trust develops in the reformers' good will, they open and move fast to gain maximum benefit from the global best practices. The key question is however, whether EDIP has reproduced the status quo, and reified local mores or challenged it; has it led to modernisation with reproduction or to transformation of the communities into new ones? Time and follow up study will tell if the new, 'global' best practices such as gender equity, active learning, critical thinking, and so on, implemented by EDIP and STEP have taken roots and changed the societies under intervention or whether they remained the same.

A related insight of this volume is the strategic preparedness of the AKU-IED, and its facilitation of the key participants and implementers for undertaking and carrying out these two large-scale projects. It is worth mentioning that a number of faculty members and staff who were involved in the STEP and EDIP projects had been involved in various small and medium projects, with international agencies such as USAID on ESRA, the Aga Khan Education Services and other NGOs. These provided them a realistic background and grasp of the education realities, developed their conceptual, emotional and social skills, and credibility to manage projects of such scale.

The success of the AKU-IED's STEP and EDIP projects, therefore, is not an accident, but a phenomenon grounded in real experience. Through STEP's three phases, AKU-IED contributed to capacity development at individual and institutional levels. AKU-IED has established structures and models, such as degree and diploma programmes, and multiple subject and area professional teacher networks in Karachi, which STEP expanded to Sindh, Balochistan, and Gilgit-Baltistan. These and other educational improvement models, mentioned above, have positioned AKU-IED as an equal and reliable partner with state, civil society, and international institutions. AKU-IED's strategic approach has been impact multiplication and amplification that were achieved through various means. These include viewing programmes and course graduates as structures and agents of change in their societies and communities; broadening experience by engaging faculty and graduates into outreach activities such as consultancies, textbook writing and curriculum development; strengthening research dissemination as well as supporting teachers professional communities that serve not only as providers of professional development opportunities but also as networks for advocacy. Another important development in IED's journey has been engaging public and private education policies. By 2006, IED had established itself as a centre of excellence and STEP was an extension of IED's vibrant, efficient, and grounded model into other areas of Pakistan. While IED has been going local and global for a while, STEP, with its remarkable scale and catchment, has firmly put IED on the national map.

The fourth insight is that STEP represents a large-scale reform both in its geographic capture as well as its conceptual and operational challenge for the Institute. This signifies a new development of AKU-IED's life. The institute was designed to remain small and vibrant and develop models that are locally grounded so that they could be replicated across different contexts. The fact that AKU-IED has been involved in a large-scale, multi-year, multi-million dollar projects across Pakistan is a testimony to at least three things: first, the institute's growing international reputation and image as a reliable, trustworthy and capable institution among local and international NGOs; second, uniqueness of the IED in being not just an academic institution, but also an institution that is grounded in the education realities and struggles; and third, the institute's confidence, maturity, and capacity to take up global educational reform ideas such as whole school improvement, cluster based mentoring and systematically try them in the most challenging contexts of developing world.

The STEP project team, headed by Ali, carried out the reform in selected districts of three provinces of Pakistan, reaching out to hundreds of schools, thousands of teachers, head teachers, community members and touching the lives of thousands of students across the three provinces. It was a comprehensive, all-encompassing, multi-dimensional, multi-stakeholder intervention, where no aspect of educational reform was left out of consideration. The project's overall framework, components of the framework (i.e. teacher education; teaching, learning and educational management; policies, practices, and networking), and its model of change (school as a unit of change; teachers, managers, and other educators, functionaries, communities as involved agents) indicate the depth and breadth of experience and thinking involved in this reform project.

As a programme, it included a number of already tried best practices locally and internationally, as described by Pardhan (chapter 2) and Ali (chapters 3 and 4). In sum, STEP was grounded in and modified some of the models of change that have been implemented by IED. STEP was a sequel to ESRA (Education Sector Reform Assistance), funded by USAID, the Government of Pakistan and a consortium of implementing agencies where IED was one of the players (2003–2007). It was at that time, that Cluster-Based Mentoring model was introduced in Pakistan. ESRA was implemented for a limited time and its key recommendation was to have a longer implementation period. STEP also borrowed the Cluster-Based Mentoring (CBM) model in order to move teacher development to the schools and to reach a greater number of teachers, particularly women in remote, rural areas of Sindh and Balochistan, by taking professional development opportunities to their doorstep

The second change model was Whole School Improvement (WSI), which denotes two key things: (i) school as the unit of change; and (ii)

the school taken as whole in the local context, culture, and structures. Chapter 9 by Ali and Ashraf presents a compelling account of how local educational governance, which includes various local groups (teachers and principals; education bureaucrats, local notables, religious leaders, and politicians) *contradictorily* and *complementarily*, individually and collectively manipulate the people, culture, religion, and structures to reproduce the status quo of illiteracy, poverty, gender, ethnic, and religious inequity and intolerance. Of course, not all are so bad: there are always some members of these groups who transform the existing cultures and customs to produce positive outcomes. Yet the sum picture emerging from the chapter is dire and depressing. The story of local tradition and elders is that children are made invisible and the teachers are tossed around; schools are closed and misused for non-educative purposes, schools funds are misappropriated for local gains; and the curriculum is controlled and suffocating. That is the local socio-political backdrop against which teachers and educational reformers such as STEP and EDIP have worked. Ali and Ashraf demystify the local and indigenous, and challenge the recent romanticisation of the local as benevolent, and the global/western as destructive (Semali & Kincheloe, 1999).

To succeed, the whole school improvement model included the following actions: (i) improved school leadership and management; (ii) decentralised professional development for teachers; (iii) enhanced community participation; (iv) continuous monitoring and evaluation; (v) effective curriculum implementation; and (vi) effective utilisation of teaching and learning resources. All of these six components geared toward the central focus that is improved teaching and learning at school (chapter 3, p. 73). Other models included Learning Resource Centres (LRS), equipped with necessary resources to support quality teaching, and establishing networks for teacher professional development (PNTD). PNTDs (Professional Networks of Teacher Development) were an extension of the already existing

Professional Teacher Association Networks (PTANs) established in Karachi since 1997 by the then graduates of AKU-IED. These subject (e.g. mathematics, science, social studies) and area focused (e.g. Early Childhood Learning, Inclusive Education) associations are voluntary civil societies that have proved as self-sustaining communities of learning, representing grass-roots movements, and reaching teachers from marginalised schools and systems.

The models also included training for multi-grade teaching. The need for this was not a part of the initial grant proposal, but a new realisation on the ground that up to 50 per cent of schools in Sindh and Balochistan are single teacher and even single class schools, teaching multiple grades. The late accommodation and inclusion of this component was, according to Ali, a clear sign of the donors' flexibility, and a clear challenge to those assertions that donors are rigid and pursuant of their own agendas only.

Be it as it may, donor bias was still evident in the last overriding component of the programme, that is gender mainstreaming, particularly that of girls. The Canadian donors of STEP and the Australian donors of EDIP made it clear that their programmes needed to include girls' empowerment, their access to, safety at and retention in schools, and their quality learning. The existing literature on the topic of gender mainstreaming as a donor's agenda has raised a number of insights and perspectives, ranging from economic (i.e. women's education leads to economic development of nations and quality of life in their homes); to liberal humanists (i.e. women are humans, equal to men in every sense and deserve equal right to education to become fully empowered and independent members of their societies); to neo-orientalist (such as gender education is part of liberating oppressed women from the patriarchy and oppressive and abusive men); and to those who consider that western secular education is haram for non-western women, as it erodes the traditional values of the roles of men and women in societies such as Muslim ones.

What the stories of this volume say is that the situation is a bit more complex and all these perspectives may apply to a certain extent. The glaring insight however, is that most parents want their daughters to study and get a good education, as long as schooling does not erode their cultural values and does not lead to insecurity or family honour problems. Of course, these concerns, as well as the approaches taken to address them by STEP and EDIP, may be seen as both valid and problematic and contested, but that is how far STEP has been able to 'push the envelope'. STEP and EDIP senior implementers placed girls' education within the Islamic tradition whereby seeking knowledge is a duty and obligation. They rarely raised questions around issues of religion, tradition, and female education beyond this. EDIP avoided using western radical jargons such as women emancipation and patriarchy and placed its discourse within local tradition of learning. Legitimately, a debate about cultural reification and fossilisation vs. cultural transformation and modernisation can be raised at this stage. Culturally relevant educational change, like culturally—sensitive pedagogy implies setting high learning expectations, promoting equity agenda and challenging oppressive status quo (Ladson-Billings, 1995). Cognizant of these, Moladad Shafa and his team, also propose that cultural changes are very gradual, very incremental, and very slow, and should come from within the communities. Their chapter does indicate subtle changes and openings taking place. There is a need to detail these small ripples that in my view have seeds for deep shifts.

The fifth insight is that STEP and EDIP provide rich understanding of the discourse of borrowing and lending. My reading of the chapters as well as discussions with the project coordinator is that the whole programme, as well as its various components present a par excellence example of borrowing and implementing the so-called best 'global practices' in a non-western context. I have also engaged this topic elsewhere (Niyozov & Tarc, 2015; Niyozov & Dastambuev, 2013). Overall, this is a central topic of post or anti-colonial research and development scholarship (e.g. Silova & Steiner-Khamsi, 2008; Steiner-Khamsi, 2004; Tabulawa, 2003).

As all social constructs, the topic of *borrowing and lending* or *policy transfer* is a contested one. It has however become more so during the globalisation, post-colonial, and post-modern era, which we live in now. There are at least three key perspectives that address the question of borrowing and lending. They all agree that borrowing and lending is a natural human quest, happens all the time and will continue to happen, as people want to improve their life conditions. They, however, disagree on the way it is happening, its open and hidden agendas, on who benefits from it and who loses, and its effects on human's ecological and social diversity, as well as equity.

Globalists suggest that while in the past westerners borrowed from the east, for the last two centuries or more, everybody is predominantly borrowing from the west, because the western technological and civilizational progresses in the last four centuries have created societies that provide good quality basic needs (often for free), developed advanced innovative and creative ideas, and have reached high levels of gender equity, human rights, intercultural, and interreligious harmony. These achievements are results of the freedom, technological development, and socio-political structures, including good governance. The fact of borrowing or buying innovative western ideas, technologies and values, and practices and policies is therefore, not a neocolonial imposition but a rational realisation of the non-western elites that these policies and methods are effective, efficient, high quality and leading to greater access and equity.

Opponents of this group, the world system theorists, suggest that in the geo-political context of core and periphery, first and third world, and colonial legacy, the notion of voluntary borrowing of ideas is not viable. What is happening is rather a hegemonic or outright forceful imposition of the western practices, policies and values upon the non-western world. These impositions are based on uncritical assessments of the western policies and promoting them as the best, unproblematic and only ways of salvation, progress and prosperity. These policies are proposed as a package that further drags the non-western societies into globalised capitalist/neoliberal world economies and cultural system, whereby the global south continues its role as the provider of human and material resources, as market for the Western products, as factories of cheaper production with tax laws on ecology and workers' protection, and as coerced consumers of western educational cultural and intellectual products. This discourse argues that local, but Western-trained elites, universities, and development institutions serve as hegemonic tools by which such transfer is domesticated, made friendly and implemented.

There is, however, a third perspective, some call as culturalist (Steiner-Khamsi, 2004), or as post-colonial (Kumar and Parthasarathy, 2007), which focuses on the context, culture, processes, agency, and complexity of the borrowing and lending. According to this perspective, while the second (world system theory) provides a deeper and more accurate analysis of the exchange, the story of borrowing is much more complex: first, there is no single lender and there is no single set of ideas that come from the west. What comes from the west is a mixed bag of ideas and polices that include those that are neoliberal (such as cost cutting, and privatisation) and neocolonial (such as English language), as well as those that are anti-neoliberal and anti-colonial (such as those focusing on empowering the indigenous, the public, and the civil society, those that speak about inclusivity and disability, and those that speak about gender empowerment from a critical-political economic perspective). Similarly, the western donors and development agencies are not monolithic, but change and represent diverse discourses. It is ironic to say that many of the innovative Muslim education practices now emerge in and spread from the west (Niyozov & Tarc, 2015). Second, while ideas and policies are being pushed around from the west, they are actually social constructs and as such, can be reshaped to serve different purposes, given the local critical awareness and creative abilities. In other words, we need to actively engage the purpose and ethics of the donors, the lenders, the borrowers and the implementers equally and critically.

This perspective also suggests that there are gaps between the policies borrowed and how they are actually implemented. This could ensue from the differences of ethics and values and agendas, but also from the differences in capacities and skills to deliver, as well as from the lack of resources and conditions to implement any policies, whether borrowed or locally developed. Most critical in this chain are teachers who can make or break the outside policies due to their value incompatibility, lack of resources, or their frustrations with their intensified and impoverished life and work conditions.

Lastly, this perspective also suggests the need to engage the grass-roots' voices about the value of the global practices. For example, most educators and parents view learner centred pedagogy, English language, and female education as emotionally, socially, and economically useful for students' overall development, rather than as western tools of subversion of their authority or the erosion of their cultural values sustaining hierarchy. In other words, there is no single voice on the ground and practitioners are more pragmatic than ideological. These voices also, as Ali suggested, see many of these progressive practices as *global* rather than *western*. Some see them as having roots in the non-western education and cultural histories and therefore 'retuning to them in an improved versions' (Niyozov & Bulbulov, 2017, forthcoming). Further, this perspective also suggests that the so called local and indigenous perspectives need not be romanticised, but engaged critically, for as the chapter 9 by Ali and Ashraf suggests, they could be abused for reproducing inequalities. The key question therefore is how can global or Western education policies and practices be used to generate local practices? This requires the learning about the processes that led to these practices' production in their original context, in this case, the west.

Given the above, where do STEP and EDIP stand? The authors and coordinators acknowledge that these are global/western practices, but suggest that they have been so deeply contextualised and modified that they have taken localised identities. While both projects were funded by donors, and the gender mainstreaming was the overarching condition, the proposal, the processes, the implantation, the additional components (such as school heads' training and multi-grade teaching) were proposed by the STEP team and accepted by the donors. Second, while the donors suggested gender mainstreaming, they did not check what ideological or value framework led that policy on the ground. For example, did the women teachers' empowerment through education lead to equality at home or did it create a double burden for these women teachers, as they moved between the home's work and the school's work. Similarly, did the girls' empowerment by EDIP lead to girls deciding for themselves or to give up on other things for their men's mercy of letting them attend schools? The STEP project team and its local partners had trustful relations with the donors, created through many years of working together. They used the common language and terms. Was there a realisation that these educational terms mean different things within different discourses and ideological frameworks (Kumar & Parthasarathy, 2007).

The fact that STEP model evolved and included more participants in capacity development (principals, community members) shows the flexibility and learning capacity at the level of the facilitators and the donor agency, in this case of the Global Affairs, Canada. As highlighted in the project's completion report[3], the project's donors were very accommodating and flexible; the project was conceived, developed and implemented without imposition: the aspects and components were all agreed upon and negotiated between the donor and the project managers. Reflecting on these experiences, the report makes it explicit by making the following recommendation:

> …large-scale, long duration reforms or developmental projects, like STEP, need to be treated as a phenomenon which can grow or evolve organically in response to emerging needs, changing situations and contingencies. Structure and scope of a large-scale project may not be precisely determined at the time of its conceptualisation. The scope and the full potential of the project to affect change are virtually determined by the circumstances, opportunities and challenges that come in the way of implementation of change and the reflective ability of the people working in the forefront and the vision of the people who work in the background. This all entails making the conceptual framework and the structure of the project flexible enough to allow necessary contextual and situational modifications and readjustments based on ongoing reflections and feedback from beneficiaries. Inflexible, budget sensitive or finance-driven reform plans in the realm of education impose limitation on the potential of the project to innovate, create, discover, and demonstrate best practices through reflective processes. These are not achievable through pre-decided plans and strategies without reflection on and maneuvering around situations, and maturing ideas and practices during the course of implementation of activities and interventions.

In my recent projects closure meeting with the donor's representative, I alluded to the various perspectives on the question of gender mainstreaming and found that she was aware of these discourses, and saw the question from human rights and economic perspectives.

Was STEP a western imposed policy? Was it borrowed uncritically? I posed these questions to my esteemed colleagues, Takbir Ali and Moladad Shafa. As we engaged in discussion around this, there was a realisation that the answer would fall within the third, the complexity/culturalist/post-colonial perspective. The ideas and words have come from the western education, but their implementation and contextualization make them local or hybrid. STEP can also be seen as creative and selective borrowing of western ideas to generate sustainable reform in Pakistan. That is how Ali articulated the case of STEP. This fits with a part of the AKU-IED's mandate of engaging global and local to create sustainable models.

What are the local alternatives to STEP and EDIP, Ali, Mola Dad, and I wondered. We acknowledged that identifying local practices would require a deep engagement with local cultures, including primarily the Islamic ones. What terms are used, how they were developed, who were their authors and would they even work better than the STEP and EDIP or earlier borrowed innovations by the IED? We recognise the need for doing more critical research in this area and this job is yet to be done.

In sum, STEP is believed to be a form of local-global, private and public encounter that has generated excitement, impact and transformation that are accepted by local, especially marginalised people as valuable and useful, and not disruptive to their cultures and traditions. For the project leadership, that is the key success.

The sixth insight is about STEP's impact. The key insight from this study is that there are various forms and levels of impact. Impact needs to be seen as a chain of effects. The chapters in the volume tell inspiring stories about successes, show examples of positive changes in teaching and learning, leading to students' improved learning outcomes; improved leadership and management practices in schools and other institutions; and tangible change in the physical and psychosocial environment of schools and classrooms. They show that despite all difficulties, improvement can be brought about in processes, practices, structures, and capacities of the schools and institutions to improve the quality of their services. For instance, AKU-IED prepared

43 Master Trainers through its graduate programme. These trainers went on to impact the teachers, the community and the students, and continue to support these stakeholders even after the project has ended. Consequently, the teachers they engaged have in turn impacted the students' learning or girls' school enrollment as the ultimate beneficiaries. More than these, AKU-IED prepared more than 130 subject-based mentors through its advanced diploma programme who went on to not only benefit their own classrooms but also teachers and community members and governments in their districts and provinces. This resulted in improved teaching at the schools that were involved in the clusters that these mentors led; increased community and parental engagement; better school environment; improved student learning outcomes and increased access, particularly for girls. So, without intermediary impacts, or second order changes, the final impact would have not been possible.

There are many other impact indicators in the book's chapters. Shafa, Baig, and Shah narrate how parents and local religious—communal leaders welcomed girls' education, constructed schools for them, and how all these led to trust and inter-communal harmony. Bashiruddin, Tajik, and Madhani enlighten the readers with how the AKU-IED graduates have become mobile, galvanised, empowered intellectually and economically, and how their transformations have become irreversible.

While all these are good points, identifying impact, measuring it and claiming it to be a result of STEP, is a very difficult task[4]. While all of the above show positive signs of impact on practice and policy, the ultimate ambition, as Ali (chapter 1, p. 22) puts it, is:

> ...envisioning a new direction for comprehensive educational reform in Pakistan...requires assessing deeper the complexity of reform in order to reinvent policy narratives and raise critical questions about the role of donor supported reform projects/programmes and the globally-

construed best practices and their compatibility with the idiosyncrasies of the local context. The focus should be on innovative, contextually grounded and culturally engaging approaches and strategies towards increasing enrolment, decreasing inequalities across gender, socio-economic status, geographic contexts (urban/rural), ethnicity, and improving and sustaining the overall quality of basic primary school education for all.

The last insight and question is about sustainability of the project. While some of the above points on impact indicate to the sustainability concerns, it is clear that the notion of 'graveyard', used by Ali in the introduction to this volume, implies how un-sustainable all the projects so far have been. This is a critical point, as the project came to its conclusion on February 29, 2016 and the funding stopped. What indicators of sustainability are there? Can we say that the long duration of the project (seven and a half years) made it develop roots on the ground so that it is a part of the system, psyche and mentality of the teachers and stakeholders; that they are convinced that STEP is genuinely valuable and the way to move Sindh's, Balochistan's, and Gilgit-Baltistan's educations forward so much so that they will continue it? Can we say that the project has created enough of critical mass and effective structures? Can we suggest that it has been intellectually rationalised to be seen as culturally and religiously important to sustain? Are there champions on the ground? These are very difficult questions to answer. What is clear is that the Project Team set the question of sustainability right at the onset, developed a research-based understanding of what it takes to make a project sustainable, and submitted a detailed sustainability plan to the local governments. The plan reflects four key factors of sustainability success: (i) 'government ownership' of the reform; (ii) the need to make reform demand-driven; (iii) a broad representation of grass-roots level educational stakeholders in choosing, planning and executing large scale educational reforms; and (iv) capacity building at the local level (for local change agents, champions and actors), which are perceived to be necessary conditions for substantive educational reform (e.g. Hargreaves & Shirley, 2009; Hargreaves, 2002).

The plan also includes continuing the Cluster-based Mentoring and Whole School Improvement models in the STEP schools as well as replicating these models in non-STEP schools in Sindh and Balochistan. This implies maintaining the STEP established Teacher and Learner Resource Centers, and the possibility of establishing new ones; and continuing professional development activities at Government Elementary Colleges of Education.

Importantly, the current weakened shape of the Pakistani public education governance system may raise critical questions about any long-term sustainability. Even though capacity was built at almost all levels via STEP, even getting some tangible outputs from some of the education managers during the life of the project was difficult. It can be hoped that teachers who have been trained as mentors, as well as the MEd graduates would continue to provide quality teaching to improve quality. The critical question is: To what extent the project really empowered the public system enough to take lead of its future reform? It should also be obvious that STEP sustainability should not be left to the government only. It is a moral duty of all sides involved: the AKU-IED, the Aga Khan Foundation, the government and Global Affairs, Canada. All these groups will have to come together and discuss the way to ensure and document the processes of sustainability of the project, a project that raised hopes and galvanised thousands of people around different parts of Pakistan.

An Epilogue

February 29, 2016 marked the closure of the funding for STEP. EDIP was closed two years ago. The story of the two projects is not over, however. Their rich stories cannot be fully covered by this single volume, however detailed and passionate the chapters may have been. We are looking for more stories to unfold on the ground, written in papers, presented at venues, and posted on websites. The true story of STEP may just be unfolding.

References

Hargreaves, A., 'Sustainability of educational change: The role of social geographies', *Journal of Educational Change*, 3/3, (2002), 189–214.

Hargreaves, A., & Shirley, D., *The fourth way: The inspiring future for educational change* (Thousand Oaks, California: Corwin, 2009).

Kumar, R. & Parthasarathy, K. 'Global interventions in educational reform DPEP and new curriculum of the case of Wayanad district in Kerala' *Journal of Education*, XXI/4, (2007), 353–371.

Niyozov, S. & Tarc, P., Working with, despite and against global best practices: Proceedings of the April 25, 2014 International Symposium at OISE University of Toronto (2015) <http://www.oise.utoronto.ca/cidec/UserFiles/File/Research/CIDE≥Accessed on October 28, 2015.

Niyozov, S. and Dastambuev, N., 'Exploiting globalization while being exploited by it: Insights from post-Soviet education reforms in Central Asia', *Comparative and International Education / Éducation Comparée et Internationale*, 41/3, (2013), Article 3.

Niyozov, S., & Bulbulov, J., Moving between Soviet and Post-Soviet Educations in Tajikistan: Institute of Professional Development as Response to Globalization, in Silova, I., S. Niyozov, eds. *Globalization on the margins. Education and post-Socialist transformations in Central Asia.* 2nd edition (Charlotte, NC: IAP, Inc., 2017)

Semali, L. & Kincheloe, J.L., 'What is indigenous knowledge? And why should we study it?', in L. Semali, L. & J. Kincheloe, eds. *What is*

Indigenous Knowledge: Voices from Academy (New York & London: Falmer Press, 1999), *59–79.*

Silova, I., & G. Steiner-Khamsi., eds., *How NGOs react: Globalization and education reform in the Caucasus, Central Asia and Mongolia* (Bloomfield, USA: Kumarian Press, Inc. 2008).

Steiner-Khamsi, G., *The global politics of educational borrowing and lending* (New York: Teachers College Press, 2004).

Tabulawa, R., 'International aid agencies, learner centered pedagogy and political democratization: A critique', *Comparative Education,* 39/1, (2003), 7–26.

Notes

1. While my summary largely focuses on and mentions STEP, I will also refer to another, Australian Government funded project called EDIP (Educational Development and Improvement Programme) that was carried out by the Institute for Educational Development (IED) in Gilgit-Baltistan and Sindh. Here, I will draw on and do justice to a single chapter of the volume devoted to EDIP written by Shafa and Baig (see chapter 5). I present similarities of the two projects and highlight the common insights and challenges they faced. In sum, EDIP, even though smaller in scale and geographic catchment, has similarities with STEP in goals (increase student enrollment; improve community participation in the school management; enhance teacher professionalism; increase gender parity; improve the schools' physical environment; upgrade the local government's leadership capacity to sustain the reform). It is also similar in the approach and models (e.g. school-cluster, multi-input, multi-level intervention, networking and consortium; community involvement). The EDIP project was carried out by PDCN and AKES, but this particular story is one of the PDCN's, which included 59 schools and 3,332 teachers. Its features such as a two tiered approach to professional development, whole school improvement model, multi-layered monitoring, inclusive nature, and respect for cultural values, are not much different from those of STEP. A particularly interesting case is the story of its extension to Diamer, a hard to reach and resistant to change district in GB. Shafa and Baig in this volume meticulously describe the outcomes

of the project in terms of students' enrollment, learning achievements, gender parity, quality and relevance, community's respect and ownership.

2. I suggest the need for an independent research not undermining the value and strength of this volume. My colleagues and I are aware of the issues of bias and positionality in research and development work and we tried to be as self-critical as possible. Yet, this volume represents the contributions of the scholars and institutions that were affectively, intellectually, and emotionally involved with the project. Therefore, we do not exclude the existence of blind spots and the impossibility of total objectivity. Most, if not all the chapters are also reflective reports and are based on data collected during the project. To that end, more research on this and other projects would only add to the value of the contribution here.
3. AKU-IED (2016). STEP final Narrative Report.
4. AKU-IED (2016). Final Project Narrative Report.

Index

C

D

L

M